"a full sweep of Merthyr's in
– Gwyn Griffiths, *The Mornir*

"a superb analysis." – Peter Stead, *Morgannwg*

Merthyr Tydfil was the town where the future of a country was forged: a thriving, struggling surge of people, industry, democracy and ideas. It was the Iron making capital of the world, and would become the crucible of modern Wales.

It was Merthyr and it's twin town of Dowlais that foretold the economic and social transformation of Welsh life and Merthyr that ignited the cultural and political furore which was to revolutionise industry and society throughout the iron and coal townships of South Wales.

It was Merthyr, from the armed rising of 1831 to the electoral radicalism of 1868 and 1900, that led the way towards democracy and civic advancement in the face of material degradation and high-handed repression. A town that encapsulated all the challenges, triumphs and aspirations of the people of an emerging country.

The major figures among the ruling class: Anthony Bacon, the Crawshays, the Guests are all portrayed; as are the Chartist leaders Morgan Williams and Matthew John, and the MPs Henry Bruce, Henry Richard, D.A. Thomas and Keir Hardie. But the heroes are the men and women of Merthyr who, with extraordinary resilience, passed through the crucible of harsh experience, and out of their communities of self-help created their own culture and an extraordinary town.

Merthyr The Crucible of Modern Wales assesses an epic history of Merthyr from 1760 to 1912 through the focus of a fresh and thoroughly convincing perspective.

Joe England was educated at Cyfarthfa Grammar School, Merthyr Tydfil and at the University of Nottingham where he studied Economic and Social History. In a varied career he has been editor of a weekly newspaper, a lecturer for the Workers' Educational Association, deputy director of the department of Extra-Mural Studies in the University of Hong Kong, a research fellow in the Industrial Relations Research Unit at Warwick University and principal and chief executive of Coleg Harlech, Wales' residential college for adults. He has travelled widely in east Asia and is well-known as a lecturer on social and industrial affairs. He is chair of the Merthyr Tydfil Heritage Forum.

"A fantastic piece of work. Highly impressive and just what is needed. An historical argument that takes in the complete sweep of industrial Merthyr's experience from the Poor Law to popular politics, from industrial developments to urbanisation – the book is all the stronger for it." – Andy Croll, University of South Wales

"This enjoyable and revealing book written in a clear and vigorous style illuminates Merthyr society but populates it with vivid character sketches of real breathing people. It shows how Merthyr was South Wales in the era of iron and then became a vital part of it in the coal age. A book accessible for those who don't know the story and fruitful for those who think they do. It contains much original research as well as a masterly pulling together of what others have written." – Neil Evans, Cardiff University.

"A must-read for anyone interested in Merthyr Tydfil and Dowlais and their extraordinary impact upon the wider world." – Huw Williams

The Crucible of Modern Wales

Merthyr Tydfil

1760-1912

JOE ENGLAND

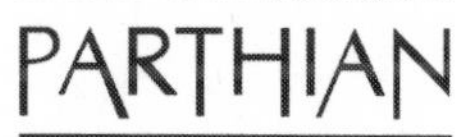

Parthian, Cardigan SA43 1ED
www.parthianbooks.com
First published in 2017
Reprinted in 2020

ISBN 978-1-913640-05-7
Edited by Dai Smith
The Modern Wales series receives support from the Rhys Davies Trust
Front cover painting George Childs, *Dowlais Ironworks*, 1840, watercolour over pencil on paper, 239 x 349 mm with kind permission of the National Museum of Wales
Back cover photograph: High Street, Merthyr Tydfil 1912
Typeset by Elaine Sharples
Printed by 4edge Limited
Published with the financial support of the Welsh Books Council
British Library Cataloguing in Publication Data
A cataloguing record for this book is available from the British Library.

To the people of Merthyr Tydfil,
past, present and future

Contents

POLITICS

Introduction

> ...it is not difficult to view the nineteenth century in Merthyr as dominated by the struggle of the people to possess their own city.
>
> **Harold Carter and Sandra Wheatley**[1]

> ...the town's radical pedigree, for all its ring of militancy, cannot be conceived of as a unified, unproblematical progression
>
> **Chris Evans**[2]

It is as an industrial town that Merthyr Tydfil exerts its fascination. Formed in the late eighteenth century, during what we still conveniently call 'the Industrial Revolution', it is the most written about town in Wales. Neither a bathing resort and centre of middle class culture like Swansea, nor a seaport like Cardiff or Newport, nor even an established county town like Carmarthen or Brecon, its true nineteenth century contemporaries were Bradford and Oldham, centres of textile manufacture, one of the two great industries that from the 1780s propelled Britain through the nineteenth century. The other was iron. And at the centre of the enormously productive iron country which straddled the heads of the South Wales valleys in the first half of the nineteenth century was Merthyr Tydfil, from 1801 to 1861 the largest town in Wales.

I have chosen dates, 1760-1912, which span years of extraordinary economic achievement, dramatic changes of

---

[1] Harold Carter and Sandra Wheatley, *Merthyr Tydfil in 1851* (Cardiff, 1982), p. 113.

[2] Chris Evans, *'The Labyrinth of Flames'*: *Work and Social Conflict in early industrial Merthyr Tydfil* (Cardiff, 1993), p. 3.

fortune, and absorbing social and political conflicts. 1760 is when a solitary iron furnace at what became known as Dowlais first produced iron bars. It marks the entry of Merthyr Tydfil into industrialisation. In 1912, when King George V and Queen Mary visited the flourishing county borough of Merthyr Tydfil, it was a place full of optimism. Its population at 81,000 was the highest ever, its affairs firmly in the hands of democratically elected councillors. Central to that optimism was the final wresting of control over local affairs from the hands of ironmasters, colliery owners and railway companies.

The allure of Merthyr's history lies in how the story unfolded through old but still relevant issues: environmental degradation, public health, labour exploitation, the relations between classes and the struggle for power between them. The central theme of this book is how for 140 years the town of Merthyr Tydfil and its twin-town Dowlais, both almost entirely working-class in composition, were dominated by two ironmaster families until finally, in the twentieth century, a democratic form of government was established.[3]

In Merthyr Technical College in the winter of 1964-5 four lectures were given to large audiences by Workers Educational Association speakers. They were subsequently published in the path-breaking volume *Merthyr Politics: The Making of a Working-Class Tradition.*[4] The lectures had been arranged by a young WEA tutor-organiser recently returned from post-graduate studies in America, Rhodri Morgan, the future First

---

[3] The interaction between class and power has been a major concern of urban history. Among many examples see R. J. Morris (ed.), *Class, power and social structure in British nineteenth-century towns* (Leicester, 1986), and Mike Savage, 'Urban history and social class: two paradigms', *Urban History*, Vol. 20 (1) (April, 1993).

[4] Glanmor Williams (ed.), *Merthyr Politics: The Making of a Working-Class Tradition* (Cardiff, 1966).

Minister of Wales. The book was edited by Glanmor Williams, the extraordinarily influential historian from Dowlais who was transforming the historiography of Wales from Swansea University, and its title deliberately echoed Edward Thompson's 1963 classic *The Making of the English Working Class*. The three lectures on the nineteenth century were given by Gwyn A. Williams, Ieuan Gwynedd Jones and Kenneth Morgan. A postscript mainly concerned with the twentieth century inter-war Slump was added by myself. The story that volume told of a community exposed to the ebb and flow of unbridled capitalist enterprise through prosperity and grim adversity was cruelly emphasised later in 1966 by the tragedy at Aberfan.

In his Foreword Glanmor Williams had asserted that in the building of a radical Wales the role of Merthyr had been crucial: 'Here the old crust of custom was melted down and fused with new aspirations flowing from volcanic social and economic change, to be remoulded and hardened into a new political democracy.' This declaration and the focus of the book upon industrial Merthyr and its working class caught the imagination of younger scholars: 'A new history of Wales was born in Merthyr'.[5] Whilst not entirely true, more than a quarter of a century had passed since David Williams' *John Frost: A Study in Chartism* had appeared in 1939 and more than 40 years since Ness Edwards' *The Industrial Revolution in South Wales* (1924) followed by his *The History of the South Wales Miners* (1926). A new generation of historians saw not just that the history of industrial Wales had been neglected but that its pursuit offered an intellectual excitement that could not be resisted. The subsequent flowering of writing about Welsh history in the nineteenth and twentieth centuries has been prolific and insightful.

[5] Dai Smith, *In The Frame: Memory in Society: Wales 1910-2010* (Cardigan, 2010), p. 157

In the intervening years I pursued other interests but the story of Merthyr and its significance always nagged at me. What happened to the consciousness of workers who fired bullets in 1831 and voted in 1868 for a Liberal pacifist? Or consider the much greater mystery of the change in behaviour between the armed insurrection of 1831 and the failure of Merthyr Chartists to join the march upon Newport in 1839, just eight years later. The shorthand version of Merthyr's political history, which runs as follows, has never seemed entirely satisfactory. From this first wholly industrial town in Wales a self-conscious proletariat engaged in strikes and riots, carried the red flag in an armed Rising out of which emerged thousands of Chartists. When in 1868 the newly enfranchised workers had an opportunity to vote they threw out Henry Bruce the ironmasters' choice and elected the radical peace-campaigner Henry Richard. When the Independent Labour Party appeared the Merthyr electors in 1900 proudly chose Keir Hardie. The march to the left, if turbulent, had been seamless.

Woven into this version is a strand of lawlessness and violence. Victorian observers of the Merthyr insurrection, the 1839 Chartist attack upon Newport, the Rebecca riots and the violent guerilla activities of the Scotch Cattle believed that certain South Wales districts 'were beyond the law'. Merthyr, with its 1831 'Rising' and as the centre of Chartism in Wales was firmly included. Its bedrock reputation as a raw 'frontier town', with its no-go area of 'China' a centre of depravity, added colour. The milestones on this march had all been highlighted in *Merthyr Politics*. The text was built around phases in the town's history represented by Dic Penderyn, Henry Richard, Keir Hardie, and the town's martyrdom during the inter-war Great Slump. Despite the sophistication of the chapters on the nineteenth century the way the book was structured made it easy for the shorthand version to be widely believed.

What actually happened is different. Rebellion by the working class was confined to the early years of industrialisation during periods of depression combined with high food prices. After 1831 resistance was orderly, usually legal, and rarely, beyond window-breaking, violent. From then on the Merthyr ironmasters established a scarcely challenged dominance. The election of Henry Richard in 1868 was mainly achieved by the votes of the coalminers of Aberdare and through the political network formed by the chapels in Merthyr and Aberdare. As late as 1888 the working men of Merthyr twice failed to nominate a working man for a vacant parliamentary seat, even when invited to do so. The election of Keir Hardie in 1900 owed most to animosity between D.A. Thomas and Pritchard Morgan, the two Liberal candidates. Labour electors were a small minority.

If one looks for 'the efforts of Welsh working people to forge a self-identity in opposition to the dominant values of a capitalist civilization'[6] the pit villages of Monmouthshire and the miners of Aberdare, free of iron company dominance, have a greater initial claim. Even there, however, early struggles were corralled as they were in Merthyr, by the grievances and organisational networks of Nonconformity. What attracts attention to Merthyr, the largest aggregation of workmen in Wales, are the bloody clashes of 1816 and 1831, the mysterious collapse of revolutionary fervour in 1831 and those dramatic parliamentary upsets in 1868 and 1900. Yet the most significant social aspects of Merthyr Tydfil in the nineteenth century are the dominance of the ironmasters and the political allegiance given to radical Nonconformity.

To address the questions thrown up by Merthyr's industrial and political history I have written about the extraordinary

[6] Evans, *The Labyrinth*, p. 2

entrepreneurial initiatives that originated in Merthyr but spread far outside, the evolution of social and industrial relations, the strength and temper of Chartism, the political ambitions and influence of the middle class, the methods by which the ironmasters wielded power, and the crucial episodes when that power was confronted and eventually broken. Glanmor Williams in his Foreword to *Merthyr Politics* claimed that Merthyr: 'more than any other Welsh town, has been the crucible and matrix of working-class political tradition'. What emerges from Merthyr's remarkable history suggests the need for a wider perspective.

The Making of Modern Wales

The Concise Oxford Dictionary defines a matrix as a place in which a thing is developed; a mould in which something is cast or developed. The record shows that from Merthyr and Dowlais capital, technological expertise, and entrepreneurial energy built the links — road, canal and rail — that made Cardiff a great port, developed iron and steel works across South Wales and initiated the exploitation of Welsh steam coal.

The dictionary defines a crucible as a melting pot but also a severe trial. In Merthyr Tydfil from the late eighteenth century onwards thousands of men and women encountered a new world and from their daily experience emerged the cultural characteristics of the people of industrial Wales. The men toiling underground with pick and shovel or in the heat and glare of furnaces; the women rearing a family on inadequate incomes, coping with disease and sickness and unceasing incursions of dust and dirt. Each depending for survival and comfort upon the help of workmates or neighbours, experiences that bred solidarity, mutual trust and moral probity. These values in turn were reinforced by their institutions: the company ironworks and collieries, the friendly societies and union branches, the terraced streets and the ubiquitous chapels.

Merthyr Tydfil was the melting pot in which its disparate immigrant population found fellowship in its many friendly societies and Welsh language dissenting chapels. It was there, in Merthyr and on a scale previously unknown in Wales, that the earth was ravaged, humans oppressed, a peasantry transformed into a proletariat, and town life enjoyed and suffered. It was there, despite severe trials, the people created their own culture and eventually found their own politics. In sporting, literary and musical competitiveness its musicians and choirs, fighters and boxers, poets and authors foreshadowed the greater South Wales cultural experience to come. From this industrial and cultural experience arose the politicians – J.J. Guest, H.A. Bruce, Henry Richard, D.A. Thomas and Keir Hardie – who each in time spoke for their Wales.

And in all this, Merthyr's small middle class played an essential role, one common to other Welsh towns, but one which until recently has been largely ignored and underestimated, especially where Merthyr Tydfil is concerned. From the early days of its industrialisation these 'middling orders' took part in civic governance – the select vestry, the poor law guardians, the local board of health, the urban district council. By the nature of their occupations they provided the shops, the medical and legal services, numerous small businesses and until the twentieth century the local politicians. Through the pages of the *Merthyr Guardian* (1832-1874)[7], *the Merthyr Telegraph* (1858-81), *the Merthyr Express* (founded 1864), and *the Merthyr and*

[7] The paper began life in 1832 as *The Glamorgan, Monmouth, Brecon Gazette and Merthyr Guardian*. In 1841 the title changed to *The Glamorgan, Monmouth, Brecon Gazette, Cardiff Advertiser and Merthyr Guardian*. R.D. Rees, 'Glamorgan Newspapers under the Stamp Acts' *Morgannwg*, Vol. 3, 1959.

Dowlais Times (1891-9) they campaigned consistently on civic issues.

Industrialisation in Britain created employment, a gradually improving standard of living and an ever-increasing supply of goods. It also brought environmental degradation and crowded disease-ridden towns and cities. To clean up the cities and towns required huge investments in social capital - drains, sewers, reservoirs — that necessarily involved an increase in rate expenditure. The politically active members of the middle class in Merthyr not only drew attention to public health problems and caused the 1848 Public Health Act to be locally applied but, accepting the financial implications in the face of determined opposition carried through the necessary works, and gave an example to other towns. They fought a tenacious and eventually successful campaign for an electorally democratic Merthyr. And in the early years of the twentieth century they worked with the emerging Labour movement to achieve educational and housing reforms.

A Narrow Base

Unfortunately, Merthyr also prefigured South Wales in its narrow economic base. The opportunity for economic diversification had been foreseen as early as 1837 by the *Merthyr Chronicle*:

> Would that we could induce our own Iron Masters or stranger speculators to manufacture our Iron into the various useful things in our domestic economy. The tools of the very workmen are made at Sheffield or Birmingham and probably from the very Iron daily issued from our Forges ...we surely ought to find the skill, the capital and the enterprise necessary for so desirable a consummation [sic]. Are we to go on in the same old

> fashioned way subject to the ebb and flow of a very uncertain trade – prices now extravagantly high, and again, absurdly low, with the fatal consequence of a discontented and excitable population. A large encampment sent merely to exhaust the mine and coal and then to fall into ruin and decay. Or are we to have ...new manufactures, a greater division of labour, fresh competition, and a boundless field for ingenuity and welfare of future generations?...Merthyr should be a second Birmingham...[8]

The *Chronicle* had posed a fundamental question. Why with its coal, iron and steel, copper and tinplate, the raw materials for engineering, shipbuilding, and a range of metal trades, did Wales fail to develop such industries? The story of Merthyr provides an answer.

An essential part of the answer lies in the sheer profitability of the iron and coal industries. The Hills, Crawshays, Homfrays and Guests made great fortunes. Capital, enterprise and skill from these giants of industry spread far afield. When iron-making faltered the ironmasters turned to coal extraction from their abundant estates and enhanced their fortunes. The growth of the regional economy produced a wealthy middle class and enabled Walter Coffin, Robert and Lucy Thomas, Matthew Wayne, David Davis (a Merthyr draper who started the Ferndale Coal Co.), Sam Thomas and W.T. Lewis, to invest in collieries in the Taff, Cynon and Rhondda valleys. Just as the railways had provided a huge market for iron rails, steam ships devoured Welsh steam coal. For these middle class entrepreneurs access to capital came through partnerships and private joint-stock companies.[9] Profits financed further developments and

[8] *Merthyr Chronicle*, 21 October 1837.

[9] Rhodri Walters, 'Capital Formation in the South Wales Coal Industry, 1840-1914', *WHR*, Vol. 10, 1980.

acquisitions. For those with the money-making instinct, iron, steel and coal (and slate in North Wales) were outstandingly profitable industries in which to invest. When such large profits could be made, why risk investing elsewhere?

Technology played a part too. Coal, due to the geological conditions in South Wales, was a pick and shovel industry right up to 1914 with little innovation that required machinery to be locally made. In the ironworks the inhouse technological advances — puddling and rolling, improvements to the blast — were related to iron-making processes. The exception was the application of steam power. Steam engines had a long history of development and there were already established steam engine manufacturers such as Boulton and Watt in Birmingham from whom the Merthyr firms bought engines. In time Dowlais and Cyfarthfa developed their own engineering departments to carry out repairs and even built railway engines within the works. By developing their own workshops and employing the engineering skills available, as well as training workmen for their own purposes, the great ironworks inhibited the development of independent engineering workshops. On the coast at Newport, Cardiff, Barry, Swansea and Llanelli the docks and ship-repairing existed only as dependent adjuncts to the coal industry.

What follows is the story of that 'long' and tumultuous nineteenth century in which the quiet parish of Merthyr Tydfil was transformed into the largest, most industrialised and technologically advanced town in Wales, whilst continuing to be a centre of radical Nonconformity. It begins with an overview of the characteristics of that industrial settlement in the early years of the nineteenth century where thousands made their home, drawn to an exploitation and transformation of the hills of Wales to an extent never previously seen.

1

A Place in the Hills

> There stood a Hill not far whose grisly top Belch'd fire and rowling smoak; the rest entire Shon with a glossie scurff, undoubted sign That in his womb was hid metallic Ore
>
> **John Milton**[10]

> The *Non-plus-ultra* of Industrialism wholly mammonish ... presided over by sooty Darkness physical and spiritual, by Beer, Methodism and the Devil, to a lamentable and supreme extent!
>
> **Thomas Carlyle**[11]

Carlyle never forgot Merthyr. 'Ah me! It is like a vision of Hell, and will never leave me, though, these poor creatures broiling all in sweat and dirt, amid their furnaces, pits and rolling mills'.[12] It was a remarkable and for some a daunting sight. On once bare hills five hundred to one thousand feet above sea level four ironworks constantly spewed smoke and flame. At night it was

> ...wild beyond conception. The vivid glow and roaring of the blast furnaces near at hand – the lurid light of distant works –

---

[10] John Milton, *Paradise Lost*, Book One.

[11] Letter dated 18 January 1854 to James Hutchison Stirling. As he notes in the same letter Merthyr was 'a place never to be forgotten when once seen'. *Carlyle Letters Online*, [CLO] Duke University Press. Accessed 23 February 2016.

[12] James Harris, 'Wales as Carlyle Saw it Forty Years Ago', *The Red Dragon*, December 1884.

> the clanking of hammers and rolling mills, the confused din of massive machinery – the burning of headlands – the coke hearths, now if the night be stormy, bursting into sheets of flame, now rapt in vast and impenetrable clouds of smoke – the wild figures of the workmen, the actors in this apparently infernal scene – all combined to impress the mind of the spectator wonderfully.[13]

Great heaps of slag glowing like lava surrounded the cottages dwarfed by furnaces and engine houses. Never completely dark, it was never silent. Thousands toiled on the scoured and quarried hill-sides and in the sprawling ironworks, or shouldered their way through the filthy lanes. It had a fearsome reputation, as did the people. Gwyn A. Williams claimed that a curate in an Anthony Trollope novel fainted when informed he must go there. One Catholic priest definitely refused to go; another found the people 'rude and uncultivated ...industrious but savage'. The Bishop of Llandaff, Charles Sumner, inducted Evan Jenkins into the living at Dowlais in 1827 and parted saying, 'I leave you as a missionary in the heart of Africa'. George Borrow at night encountered 'throngs of savage looking people' and fled after two hours of daylight, complaining of edifices 'of a gloomy, horrid Satanic character'. For Barclay Fox 'The men of Merthyr are the crudest looking material in human shape I have yet seen'.[14] It

---

[13] Charles Frederick Cliffe, *The Book of South Wales, the Bristol Channel, Monmouthshire and the Wye* (1847).

[14] Paul O'Leary, *Immigration and Integration: The Irish in Wales 1798-1922* (Cardiff, 2000), p. 57; Ursula Masson, 'The Development of the Irish and Roman Catholic Communities of Merthyr Tydfil and Dowlais in the Nineteenth Century', M.A. Dissertation, (University of Keele, 1975); Ieuan Gwynedd Jones, *Mid-Victorian Wales: The Observers and the Observed* (Cardiff, 1992), p. 4; George Borrow, *Wild Wales: Its People, Language and Scenery* (First published 1862; Wrexham, 2009), p. 458; R. L. Brett (ed.), *Barclay Fox's Journal* (1979), p. 190.

was the largest gathering of Welsh people on earth and no place made more iron.

Carlyle first visited in 1843. When he visited again in 1850 the age of iron had reached its zenith. From the late 1780s Merthyr had been the epicentre of a phenomenal expansion of the South Wales iron industry. Its four main works – Dowlais (1759), Plymouth (1763), Cyfarthfa, (1765), Penydarren (1785), each within a two-mile radius of the old village – had set the pace for the works that sprang up along the north-eastern rim of the coalfield: Hirwaun (1757), Blaenafon (1789), Ebbw Vale (1789), Nantyglo (1791), Tredegar (1800), Union (1800), Aberdare (1800) and Abernant (1802). By 1806 the four Merthyr works were producing half of the pig iron produced in South Wales and in 1812 one-fifth of all British pig iron. In the late 1840s the largest furnaces at Cyfarthfa and Dowlais were smelting 120 tons a week when the mean for Britain as a whole was 89.[15] The details of this explosive development based upon the easy accessibility of iron ore, coal and limestone on cheap long-term leases, the sources of investment, the adoption of new technologies – particularly coal smelting and Cort's puddling process – the stimulus provided by the wars of the eighteenth and early nineteenth centuries, the increasing use of iron for domestic purposes as well as for the building of bridges and then the ever-increasing demand for locomotive rails in Britain and abroad, have all been well rehearsed.[16] But time and place are fundamental to understanding social relations in Merthyr Tydfil during the nineteenth century.

---

[15] David S. Landes, *The Unbound Prometheus: Technological Change and Industrial Development in Western Europe from 1750 to the Present* (Cambridge, 1969), p. 180.

[16] Michael Atkinson and Colin Baber, *The Growth and Decline of the South Wales Iron Industry 1760-1880* (Cardiff, 1987); A. H. John, *The Industrial Development of South Wales* (Cardiff, 1950).

This irruption of industry came to an underdeveloped Wales where an increasing population outpaced the meagre resources available, where people subsisted mainly upon barley bread and potatoes, and where 'the labourer and the small tenant farmer lived constantly on the edge of poverty'.[17] From the last quarter of the eighteenth century Merthyr was the place where money could be made. There were good years and bad years but the long-term trend was up. In 1786 wages at Ciliau-wen, in Pembrokeshire were 6d. [0.25p] a day, 'out of which the labourer paid nine shillings [45p] cow hire and 28s. [140p} a year for a cottage and some land'. Four years later, the day rate for labourers in the vicinity of works in Glamorgan was 1s.2d. [5.08p]. The gap between the living standard of the Welsh farmer and the industrial wage-earner continued to increase during the first half of the nineteenth century.[18]

The scent of money in those early years was irresistible. The iron companies bought land leases from local farmers: 'One hundred pounds in shining gold ...They did not know what to do with it, or make of it ...every one congratulated himself on having lived to see the golden age'.[19] Quarrels over land rights followed the quarrying, mining, scouring and tipping that

[17] A. H. John, *The Industrial Development...* , p. 17. Between 1801 and 1851 the population of rural Wales, outside the semi-industrialised counties of Glamorgan and Monmouth, increased naturally by 64 per cent, David W. Howell, *Land and People in Nineteenth Century Wales* (1977), p. 96.

[18] A. H. John, *The Industrial Development...* pp. 80-81, 83, 87. For discussion of rural migration into the coalfield see John, pp. 53-66 and Howell, pp. 96-8. For the long tradition of workers migrating to ironworks see T. S. Ashton, *Iron and Steel in the Industrial Revolution* (Manchester, 1924), pp. 197-205.

[19] Charles Wilkins, *The History of Merthyr Tydfil* (Merthyr Tydfil, 1908), pp. 227-8.

encroached across fields and unenclosed commons. Feelings ran high – 'You and the Iron Masters came into the Country to make your fortunes by imposing on the natives' – and litigation could follow. There were second thoughts about the compensation received and the high-handed methods of the iron companies. Wilkins the local historian picked up the resentment:

> ...about twenty farms were swallowed up by the Cyfarthfa works, and Dowlais, equally ruthless, not only converted some into agents' houses and warehouses, but tipped over many, and so undermined the foundations of others by coal and mine works that they have long since tumbled in ...snug little estates were given away for a mess of pottage ...The old tale! Bad harvests, money borrowed, farm sold. [20]

But local farmers gained lucrative contracts for haulage, land prices boomed as the ironworks spread. Thomas Rees in 1815 recorded the impact: 'one farm in the neighbourhood, which at the time of the erection of the first furnace, about A.D. 1755, let for the annual rent of two pounds ten shillings, is now rented for fifty pounds; and another, which at the same period let for five pounds, has been advanced to one hundred pounds.'[21] In a journalistic flourish Wilkins envisaged money in these early days as 'absolute trash'.

For the ironmasters it was seed corn that brought golden harvests. The enormous profits accruing to the families who by the end of the eighteenth century had gained control of the works – Crawshays at Cyfarthfa, Guests at Dowlais, Homfrays at Penydarren, and Hills at Plymouth – were used to finance expansion. The capital of Cyfarthfa Works grew from £14,369

---

[20] Wilkins, *History*, p. 145.

[21] Thomas Rees, *The Beauties of England and Wales: South Wales* (1815), p. 646.

in 1790 to £103,908 in 1798, and then accelerated. Between 1813-19 William Crawshay I expended £250,000 to £300,000 from the profits of his London merchant house in buying out partners, and in building additions to the Cyfarthfa Works. By 1820 the Crawshay total investment at Cyfarthfa and their works at Hirwaun lay in the region of £400,000. Penydarren, Plymouth and Dowlais expanded by the same method. Under Josiah John Guest in the 1820s Dowlais began to catch up with Cyfarthfa, finally exceeding its output in 1830 and consolidating that superiority through rigid financial controls and investing in capital projects directly from profits. In 1840 Dowlais employed over 5,000 people, Cyfarthfa 3,000, and Plymouth and Penydarren each had around 2,000. They were giants of British industry. Five years later the Dowlais workforce was 7,300. The amount paid out in wages by the four works in 1847 was estimated to be one million pounds.[22]

An Environmental Disaster

All that lay in the future. The village of Merthyr Tydfil, inland, 500 feet above sea level and some distance from existing towns – 24 miles from Cardiff, 32 miles from Swansea, 18 miles from Brecon – was situated at the northern and widest part of a parish nine miles long from north to south, that covered about 27 square miles of upland sheep tracks. Within that territory in the middle of the eighteenth century there were ninety-three scattered farms with a total population of probably less than a thousand. The village consisted of forty or so thatched houses

---

[22] A. H. John, *The Industrial development*...pp. 35, 41-2; Atkinson and Baber, *The Growth and Decline* pp, 52-6; T. E. Clarke, *A Guide to Merthyr Tydfil and the Traveller's Companion* (Merthyr Tydfil, 1848; Cardiff 1996 reprint), p. 28.

close to the parish church. The four ironworks, each at a discrete distance, like medieval castles attracted settlements where the workers found shelter and were known as 'the Inhabitants of the Ironworks' to distinguish them from 'the Inhabitants of the village'. Each settlement – Plymouth, Cyfarthfa, Penydarren, Dowlais and the village itself – retained its distinct character, only gradually coalescing into an urban identity as the flood of immigrants continued. The southern end of the parish untouched by these developments remained entirely rural.

During the last third of the eighteenth century the parish population rapidly increased until in 1801 the total approached 8,000 and still the flood of immigration came, creating the largest industrial metropolis seen in Wales, only slowing after 1851.

Date	Population	Date	Population
1801	7,705	1861	49,794
1811	11,104	1871	51,949
1821	17,404	1881	48,861
1831	22,083	1891	59,004
1841	34,977	1901	69,228
1851	46,378	1911	80,990

Source: Census.[23]

Overwhelmingly the immigrants came from rural Wales, although by the 1840s some 12 per cent were English, with increasing numbers of Irish, a small colony of Scots traders and even some émigrés from continental Europe. As late as 1851 three-quarters of those aged twenty and over had been born

[23] The numbers do not include the populations of Cefn Coed or Vaynor.

outside the parish and about two-thirds of these came from the Welsh counties of Carmarthen, Brecknock, Pembroke and Cardigan.[24] Practically all of those born within the parish were the children or grandchildren of immigrants. By the 1820s the Irish had begun to arrive, driven by famine and drawn by the promise of work. During the Great Famine many more came so that by 1851 there were over 3,000 Irish-born in Merthyr and Dowlais, approaching 7 per cent of the population. Altogether, between 1801 and 1851 the population increased six times over; half was under 25-years-old.

In a ceaseless search for iron ore, coal and limestone, all close at hand, the works devoured land. Where once had been farms, gorse, bracken, scrubland and grazing for sheep, the land was scoured, pitted and quarried. Coal tips and slag heaps daily encroached upon more land. The waves of incoming humanity compounded the environmental disaster by overwhelming the scanty accommodation. Shanties – *tai-unnos* –were swiftly flung up on the periphery of the village and around the works – sometimes within them – in total disorder. Local speculators – shopkeepers, farmers, publicans, builders – borrowed to build and sought the maximum return by randomly cramming houses without drains or lavatories into every available nook and cranny. Faced with this urgent human need the ironmasters were slow to respond. In 1798 when Cyfarthfa employed almost 1,000 it owned 70 workers' houses, Penydarren 49, Dowlais 58 and Plymouth 15.[25] These were homes for the imported skilled workers, the core of the labour force, for whom additional houses of good quality were later built near Cyfarthfa

---

[24] Brinley Thomas, 'The Migration of Labour into the Glamorganshire Coalfield (1861-1911)', *Economica* X (1930), reprinted in W. E. Minchinton, (ed.), *Industrial South Wales 1750-1914* (1969).

[25] Evans, *Labyrinth*, p. 153.

at 'Williamstown' and 'Georgetown' and at Dowlais as the works expanded. Anthony Hill built 'the Triangle' for his core workers at Pentrebach. The unskilled and their families had to fend for themselves.

The result was extreme squalor, filth, disease, and appalling rates of mortality, all compounded by the delay of the ironmasters in making clean drinking water generally available. The situation deteriorated further as the population grew. In 1852 the average age at death in Merthyr was 17.5 years. More than half of all children died before reaching the age of five and more than a quarter died before reaching one. The overall death rate was 36 per thousand against the, then, accepted norm of 20.

Disease apart, violence to the person was ever present. *The Morning Chronicle* correspondent in 1850 reported: 'I believe there are in Merthyr more men with wooden legs than are to be found in any town in the kingdom having four times its population. I once passed in the street three, within a hundred yards, and five in going through the entire street, which was not a long one.'[26] The main occupations – mining iron ore and coal, quarrying limestone, iron-making around furnaces and machinery – were dirty and dangerous, leading to lung diseases, deafness, blindness, loss of limbs and death through rock falls, explosions, burns and scalds. The evidence of seventeen-year-old Thomas George, speaks volumes.

> About a year ago I lost my left arm above the elbow; I slipped my foot and fell down, and my arm got into the rolls. I was only saved from going through them by being caught hold of by the men ...while I was at the Dowlais forge there were two men killed by the rolls and wheels, and two boys lost their left legs

[26] Jules Ginswick (ed.), *Labour and the Poor in England and Wales 1849-1851: Vol. III South Wales – North Wales,* (1983), p. 49.

> in the rolls and by the locomotive engine ...my eldest brother was killed at Aberdare, 23 years ago, by the rolls; and my youngest brother, aged eight years, has lost his left leg above his knee, from white swelling. My mother died about four months back'[27]

Most fatal accidents occurred underground and child deaths were not uncommon. Coroners were loath to hold inquests. Employers did not keep records of accidents. [28]

A Frontier Town

It has become a cliché to liken Merthyr in those early industrial years to an American frontier town or mining camp. The comparison is understandable. In August 1829 the *Cambrian* reported:

> The notorious David Davies or Dai Gam and Dick Parry were apprehended at Merthyr Tydfil, the last remnants of a numerous and atrocious gang who had infested Merthyr and its neighbourhood for the last twenty years, the successors of the gang that was broken up when John the Fox and Nehemiah Lee were transported.[29]

Merthyr's macho image was early established. By 1790 the

---

[27] Parliamentary Papers. *Children's Employment Commission, Appendix to First Report of Commissioners. Mines*, Part II (1842). Evidence collected by Rhys William Jones, p. 641.

[28] Keith Strange discusses accidents and their causes in 'Accidents At Work in Merthyr Tydfil c 1840-1850', *Merthyr Historian*, Vol. 3, (1980).

[29] Quoted in Russell Davies, *Hope and Heartbreak, A Social History of Wales and the Welsh, 1776-1871* (Cardiff, 2005), p. 217.

number of young unmarried men in Merthyr, 'a set of people ...naturally turbulent', was causing concern. Some, like William Jones the Tregaron tinker and army deserter, and Thomas Evans of Penboyr, a well-known thief, were on the run. Judge George Hardinge at Cardiff advocated marriage as a cure for restlessness but females were in the minority in Merthyr throughout the early decades of the nineteenth century. In the years following the end of the war against Napoleon in 1815 redundant soldiers and sailors finding life too quiet in their native parishes after the traumas and turbulence of war were among those attracted to Merthyr. It was not only work that attracted young men, it was liberation from the dullness of life on isolated hill farms, a quest for freedom, even licence, that brought them the 'wages of sin and savagery'. For fugitives it was an opportunity to achieve anonymity and in the process, as family history researches have revealed, to change their name. The restless movement of young males in and out of Merthyr and over the Monmouthshire hills was regarded as a prime cause of 'unruly behaviour'.

Rural pursuits, but now in an urban setting, continued well into the nineteenth century. Gambling accompanied foot and horse races, pitch-and-toss, dog and badger baiting, cock fighting and savage bare-fist mountain fights. Drunken street fights were common. Violence could also take the form of retributive mob justice. In 1833 a man who whipped a tram boy was beaten to death, and thirteen years later a stepmother accused of cruelty to a child was almost lynched.[30]. Responses were not always violent. A collier 'worsted in inglorious conflict' by his wife was carried through the streets on the shoulders of fellow colliers amidst a crowd of over 2,000 'without a breach of the peace'. Robert Thomas, a married man found penniless in the prostitute district

[30] David J. V. Jones, *Crime in Nineteenth Century Wales* (Cardiff, 1992), p. 83.

known as 'China' in 1845, was placed in a chair, carried on the shoulders of four men, and publicly humiliated and lectured. These reflected the rural mock trials that asserted community morality. An amicable instance of wife-selling was reported in 1863. The town was well-known for practical jokes, a favourite being the exchange of shop signs, with a butcher's sign placed above a doctor's surgery or, as the worshippers at Pontmorlais Wesleyan chapel found one Sunday morning, their chapel adorned with the pub sign of the *Jolly Sailor*.[31] On 4 August 1831 Thomas James was sent to Swansea prison for running naked through Merthyr streets for a sixpenny (2.5p) bet.[32]

Pubs and beer shops, usually open from six a.m. until midnight, proliferated; accounts of the number vary widely. Allegedly, at one time there were 200 in the Dowlais district alone. At Cefn Coed the population of about 1,500 in 1841 was served by 13 licensed houses. The estimate given to the *Morning Chronicle* in 1850 was of 305 in Merthyr and Dowlais, one to every 24.5 houses. Superintendant Wrenn of the Merthyr police told a Select Committee in 1854 that there were 208 public houses and 298 beer houses, making a total of 506 for a population of 63,000. Out of the 298 beer shopkeepers 158 were employed in the works 'being petty agents, who have very great influence in attracting and compelling men to their houses'.[33] Beer and cider were safer to drink than the water available, gin and brandy were 'medicinal' and kept babies quiet.

---

[31] *MG (Cardiff and Merthyr Guardian),* 23 April 1836; Russell Davies, *Hope and Heartbreak*, p. 269; 'Reminiscences of Merthyr Tydvil', *The Red Dragon,* Vol. 2 (n.d.), pp. 337-43; David Jones and Alan Bainbridge, 'The "Conquering of China": Crime in an Industrial Community, 1842-64', *Llafur*, Vol. 2 no. 4 (Spring 1979); *ME (Merthyr Express),* 17 June 1899.

[32] *Cambrian*, 13 August 1831.

[33] *MG*, 23 June 1854.

Pubs provided the gaiety and warmth often missing from houses. They gave blind harpists and ballad singers the chance to pick up an income, they provided a venue for dancing, for *gymanfa ganu* and *eisteddfodau*, for newspapers to be read aloud and benefit clubs to meet, for gossip, for wages to be paid out, and for newcomers to gather news of job opportunities and be hired. In the absence of public buildings they were the site of most public functions. Drink was essential to ironworkers. The furnaces at 1500 degrees centigrade sucked men dry leaving their eyes sunken, their features waxen and their limbs gaunt and thin, yet with muscles like wire.[34] Tea and beer were drunk in prodigious quantities. Home brewing, a rural art, was practised extensively in the growing town but by 1830 it had two well-known commercial breweries – Giles and Harraps Merthyr Brewery and the Pont-y-capel brewery at Cefn Coed. Evan Evan's brewery at Penyrheolgerrig and the Cyfarthfa brewery in Georgetown soon followed.

Law and Order

Arrangements for law and order before the 1840s were primitive. C. H. James who was born in 1817 and became a solicitor and then MP for Merthyr remembered that the parish constables 'were a dissolute, disreputable, corrupt set of men'. The stocks 'were a living institution' and next to them in Cross Keys street was

> the black hole, which was the only place where a man could be confined from the time he was taken up till he was taken before the magistrates. Twas literally a black hole...a building about ten or fourteen feet square, no windows to it, no fireplace, a

[34] Ginswick, p. 39.

> door studded with nails; there men often half drunk, and sometimes very drunk, were pushed in and there remained till had to go out before the justices. Twas a most barbarous business.[35]

The large keyhole to this building was often used 'by friends of tipplers to supply them with a little refreshment'. The stem of a tobacco pipe was inserted into the keyhole and into the protruding bowl was poured gin or brandy.[36]

There were no resident coroners or magistrates and consequently in 1793 all the local ironmasters were made justices of the peace. Not until 1829 was a stipendiary magistrate appointed. Before the police court was built in 1846 the magistrates held their sittings in public houses. The local newspaper in condemning this practice drew attention to an unintended consequence:

> This is not only disgraceful, but a positive grievance as to the prompt administration of justice. Persons who ...have to appear before the magistrates, are frequently attracted to spend the time, previous to their being called forward, in the bar or taproom; and not a few instances have occurred where witnesses have been brought forward in a state of ebriety, [drunkeness] in which all idea of administering to them the solemn obligation of an oath is out of the question.[37]

But it was the district known as 'China' that earned Merthyr a reputation for immorality. Reputed to be as bad, if not worse, than the 'Little Sodom' areas of Liverpool, Nottingham and

---

[35] C. H. James, *What I Remember about Myself and Old Merthyr* (Merthyr, 1892), p. 21.

[36] Wilkins, *History*, p. 364.

[37] Wilkins, p. 363; *MG*, 1 November 1834.

Derby its recognised leaders were known as the 'Emperor' and the 'Empress'. When one pair was transported, as happened in 1841, another pair succeeded them. These in turn were transported in 1847, only to be succeeded by another pair (who migrated to America in 1852). The area, properly known as Pont-y-Storehouse, was neither an ironworks community nor a part of the old village but a maze of alleys, narrow courts and tortuous lanes along the bank of the Taff from the lowest point of the High Street towards Cyfarthfa. Analysis of the 1851 census indicates an area high in lodgers, Irish-born labourers, and paupers so that it was by no means exclusively inhabited by criminals. Nor was it the only part of Merthyr or Dowlais where there were brothels. 'China' nonetheless captured public imagination.

There are two contemporary accounts. The *Morning Chronicle* correspondent investigated the area in the company of J.C. Campbell, the Rector of Merthyr and declared:

> Here it is that, in a congenial atmosphere, the crime, disease, and penury of Merthyr are for the most part located. Thieves, prostitutes, vagrants, the idle, the reckless, the dissolute, here live in a miserable companionship...what I that day saw of misery, degradation, and suffering, I shall remember to the end of my life.[38]

Ten years later in 1860, after the area had been 'cleaned up', an Anglican scripture reader and preacher kept a journal of the five months he spent trying to 'save', largely without success, the prostitutes who lived there. He noted ten girls in one brothel and gave the names of 36 prostitutes and of the men living off them. 'There is always a much smaller number there when the

[38] Ginswick, pp. 86-8.

works are slack than when they are going on briskly', he was told by Lewis Thomas, 'a poor man who earned his livelihood by carrying goods for people with his little donkey'. Thomas had an explanation of how 'China' had become the home of so many prostitutes. Originally

> many of the houses, as they were small and inconvenient (built when Merthyr was not intended to be what it is) were taken over by the parish and the aged poor were sent there to live – so that it was always a place where vice and crime would be met with less opposition than any other part of the town.
>
> The first prostitute arrived about 1825, others came, and as the old people 'were dying those girls were waiting to pay more money for the houses [rent] ...and so they were occupied one after the other until it became to its present aspect'.[39]

It was not until after the formation of the Glamorganshire police force in 1841 that serious efforts were made to bring to court the pimps and 'bullies', the prostitutes, brothel keepers, female pick-pockets and receivers. Initially there were only four full-time police officers. By 1847 there were 12 officers to cope with a population over 40,000. For more than twenty years the police raided China, fighting their way on occasions past 'bullies' who included, until he went to Carmarthenshire and was involved in the Rebecca Riots, the prize fighter John Jones (*Shoni Sguborfawr*).[40] The most colourful accounts are in the reports of court cases. Many of the 'Rodnies' (street urchins) had been orphans farmed out to residents of China and brought up to a life of crime. A number

---

[39] *The Scripture Reader's Journal,* NLW. M.S. 4943B, pp. 81-3. The hand-written journal covers January-May 1860.

[40] For John Jones (*Shoni Sguborfarw*) see David Williams, *The Rebecca Riots* (Cardiff, 1955, reprinted 1998).

of the women were deserted wives.[41] Where the name China came from is unknown but it probably came from an imaginative journalist who saw the district as mysterious and dangerous. From the early 1840s Britain was involved in 'Opium Wars' with China.

The criminal aspects of nineteenth century Merthyr were a significant part of its urban life but drunkenness, assault, petty larceny, poaching, sheep stealing, horse stealing, and even arson were prevalent in the rural villages and market towns of England and Wales, and 'many of the migrants to Merthyr Tydfil took their delinquent behaviour and rebellious instincts with them'. In the countryside the sanitary condition of accommodation for labourers was 'atrocious'[42] And, in all the newly industrialised towns of Britain squalid twilight zones existed that were cleared only gradually by the combined efforts of the police and public health authorities during the second half of the century. 'China's' criminal sub-culture was quite distinct from the drunkenness and disorderly conduct that featured in the Merthyr courts. Gradually, as in Wales generally, this behaviour diminished. 'In the context of unprecedented urban and industrial growth, and the great shifts of population, the improvement in social behaviour seemed remarkable. For

---

[41] David J. V. Jones, *Crime in Nineteenth Century Wales* (Cardiff, 1992), pp. 93,211. See also Jones and Bainbridge, 'The Conquering of China: Crime in an Industrial Community, 1842-64', *Llafur*, Vol. 2, No. 4 (Spring 1979) and Keith Strange, 'In Search of the Celestial Empire. Crime in Merthyr, 1830-60', *Llafur*, Volume 3 no. 1 (Spring, 1980), and David Jones, *Crime, Protest, Community and Police in Nineteenth Century Britain* (1982), chap. 4.

[42] Pamela Horn, *Labouring Life in the Victorian Countryside* (Dublin, 1976), chapter 11; David Jones, *Crime in Nineteenth Century Wales*, (Cardiff, 1992); David W. Howell, *Land and People in Nineteenth Century Wales* (1977), pp. 104-7.

many people, it had been an essential ingredient in the economic miracles of the period'.[43]

An Iron Town

Above all, Merthyr was defined by its industry. It was where Cort's puddling process was perfected, where Richard Trevithick's steam locomotive in 1804 pulled a load on rails for the first time in world history (characteristically for a bet), where Watkin George built a cast iron water wheel 'the greatest the world has seen', where Adrian Stephens invented the steam whistle, where rails for the Russian steppes and the American plains were rolled and where the South Wales Institute of Engineers was formed in October 1857 with Menelaus of Dowlais as its first president. It was where Robert and Lucy Thomas laid the foundations of the Welsh steam coal trade and where thousands first entered the industrial world and became proletarians, subject to capitalist authority and the harsh disciplines of market forces.

Merthyr was an 'iron town' as other towns were 'cotton towns' or 'railway towns'. The phrase connotes more than the means by which people earned a living; it suggests correctly that the whole social order was informed by the dominance of a single industry, its processes and its masters. One aspect found its way into every corner. The iron industry was intensely affected by the booms and depressions of the trade cycle. Every boom brought increased wages, jubilation and immigrants; every depression brought wage cuts, unemployment, poverty and fear of pauperism. For all its growth the keynote of the local economy was its roller-coaster vulnerability.

That was one reason why benefit or friendly societies

[43] David J. V. Jones, *Crime in Nineteenth Century Wales*, p. 244.

flourished in Merthyr. Open to anyone who could pay the contributions, the societies made weekly payments to members out of work because of sickness or infirmity, and provided a lump sum at death. Between the 1793 Act, which gave legal advantages to such societies and 1832, thirty-two friendly societies in Merthyr were registered with the Glamorgan Clerk of the Peace. Other societies existed but chose not to register. Societies multiplied faster than the population. In 1848 the *Merthyr Guardian* reported that 'in the Merthyr District, comprising Merthyr, Dowlais, Aberdare, Hirwaun and part of Gelligaer,' there were 144, with 13,342 members. The great majority of members would have been in Merthyr and Dowlais. It means that approaching 30 per cent of Merthyr's total population were members. Their monthly lodge meetings, usually held in pubs, were occasions for fellowship, discussion of current affairs, gossip and conviviality. In this they represented a half-way house between the chapels and the raw drinkers. Of the friendly societies registered in Merthyr between 1796 and 1848, twenty-one were for females. These also met in pubs: The Iron Bridge, The Miners' Arms, The Swan, The Globe, The Duke of York, The Cross Keys, Dowlais Inn, The White Lion, The Greyhound, The King's Head, The Old Angel, The Ivy Bush and the Vulcan Inn, Dowlais.[44]

But Friendly Societies had a serious purpose. The Victorian values of prudence, respectability, self-help and self-respect found concrete expression in the members' monthly contributions that built toward insurance against sickness, help for women during confinement, and a modest burial rather than a pauper's grave. A constant fear in skilled workers' lives was that accidents, illness and old age would precipitate a descent to the ranks of the labourer, or after 1853 the hated workhouse.

[44] Dot Jones, 'Self-Help in Nineteenth Century Wales: the rise and fall of the Female Friendly Society', *Llafur*, Vol. 4, No. 1 (1984).

The ability to work as a puddler was reckoned to last not much beyond forty years of age. The societies were a barrier, although ineffectual in many cases, against the 'cold and heartless nostrums' of the political economists and the harsh treatment that the Poor Law Guardians and their officers could deal to the poor.[45] Some, at times, may have been quasi-trade unions. There is no hard evidence.

A Nonconformist Town

A civic society needed more than an industrial base. Immigration was not a once-for-all phenomenon. It continued for the best part of a hundred years and those who settled in the mid-nineteenth century found a very different Merthyr from those who had arrived in the 1790s. The later immigrants found kin, chapels for their faith, benefit societies, a growing middle class, a flourishing market place and shops, appalling sanitation, a police force, and a working class that had been through the armed insurrections of 1816 and 1831. The process of building an urban industrial society on a scale unknown in Wales was in hand, and it was the people who had to do it. The immigrants brought their language, their country customs, and their religious beliefs.

It has been claimed that Victorian England was a country

---

[45] J. Burn, *An Historical Sketch of the Independent Order of Oddfellows* (Manchester, 1845), p. 33. Quoted by Trygve R. Tholfsen, *Working Class Radicalism in Mid-Victorian England* (1976), p. 294. Gwyn A. Williams, 'Friendly Societies in Glamorgan, 1793-1832', *Bulletin of the Board of Celtic Studies*, Vol. XVIII, (Nov. 1959); Dot Jones, 'Did Friendly Societies Matter? A Study of Friendly Society Membership in Glamorgan, 1794-1910', *Welsh History Review*, Vol. 12, No. 3 (June, 1985), *MG*, 9 December, 1848.

whose essence was a literal belief in the Bible, a certainty about an after-life of rewards and punishments, and consequently a conviction that this life is only a preparation for eternity.[46] For England see Wales, writ large. A parish church had been established at Merthyr since at least the thirteenth century, but it was Dissent not Anglicanism that predominated in the parish. Dissent in the Merthyr parish was strong and continuous from the Cromwellian Commonwealth of the seventeenth century when it was 'the centre of one of the most powerful concentrations of Puritan believers in Wales'.[47] The rector reported in 1763: 'above three fourths of the above mentioned inhabitants are professing themselves for the most part Arminians, with a few Calvinists, and fewer Anabaptists, and among all these I am afraid are too many Deists'.[48] In the last quarter of the eighteenth century this stream of dissenting ideas was swollen and given fresh impetus by the American and French Revolutions. In 1792 Richard Crawshay was concerned that 'An evil Spirit prevails amongst our Dissenters from the Damnable Doctrines of Dr. Priestley and Payne'.[49]

These authors were believed to be amongst the reading matter of certain members of the Cyfarthfa Philosophical Society founded in 1807. The Unitarian missionary Lyons preached in Merthyr in 1811 and found 'many of the workmen are of a reading and inquiring turn of mind'.[50] In 1812 a meeting place

---

[46] R. C. K. Ensor, *England, 1870-1914*, pp. 137-8.

[47] Glanmor Williams, 'The earliest Nonconformists in Merthyr Tydfil', *Merthyr Historian*, 1 (1976).

[48] John R. Guy (ed.), *The Diocese of Llandaff in 1763: The Primary Visitation of Bishop Ewer* (Cardiff, 1991)

[49] Chris Evans (ed.), *The Letterbook of Richard Crawshay 1788–1797* (Cardiff, 1990), p. 132.

[50] D. Elwyn Davies, *'They Thought For Themselves'* (Llandysul, 1982), pp. 127-8, 139.

for Unitarians was licensed in Merthyr and a Unitarian church opened in 1821 in Twynyrodyn close to the heart of Merthyr village. Its first sermon was preached by Thomas Evans (Tomos Glyn Cothi) – the minister at Trecynon, Aberdare – who had spent two years in gaol for insulting the king. Another visitor was the Unitarian republican Edward Williams (Iolo Morgannwg) who had turned his bookshop at Cowbridge into 'a Jacobin den' and whose influential collection of Unitarian psalms and hymns was published in Merthyr in 1812.

Both these pioneers of Welsh Unitarianism had been associates of Joseph Priestley and of the Welsh moral philosophers Richard Price (who had provoked Edmund Burke into writing his *Reflections on the French Revolution*), and David Williams whose *Lectures on Political Principles* was published in Merthyr in 1817. Iolo Morgannwg sometimes called at the home of William Williams of Penyrheolgerrig, the Unitarian weaver and cloth manufacturer. His presence attracted the 'sturdy old Republicans' of the district and William Williams' young son Morgan, the future Chartist leader, listened by the fireside to their discussions.[51] Iolo's son Taliesin Williams (ab Iolo) recalled that in 1815, when he came to live in the town, Napoleon and Cobbett were extolled by Merthyr's radical middle class.[52] Merthyr, a raw frontier town in the hills but also a centre of technological innovation, was saturated with radical ideas.

Like no Other

While the working class was creating a culture based on pubs,

---

[51] Geraint H. Jenkins, 'The urban experiences of Iolo Morgannwg' *Welsh History Review*, 22 (3) (2005); Morgan Williams, 'Notable Men of Wales: Iolo Morgannwg', *The Red Dragon*, Vol. 2, pp. 97-104.

[52] *MG,* 3 January 1835, correspondence.

chapels, the perils and fellowship of the workplace, the competitive creation and performance in *eisteddfodau* of poetry and music, and later in the century through organised sports, the ironmasters' contribution to Merthyr's evolving urban identity was miniscule. One verdict was pronounced in 1850 when T. W. Rammell, despatched to inquire into the sanitary condition of Merthyr Tydfil, was astonished to discover a town of 50,000 'as destitute of civic government as the smallest rural village of the empire'.[53] Attempts by the small group of middle class activists to institute a town council were blocked by the ironmasters throughout the whole of Victoria's reign. It can be safely said they did nothing that threatened their wealth or power.

Merthyr Tydfil, a town Welsh in language and culture, was also by the nature and scale of its industrialisation, the size of its proletariat and its concentration of Nonconformist worshippers, like no other Welsh town then existing. The inhabitants' rural roots, ongoing experience of industrialisation and their cultural inheritance produced a society that was both unique and foreshadowed the future South Wales. As early as 1831, 96 per cent of families worked at non-agricultural jobs. It displayed in full the worst characteristics of early capitalist industrialisation – rapid population growth, careless destruction of the natural environment, squalor, disease, crime, and great wealth, all cheek by jowl with desperate poverty. Merthyr Tydfil, with its early nineteenth century contemporaries Manchester, Liverpool, Birmingham, Bradford and Oldham, exemplified the industrialisation of Britain. At Merthyr the lives of thousands depended on just four family-owned ironworks whose heads wielded power comparable to that of the great medieval landowners. They were the Masters.

---

53 T.W. Rammell, *Report to the general Board of Health... into... the sanitary condition... of Merthyr Tydfil* (1850), p. 12.

2

The Masters

> The Masters are *very few* and very distant towards their men excepting *in the works.*
>
> **Henry Scale**[54]

> The very term 'ironmaster', so long applied in no other trade, has a strong flavour of power.
>
> **George T. Clark**[55]

As employers, landlords, magistrates, and patrons the ironmasters expected and received obedience and deference in the towns which they had largely brought into existence. They were not philanthropists: their chief interests were money and power. 'I have but one ambition and that is to be King of the iron trade' declared Richard Crawshay (1739-1810). His dictatorial son William I (1764-1834) and volatile grandson William II (1788-1867) shared this obsessive drive. All three are said to have turned down honours, proud to be known as Iron Kings. But in late eighteenth century Britain the men pursuing great fortunes inadvertently created a new society. Wealthy traders turned themselves into industrialists. Technological innovation became the norm. Steam replaced

---

[54] Cardiff Central Library, Bute MSS, XX/75: Scale to Bute, 19 November 1839. Italics in the original.

[55] George Thomas Clark, Inaugural Presidential Address to the British Iron Trade Association, 24 February 1876. NLW.

water as a source of energy. Iron replaced wood and stone. Steam and iron combined in machinery that brought even greater changes and more wealth. Men, women and children entered factories and mines in large numbers, relationships changed, a mass proletariat was born. Inequality grew. This revolution, the creation of a new civilisation spreading throughout Britain's industrial areas was as profound in Merthyr Tydfil as anywhere.

In Merthyr two men stand out as pioneers of this revolution – Anthony Bacon and Richard Crawshay. Both were traders and both were extremely rich before they appeared in Merthyr. The deeds of later ironmasters have overshadowed Bacon (1717-1786), but he had a massive influence upon the development of Merthyr's iron industry. Born in Whitehaven, Cumberland, he became involved in the import-export trade of that port as a teenager, went to America and ran a store in Maryland, mixed with leading tobacco planters and slave owners including George Washington and, before he was thirty, was trading in London. Government contracts to supply provisions to British troops in Africa and the West Indies brought him increasing wealth but it was as a slaver, selling men and women from Africa to the Caribbean, to Virginia and North Carolina, that he became super-rich. By 1765 when he invested in Merthyr he was the MP for Aylesbury, the owner of coal mines on Cape Breton Isle in Canada, and of a colliery near Workington. And at Whitehaven he had already experimented with using pit coal to make wrought iron.

He was not the first to invest in the Merthyr parish. Anthony Morley in the sixteenth century had established charcoal fired furnaces and forges in the area and in Bacon's day furnaces had already been established at Dowlais and Plymouth. But Bacon invested on a scale that outweighed all others. In 1765 he secured from the Llancaeach estate the mineral rights over

4,000 acres for 99 years at a rent of a mere £100 per annum. On this the industrialisation of Merthyr was founded. In 1766 he began to build a furnace and forge beside the river Taff at Cyfarthfa, introducing the latest technology – Abraham Darby's method of smelting iron ore with coke and Charles Wood's process for refining pig iron with coal. That same year he bought into the Plymouth furnace and its mineral rights. Early in the 1770s he added a foundry at Cyfarthfa and secured a contract to supply the East India Company with cannon. That led to lucrative British Board of Ordnance contracts to supply armaments. In 1780 he bought the furnace at Hirwaun so that its pig iron could feed the cannon foundry at Cyfarthfa.

In 1782 Bacon faced a dilemma. Should he give up his Parliamentary seat or his lucrative government contracts? A change of government had brought an attack upon corruption and Clerke's Act barred government contractors from sitting in the Commons. Bacon unscrupulously found a way around the legislation by having the contracts transferred to Francis Homfray a Staffordshire ironmaster. Homfray carried out the work at Cyfarthfa, paying rent to Bacon and using materials supplied by Bacon. Bacon kept his parliamentary seat. [56]

The scale of his investment and use of state-of-the-art technologies at Cyfarthfa, his employment of Richard Hill as manager at the Plymouth works, and then his introduction of Francis Homfray to the area, laid the foundations of Merthyr's iron industry. Homfray did not stay but he bought land in the

---

[56] On Anthony Bacon see Chris Evans, *Slave Wales: The Welsh and Atlantic Slavery 1660-1850* (Cardiff, 2010); L.B. Namier, 'Anthony Bacon, MP; an eighteenth-century merchant', *Journal of Economic and Business History*, Vol.2 (1929) reprinted in W.E. Minchington (ed.), *Industrial South Wales, 1750-1914: Essays in Welsh Economic History* (1969).

Merthyr area and his sons Jeremiah and Samuel became ironmasters at Penydarren. Above all, Bacon introduced Richard Crawshay to Cyfarthfa in 1777 as a partner. When Bacon died in January 1786 his three sons were minors and the Court of Chancery ruled that the Plymouth furnace should be leased to Richard Hill and the Cyfarthfa property to Richard Crawshay.

Richard Crawshay

Heavy-jowled Richard Crawshay is the supreme example of that key figure in the industrial revolution, the merchant who becomes an industrialist, not simply bringing capital but organizing and planning production, imposing the dictates of the market and the disciplines of industrial production upon large numbers of workers. Bacon had made that revolutionary move but he lacked Crawshay's consuming ambition.

Richard Crawshay's early years are the stuff on which the legend of heroic self-made men is founded. He came from a respectable farming family in the village of Normanton, Yorkshire, but at sixteen quarrelled with his father (all the Crawshays did that), made his way to London, sold his pony for £15 and found a job cleaning and running errands in a warehouse that sold smoothing irons. Through hard work, ability and unfailing self-confidence he was eventually put in charge of sales, and when his employer retired he left the business to twenty-four-year-old Richard. He went on to make his fortune by importing high grade iron bars from Sweden and Russia through his own wharves and warehouses and became London's leading iron merchant. But this was not enough. He determined to be an ironmaster in his own right and joined his fellow London merchant Anthony Bacon in a partnership at Cyfarthfa. It was a good time to be in the arms-trade. Britain was at war with France, Holland and the American colonies throughout 1775-83, and, with a one-year pause, with the French from 1793 to 1815.

After Bacon died Crawshay took over management of the works at Cyfarthfa. In 1792, aged fifty-three, he moved from London to Cyfarthfa to take personal control and in 1794 he bought the works. His ambition and indefatigable energy had been the driving force behind the completion of the Glamorgan Canal that same year, vastly increasing the ability to send iron from isolated Merthyr into the world via the port at Cardiff. He had already revolutionised the iron industry. In 1787 he had taken out a licence under patent to use Cort's method of making wrought iron, brought Cort's workmen to Cyfarthfa to train local workers and by trial and error perfected Cort's method. The completion of the canal together with the improvements to Cort's puddling and rolling methods dramatically reduced the price of a ton of bar iron, enabling much greater quantities to be produced at a lower price.

Through technological innovation, rigorous attention to detail and reinvestment of profits Richard Crawshay made Cyfarthfa the most modern works in Britain and the largest capitalist enterprise on the planet. A man of irrepressible ego, he let nothing and no-one stand in his path. He ruthlessly disposed of partners and quarrelled incessantly with fellow ironmasters. When he died at Cyfarthfa on 27 June 1810 he left over £1 million, an extraordinary sum for those days, equivalent to some £100 million today.

Investment and Innovation

Anthony Bacon and Richard Crawshay were exceptional among Merthyr's early ironmasters in being rich merchants who moved into manufacturing. The other entrepreneurs associated with Merthyr's iron industry were already ironmasters. Francis

Homfray owned forges and mills in Staffordshire and Worcestershire. John Guest was associated with a small furnace in Broseley, Shropshire. Isaac Wilkinson, one of the original partners in the Dowlais furnace in September 1759, was the master of the Bersham works, Denbighshire. Richard Hill had been brought from Cumbria by Bacon to be his agent at Cyfarthfa. He was married to Bacon's sister-in-law. These men, steeped in the culture and skills of the iron trade had technological expertise, marketing experience and access to skilled workmen but their capital resources were far below those of Bacon and Crawshay.

In 1763 Wilkinson, who through his involvement at Dowlais saw the industrial potentialities of the area, contacted John Guest and they built a furnace to the south of Merthyr village on land leased from the earl of Plymouth. They named the furnace after their landlord. When Bacon bought them out in 1765, Wilkinson left the Merthyr district. John Guest was appointed manager at Dowlais two years later. Originally the Dowlais furnace was owned by nine partners who had raised the £4,000 capital between them. With four of them merchants from Bristol, it is highly likely that slave-trade money financed Dowlais as well as Cyfarthfa, Plymouth and Hirwaun. As at Cyfarthfa the foundation of the future wealth at Dowlais was underpinned by an advantageous lease – 2,000 acres of mineral bearing land at a rent of £38 per annum for 90 years.

Once launched, the ironworks enjoyed steady success providing munitions for the wars of the eighteenth and early nineteenth centuries and wrought iron for the expanding home market – tramroads, railings, ballast for ships, steam engines, pipes, bridges (the metal in London Bridge came from Cyfarthfa), pit cages and lamp standards. The Crawshays sold iron through their own London House, George Yard. The other works employed agents to pick up contracts all over Britain and

Ireland. Success brought increasing profits, but also the need for new furnaces, forges and rolling mills. A second furnace was built at Dowlais in 1789. At Cyfarthfa Richard Crawshay poured money into expansion. By 1796 it had three furnaces and in 1801 a subsidiary ironworks to Cyfarthfa was built nearby at Ynysfach. His son, William Crawshay I (1764-1834) continued the investment and by 1820 total investment at Cyfarthfa and Hirwaun lay in the region of £400,000. These vast sums were financed by ploughing back profits. Investment in furnaces and machinery at the other works was similarly funded. It was a characteristic of the first generation of ironmasters (and industrialists in other fields) that they took the long view, exercising restraint on personal spending in order to invest for future wealth. As William Crawshay I wrote to his son, 'Early economy will make mature wealth'. In the interests of economy he even insisted that private correspondence should be written on a single sheet of foolscap.[57]

Entrepreneurship, new technology and invention went together. Behind the apocryphal stories of Crawshays drenched in sweat as they worked the molten ore is the reality that Richard Crawshay at Cyfarthfa drove the workmen through trials and improvements and numerous setbacks until Cort's puddling process was brought close to perfection. Watkin George, Richard Crawshay's engineer, was given a share of the profits in return for his imaginative designs of aqueducts, bridges and the massive Aeolus waterwheel, measuring 50 feet in diameter, six feet across, and weighing 100 tons. Fed by

---

[57] John P. Addis, *The Crawshay Dynasty: A Study in Industrial Organisation and Development, 1765*-1867 (Cardiff, 1957), p. 53. This is largely a business history and a full assessment of this remarkable family has yet to be written. Margaret Stewart Taylor, *The Crawshays of Cyfarthfa Castle* (1967) provides an interesting but sentimentalised version.

water brought by a double aqueduct on stone pillars 60-70 feet high it was the subject of a popular song heard in Merthyr's streets. The founding of the Cyfarthfa Philosophical Society in 1807 with its focus upon scientific discoveries and radical thought reflected the national fascination with scientific discoveries, together with the excitement surrounding local inventions and technological advance.

It was not an accident that Trevithick's world-changing experiment of putting wheels on a steam engine and making it pull a load on rails took place at Merthyr. At Penydarren, where in the 1780s the Homfrays benefitted from the capital investment of the London financier Richard Forman and later from the wealthy City dealer William Thompson, Samuel Homfray also worked on Cort's process with success. More significantly Homfray was an early user of Richard Trevithick's efficient high-pressure stationary engines. In 1802 the six feet two powerful Cornishman was at Penydarren installing an engine and was there again, of course, in the winter of 1803-4 developing his revolutionary locomotive. In 1804 when Davies Giddy, a future President of the Royal Society, and the Cornish patron of both Trevithick and Humphrey Davy, stayed at Penydarren House to see Trevithick's world-changing locomotive, he noted that one of Trevithick's stationary engines at Penydarren consumed eighteen tons of coal compared with a Watt engine at Dowlais which required feeding with forty tons to get the same result.[58] The astute Homfray held a share in Trevithick's patent for these machines.

The Plymouth works too had a reputation for high quality iron and innovation. Anthony Hill (1784-1862), the manager under his father Richard and subsequently sole owner from 1844, was known as a scientific ironmaster and good practical

[58] A. C. Todd, *Beyond The Blaze: A Biography of Davies Gilbert* (Truro, 1967), pp. 86-7.

chemist. He patented various chemical processes and shortened the conversion of pig iron into malleable iron by applying blast to it as it ran from the furnace. He was a Fellow of the Geological Society and counted among his friends I. K. Brunel and Mushet the metallurgist.

At Dowlais John Guest's brother-in-law Peter Onions patented in 1783 a coal-fired method of refining iron similar to Cort's method but the final stage consisted of hammering whereas Cort's patents of similar date specified rolling. Further innovation at Dowlais, however, was slow with the work's main role being to produce bar iron for use at Cyfarthfa and Penydarren.[59] Puddling was introduced at Dowlais in 1801 but it was not until Guest's grandson, Josiah John Guest (1785-1852), was in sole charge from 1814 that significant technical innovations were introduced and profits ploughed back. Guest, with Adrian Stephens, is credited with inventing the steam whistle and in 1833 devised a 'running out furnace' that eliminated a wasteful cooling process. He was elected a Fellow of the Geological Society in 1818 and a Fellow of the Royal Society in 1830.

The Entrepreneurial Tradition

The values of hard work and financial discipline were instilled into the younger members of these family firms, not always with success. The significance of accumulating wealth which, if reinvested would bring more wealth was a lesson particularly appealing to William Crawshay I. He was twenty-eight when his father Richard moved to Cyfarthfa and William was put in charge of the London House. Trading and money dealing were the major part of his life until, when he was forty-seven, Richard

---

[59] J. England, 'The Dowlais Iron Works, 1759-93', *Morgannwg*, Vol. III, (1959).

died. William then spent £247,000 to consolidate the Crawshay family grip upon Cyfarthfa and Hirwaun by buying out other shareholders; and went on to invest huge sums in the plant and machinery. But he remained in London and left the management of Cyfarthfa to his twenty-two-year-old son, William Crawshay II.

It is a curious coincidence that William Crawshay II was twenty-two when given charge of Cyfarthfa, that *his* son, Robert Thompson Crawshay (1817-1879), was the same age when he took charge of Cyfarthfa in 1839, that Samuel Homfray was also twenty-two when he, with his father and brothers started the Penydarren Works in 1784, and that Josiah John Guest was also twenty-two when he became manager at Dowlais in 1807. Coincidence it may be, but it points to an important fact. These sons of wealthy fathers were not sent to exclusive schools, least of all to a university. Their formal education ended early and from their teenage years they were immersed in the works and the ways of making iron. They learned the technology of furnace, foundry and forge, they gained personal knowledge of the key workmen and were taught the ways and importance of making money.

Trained as they were, there was a further step. Marriage was a way of safe-guarding financial interests, enhancing business opportunities, strengthening power-bases and reinforcing the money-making value system. The Crawshays and Homfrays were at the heart of an extensive and remarkable industrial and political network. In 1793 when Samuel Homfray was thirty-one he married Jane, the daughter of Sir Charles Morgan of Tredegar Park. By this one move he was linked to landed wealth, social position and enormous political power. It was a marriage of financial benefit to both families. He obtained from his father-in-law a lease on 3,000 acres of mineral land at Tredegar for ninety-nine years at £500 a year and began the

Tredegar Works in 1800. In return his father-in-law insisted that Homfray invest £40,000 in the Tredegar works and that all the exports from the works were carried through the Morgan wharves at Newport. Samuel became High Sheriff of Monmouthshire in 1813 and in 1818 MP for the county of Staffordshire. Earlier, the Homfray brothers had quarrelled, (a normal happening with them; unlike the Crawshays whose quarrels were intergenerational) and Jeremiah the elder brother left ill-tempered Samuel at Penydarren and founded the Ebbw Vale works in 1789 and then the Abernant works in 1801. So, three of the new works along the heads-of-the–valleys, Tredegar, Ebbw Vale and Abernant had their origins in Penydarren.

In addition to the works at Cyfarthfa and Hirwaun the Crawshays owned the largest tinplate works in the world at Treforest near Pontypridd, mines and works in the Forest of Dean, and a major export business in London. Richard Crawshay's daughter Charlotte married Benjamin Hall, a barrister educated at Christ Church, Oxford and Lincoln's Inn. He became MP for Totnes in 1806 and for Glamorgan County in 1814. He was a partner with his father-in-law Richard Crawshay in the Union ironworks in the Rhymney valley, and by Richard's will was bequeathed a three-eighths share in Cyfarthfa and the whole of the Union works. (Big Ben, the Westminster bell, was named after Benjamin Hall's six foot three inches tall son, also named Ben, who was Minister of Works when the Palace of Westminster was rebuilt after the disastrous fire of 1834. So, Big Ben is named after a grandson of Richard Crawshay).

Two of the sons of William Crawshay I married daughters of Samuel Homfray. Richard II married Mary, went into farming and land-ownership and largely disappears from view so far as industry is concerned. William Crawshay II married another of Homfray's daughters – Elizabeth – and after she died in 1813 he married Isabel Thompson, sister of Alderman Thompson, a partner in the Penydarren works and after the departure of Samuel Homfray to Tredegar its owner. Thompson was MP for the City of London 1826-32, Lord Mayor of London 1828-9 and a Director of the Bank of England 1829. In 1817 Thompson in turn married Amelia, yet another daughter of Samuel Homfray. He therefore had William Crawshay II as a brother-in-law and Samuel Homfray as his father-in-law. In the 1830s he was head of the Santiago Company that invested in copper mines in Cuba.

But it was George, another son of William Crawshay I, who upset his father and brothers by recruiting Merthyr puddlers and taking them to France to train French workmen. He had married Louise Dufaud the daughter of Jean Georges Dufaud a French ironmaster who William I thought was a French government spy. For several years George worked with Dufaud at his works at Grossouvre and later at his new works at Fourchamboult in the Nieve district. A brewery was built at Fourchambault for the Welsh workers, a number of whom married French women.

Another line in the 'Crawshay Dynasty' came when Richard Crawshay's sister, Susannah, married John Bailey, a Yorkshire farmer, and had two sons about whom a legend 'echoes' the life experiences of Richard himself. The story goes that Matthew Wayne, furnace manager at Cyfarthfa, was enjoying a drink at an inn at Quakers' Yard when a ragged boy walked in and asked if anyone could direct him to Mr. Crawshay, his uncle. The boy was fifteen-year-old Joseph Bailey (1783-1858) who had walked from Yorkshire. He was given employment in the works and, like his uncle, through hard work and ability gained promotion, became works manager and received a share in the profits. In 1801 he was joined by his twelve-year-old brother Crawshay Bailey (1789-1872). He too, it is said, had walked from Yorkshire. Unfortunately, neither story is likely to be true as both boys were born in Sussex to which their parents had moved from Wakefield.

However, the remainder of their story is indeed remarkable. Richard Crawshay left Crawshay Bailey £1,000 in his will and to Joseph he left 25 per cent of Cyfarthfa works. Joseph sold his share to William Crawshay I and with Matthew Wayne as a junior partner leased the Nantyglo works in 1811. In 1820 Wayne sold his share in the Nantyglo Works to Joseph Bailey who, together with his brother bought the Beaufort ironworks in 1833 for £45,000. Both moved into politics. Joseph bought the Glanusk estate near Crickhowell, went on to be MP for Worcester in 1835, MP for Breconshire in 1847 and was knighted in 1852. Crawshay Bailey became an industrial magnate in his own right, owning ironworks, financing railways and leasing vast coal reserves in the Rhondda. He was MP for Monmouth boroughs 1852-68 and in 1871 sold the Nantyglo iron company for £4 million.

Matthew Wayne bought the Gadlys works at the head of the Cynon valley after he left the Nantyglo works, supervised the building of the Victoria ironworks at Ebbw Vales, and was chairman of the Merthyr Aberdare Coal Company, the first to exploit the steam coal resources of the Cynon valley. Watkin George left Cyfarthfa for his native Pontypool where he became part-owner and manager of the Pontypool works.

The Merthyr iron industry was the seedbed from which ambitious men, ruthless and well trained in the arts of iron and money-making, planted ironworks throughout the heads of the valleys and beyond. Penydarren spawned the works at Tredegar, Ebbw Vale and Abernant. Capital and enterprise from the Cyfarthfa works went into the Union works at Rhymney and those at Nantyglo, Beaufort, Aberaman, the Victoria works at Ebbw Vale, Pontypool, and the Merthyr Aberdare Coal

Company. Cyfarthfa and Dowlais were models of integrated iron production that heavily influenced French ironworks in Burgundy and Aveyron where Welsh workers, including those from Merthyr, were employed.

The transfer of iron-making skills to America through the employment of Welsh workers is well documented. One of many links was the marriage in 1838 of Isabel, daughter of William Crawshay II into the Ralston family, leading Philadelphia merchants with an interest in the Farrandsville works in Pennsylvania. The works had already recruited Edward Thomas from the Plymouth works. In 1842 Giles Edwards, a pattern-maker from Merthyr emigrated to Carbondale, Pennsylvania. He went on to manage and own ironworks in Alabama.[60] A later and more spectacular development came in the 1860s when John Hughes, one-time apprentice at Cyfarthfa founded the ironworks, mines and city of Donetsk, initially called Hughesovska, in the Ukraine.

If Cyfarthfa was the cradle of entrepreneurs, Dowlais was the nursery for managers and technical innovators. When Sir John died there was no family member competent to take over, except for his remarkable widow Lady Charlotte. His eldest son Ivor was seventeen and had not been bred up in the iron trade. He was being privately tutored by Charles Schreiber, Fellow of Trinity College, Cambridge, who Charlotte, fourteen years older than Charles, soon married. Because of the youth and the upbringing of the Guest children the influence and expertise of Dowlais was not spread by family members but by those who had worked and received their training there. Among them were William Jenkins, general manager of the Consett works in

---

[60] Anne Kelly Knowles, *Managing Iron: The Struggle to Modernize an American Industry, 1800-1868* (Chicago, 2013) is a valuable source for the influence of the Merthyr ironworks upon early developments in France and America.

County Durham 1869-1894 who made it efficient and profitable; Edward Pritchard Martin a successful innovator at Port Talbot and Blaenavon who returned to Dowlais as General Manager where he had first learned his trade; and John Vaughan and Edward Williams (grandson of Iolo Morgannwg) both products of Dowlais and both hugely involved in the Teeside firm of Bolckow-Vaughan and the rapid rise of Middlesborough, the fastest growing city in late Victorian England.[61]

It was in the works, as Henry Scale pointed out, that iron-making, its skills and its acknowledged special culture, formed a bond between employers and workers, one enhanced by the physical presence – 'the Master's Eye' – in and around the works. The Masters' knowledge of the iron trade recognised (and embellished in the telling) by those who toiled over the mysterious chemical processes of iron-making, contributed to the aura surrounding individual ironmasters, who were, in any case, commanding personalities. Amidst the shock of the new, the ironmasters' technical knowledge, parliamentary connections, and national prominence in the iron trade enhanced their local aura.

Quarrels and Competition

Inter-marriage did not prevent quarrels between the ironmasters. They were fiercely competitive and quarrelled with each other over a whole range of issues – the price of iron, transportation, the recruitment of skilled labour, access to water, coal and iron ore. A visitor in 1797 found Richard Crawshay and his son William I in such bad temper that they refused to sit in the same room together, sending each other

[61] Asa Briggs, *Victorian Cities* (Harmondsworth, 1968), chapter six. Joe England, 'What Has Merthyr Tydfil Ever Done For Us?', *Merthyr Historian* Vol. 27, 2015.

letters from one room to the next.[62] But this was merely one incident among many across the generations.

The early works depended upon water as a source of power. When in 1790 Richard Crawshay set out his plans for a canal to run from his works to Cardiff, Richard Hill at Plymouth objected that diverting water from the Taff into the canal would injure his works. Despite a clause in the canal Bill that safeguarded Plymouth's water supply the dispute between Crawshay and Hill dragged on for years, including physical attacks by Hill upon a canal lock, and litigation that went all the way to the Court of Chancery. Richard Hill called Richard Crawshay 'a tyrant'. Samuel Homfray who quarrelled with him over access to the canal called him 'a damned scoundrel'.

There were also fierce quarrels between Dowlais and Penydarren over access to coal and iron ore in the narrow valley of the Morlais. More than once labourers and miners on each side fought each other with the full support and sometimes leadership of their employers. An armed clash between Penydarren and Dowlais men in 1809 led to twenty-four-year-old Josiah Guest being indicted for riotous assembly and assault. So bitter were these rivalries that when Taitt of Dowlais left the bulk of his fortune to Josiah he stipulated that if he helped Samuel Homfray in any way the bequest would be forfeited and 'irrevocably null and void'. Josiah John Guest's promotion of the Taff Vale Railway, opened in 1841, was a source of bitter dispute between Guest and the Crawshays who, correctly, saw it as a threat to the traffic on the Glamorganshire Canal, which they owned.

These quarrels were a powerful early ingredient in the mix that caused workers, as contemporaries noted, to be strongly attached to 'their' works. The memory of violent skirmishes

[62] Chris Evans, *The Labyrinth*, p. 123.

sanctioned and supported by their employers established allegiances and a company chauvinism that ran throughout social relations in the nineteenth century.[63] Originally, this localism arose from the geographic distances between Plymouth, Cyfarthfa, Penydarren, and Dowlais, and the neighbourhoods that grew up around them. From this topography, the loyalty induced by company quarrels, and the personal attributes of each ironmaster, there evolved separate and distinct cultures, most notable at Cyfarthfa and Dowlais.

The aristocratic Lady Charlotte Guest had her own assessment of these businessmen. William Crawshay II, she noted, drove his family to church in a coach and four with liveried coachmen. He was 'beyond all rule and description and is quite one of those meteoric beings whom it is quite impossible to account for'. 'Mr. Anthony Hill is a gentleman – Mr. Bailey has a low born purse cunning – Mr. Thompson is the Alderman in every sense, and has not the uprightness which I should be inclined to give most City Merchants credit for – the Harfords [ironmasters at Ebbw Vale] are Quakers of a rather American stamp'. [64]

Droit de Seigneur

In September 1839 William Crawshay II suffered a terrible blow. His son and heir to Cyfarthfa, William III, drowned whilst crossing the Severn. The question of succession was urgent for

---

[63] Chris Evans, *The Labyrinth*, pp. 107-120; ibid, 'Work, violence and community in early industrial Merthyr Tydfil', in P. J. Corfield and D. Keene (eds.), *Work in Towns 850-1850* (Leicester, 1990); E. A. Havill, 'William Taitt and the Dowlais Ironworks', *Transactions of the Honourable Society of the Cymrodorrian*, 1983.

[64] Revel Guest and Angela John, *Lady Charlott Guest: An Extraordinary Life* (Stroud, 2007) p. 43.

William had already begun to withdraw to Caversham Park, near Reading. He decided that his other two sons by his first wife were unsuitable to take over the Cyfarthfa Works. Francis was lazy and eccentric to the point of being regarded by his father (and others) as unstable, while Henry, an extremely capable businessman and manager of the Hirwaun works, had offended social convention by marrying Eliza Harris a woman working in the works. Consequently, the management of Cyfarthfa fell to twenty-two-year-old Robert Thompson Crawshay, the eldest son by William II's second wife. It was an unfortunate decision for the future of Cyfarthfa. Robert's initial popularity ended with his gravestone in Vaynor churchyard engraved, at his own wish, with 'God Forgive Me'.

Whether this guilt-ridden epitaph arose from his well-known lechery or the disinheritance of the children of his daughter Rose Harriette or the five-year lock-out of his workmen that began in 1874 is unknown. The Cyfarthfa bandsmen used to recount how a workman, cap in hand, complained to William II that his son, Robert, had made his daughter pregnant. 'Be proud, my man, be proud' was the response, 'and here's a golden guinea for you'. Probably apocryphal – the tale is told about other ironmasters – it was rooted in fact. Robert, who had a procurer, was not alone; his brother Francis had the same reputation. Francis, sent to manage the Crawshay's tinplate works at Treforest, is reputed to have had a large number of illegitimate children by local women, rewarding them and their offspring with £100 and a job in the works. Their uncle George when eighteen had had an affair with a girl employed at the works and had been a constant worry to his father. The Merthyr parish registers reveal that Samuel Homfray of Penydarren was the father of at least three illegitimate children. A visitor in 1852 picked up reports of how 'the young masters ...played the parts of so many sultans' with the young women in their employ promising 'higher pay and lighter work' on the one hand and menacing them on the other with threats 'to be dismissed ...these and a score of other reasons may be given'.[65]

Nor, in the frontier town phase, were the ironmasters above brawling. Samuel Homfray had a reputation as 'a bull necked, snub nosed bruiser', with a temper 'explosive and vengeful' a tongue 'uncontrollably abusive, and his disposition libidinous'. George Crawshay told his brother, William II, in May 1823 that Richard Fothergill of Aberdare: 'drank 2 bottles of port the night before and then finished with grog. We told him we hoped he had not broke any body's head which he might do if he ever got fighting. I do not think he knows you hit him, he was too infernally drunk'.[66]

The Guest family by contrast were staid. Or so it seemed. But before settling down and becoming a dampening presence upon any frivolity, Thomas' son Thomas Revel Guest (1790-1837) had fought a duel in France, fathered two illegitimate children (who were despatched to Australia) and been unfrocked.[67]

Houses and Country Estates

The houses of the first generation of ironmasters were actually in or near the smoke and clamour of their works, but later generations lived more grandly. The pace was set by the Homfrays who about 1786 built, on what workmen discovered to be the site of a Roman fort, Penydarren House with its planned gardens, fishponds and grape houses and every modern convenience. That was outshone when William Crawshay II

[65] Edwin F. Roberts, *A Visit to the Ironworks and environs of Merthyr Tydfil in 1852* (Swansea, 1853), p.42.

[66] Evans, *The Labyrinth*, p. 124. G. A. Williams, *The Merthyr Rising*, p. 40.

[67] Guest and John, *Lady Charlotte Guest*, p. 126.

built in 160 acres of parkland, against his father's wishes, the imposing mock medieval Cyfarthfa Castle. The workmen who, in 1825, saw it rise on the skyline and look down on them understood its message of wealth and power. But William I thought it an extravagant folly 'A great House and expensive establishment will not fight our Battle in the Trade'.[68] Lady Charlotte, who visited in 1835, was unimpressed. The 'fine rooms' were 'ill lit', with 'wretched furniture': 'I never saw such splendid misery!' Less opulent, the solidly built Georgian Dowlais House where Sir John and Lady Charlotte lived was dubbed by her mother 'the Cinder hole'.[69]

The third generation moved to land ownership, a first step to leaving behind the sooty region where their fortunes had been made. It was time to enjoy that money. Between 1830 and 1848 the Dowlais partners drew from the works an average of £64,000 a year.[70] The Guests by the 1840s, in addition to prestigious London addresses, usually rented, were installed at Canford in Dorset. The estate with its mansion, 5,000 acres of prime land and 5,000 acres of poor land was bought for £335,000 with a further £19,000 paid for extra land.[71] Charles Barry (architect of the Houses of Parliament) was engaged to make alterations that cost a further £30,000. With Sir John's parliamentary duties, Lady Charlotte's determination to succeed in London Society, and months spent in foreign travel as well as residence at Canford, the Guests were frequently absent from Dowlais for long periods.

In 1825, the same year that Cyfarthfa Castle was completed,

---

[68] Addis, p. 54.

[69] Anon., 'A Run on the Rails and a Few Days amongst the Furnaces of South Wales', *Bristol Times*, 21 February 1851, quoted by Carter and Wheatley, *Merthyr Tydfil in 1851* (Cardiff, 1982), p.12.

[70] J. H. Morris and L. J. Williams, *The South Wales Coal Industry 1841-1875* (Cardiff, 1958), p. 86, note 3.

[71] Guest and John, *Lady Charlotte Guest*, pp. 136-7.

Joseph Bailey had a house built at Glanusk Park by Robert Lugar the designer of Cyfarthfa Castle. By 1830 Bailey had retired from active management to live the life of a country gentleman with major holdings in Breconshire, Herefordshire and Glamorgan. Crawshay Bailey, unlike his brother, continued in active management for most of his life until eventually retiring to Llanfoist House, near Abergavenny. William Crawshay II, who enjoyed investing in land, bought Hensol Castle one year after Cyfarthfa Castle was completed then, realising he had made a mistake, struggled to sell it, until finally successful in 1839. He next rented the elegant classical mansion at Caversham Park, near Reading, before buying the whole estate in 1848. Extraordinarily he had not insured the house. When it burnt down he spent another fortune building a new mansion on the same spot, using wherever possible iron instead of wood for the interior fittings. From 1839 he spent more and more of his time at Caversham while his heir, Robert Thompson Crawshay, lived in Cyfarthfa Castle. The exception to this pattern of expenditure was the Hill family who despite their considerable wealth bought neither a country estate nor a prestigious house. It was not until 1850 that Anthony Hill built the mansion at Pentrebach where he lived until his death in 1862.

In politics Anthony Bacon and Richard Crawshay were Tories and high Anglicans, as were William Taitt and Anthony Hill, a fact that together with their Englishness separated them from their Welsh-speaking Nonconformist workmen. Richard Crawshay was buried at Llandaff Cathedral, Anthony Hill in the Church of St. John the Baptist at Pontyrhun, near Merthyr, a church he paid for in 1853 on condition that he would be the only one buried there. He lies in a brick-lined vault below the altar in an elm coffin encased in a lead coffin which is within an oak coffin. When he died his workmen were given the day off to attend his funeral, with full pay, but out of respect for him they each donated their day's pay to purchase the stained glass window on the east side of the church. Neither the Crawshays nor the Hills pursued personal political ambitions, unlike J.J. Guest who had a lengthy parliamentary career.

It is a ruthless ambition for money and the power to protect it that most clearly defines these ironmasters. They provided the capital investment, technology, entrepreneurial energy and imagination that created an industry at the heart of the first Industrial Revolution. The communities they had caused to come into being were to them merely by-products of that process.

3

Protest and Control

> Now is the time to be masters or slaves to the men
>
> **Crawshay Papers, 8 June 1813**[72]

On 7 June 1815 a Dowlais worker named Lalby was sacked. It was reported that he ' have been in a state of Intoxication since Saturday Night Last & have not sleept at home until Last night, & have Left work this Day for the purpose of gitting drunk.'[73] He was not exceptional. The first generation of industrial workers the world over did not take easily to the new disciplines of time-keeping, regular work routines, the demands day and night of the iron-making processes. Money in their pockets was another new experience.

On Merthyr's hills a new society was being created, a learning process for both masters and men. In the final years of the eighteenth century the pace of change became frenetic. The war against Revolutionary France that began in 1793, the assumption of complete control of Cyfarthfa by Richard Crawshay in 1794, the completion of the Glamorganshire canal from Merthyr to Cardiff, the increasing use of steam power and the successful application at Cyfarthfa and Penydarren of the puddling process for making wrought iron, all fuelled an accelerating industrialisation. In 1785 when the new works at

---

[72] NLW: Crawshay Papers, 8 June 1813. Quoted by A.H. John, *The Industrial Development of South Wales* (Cardiff, 1950), p.95, note 3.

[73] Elsas, p. 22. Thomas Bridges to William Taitt.

Penydarren began to produce there were only four blast furnaces in Merthyr, one in each works. By 1812 there were eighteen furnaces and by 1831 there were thirty-three. Between 1817 and 1830 the tonnage of iron sent down the Glamorganshire canal from the four Merthyr works increased by 180 per cent.[74] However gradually 'the industrial revolution' developed in other parts of Britain, in the South Wales iron district, and in Merthyr in particular, the pace of change in those years was ferocious. But that headlong growth was punctuated by sudden plunges into recession that added to the stresses caused by technological innovations, immigration and food shortages.

Recurring boom and slump reached into every household in Merthyr and in the first third of the new century issues that began in the workplace spilled over into district-wide bitter protests that tested the determination and resources of both masters and men to the limit. South Wales in the early nineteenth century was in a seemingly constant state of civil unrest and violence as workers encountered the realities of industrial discipline.[75] Riots erupted in Merthyr in 1800, 1816 and 1831 each one growing in scale and ferocity. But daily life could not be lived at that level of violence and turmoil. Within the ironworks masters and men found ways of settling disagreements, sometimes through conflict but often peacefully, that enabled workers to live their lives and produce the iron that drove Britain's economic expansion and made their masters' fortunes. These compromises, developed in the early years, continued after the days of riots had passed.

---

[74] Edgar Jones, *A History of GKN Vol 1: Innovation and Enterprise, 1759-1918* (1987), p. 65, Table 3.2.

[75] Ivor Wilks, *South Wales and the Rising of 1839* (Llandysul, 1989); David Jones, *Before Rebecca* (1973); idem, *The Last Rising. The Newport Insurrection of 1839* (Oxford, 1986).

Work and the Workers

Welsh agricultural workers knew little about the production of iron but around the works, mines and quarries there were tasks such as breaking limestone, loading and unloading trams, lifting and piling iron, stacking coal at the coking pits, wielding pick and shovel, to which they – men, women and children – adapted. They laboured in low-paid open-air jobs with little chance of advancement, often like sixteen-year-old Jane James at Dowlais, employed by a sub-contractor. She explained to the 1842 Children's Employment Commission: 'I went to keep an air-door [underground] when I was nine years old, and have been "polling" or cleaning mine on the mine banks for five years...I work for another girl, she employs me, and pays me 6s.[30p] per week; she has the "polling" at this bank by the job.'

Initially, iron ore ('mine') was so close to the surface that it could be obtained merely by digging, or through releasing pent-up dams, scouring the top soil and revealing the ore. Later, the ore was worked underground. Coal for smelting the ore was obtained through driving 'levels' into the hillsides as well as sinking mine shafts. Miners (who dug the ore) earned about 50 per cent more than labourers while colliers (who dug the coal) earned about 70 per cent more than labourers.

In all these jobs conditions were harsh beyond twenty-first-century Western sensibilities; the competition for employment constantly heightened by fresh immigrants and by children sent into the labour market to earn a few extra pennies. Competition meant that the irresponsible soon found themselves on the margins of employability or cast aside. Recessions threw many out of work and into destitution. The normal working day for men, women and children ran from six in the morning to six at night in a working week of six-and-a-half days. There were two days holiday a year – Good Friday and Christmas Day. Those who made iron worked alternate shifts, days one week and nights the next. Beyond the works a small but slowly growing number, both skilled and unskilled, were occupied in construction, transport, wholesaling, retailing and other services.

The Children's Employment Commission collected evidence in 1841 from the south Wales ironworks and collieries. Robert Eldridge, aged thirteen, came from Sydenham in Kent.

> His mother is dead. His father brought him down to this country, and left him on the mountain. He ran away and has not seen him since. He got into the [Dowlais] engine house, and got scalded bad; he was taken in by a widow woman of the name of Margaret Williams, who got a doctor for him, and took care of him. He works for a 'filler' and gets 5s.[25p] per week. 'He gives his wages to Margaret Williams who ...kept him for eight or nine months while he was ill, and paid the doctor for him'.

Benjamin Jones, aged eight, deformed by rickets, worked with his father at Dowlais 'straightening bars.

> I hold the "set-hammer". I work the same time that he does. In summer from "six to six"; in winter from "light to light" ...My wages are 3s.[15p] per week. My father holds the bars, and another man straightens them with the sledge. That man pays a part of my wages; my father has the money'.

Morgan Davies, aged seven kept

> a door in Tommo's Level [the upper four feet level]; I go down at six o'clock, the same time as the men, and come up again

> with them. I take bread and cheese and bread and butter with me, and eat it when I want it; I eat it sometimes in the morning soon, and then have none all day; the rats run away with my bag sometimes.

Mary Richard, aged twenty-five, was a limestone breaker at Penydarren.

> My father took me to work with him when I was nine years old ...I work at the top of the furnace; there is no cover over head, and when it rains I get wet. I break the stones for one furnace, about 14 trams full every day; they hold more than a ton each. I am paid by the ton of iron made. I have my own time for meals provided I keep the furnace supplied.

A family 'helper' underground brought additional income. Frederick Evans, clerk and accountant for the Dowlais Collieries gave evidence:

> I have known instances of a father carrying his child of four years old on his back to the work, and keeping him with him in the stall all day for the purpose of obtaining an additional tram allowed him. Children are generally brought to work about six years old, and the first work at which they are employed is to stand by an air-door, opening and shutting it after each horse that passes that way... Girls generally begin to work about seven years old, and they are few in number in comparison to the boys...In most cases it is the extreme poverty of the parents that compels them to send their young female children to work.[76]

[76] British Parliamentary Papers, *Children's Employment Commission. Appendix to First Report of Commissioners.* Mines. Part II. Report by Rhys William Jones, pp. 633-659.

Similar evidence was given for workers at Cyfarthfa and Plymouth and for those at mines and ironworks throughout South Wales and Britain. After such evidence the 1842 Mines Act prohibited the employment underground of women, and boys under ten. The legislation was not always observed, parents often claiming that children were older than they actually were.

Women at work

Reliable data for the number of females in employment before 1851 does not exist. After that date numerous detailed problems exist with the way persons and jobs were classified from one census to the next. However, by dealing in broad occupational categories comparisons have been made between England and Wales and between Cardiff, Swansea, Merthyr Tydfil and Rhondda 1851-1911.[77] The data for 1851 revealed that 4,894 females were in paid employment in Merthyr Tydfil, 23.3 per cent of the total number of females aged ten years and over, and 12.7 per cent of the total occupied labour force. The largest number of women employed were in Domestic Offices or Services, 39.6 per cent; followed by Dressmaking, 23.5; Mines and Quarries, 9.7; Metals, Machines etc., 8.7; Food, Drink, Lodging, 5.5; Agriculture, 2.1; Professional Occupations, 1.7.

The correspondent of *The Morning Chronicle*, was given access to the ironworks and reported in 1850 that of the 6,000

[77] L.J. Williams and Dot Jones, 'Women at Work in Nineteenth Century Wales', *Llafur* Vol. 3, No. 3 (1982). The figures exclude the wives of Innkeepers, Shoemakers, Shopkeepers, Farmers and Graziers, Butchers, Licensed Victuallers and Beershop Keepers, Lodging and Boarding House Keepers; the daughters, grand-daughters, sisters and nieces of Farmers and Graziers.

employed at Dowlais only 180 were females, of 5,000 at Cyfarthfa 150 were females, and at Plymouth only 175 out of 2,750. He was denied access to the Penydarren works but estimated it employed 120 females. Altogether, he put the total number of females employed in the manufacture of iron in Merthyr and Dowlais at 625 out of almost 16,000 male and female employees: equivalent to 3.9 per cent, an estimate less than half that indicated by the Census. (An illustration of the gender difference between the labour used in the two major industries of the nineteenth century is that in 1850, 55.8 per cent of the 331,000 employees in cotton factories were females aged above thirteen years.[78])

The eye-witness accounts and interviews conducted by *The Morning Chronicle* correspondent vividly illustrate the work done by women. The task of 'poll-girls' was to lift lumps of iron ore from the trams, separate it from stone shale and then pile it ready for the furnaces. A twenty-one-year-old explained:

> I work eleven hours a day in the open air, and am paid by the ton. My earnings come to 3s 9d [15.75p] per week – not more. I clean and stack about four tons of mine a day. The mine is often so flinty that it cuts my hands. (Her hands were horny with callouses.) I live on bread and cheese.

The reporter next describes the work of 'coke-girls'. He saw them on a day of heavy rain and high wind, working on the mountain side 'with the rain literally running off their coal-bedaubed petticoats over their boots, in black streams, to the ground.' They were not paid by the ton but by the day and as the furnaces constantly required coke they had to work in all

[78] Ginswick, p. 30; Neil J. Smelser, *Social Change in the Industrial Revolution: An Application of Theory to the Lancashire Cotton Industry 1770-1840* (1959), p. 202.

weathers. A twenty-four-year-old 'coke-girl' who worked at Penydarren reported:

> I earn five shillings [25p] a week, but pay out of that a trifle for the doctor and 'fund' [provision for sickness.] I have often to lift from the trams pieces of coal which weigh over a hundredweight, and carry them to the pit. I work eleven hours a day taking the year through... Without the assistance of my mother and father I could not live.

The 'lime-stone girls' who with hammers broke up the limestone before it was put in the smelting furnaces at Dowlais earned seven shillings [35p] a week. They paid a shilling [5p] for lodging, and their boots which 'the work rapidly destroys' cost eight shillings [40p] a pair. Their diet was chiefly tea and bread and cheese but sometimes 'animal food'. They were better off than the 'tippers' who worked with men and boys in all kinds of weather and cleared the trams of their loads of burning cinders for four shillings [20p] a week. 'Pilers' worked in the intense heat of the mills and forges piling and weighing the iron cut by the shears. A nineteen-year-old explained:

> I work by day one week and by night another. When the mills are working "rails", two other girls and myself pile on an average 35 tons a day between us. We have to lift up the pieces from the ground as high as my middle. Sometimes the iron is very hot, and we can't take hold of it without thick leathers. I have burnt my hands shockingly, and so have the other girls who do the same work. I live here with my father; sometimes I earn 4s [20p], and at others 5s [25p] a week.

The manufacture of fire-bricks at these works was done exclusively by women and in the opinion of the correspondent 'a more humiliating and uncongenial occupation for the sex is hardly to be found through the entire range of our industrial economy'. The local fire-clay was ground by machinery and then saturated with cold water by the women who next rapidly trod it with their bare feet, with the clay and water reaching calf height.

> This operation completed, they grasp with both arms a lump of clay weighing about 35 pounds, and supporting it upon their bosoms, they carry this load to the moulding table, where other girls, with a plentiful use of cold water, mould it into bricks.

On average they earned six shillings [30p] a week when at work but there were numerous weeks when clay was not available and then they were unemployed, going into debt to live. On Sundays they went to school and worked twelve hours a day on the other days of the week.[79]

The Morning Chronicle correspondent recorded *en passant* that female domestic servants were prized as wives compared with those who laboured in the ironworks or brick works, because they knew 'middle class ways' and how to run a home. The arduous, exhausting and essential housework of wives and mothers in industrial communities remains largely unrecorded.[80]

The Skilled Workers

There was little difficulty in inducing field labourers to desert hoeing turnips for better paid unskilled jobs in the quarries and

---

[79] Ginswick, pp. 29-35.

[80] General comments appear in R. Page Arnot, *South Wales Miners, Glowyr de Cymru: A History of the South Wales Miners' Federation 1914-1926* (Cardiff, 1975) and Lady Florence Bell, *At the Works: A Study of a Manufacturing Town* (1907). See also Elizabth Andrews, *A Woman's Work is Never Done* (Dinas Powys, 2006).

ironworks, but the recruitment of skilled furnace-men was another matter. In the early years companies were constantly on the look-out for 'sound' men and recruited them from the established centres of iron working in Scotland, Staffordshire and Shropshire. Apart from the higher wages their skill brought them, these men could ask for housing with low rent, or even rent-free houses, together with free coal and an assurance that there would be work for their children. Most important were the process workers who actually smelted the ore, made wrought iron and turned it into bars and rails. Within the works, vast by the standards of the day, tasks were broken down into different 'shops' – smelting, rolling, forging, founding, moulding – where human intervention was vital. The adoption of Cort's method of making wrought iron, increasingly at Cyfarthfa from 1790 and thereafter by other works, created tasks for refiners, puddlers, shinglers, ballers and rollermen, all of whom were regarded by their contemporaries as skilled men. These central iron-making processes required team-work and the master workman whose skills gave him a recognised authority controlled the team. With strength, vigilance, and judgement they controlled the stages of production, the puddler in particular having a key role.

> ...a task that was simultaneously highly skilled and exhausting, turning a viscous mass of liquid into metal. He worked in conditions of tremendous heat, violently agitating the metal as it boiled, rabbling it from side to side in the furnace, and then gathering it at the end of a rod while the molten liquid thickened and the supercharge of carbon burnt out. [81]

[81] Ginswick, pp. 20-27; Raphael Samuel, 'The Workshop of the World: Steam Power and Hand Technology in mid-Victorian Britain', *History Workshop* 3, Spring 1977.

A second key group were the ancillary 'artisans' or 'tradesmen', essential to each works: millwrights, engineers, carpenters, pattern-makers, blacksmiths, wheelwrights, furnace masons, locomotive and boiler-men. In both categories skill was acquired by working alongside the acknowledged master workman through formal or informal apprenticeships. Amongst the artisans it was natural and common for young family members to be recruited into these assistant positions, so retaining better paid jobs within families and passing skills from one generation to the next as a family heritage.[82]

Only certain people were allowed to acquire 'skill'. Women and Irish were excluded. The recruitment policy at Dowlais was firmly stated in 1867 by G. T. Clark in evidence to the Royal Commission on Trade Unions: '...but the place of the skilled Welshman cannot be filled by an Irishman. The men we get for that purpose are men who have been bred up in the rural districts, they speak Welsh only...'.[83] In the ironworks 'skill' usually entailed physical strength, an expertise learned by practice and observation, and the exercise of judgement. Entry to these occupations was often in the hands of the master workman, whose skills gave him a recognised authority. Once in the team a worker by sustained observation would gradually comprehend the almost intuitive practice of the master workman and through a ladder of promotion determined by seniority could move from helper to under hand to first hand, a process that led to a well-paid job. Boys as young as eleven began by raising the furnace doors.

These male, skilled, comparatively well paid workers constituted close to 40 per cent of the ironwork's labour force.

---

[82] Eric Hobsbawm, *Worlds of Labour: further studies in the history of labour* (1984), pp. 264-5.

[83] PP 1867-8 XXXIX, Fifth Report of the Royal Commission on Trade Unions, p. 92.

'It was estimated [for South Wales] in 1839 that each blast furnace employed between 280 and 300 persons, of whom 25% were labourers, 37.3 % miners and colliers, 14.7% artisans, and the remainder furnacemen.'[84] That would make furnacemen 23 per cent of the labour force. Added together the furnacemen and artisans come to 37.7 per cent of the labour force. Two other reports, one by Education Commissioners in 1840 and one by William Menelaus, manager at Dowlais, in 1866 indicate similar percentages.

Abenteeism and Drunkenness

The immigrant farm labourers were accustomed to working for wages but not familiar with the rhythms and disciplines of industry. They 'were non-accumulative, non-acquisitive, accustomed to work for subsistence, not for maximisation of income [and] had to be made obedient to the cash stimulus... '[85]. The employers' problem, in other words, was how to get consistent work out of the workers. Whilst they could buy the workers' ability to work – their labour power – they could not buy the workers, who persisted in old habits and attachments. The men and women who peopled the 'iron country', the great majority from rural Wales, were not a mere 'factor of production'. They came with memories, affiliations and experience. They came from a society that combined servility with violent lawlessness, deference to manorial lords with a sense of right and wrong that throughout the eighteenth century erupted in corn riots, assertions of the right to purchase food at fair prices.[86] They were new to industrialism but not to

---

[84] A. H. John, pp. 59-60.

[85] Sidney Pollard, *The Genesis of Modern Management: A Study of the Industrial Revolution in Great Britain* (1965), p. 161; A. H. John, p.70.

participating in their own history.

Workers rebelled against the new disciplines in a variety of ways: missing a day's work like Lalby, temporarily walking off the job, thieving, committing sabotage, going on strike or joining the gangs who roamed the hills from one job to the next. Drunkenness and absenteeism, particularly on Mondays after heavy weekend drinking was a major problem in the iron towns, as it was in many of Britain's new industrial areas. Work at the furnace or coalface was hot and exhausting. Pubs proliferated faster than the expanding chapels and there were no other diversions. There was a phase when companies paid men in beer tokens or gave them beer allowances. The Rhymney Iron Company opened its own brewery in 1839 'for the supply of beer to all persons employed in the works'. It was customary for gaffers and master workmen to pay their helpers in pubs where they had a financial interest and where change was available; a situation which encouraged prolonged drinking sessions. At Dowlais attempts were made on various occasions to get gaffers and contractors to give up their public houses. Cyfarthfa contractors were debarred from owning public houses in 1848. Dowlais arranged in 1841 that men could be paid through the office rather than in pubs and Robert Crawshay in 1859 informed his father that 'all the men, colliers and miners' were being paid directly.[87]

Nonetheless, drink and drunkenness were continuing problems and regular working habits came slowly, particularly to those working the coal levels. As late as 1846 it was alleged

---

[86] David W. Howell, 'Riots and Public Disorder in Eighteenth Century Wales', in David W. Howell and Kenneth O. Morgan (eds.), *Crime, Protest and Police in Modern British Society: Essays in Memory of David J. V. Jones* (Cardiff, 1999), pp. 42-72.

[87] Elsas, p. 79. W. R. Lambert, 'Drink and Work-Discipline in Industrial South Wales, c. 1830-1870', *Welsh History Review,* Vol. 7, (1974-5).

that colliers and miners employed by the ironworks lost one week in five and in 1869 it was noted that the first Monday in the month after Saturday payday was 'the noisiest night in Merthyr'.[88] The relationship between the level of wages paid and the incidence of drunkenness was frequently commented upon. Drunkenness and absenteeism increased when wages did, and fell when wages fell. John Evans, the general manager at Dowlais, resisted miners' requests for higher pay in 1855 on the grounds that extra money would be spent on drink, and coal and mine production would falter. 'I think that the Men are better off at present than they were before the last reduction. They work more regularly and earn as much money as before.'[89]

Fines and Imprisonment

Individuals like Lalby, drunk and incapable, were dismissed; with cases dealt with on an *ad hoc* basis until in July 1828, after 'several workmen have recently very much neglected their work', Guest at Dowlais introduced printed rules governing the exaction of fines from workmen who absented themselves without permission.

> And to prevent frivolous excuses, notice is hereby further given, that no plea of illness will be allowed unless notice of such illness shall have been given to the foreman at least six hours before the commencement of the turn, or a certificate from the surgeon that he was unable to attend to his work.[90]

---

[88] John, pp. 66, 71-2; 'The Merthyr Iron Worker: Toiling and Moiling', *Good Works*, 1 January 1869, pp.35-44.

[89] Elsas, p. 57. See also the examples quoted by Lambert in note 87.

[90] *Parliamentary Papers*, *Children's Employment Commission,* Appendix Part II, 1842. Evidence collected by Rhys William Jones, p. 651.

The fines went into a fund that paid the surgeon, supported sick workmen, and paid the schoolmaster. Formal and impersonal, such rules symbolized the new industrial relationships. At Penydarren no formal rules existed but 'the men, and children, and young persons, are generally fined for misbehaviour and neglect of work'. Some events were beyond management control, as in 1854 when panic and drunkenness – 'beyond everything, worse than ever and all from spirits' – seized Dowlais furnace workers facing the cholera outbreak.[91]

Organised opposition to the master's will was not tolerated and trade unions when they appeared in 1831 and 1834 were broken by lock-outs that pushed families to the verge of starvation. The main weapons commonly used in the South Wales iron-making district against 'troublesome' workers were the lock-out, the discharge note which made clear to a future employer whether the worker had left his previous employment legally, the common law of conspiracy, and criminal proceedings under various statutes dating back to Elizabethan times for breach of contract, such as leaving work unfinished.[92] Legally binding contracts were used to tie workers to a period of employment that could be a month, a year or longer. When workers broke the contract by not giving due notice, by leaving before the term of the contract was expended, or by striking not performing the duties expected, the masters did not hesitate to prosecute and exact fines or imprisonments in the 'Bridewell'. It helped that the iron-masters and their friends were also the magistrates.

J. J. Guest wrote to James Wise his confidential clerk in May

---

[91] Elsas, pp. 73-4

[92] John Rule, *The Experience of Labour in Eighteenth Century Industry* (1981), p.175. S. Deakin and F. Wilkinson, *The Law of the Labour Market: Industrialization, Employment, and Legal Evolution* (Oxford, 2005), pp. 61-7.

1826 urging that 'two or three of the worst' of the colliers in question should be taken 'before a Magistrate and punish them by *committal* for neglecting their work'.[93] Breach of contract by a worker remained a criminal offence until 1867 and even then sanctions against workers taking industrial action remained. In 1872 alone there were 10,400 convictions. The repeal of the Master and Servants Act in 1875 swept away these sanctions. Another weapon available to the employer was that skilled workers were given priority when cottages owned by a company were allocated, which helped to tie the men to the company. But the cottages were usually leased on the term of notice that terminated employment. Dismissal could also mean eviction.

Theft and pilfering from the growing number of coal levels that were too numerous to be policed became a serious problem for the ironmasters. In 1800 an 'Act for the security of collieries and mines, and the better regulation of colliers and miners' was promoted by the South Wales ironmasters and colliery owners who met at Merthyr in March 1800. Parliament passed it in the summer. It prescribed a prison sentence of six months for sabotaging, stealing from, or in any way interfering with a colliery or mine. Initially the ironmasters had wanted a sentence of seven years transportation. The Act remained in force until 1836.[94]

A Fragmented Working Class

The fundamental characteristic of the Merthyr labour force was that whatever skills men and women possessed, their livelihood depended upon selling their ability to work. In this sense it was a working class. But it was a working class fragmented by the

[93] Elsas, p. 24.

[94] Chris Evans, '*The Labyrinth*, pp. 104-7.

immigrants' place of origin, dialect and language, place of employment, gender, religious affiliations ranging from Roman Catholicism to Unitarianism, and a gulf in income and status between the master rollerman or puddler and the unskilled labourer. Many were not directly employed by the ironmasters but by another worker, or by mining subcontractors, or were subject to the authority of team leaders, 'the upper class of workmen'. Relationships with employers were not therefore a simple matter of proletarians versus capitalists. On the contrary, in these early years the anger of the crowd was more often turned against the shopkeepers. The ironmasters were seen, correctly, as providers of work. These divisions and ambiguities meant that class solidarity was fragile. The need for work was the only reason they were in 'Taff's wide vale'. Workers were by definition dependent, even though there were times when they rebelled against that condition.

Those who were least dependent were the skilled process workers, not powerless wage hands but men with status and authority who were not slow to assert their independence when circumstances favoured them. The acquisition of skill was a pathway that, apart from higher income and prized social status, gave the skilled worker a command over materials and tools (the tradesmen had their own tool-kit), over the way work was done (the labour process), and the quality of the finished product.

For the employers the punishment of individuals was essential for maintaining discipline but just as important was to find methods of management that combined discipline with the recruitment of reliable workers. As these highly capitalised and technologically advanced ironworks grew in size and complexity so their management systems evolved. An early development was to sub-contract the recruitment and management of labour. At Dowlais this had a long history. As early as 1767 the partners in the infant but flourishing enterprise had handed over these functions to Josiah Guest's grandfather John Guest when they appointed him manager. With continuing growth and success the ironmasters' primary concerns became the intimately related strategic and entrepreneurial issues of investment, product range and output, pricing policy, transportation, and marketing. They sat on top of a pyramid of authority with tasks assigned to trusted relatives, managers, 'agents' who performed a variety of supervisory functions, foremen, clerks that kept account books and sales ledgers, the master workmen and sub-contractors who supervised the processes of iron-making and mining iron ore and coal and dealt directly with the workers,

This delegation of labour issues kept to a minimum the costs of supervisory staff as the master puddler, furnace keeper or mining sub-contractor did the directing and disciplining of his work team. In iron-making the arrangements for payment could vary from one works to another, but the general procedure was for the master worker to receive payment based on the tonnage made and then to pay team members from his earnings.[95] A variation on that was for the members of the team to be paid directly by the ironmaster on a tonnage basis and then, the master puddler or furnace keeper, in recognition of his superior skill, would receive from the members of his team a supplementary payment. The arrangements varied considerably in the getting of coal and mine where bargains between

[95] Bernard Elbaum and Frank Wilkinson, 'Industrial Relations and uneven development: a comparative study of the American and British steel industries', *Cambridge Journal of Economics*, vol. 3 (1979), pp. 275-303; N. P. Howard, 'The Strikes and Lockouts in the Iron Industry and the Formation of the Ironworkers' Unions, 1862-1869', *International Review of Social History*, vol.18, No. 3 (1973).

ironmasters and individual contractors depended upon the accessibility of the seam, the amount of rubbish to be carried away, and numerous other factors.[96] In such cases the contractors would themselves hire and pay colliers. These management methods were effective in containing and dealing with day-to-day grievances over wages and earnings. But their efficacy always depended upon the prevailing industrial, social and political context.

It was not until 1846 when Dowlais was the largest ironworks in the world, the industrial relations climate much calmer, and deeper capital-intensive pits were being sunk that the sub-contracting system of mining coal was largely abolished except for patches and small levels. Instead a hierarchy of agents, managers and overmen in the direct employ of the company was introduced.[97]

Workplace Bargaining

Instinctively the ironmasters knew it was in their interests to act together to control the price of iron and what men could earn. Yet they did not always get their own way. Booms and slumps and their own rivalries meant they had uncertain success on both fronts. In a long established industry like iron-making, skilled workers were accustomed to bargaining over terms and conditions. Their methods included 'humble' petitions, delegations to 'the office', and giving legal notice of the intention to quit unless wages were increased. Although workers who 'combined' were dismissed, negotiation with individuals or with work groups was common. Arguments over piece-rates frequently involved comparisons with workers in

---

[96] Evans, *The Labyrinth*, pp. 101-3.

[97] E. Jones, *GKN*, p. 249.

similar circumstances in the same or different works. Both masters and men were aware of the potency of comparisons that could help to smooth problems and keep wages in line, even when there was no formal agreement.

The buoyancy of the 1790s product market, combined with the quickening pace of industrialisation, increased workers' assertiveness. A tactic when the demand for iron was high was simply to walk off the job to draw management's attention to a grievance. Such a 'downer' occurred at Dowlais in 1792 when 'the Colliers who came out of their work this morning without saying a word to any Body previous to doing so, and said they wanted to have the Cutting of the yard Coal by the dozen'. The grievance was over colliers' piecework, of which concern 'there was no end of at present'.[98]

A greater issue appeared as technological changes to the processes of iron-making made production targets obsolete and, to the dismay of employers, earnings of production workers rose to unprecedented levels. By the late 1790s furnaces at Cyfarthfa and Dowlais were producing over forty tons of iron per week compared with just twenty tons ten years earlier. The result, as Richard Crawshay complained in 1797, was that furnace men receiving 7d [0.7p] a ton were 'makeing such excessive Wages as are Scandalouse for us to pay'. Two years later a customary bonus payment was withdrawn from furnacemen at Dowlais because of similar increases in productivity. When they asked for a higher piece-rate William Taitt of Dowlais wrote,

> They must abide by their agreements or be sent to Bridewell by a magistrate. It is a Rascally demand & must be resisted in the first Instance. The encreased Quantity of Iron made is a

[98] Elsas, p. 33. [? Robert Thompson] to William Taitt. The term 'downer' became current in the British car industry in the 1960s but the practice has a long history.

> Sufficient encrease of wages to them & especially as it cannot be attributed to any exertions of theirs: but to our having expended £3000 to improve our Blast.[99]

When the men combined to insist on receiving the bonus, Taitt's response was uncompromising. 'I advise you', he wrote to Thomas Guest, 'going to Mr. Homfray or Mr. Crawshay [both of them magistrates] & get them to Commit to Bridewell 2 or 3 of the Ring leaders...they may afterwards be Indicted for the Conspiracy notwithstanding the Commitment'.[100] Puddlers were prominent in making demands, as when the Penydarren puddlers struck for an increase of two shillings [10p] a ton in February 1797. In the face of 'insolence' Samuel Homfray sacked them all and somehow found replacements. A strike by Penydarren puddlers in February 1838 resulted in fifteen of them being sent to Cardiff's House of Correction and only released when they submitted to the Company's terms. But in boom times workmen would usually play the market by offering themselves to a neighbouring works at an enhanced wage; the opposite side of that coin being the enticement of workers by employers. In April 1790 Taitt of Dowlais, adopting the high moral ground, wrote to Samuel Homfray at Penydarren:

> You do not make (or will not understand) a distinction between men offering themselves and Masters enticing them from their present employers. If you will recollect I told you some time since that I would take any of your men who offered but I wou'd not send into your Works to entice any of them away – this was

---

[99] Elsas, p. 34. The impact of technological change and capital investment upon the earnings of iron and steel workers has been an issue for more than two centuries; see E. Owen Smith, *Productivity Bargaining: A Case Study in the Steel Industry* (1971), p. 49.

[100] Chris Evans, *Labyrinth*, p. 93.

> in consequence of your taking several Miners which had come from Pontypool at our Expence ...You (if I may Credit what I am just now told) have sent repeated Messages to one of our Founders to come down and Engage with you – this is *Illegal* and extremely unhandsome ...We have Repeatedly been Sufferers by your taking our Men before, & are determined not to put up with it any longer.

In fact, from the 1790s into the 1840s and possibly beyond, Dowlais in boom years poached skilled workers as did all works in the iron districts.[101]

Wages and the Trade Cycle

The swings of the trade cycle from boom to slump were at the core of how wages were determined. When demand for iron increased, production increased, the need for labour increased, the price of iron bars increased, and wages increased. When demand fell, the opposite occurred: wages were cut, jobs were lost, debts increased, too many people looked for too few jobs, the unemployed and their families became destitute; and skilled workers, rarely made redundant, tried to resist wage cuts and hoped for better times. Changes in the product market fed through directly to the labour market.

How this worked out in practice depended upon how long an economic depression lasted. If expected to be of short duration, and many were, ironmasters were reluctant to cut back production by closing down a furnace. That would risk losing workers needed when the economy improved. Moreover, shutting down a furnace completely was not lightly undertaken; getting it back fully into blast was a lengthy process. Richard Crawshay on

---

[101] Elsas, pp. 64-9.

at least one occasion employed men on half-pay to clear the ground of stones 'when his works were at a stand' and then cultivated the land.[102] The usual reaction was to maintain production but to lower the price of iron in order to capture sales. Price competition between the smaller firms in the industry became intense at such times but larger firms like Dowlais and Cyfarthfa avoided price cutting as long as they could, relying on the quality of their iron to gain sales and their immense financial resources to weather the storm. Both made iron for stock during recessions, hoping to be ready for swift sales when the market improved.[103] But even they had to cut their prices when recessions were prolonged and the fall in profit margins reached the point where actual losses were being incurred. They then cut wages. The issues are clearly illustrated by a letter from William Forman of Penydarren to Taitt in March 1813:[104]

> In consequence of the further reduction of Bar Iron [prices], I think something may be done by the Iron Masters to reduce the Wages. The best time to effect it is when the Trade is in that state that the Master is full as much benefited by the works standing still as going on. That period is now arrived ...All the works must be of one mind or nothing efficient can be done ...

Here is the pressure to cut costs as profits fall; the pointlessness of continuing to produce when losses are building up; and the caution that unless the ironmasters act together to reduce wages there could be the loss of skilled workmen. However, less than a month later the decisive William Taitt wrote to his nephew:

---

[102] J. H. Manners, *Journal of a Tour through North and South Wales* (1805), quoted by C. Evans, *The Labyrinth*, p. 83.

[103] Martin Daunton, 'The Dowlais Iron Company in the Iron Industry, 1800-1850' *WHR*, vol. 6, No. 1 (June 1972).

[104] Elsas, p. 38.

> ...I do not expect that much dependence can be placed upon our Neighbours for reduction of Wages ...I think you should give our Men Notice tomorrow (those who are not under unexpired Agreements) that we must reduce the prices owing to the very depressed State of the Trade, from the end of the Current Month ...

The lesson that was repeated over and over was that the price of labour was determined by the price of iron in the marketplace and not by workers' needs. In due time, when trade improved workers expected the cuts to be restored or they would find another employer.

In depressions resistance to this link between the price of iron and the level of earnings was expressed through strikes of varying degrees of intensity and in extremity, by riots. Strikes were also used to gain wage increases as the iron trade came out of recession. But strikes were not the invariable response. A puddlers' petition to J. J. Guest in 1824 gives a fascinating glimpse of what was evolving.[105]

> Your pettioners most humbley beg you will be pleased to recall to recollection the promise you made to the Puddlers when you reduced the Price of Puddling. You then made a promise that whenever other ironworks would advance the price for Puddling you would do the like, and we'v bin convinced that other ironworks has advanced above a month ago. We therefore did not send inn our pettion immediately, tho' many of us have need enough, for we have a large family to supporte and a heavy rent to pay. Therefore, we Sincerely hope you will Most honourabley take those things into consideration and advance our wages to the same proportion as other works have don, and your

[105] Elsas, p. 40.

> petitioners will ever pray for your Good Success & prosperity.

This reveals that even in the pressure-cooker years relations between masters and men could be orderly and respectful as well as confrontational; it demonstrates the use of comparisons between works in wage negotiations; it reveals that by the 1820s works were regularly restoring cuts made in difficult times and that Guest, when cutting wages, had *promised* to restore them when times were better. The traditionally deferential language cannot obscure the puddlers' determination to hold Guest to his promise. Here is the seed of a system of determining wages that, given favourable circumstances, could bring industrial peace; a relief to both masters and men. Even a man as strong-willed as William Taitt had written to his nephew J. J. Guest on 7 November 1792, 'to be battling with the men is disagreeable'.[106] When that seed blossomed it underpinned the dominance of the masters for many years. But that dominance had yet to be established.

During the years 1795 to 1834 Merthyr was a society full of frustrations and insecurities over new work patterns and disciplines, housing and health, and recessions that brought wage cuts, unemployment, deepening debts, and border-line starvation. These were the 'wants' that Major-General James Willoughby-Gordon had forecast in 1817 could result in rebellion. He was right. But his analysis was incomplete. The necessity to rebel based on 'wants' was accompanied by democratic yearnings that became increasingly significant as riots in Merthyr in 1800, 1816 and 1831 grew in scale and ferocity.

---

[106] K.T. Weetch, 'The Dowlais Ironworks and its Industrial Community', (M. Sc. Econ. thesis, London University, 1963), p. 55.

4

Riots 1800 and 1816 [107]

> This place certainly gives the tone to the whole *iron country*, and I am fully convinced that your Lordship cannot keep too vigilant an eye upon it. Their numbers are formidable, and they have no other principle of action than what proceeds from their wants. In a moment of distress, therefore, they may be impelled to mischief, without combination or forethought, and they have the power (unless curbed by the presence of some force and by the apprehension of more) of doing the most extensive mischief, both private and national, in a very short time ...
>
> **Major-General James Willoughby Gordon, 14 March 1817**[108]

The prescient Major-General was writing in the aftermath of the 1816 Merthyr riot and midway between 1800 and 1834, years of headlong economic growth in the iron district but also marked by hunger and distress, strikes, armed rebellion,

---

107 The following abbreviated account of events given in this and the next chapter is based upon David Jones, *Before Rebecca: Popular Protests in Wales 1793-1835* (1973), Chapter 6; D. J. V. Jones 'The South Wales Strike of 1816', *Morgannwg*, Vol. XI, 1967; Evans, *The Labyrinth,* pp. 170-7; D. J. V. Jones, 'The Merthyr Riots of 1831', *WHReview,* iii, 2 (1966); and Gwyn A. Williams, *The Merthyr Rising* (1978).

108 In a letter from Merthyr to Viscount Sidmouth, the Home Secretary, urging that the troops in Merthyr should be separated from the civilians: H.O.42/161; Aspinall, p. 231.

repression and martial law. The first determined challenge to the existing order came on Saturday 20 September 1800 over the most basic issue of all, food.

How to feed Merthyr's rapidly growing population had become a major problem. The sheer quantities of food required were beyond the resources of local farmers or the small number of shops. For every four hundred people in Merthyr in 1822 there was one shop. In York, a town of roughly the same size, there was a shop for every seventy people.[109] The ironmasters, fearful of corn riots, reluctantly bought food in bulk. Cyfarthfa imported 1,200 tons of American flour after the 1792 harvest and in the bitter winter of 1794-5, when shortage of supplies caused famine and riots in parts of Wales, the Dowlais Company brought in pickled pork, peas, flour, sugar and dried fruit. At Penydarren a works' shop was opened in 1793 and a works' shop at Dowlais followed in 1799.[110] Richard Crawshay at Cyfarthfa and the Hill brothers at the Plymouth works had principled objections to company shops (the truck system) and refused to open shops. But food shortages and high prices were endemic in the iron country in these years, and when high prices coincided with wage cuts it was a recipe for violent protest.

Riot in 1800

In the autumn of 1800 the price of food in Merthyr was double what it had been twelve months earlier and some families were becoming desperately hungry. On Saturday 20 September in the village marketplace a crowd suspecting fraud seized weights and

---

[109] Carter and Wheatley, *Merthyr Tydfil in 1851*, p.18.

[110] Evans, *'The Labyrinth,* p.159; E. A. Havill, 'William Taitt and the Dowlais Ironworks' *Transactions of the Honourable Society of the Cymmrodorian*, (1983), pp. 106, 109.

measures from dealers. Scarcely one was accurate. The Penydarren workmen were already complaining that Homfray was cheating them at his shop. Workers from the four ironworks decided to force shopkeepers to reduce their prices. The cry 'we want bread' was taken up, echoing the cry of the market women who marched on Versailles in October 1789 and the crowds in Paris protesting against famine in 1795. By Monday afternoon the Penydarren company shop had been totally demolished, the goods plundered, and demands for food and drink made at the homes of the 'respectable inhabitants'. In the aftermath it was claimed that 'thousands of pounds worth of damage' had been done to bakers' and shopkeepers' premises. Intimidated shopkeepers agreed to sell flour, butter and cheese at reduced prices and signed a paper to that effect. The Dowlais shop was saved from destruction by a swift reduction in prices.

The excitement of rebellion brought workers pouring into the town from neighbouring settlements. Work at Penydarren and Cyfarthfa stopped. On Wednesday afternoon twenty Inniskillings (7th Dragoons) sent for by Samuel Homfray, iron-master and magistrate, reached Merthyr from Gloucester. Their arrival in the village was memorable. 'One of them, to show his skill, cut a dog in two in front of the Star and another sliced off the crown of an old man's hat, and bade him go home in safety'.[111] Homfray imposed a curfew. Troops continued to arrive, fifty prisoners were taken and gradually order was restored. But it was not until two days later that Homfray felt free to revoke the price schedule signed by the village's shopkeepers. Three men, Aaron Williams, Samuel Hill and James Luke, were tried in Cardiff and sentenced to death. The sentence on Luke, aged eighteen, was commuted to transportation for life. Aaron Williams was found guilty of

[111] Wilkins, *History*, p. 317.

helping James Luke to steal nine gallons of porter; Samuel Hill was convicted of assaulting Dr. Bannister's wife and robbing her of half a guinea. Both men were hanged. A pattern had been set. Disaffection over earnings, distress and hunger, determined violence and looting for food, gangs descending from the surrounding hills, a small and frightened middle class, the sending for troops, rounding up of protestors, death sentences to make an example and then a return to normality.

Were the events of September 1800 really 'a corn riot'? Fundamentally they were. People were certainly hungry and angry about high prices; yet the causes were more than those alone. There was the deterioration in employment relations as earnings were held down; the resentment against prison sentences freely handed out to workers in industrial disputes by magistrates who were also employers; the suspicion of fraud by market traders and company shops. There was the magnetic attraction of an attack on authority in this the largest aggregation of people in Wales, the centre of the iron district. Workmen from The Hills came to watch and to participate.

And a whiff of democratic ideology was also in the Merthyr air. Samuel Homfray believed that 'political Principles have in some degree influenced the Minds of the lower Class of People'. On the day of the workers' meeting on 20 September John Thelwall was seen near the crowd. Thelwall, a leading London radical who had been tried and acquitted of high treason in 1794, was living in 'exile' at Llyswen, and came more than once to Merthyr. In 1795 he had published 'Natural and Constitutional Rights' which argued that

> If, once in every year, the poor man's vote were as important as his employer's, the poor could not be forgotten. But it is property we are told, that ought to be represented, because by property government is supported. What? Does property man

> the navy or fill the ranks of the army? ...Let us not deceive ourselves! Property is nothing but human labour.[112]

What had drawn him to Merthyr? The answer lies perhaps in the well-known story that while walking in the Quantocks with Coleridge in 1797 they had come upon an enchanting 'secret' dell. 'Citizen John' said Coleridge, 'this is a fine place to talk treason in'. Thelwall replied: 'Nay, Citizen Samuel, it is rather a place to make a man forget that there is any necessity for treason.'[113] On 14 April 1801, as the Spring Assizes were held in Cardiff, a document found near Merthyr declared:

> we the workmen of the Ironworks on the Hills have come to the following resolutions, that they are determined to assemble on a certain day, to consider the most effectual method to be adopted in extricating ourselves and the rising Generation from the Tyranny and Oppression of the times...

In Brecon 'respectable inhabitants', not for the last time, feared the Merthyr insurgents would come visiting and steps were taken to site a barracks there.

Towards 1816

The rest of the decade was largely peaceful with low food prices coinciding with high levels of employment and a growth in real wages. But from 1810 trade and employment relations again deteriorated with the return of recession and falling prices for iron. The first indication of labour struggles came

---

[112] Quoted in Max Beer, *A History of British Socialism* (1919), p. 124.

[113] E.P. Thompson, *The Making of the English Working Class* (Penguin, 1991) p. 193.

in April 1810 when the earnings of furnacemen at Dowlais were reduced. The result was a month-long strike, the men acting as one, a tendency increasingly apparent. These 'combinations' were not permanent organisations but *ad hoc* associations as workers learned the need for solidarity to defend customary work practices and the level of earnings. Under common law they were illegal conspiracies acting in restraint of trade. The criminal penalties for conspiracy were harsher than the penalties under the new Combination Acts of 1799 and 1800 that had made trade unions illegal. The ironmasters therefore usually used the conspiracy laws against workers' combinations.

In April 1813 came the fiercest confrontation over workplace issues so far. With the price of iron falling, the employers cut piece-rates at all the works whilst at the same time closing the Glamorgan Canal for repair, so reducing the impact of any strike. Again it was the puddlers who took up the challenge after swearing oaths to stick together (oaths that William Crawshay fashionably labelled 'Luddite' although there was no machine-breaking). The masters blew out furnaces, dismissed the strikers, and the Cyfarthfa works replaced the puddlers with men from Staffordshire. This assertion of authority did not go unchallenged for long.

The end of the war against Napoleon in 1815 brought recession, unemployment, falling wages and the release of 300,000 redundant soldiers and sailors onto the British labour market. Radical calls for Parliamentary reform, stifled by patriotism and repressive legislation during the war, vigorously returned. In Lancashire, Yorkshire, Leicestershire and London there were mass meetings; radical political clubs multiplied. With excess capacity in the iron trade, furnaces were taken out of blast in Shropshire and Staffordshire, works were sold off and thousands of ironworkers and miners were thrown out of work.[114] In Merthyr iron production fell from the beginning of 1816 and in July the puddlers at Cyfarthfa briefly went on strike when given notice of a wage reduction. The prospect of a poor harvest increased the average price of wheat per quarter from 65s [£3.25p] in early June to 107s 4d [£5.35.6p] in October. Throughout the summer the whole South Wales iron district simmered with discontent. On 15 June the Rev. William Powell of Abergavenny informed the Home Secretary that Merthyr 'is the spot, at which we anticipate the next explosion ...emissaries from that quarter have spread themselves all over the hills to the different works'.[115]

On Tuesday 15 October, the puddlers, forgemen and others at Tredegar were given notice of pay cuts of up to 40 per cent to take effect in November. The news, with its implications for the whole district, spread rapidly and by that evening a deputation from Merthyr had persuaded a hundred Tredegar forgemen to leave work. The next day over a thousand ironstone miners and colliers at Tredegar stopped work and about half set off for Merthyr where they stopped the Plymouth, Cyfarthfa and Penydarren works. William Crawshay II sent an urgent message to Guest at Dowlais:

> The enemy in too great strength to oppose with any probability of success, have possessed themselves of all our Works & wholly stopped them. They are yet exulting in their victory & are about to proceed to Pendarren and Dowlais. My spies tell me they threaten hard your shop, for they are hungry. I have been in the midst of them all & found as usual argument useless. I have just had a messenger from Mr. Hill. He says all his works are stopped same as ours.[116]

---

[114] T. S. Ashton, *Iron and Steel in the Industrial Revolution* (Manchester, 1924), pp.153-4.

[115] David Jones, *Before Rebecca*, p. 166

[116] Elsas, pp. 39-40.

By the time the men reached Dowlais it was late in the evening, their numbers had reduced, and Guest, never known to shirk a confrontation, was able with allies to resist attack. For most of Thursday the action moved to Monmouthshire where blast furnaces from Tredegar to Llangynidr were put out but in late afternoon a large crowd returned to Merthyr intent on dealing with Dowlais.

The mood was now violent. In expectation of an attack 200 special constables had been sworn in and stationed at Dowlais but that evening they were swept aside in a hail of stones and bricks, the works brought to a halt and Guest's residence attacked. A direct attack upon an ironmaster in Merthyr was unprecedented. Guest's people fired into the crowd wounding several, one of whom later died.

The next morning around 5,000 gathered early in the town but after the Riot Act had been read they dispersed moving again into Monmouthshire to persuade workers to leave work; when men of the Glamorgan Militia arrived later that day the town was quiet. By Saturday thirty cavalrymen had arrived from Cardiff, Merthyr's furnaces had been restarted, and troop reinforcements were on their way from Swansea and Newport. But early that Saturday afternoon 8,000 to 10,000 workmen assembled before the Castle Inn where ironmasters and leading tradesmen had gathered. At the same time 120 men of the 55th Regiment and the Swansea Cavalry arrived. A deputation from the workmen entered the inn and argued for a return to the wages of six months previously. The High Sheriff, Richard Hill, refused to bargain with them in their 'present riotous state'. The men asked for this response to be put in writing, which it was. As the deputation left the inn the crowd surged forward, perhaps to hear what had been decided. The Riot Act was read and the crowd was warned that they would be fired on. Abusive and defiant, they stood firm. The cavalry were ordered to charge and using bayonets and the flat side of their swords they dispersed the crowd, arresting around thirty. The climax was over. Strikes and protests continued across the coalfield reaching as far as Swansea, but by Wednesday all were back at work in Merthyr.

Throughout the autumn and winter soldiers remained stationed in Merthyr. One was attacked at night, his legs cut with a knife. Several deserted. Major-General Gordon recommended that they be separated from civilians. Political radicalism was no longer in the background. A speech by 'Orator' Hunt found a receptive audience when translated into Welsh. A paper found near Penydarren in January 1817 spoke of London groups petitioning for reform, the necessity to disarm and shackle soldiers, and that 'nothing short of a revolution can save the country from ruin, and the population from starvation...'[117]

The events of 1816 are a notable escalation on 1800. Gangs strode across the hills of north Monmouthshire putting out furnaces, persuading and coercing fellow workers to join the action. The range of workers involved was wider than previously – skilled process workers but also colliers, miners, and labourers — and the level of violence much higher. With deepening poverty in the iron districts, an impending wage cut of 40 per cent, and the ruthless suppression of attempts to form unions, 'collective bargaining by riot' was wholly predictable. The reaction of William Wood, the Dowlais Company's London agent, upon hearing of the 40 per cent cut is illuminating: 'the Welsh iron masters are attempting to reduce Wages below what the men can exist upon to enable them to sell against Staffordshire'. 'As well die as starve', said one of the rioters to Merthyr's High Sherriff.[118]

---

[117] Jones, *Before Rebecca*, Appendix Three, pp. 231-4.

[118] Jones, *Before Rebecca,* p. 71.

Yet, by the winter of 1817-18 trade had improved so much that Cyfarthfa increased piece rates by 23 per cent, and the price of iron climbed from £8 to £14 a ton. Three years later earnings were again being cut and trade only picked up in late 1823, continuing for the next two years. In 1824-1825 Cyfarthfa Castle was built, a symbol of William Crawshay II's power and ego and of his confidence in the future. Miners and skilled men felt able to agitate for wage increases and on 16 June 1825 William Crawshay I wrote to William Crawshay II recommending an increase for puddlers: 'which policy should be followed whenever necessary to keep the Works in production'.

Towards 1831

Then, in December came a financial and stock market crash, several banks failed, there were riots in the north of England, a slow recovery in 1827-28, and depression again in 1829-31. Wheat prices increased, food became dearer, the price of iron fell and earnings stagnated before being reduced. Dowlais shut down three furnaces, Penydarren and Plymouth two each, Cyfarthfa one. Protests against unemployment, debt and 'distress' gathered strength across Britain. In the summer of 1830 in the southern and eastern counties of England agricultural labourers revolted against the miserable struggle to exist, burning ricks and smashing machinery.

And the smouldering agitation for electoral reform burst again into flame in 1830 with news of the death of King George IV in June, the overthrow of Charles X and his reactionary government in a French bloodless July revolution, and the coming to power at Westminster in November of a Whig administration pledged to electoral reform. That autumn radicals in Merthyr – as did those in Manchester, Liverpool,

Birmingham, Sheffield, Newcastle and other major industrial centres — formed a Political Union 'to collect and organise the moral power of the country for the restoration of the people's rights...' Nowhere did this combination of recession and reform resonate louder than in Merthyr Tydfil.

On 9 August 1830 William Crawshay II, wrote, 'I should have liked to have been in Paris with my double gun within reach of the King!! I would rather have one shot at him than ten thousand Woodcocks'.[119] Reform fever had seized him, as it had the nation. In Merthyr the Political Union brought workmen together with, and ostensibly under the influence of, the radical lawyers, shopkeepers, and traders associated with the influential and Unitarian James family that throughout the nineteenth century remained prominent in Merthyr public life. The head, Christopher James, had made a fortune from dealings with the Glamorganshire Canal and turnpike roads. His brother William owned the Globe and Swan inns and much other local property. Another brother, Job, a former naval surgeon in the West Indies who combined private medical practice with selling books and pamphlets was an ardent admirer of William Cobbett. But it was Christopher's eldest son, David William James, trader and early investor in coal mines in the Rhondda, who was the leading local politician.

In the autumn thousands signed petitions at anti-truck and anti-Corn Laws agitations. On 23 December a crowd of over 800 turned up for a meeting on parliamentary reform that, because of the number, had to be held in the parish church. There a petition was drafted that called for annual parliaments, abolition of rotten boroughs, representation for large towns and populous districts, the secret ballot, and the vote for all who contributed, directly or indirectly, to national or local taxation.

---

[119] William Crawshay II to Walter Coffin, 9 August 1830. NLW, Crawshay Papers.

These demands looked back to those of the 1790s and forward to those of the Chartists. They were not, of course, on the agenda at Westminster. David John a blacksmith, teacher, and pastor of the Unitarian church at Twynyrodyn caused uproar by denouncing bishops for starving their clergy – the meeting was in Merthyr's Anglican parish church – and by proclaiming that the poor were living on carrion.[120]

The first Reform Bill was presented to Parliament on 1 March 1831 and on 9 March a meeting was held in Merthyr at which a petition was drawn up calling for Merthyr to be included in the Bill. To justify Merthyr's claim for a MP it was decided to have a census that would provide evidence of the size of the population. On 8 April another meeting attended by the ironmasters decided to press the case. In mid-April the Reform Bill was rejected by eight votes, the Commons was dissolved and a general election called, the sole issue being Reform. The decision lay in the hands of the small unreformed electorate but the whole country was convulsed with the issue. At a meeting on 27 April Christopher James, his son David William, the radical lawyer William Perkins and the schoolteacher Taliesin ab Iolo spoke of 'rescuing the land from thraldom and misery'. Excited crowds thronged Merthyr streets demonstrating in favour of reform. Crawshay encouraged 'his' miners to join them and helped them to draft a petition. But they were finding their own leaders.

---

[120] Gwyn A. Williams, *The Merthyr Rising*, p. 96.

5

1831: Armed Insurrection

> 'Chartism, my Lord, began in 1830 and 1831. Although it was then called by *another name* the populace understood it in the sense they do now – a *Re*-forming of society'
>
> **Henry Scale[121].**

On 2 May 1831 workers, acting independently of the radical middle class, held a mass meeting. Parades and demonstrations in favour of Reform continued throughout the week, effigies were burned, there were arguments and fist-fights. Then on 9 May some 5,000 massed outside the home of James Stephens, a well-known trader. Thomas Llewellyn, a Cyfarthfa miner, declared that everyone who was an enemy of Reform should be hanged on a gallows and he was the man to do it, free of charge. Later, in the evening Stephens' house was stoned and windows broken. The Court, home of William Thomas a major Merthyr landowner, was also attacked. Both men were Tories and opposed to Reform.

James Stephens complained to the magistrate J. B. Bruce. The two ringleaders were brought before him and, as they did not have money for bail, were sentenced to gaol. The hearing had taken place in the Bush Inn. On hearing the sentence a crowd of 3,000 stormed the Bush, released the prisoners and forced Bruce to sign an acquittal. The official weakness and

[121] G. A. Williams, 'The Merthyr Election of 1835', *Welsh History* Review, 10 (1980), pp. 369-70.

subsequent failure to deal with this openly violent and successful lawless action caused the Marquess of Bute to note: 'From that moment the people thought they were irresistible and could act with impunity'.[122]

By June 1831 REFORM was on everyone's lips. But there was confusion over what Reform meant. To the small shopkeepers who did not have the vote, to the Nonconformist radicals who had ideological objections to aristocrats, bishops, and privileged elites, to Guest and Crawshay who wanted free trade and the new voice of industry to be fully represented in the Commons, Reform meant a change in the franchise to enable their interests to be heard and acted upon. To the workmen Reform meant something completely different. To them it meant a lifting of life's injustices; a new start; a wiping out of humiliations, misery and want. As the astute Henry Scale remarked, they wanted 'a *Re-forming* of society'. And a militant core was convinced that physical force was the only way to get it.

The differences over reform were perfectly illustrated in the last days of May. With no wage increase for twelve months, food becoming dearer and debts increasing, ironstone miners at Cyfarthfa and Hirwaun had their pay cut on 23 May and on the next day eighty-four puddlers were sacked. Why would Crawshay do this? With a glut of iron throughout the industry, the Hirwaun works losing money, and the price of iron down to £5 a ton from £15 10s [£15.50p] in 1825, these were to him necessary business decisions. Indeed, they were a last resort. He had stockpiled 78,000 tons of ironstone and for several months had held back from cost-cutting.

For the men the imminent prospect of hunger and deeper debt increased their desperation. On Monday 30 May about 2,000

[122] Jones, *Before Rebecca*, pp. 135-7; Williams, *The Rising*, p. 98.

workmen, many of them Cyfarthfa miners, attended a pre-arranged meeting at Twyn y Waun to support a petition that Crawshay had helped to word. The banners and flags all cried for Reform. But the issues they debated were economic. Abolition of Merthyr's Court of Requests, established for the recovery of small debts, usually by selling debtors' furniture; the abolition of imprisonment for debt and the seizure of goods from those in debt; the prevention of traders buying foodstuffs in the cheapest market and then selling in the dearest; and the prohibition of any miner or collier taking a vacant stall except at an increased rate of earnings. These were at the heart of their cry for reform. *Reform* to those workers was synonymous with economic improvement. A few years later it would be called 'bread and cheese Chartism'.

A decisive moment came when 'a stranger' – most likely a representative of the colliers' union in north-east Wales – argued that petitioning the King or Parliament about reform or grievances was fruitless. He called upon them to stop work and apply for parish relief. This would put such pressure on the rate-payers that something would have to be done. The Court of Requests should be ended. A resolution to stop work was carried with acclamation. From that point Crawshay and the middle-class reformers were irrelevant.

The next day, Tuesday 31 May, in Penderyn a crowd physically prevented bailiffs working for the Court of Requests from seizing property belonging to a miner named Lewis Lewis. J. B. Bruce, the stipendiary magistrate, stepped in and arranged that Lewis would pay sixpence [2.5p] per week towards his debt of £18 19s 0d [£18.95p] and the shopkeeper to whom the debt was owed would hold as surety a trunk belonging to Lewis.

On Wednesday 1 June hundreds of men marched to Aberdare, confronted Richard Fothergill the local ironmaster, and made him retract an alleged statement that Cyfarthfa's ironstone miners were being paid too much. At the same time a crowd in Hirwaun forcibly took back Lewis' trunk from the shopkeeper. Lewis was there, and mounting the trunk spoke to the crowd. Later that day fireballs were thrown through the windows of Joseph Coffin, president of the Court of Requests. These were just the preliminaries.

The next day, Thursday 2 June, over one hundred houses and shops in Cefn, Merthyr and Dowlais were visited by bands of men and women carrying 'Reform' banners. They located goods taken by order of the Court of Requests and restored them to the original owners. These acts of redistributive justice were carried out with threats and sometimes actual physical violence. Lewis Lewis marched at the head of a crowd that carried his rescued chest and a Red Flag with a loaf speared on the pole. It was not, as often claimed, the first time the red flag had been flown in Britain, but it was the first time in Wales. (A red flag had been displayed by the naval mutineers in 1797 and in April 1820 several hundred armed Barnsley weavers had marched behind it to Grange Moor, inscribed with 'Hunt the intrepid defender of the Rights and Liberties of the People': a reference to 'Orator' Hunt.)

Bruce, stationed in the Castle Inn, sent a message to Brecon asking for troops to be ready to leave if required. In the afternoon, alarmed by attacks upon houses and accompanied by Anthony Hill, he read the Riot Act to a 'very furious' crowd of 2,000. He was ignored and goods continued to be returned to their former owners. That evening Joseph Coffin's house was wrecked, even the wallpaper stripped from the walls while the Court's account books were found and ripped up. His furniture and books were thrown through the windows into the street and burnt. By early evening forty-two shopkeepers were at the Castle inn, complaining of looting. Bruce urgently sent for troops from Brecon, Llantrisant and Neath. In a switch of tactics the insurgents marched to Cyfarthfa, stopped the works and after midnight set off for Penydarren and stopped work there.

At the Castle Inn

From 7 a.m. on Friday 3 June thousands of workers – many carrying bludgeons, pit timber, hedge stakes, even the side of a wheelbarrow – paraded around Merthyr gathering more numbers along the way. Ropes were stretched across the street to prevent anyone from running away. About 10.00 a.m. some eighty men of the Argyll and Sutherland Highlanders marched into town and, sweating in the sultry air, drew up outside the Castle Inn. They had marched for seven hours from Brecon. A crowd of 7,000 to 10,000 massed around the inn. At the front was the determined hard core still carrying their Red Flag topped by a loaf. The scene was set for confrontation, as in 1816.

At 10.40 a.m. Richard Jenkins the High Sheriff of Glamorgan read the Riot Act and Bruce repeated it in Welsh. The crowd roared defiance. The Highlanders meanwhile were ranged before the entrance and along the wall of the inn, their muskets with fixed bayonets pointing straight up to the air. The muskets were not loaded. Someone, several thought it was Lewis Lewis, shouted: 'There's no need to fear the soldiers. The game is ours. They're no more than gooseberries in our hands.' Eighty faced thousands. Amidst the shoving and shouting, Anthony Hill called for a dozen or so delegates to talk with the magistrates and ironmasters, again as in 1816. After ten or twenty minutes the men came out. Nothing had been settled. An hour passed since the reading of the Riot Act. The crowd was told in English and in Welsh to disperse or face death. Men edged forward, working themselves round and between the soldiers and the inn wall.

The crowd called for Guest. Twice he spoke from an upstairs window. It was violence that had caused the Inhabitants to send for the soldiers. If the crowd would disperse he would do what he could for them. 'I have done all in my power. You must take the consequences upon yourselves'. An eyewitness claimed that Guest was in tears. The crowd continued to press forward. Soldiers with loaded muskets appeared at the upstairs windows of the inn. Crawshay spoke from a window, 'So help me God, I will not listen to people coming in arms in this violent manner'. He only provoked greater anger. Lewis Lewis was hoisted up and held on to the lamp iron by the front door and then, after shouting 'Take their arms away. Off with their guns' he jumped down. Like a great wave the crowd surged forward.

In the violent struggle that followed four or five soldiers were instantly laid out, muskets were seized, two rioters were bayoneted, Private Black was stabbed in the thigh. Major Falls, the commanding officer, stumbled into the inn blood pouring from a severe head wound. Rebels repeatedly fought their way into the passage of the inn and were driven back hand to hand. Finally an officer ordered the soldiers at the upstairs windows to fire. Hundreds ran in panic but others fired back, and persistently did so in the face of shot after shot from the soldiers. Others attacked the back of the inn, firing marbles when they ran out of shot! When the shooting stopped it was not yet 1.00 p.m. How many of the crowd died is not certain. The *Cambrian* put the figure at eighteen with seventy wounded, but some of the wounded may well have died in secrecy later and estimates have put the number of dead as high as twenty-six. Sixteen soldiers were wounded, six of them severely.

The ironmasters and the Highlanders abandoned the town and retreated to Penydarren House. The insurgents set up positions in Cefn and on the Swansea road. At Hirwaun a calf was sacrificed, and a flag bathed in its blood. Cyfarthfa Castle that night was fired upon for several hours. The 47-year-old Anthony Hill rode desperately throughout the day to London, alerting troops in Cardiff and Newport along the way. In London he spoke that evening to Lord Melbourne, the Home Secretary, who informed the King.

Saturday, 4 June was remarkable. Armed bands seized guns, powder and ammunition from shops, houses, depots, works and farmhouses. Men, mainly from Cyfarthfa and Hirwaun, began to drill, presumably under ex-soldiers. Road blocks were set up on the routes to Brecon and Swansea. The ironmasters called for a return to work, while sending for more reinforcements from Brecon. The reinforcements were stopped from getting through by boulders across the road above Cefn Coed and gunfire from the mountain above. In the afternoon the Swansea Yeomanry on its way into Merthyr was ambushed, disarmed, and sent packing. Morale among the rioters was sky-high; at Penydarren House the ironmasters were frustrated and anxious. Three separate delegations from the insurgents went up to Penydarren House, one a single individual, but there was no apparent agreement. We know little about these events. Troop reinforcements were, however, getting through from Cardiff.

Late that Saturday afternoon came a decisive encounter. A delegation that had been to Penydarren House met, at the gates of Cyfarthfa Park on the Brecon road, a large armed crowd coming from Cefn and apparently determined to attack Penydarren House. Discussions about the situation at Penydarren House and the attitudes of the ironmasters ended in disagreement. The great crowd broke up with groups going in different directions; some to Cefn, some towards Hirwaun, others into Merthyr. But the march on Penydarren House had been aborted. After that, the balance of power shifted. Troops arrived in numbers. On Sunday 5 June the ironmasters seized the initiative by issuing a statement warning that those carrying offensive weapons could be found guilty of High Treason and Rebellion. The insurgents meanwhile planned a mass meeting at the Waun on Monday morning. Merthyr delegates travelled to the ironworks at Ebbw Vale, Nantyglo and Tredegar, urging workmen to attend that meeting.

Very early on Monday 6 June Merthyr delegates went to the works at Blaenavon, Llanelly and Pontypool to recruit support. They were so successful that by 10.00 a.m. a crowd estimated to be well over 12,000 approached Dowlais Top. There they were confronted by magistrates and 450 troops determined to prevent the crowd joining the militants at Cefn Coed. Guest energetically appealed for calm and negotiation but without success. He then read the Riot Act and the troops were ordered to advance slowly with fixed bayonets. One report asserts they were 'on the point of firing'.[123] The crowd gave way and Guest, on reaching the Dowlais Ponds, persuaded a large crowd to disperse. Some joined the insurgents at Cefn Coed, many returned to Monmouthshire complaining that the Merthyr armed militants had not turned up.

The drama was not yet over. 'Immense' numbers were seen exercising with firearms, excitedly firing in the air. Two black flags suddenly appeared on the road to the north. The watchers from the Cyfarthfa tower were convinced that an attack was imminent. But then, unexpectedly, the men dispersed, throwing away or breaking their weapons. A core of the militants remained for most of the afternoon but the troops moved from Penydarren House and into the town. By the end of that day the whole movement had collapsed and troops were already rounding up the leaders. The true nature of the dramatic encounters at Dowlais Top, the thoughts and emotions of individuals, the urgent debates in the insurgents' camps remain

[123] 'Fair Play' in *Cambrian*, 18 June 1831.

a mystery. 'It is possible only to report, not to explain these events'.[124] The next day, Tuesday 7 June, men began to return to work.

At the July assizes in Cardiff twenty-eight people, two of them women, were charged with various offences. Some were acquitted; six, including the two women, were given one year's hard labour; some received lesser gaol sentences; three were sentenced to death later commuted to transportation for life; Lewis Lewis and a twenty-three-year-old miner called Richard Lewis, known as Dic Penderyn, were sentenced to death. Dic Penderyn was accused of stabbing Private Robert Black in the thigh. Apart from the fact that he was one of the delegates that went into the Castle inn on 3 June, his activities during the Rising are unknown. He was certainly not the leader. If anyone was, it was 34-year-old Lewis Lewis, against whom evidence of his leading role was compelling. Yet two weeks later his death sentence was changed to transportation for life. Despite various theories the circumstances surrounding this clemency remain mysterious.

Richard Lewis, almost certainly innocent of the charge against him, was hanged in Cardiff on 13 August. Large demonstrations, three petitions – one from Merthyr had 11,000 signatures – and appeals for clemency from 'respectable persons' who unearthed fresh evidence, were all brushed aside. An example had to be made. Private Black could not identify his attacker and in America in 1874 Ianto Parker made a death-bed confession to the stabbing. Dic Penderyn with his 'martyrdom' has become a symbol of Welsh working-class struggles against oppression.

---

[124] Williams, *The Rising*, p. 158.

Accidental and Isolated?

Reflecting upon what happened in Merthyr in the first week of June 1831 Evan Thomas, chairman of the Glamorgan Quarter Sessions, reported to Lord Melbourne, the Home Secretary: 'The causes of the Ebullition were neither momentary nor specific, but rather the effect of a high state of excitement for a long period, which burst out here prematurely by accident'. The thought that what occurred was an 'accident' was picked up by the historian David Jones who suggested that unlike Peterloo in 1819 or the 1839 march on Newport, 1831 in Merthyr was 'an isolated and almost accidental occurrence'.[125] As to whether it was 'accidental', there is certainly room to wonder what would have happened if, instead of foot soldiers weary after a seven hour march, there had been cavalry confronting the crowd outside the Castle Inn, as in 1816.

'Isolated' it was not. As the Duke of Wellington had declared, Britain 'was in a state of insanity about Reform' and so was much of Europe. In July 1830 the Bourbons were overthrown in the Paris uprising, in August there was revolution in Belgium, there were uprisings in Poland. In early 1831 there were armed struggles in Hungary, Italy and Portugal and in Spain civil war broke out. These were not far away countries of which Merthyr people knew nothing. Apart from the struggles being widely reported – *The Cambrian* carried regular accounts – Merthyr's population contained men from Wellington's armies who had fought across Europe from Spain to Belgium. Henry Scale, the Aberdare industrialist, informed the Marquess of Bute that the words 'Remember Paris' and 'Think of the Poles' were 'on the mouths of many of the so called ignorant men of the mountains' during the uprising. Crucially, there was an established two-

[125] Jones, *Before Rebecca*, p.134.

way traffic between Merthyr and France. Puddlers and other skilled workmen from Merthyr had been moving, at the invitation of George Crawshay, from Merthyr to the ironworks at Grossouvre in the centre of France since 1818 and subsequently to the new works at Fourchambault founded in 1824.[126] In Britain the Merthyr insurrection was preceded by the Carmarthen riots in May and followed in the autumn, after the Lords had rejected the second Reform Bill, by those in London, Derby, Nottingham and Bristol. Reform was a nation-wide demand. Nor did the 1831 'Rising' come out of a clear blue Merthyr sky: it came after a 'high state of excitement for a long period' and was yet one more cathartic release of the economic and communal conflicts in the pressure cooker that was Merthyr Tydfil.

Beginning or End?

The armed insurrection that erupted in Merthyr in June 1831 was a rare revolutionary moment in British nineteenth century political history. Melbourne, reflecting on it later declared 'The affair we had there in 1831 was the most like a fight of anything that took place'.[127] But did it mark a decisive change in the history of Merthyr's working class? At the end of his remarkable account of *The Merthyr Rising*, as he called the events of 1831, Gwyn A. Williams asserts that it represents 'one of those structural, almost geological shifts which

---

[126] George Crawshay, son of William Crawshay I, had visited the works at Grossouvre, married a daughter of Georges Dufauy the owner of the works, and arranged for Welsh puddlers and other skilled workers to work in France and train French workers. See Chapter two.

[127] *The Rising*, p. 165, quoting a letter from Melbourne to Normanby, 5 November 1839.

accompany a profound change in opinion and attitude.' And he ends: 'In Merthyr Tydfil in 1831, the prehistory of the Welsh working class comes to an end. Its history begins.'[128] Put to one side that flourish about the *Welsh* working class; his assertion clearly is that the Merthyr working class had been through a baptism of fire (literally) and emerged with a consciousness of its class identity, separate and different from men and women with other interests. By implication also it was ready to undertake its historic Marxist role of being the engine of revolutionary change.

Without question 1831 is the culmination of 35 years of accelerated capitalist development during which Merthyr workers had daily engaged in workplace confrontations great and small, endured severe hunger and distress, had taken part in riots, confronted the soldiers of the Crown, and been increasingly exposed to radical political ideas to which they were receptive. The strikes and riots of 1816 provide ample evidence of militant working class action and the deliberate co-ordination of such action across the iron district by Merthyr workmen. In the heat of 1816 volatile William Crawshay II defined workers as 'the enemy'; a clear statement of a relationship, although not one he consistently used. A sense of class separateness and a willingness to organise and act together in periods of distress are evident *before* as well as during 1831.

That sense of class separateness further emerged in the peaceful turn to trade unionism that followed. But during the insurrection it is clear that there were deep divisions among the workers. The use of guards and a rope to keep people in the High Street on 3 June and on other occasions points to intimidation. The argument on 4 June between factions at the gates of Cyfarthfa Park about what to do next, the failure to

[128] *The Rising,* p. 230.

agree, and the swift falling apart of the whole enterprise on the afternoon of 6 June, testify to deep schisms. Most telling is the split between Cyfarthfa and Dowlais. At the height of the insurrection on 4 June hundreds of Dowlais workers defected to Brecon in order to avoid being embroiled. (A fund in gratitude was raised for them in Brecon.) This defection laid bare the cultural differences between the west of the town with its associations with Unitarianism, the Cyfarthfa Philosophical Society, the physical presence of the Court of Requests, and the proximity of China, compared with the Dowlais community under authoritarian paternal rule and strong Methodist influence. William Crawshay II and his workers felt betrayed, each by the other; there was no such ambiguity in Dowlais. These divisions apart it is clear this was not the beginning but the end of a revolutionary phase. Merthyr's workers had had their revolutionary moment. Merthyr's 1831 would be Monmouthshire's 1839.

6

Breaking the Unions

> ...is not this "Union" a confederacy that will bring you into those places where as men fearing God you should not be found...
>
> Thomas Revel Guest[129]

The Rising had been defeated. Without a national uprising comparable to those in Europe it could not have been otherwise. By the shootings, the hanging of Richard Lewis, the imposition of martial law and the stationing of troops in Dowlais, Abergavenny, and Brecon, the capital of the iron country had been subdued. But the urge for reform, for a better life was still strong. The answer lay to hand. With startling suddenness lodges of the Friendly Society of Coalmining appeared in Merthyr as early as 3 July. Undoubtedly the ground had been prepared. Everything, short of certainty, suggests that 'the stranger' who made such an impression at the Waun was an activist from the colliers' union.[130]

Founded in March 1830 with headquarters in Bolton, it had affiliated in April 1831 to John Doherty's National Association for the Protection of Labour, which saw no boundaries to recruitment. The indefatigable Doherty repeatedly urged in

[129] Thomas Revel Guest, *A Plain Address to such Members of the Union Lodges as are in connexion with Christian Churches* (Cardiff, 1831) quoted in Elsas pp. 61-2.

[130] Gwyn A. Williams, *The Rising*, pp. 110-11.

public speeches the need for trade union unity and the rights of labour. In 1830 union lodges spread rapidly in all the industrial centres of the north of England and during the winter of 1830 the miners' union had conducted a successful strike in north-east Wales. The next target was industrialised South Wales with Merthyr, the largest and most working class town, the prize. Unions appeared over the whole coalfield. [131] In all four Merthyr works iron-workers as well as colliers and miners joined the union, clear evidence of a readiness to combine with fellow workers against the interests of their employers. They had moved with growing confidence from 'downers', to informal combinations without permanent association, to the point where in the bitter aftermath of revolt they were ready to take the step to formal organization.

The fact that since the repeal of the Combination Acts in 1824 and 1825 trade unions were legal gave legitimacy and reassurance to the men. William Crawshay I recognised this and went so far as to say, 'The men have in my opinion as much Right to have unions as the Masters' and with an oblique reference to the laws of conspiracy added, 'the Old Laws are quite sufficient if acted upon between Masters and Men'.[132] Josiah. J. Guest, who, following the example set by Taitt, was all his life fiercely anti-union, reacted differently and called for united resistance to this alien force that challenged the masters' authority. On 27 August he wrote to employers in Wales and in the north of England where unions had appeared, inquiring about their strength and how they were being dealt with. Of the various replies received the most decisive was from W. H.

---

[131] Eric Evans, *The Miners of South Wales*, (Cardiff, 1961), Chapter 3. See also Elsas, pp. 62-3; E.D. Lewis, *The Rhondda Valleys* (1959), pp. 156-7.

[132] W. Crawshay I to W. Crawshay II, 27 August, 7 September 1831. Crawshay Papers (NLW)

Bevan of Beaufort who argued for discharging all union members and on 2 September provided one of the earliest known examples of 'the Discharge Note'.[133]

> "I hereby certify that the Bearer William Jones Collier, 'not being a member of any Union or other Society combined for the purpose of Regulating Wages', is this day discharged from the employ of Messrs. Kendalls & Bevan, in pursuance of notice of that effect given by (or to) the said William Jones on the 2nd of August last. W. H. Bevan."
>
> Would not the above form answer all purposes? Should the man be a Member of the Union the words between the Commas being drawn through with the pen would be a sufficient hint.
>
> The Notices should be printed in duplicate so that a Register would be Kept of each man's discharge. The Words scored under, to be left blank. Will Mr. Guest give it his Consideration.

The idea was taken up and Dowlais and Plymouth gave notice that union members would be dismissed.

On the same day, 27 August, that Guest wrote to employers seeking information Major Digby Mackworth, sent down by the War Office on a special mission, wrote, 'I am told by the magistrates of Merthyr that every individual miner there is a member of a Secret Society and has taken Oaths of Secrecy'[134]. Two of the magistrates were, of course, Guest and Hill who were about to dismiss trade unionists from their employ. Much was made at the time of the fact that the initiation ceremony into the union included the swearing of oaths of secrecy.

---

133 Elsas, pp. 58-61.

134 *Rising*, p. 210.

However, there was nothing new about taking oaths or 'obligations' of secrecy. It was a normal part of craft guild and trade union practice; it was a standard aspect of initiation into Friendly Societies, with which Merthyr workers were familiar; it was essential to the initiation ceremony into Freemasonry, through which J. J. Guest had passed in 1810 and to initiation into the Orange Order whose Grand Master was the Duke of Cumberland.

The Acts of 1824-25, which had legalised combinations whose aim was to raise wages, had also repealed all previous acts relating to such combinations, including those relating to the taking of oaths. Combinations to raise wages (trade unions) were legally separated from other combinations that acted as mutinous societies. Consequently, the attack on oath-taking came not on legal grounds but on biblical. Workers who took the oaths were said to be disobeying the Third Commandment. An anonymous pamphlet, *On the Oaths Taken in the Union Club* by *Looker-On* took this line as did Thomas Guest's *A plain Address to such Members of the Union Lodges as are in connexion with Christian Churches* which was widely circulated. The same arguments were heard from local pulpits.

From late September to mid November 3,000 to 4,000 workers at Dowlais and Plymouth were locked-out. Despite financial support from those in work at Cyfarthfa and Penydarren, and from further afield, the men and their families were brought to the verge of starvation and by the end of November even the most determined had returned to work. Throughout this harsh and bitter dispute the men behaved peacefully. The legality of their action after what had occurred in June was of huge emotional and psychological importance. This was not treason, it was not violent, it was lawful.

The workers were asserting their right to belong to a legal institution, Guest and Hill were clear that at issue was their right to be masters in their own house. Their desire was echoed by those in government who saw 'the unions' as a challenge to their power. Melbourne, who in March 1831 had ruthlessly repressed the labourers' revolt in the southern counties of England, now connived in an illegal refusal of poor relief to the locked-out union members. The Merthyr magistrates, and in particular J.B. Bruce the Stipendiary, inquired of Melbourne whether poor relief could be paid to the men. 'The workmen say', reported Bruce, 'they do not wish to control their masters and they do not exceed the powers given them by 6 George IV cap. 129 [which legalised trade unions] and that therefore the Masters have no right to annex any conditions to their returning to work.' [135] Melbourne's response was ambiguous, assuring the magistrates that he was sure they would act with firmness and discretion. The Home Office received the formal Opinion of the law officers on the question of whether the locked-out men were entitled to relief. In it the law officers stated:

> ...The question submitted to us therefore taken in connexion with the Magistrate's letter seems to resolve itself into this: whether the union societies of which the workmen are members are illegal societies. If not, we think that the workmen are entitled to parochial relief and we see no grounds stated for thinking that they are illegal.

This Opinion never reached Merthyr. The men were refused relief and not for the last time faced starvation or submission.[136]

A treacherous and shameful event during the struggle was that William Twiss, the union organiser who had been sent to help the men and raise funds, absconded on the morning of 15 November

[135] *Rising*, p. 215.

[136] Gwyn A. Williams, 'Merthyr 1831: Lord Melbourne and the Trade Unions', *Llafur*, Vol.1, No. 1 (May 1972).

taking what union funds remained.[137] It was a betrayal long remembered. Thirty-eight years later a rollerman was asked whether he belonged to a trade union. He replied: 'No, we did have a union once, but the young man run away with the money.'[138]

In 1834 another attempt at unionisation came during a period of relative prosperity. Robert Owen's Grand National Consolidated Trades Union was gathering members throughout Britain and Cyfarthfa puddlers and ironstone miners became union members. Crawshay changed his tune and once again magistrates and employers acted against 'the intolerable tyranny of the Trades Unions'. Membership crumbled in the face of this opposition and only at Cyfarthfa and Hirwaun was there resistance where men were locked-out until they caved in by mid-August.[139] In both 1831 and 1834 trade unionism had come from outside Merthyr, finding fertile ground. On both occasions its growth had been ruthlessly stamped out.

A New Arena

In the fever of the Reform Crisis the 1830 Political Union had brought together a wide range of interests, but the insurrection ended that alliance. Most of the shopocracy, not surprisingly, for they had been as much or more the target of angry crowds as the ironmasters in 1800, 1816 and 1831, enrolled as Special Constables. The small group of idealistic radicals were appalled by the violence towards persons, particularly the treatment of the Unitarian Joseph Coffin, his wife and children. For the next fifteen years fear of 'the mob' was a constant theme in Merthyr's politics, strongly influencing reaction to the next

[137] Evans, *The Miners of South Wales*, (Cardiff, 1961), p.47.

[138] *Good Words*, 1 January 1869, quoted in John A. Owen, *The History of the Dowlais Iron Works 1759-1970* (Risca, 1977), p. 73.

[139] Evans, *The Miners,* pp. 53-5.

phase of working class action. On 1 August 1831 ninety inhabitants, including the radicals, petitioned Melbourne to keep the troops in Merthyr to protect them from a 'licentious and senseless rabble'. In the aftermath of the insurgency an estimated 5,000 people left Merthyr to seek work, escape victimisation, or find peace. So many Irish left that the town was without a Catholic priest for two years.[140]

With troops parading the streets the Unitarian radicals were soon visible again in local politics. In an alliance with the ironmasters they had since March 1831 been effectively governing Merthyr through a standing committee of the Select Vestry. As an uneasy calm returned, their appetite for insider politics was fed further by the final amendment to the third Reform Bill that made Merthyr a Parliamentary constituency that included Aberdare and Cefn Coed. Out of a Merthyr population of well over 20,000, the Reform Act gave 452 people the vote. Another fifty received the vote in Aberdare. But a new arena for local political debate had been opened. The James faction rallied behind Josiah John Guest who became Merthyr's first MP.

Not until the last moment did Parliament grant Merthyr the status of a single borough with the right to elect a Member of Parliament. In an account of the exhausting committee debates and the parliamentary dynamics of carrying the Bills through the Commons Ted Rowlands (a member of the House of Lords and former MP for Merthyr Tydfil) sees the answer in concessions made by government ministers to ensure the successful passage of the Bill. What made the final difference, he argued, was the successful repression of the trade unions. Merthyr Tydfil was now in government eyes a safe place to enfranchise.[141]

---

140 O'Leary, *Immigration and Integration: The Irish in Wales 1798-1922* (Cardiff, 2000), p. 65.

141 Ted Rowlands, 'Rebellion and Representation: The Making of the Merthyr Tydfil Constituency, 1831-2', *WHR*, vol. 26/3 (June 2013).

If 1831 was the moment that confirmed a self-conscious working class, the Reform Act of the following year sealed its distinctiveness. It was excluded from the franchise and the stage was set for the formal emergence of Chartism. When it came, the younger generation of Merthyr Unitarians allied themselves with the workers' cause. The lone emissary who had gone to Penydarren House at the height of the rebellion was Matthew John, aged twenty-four, son of David John the Unitarian minister at the Twnyrodyn chapel. It was a meeting the ironmasters described as 'chilling'. Matthew John had been utterly intransigent and 'lived in hourly expectation of a general insurrection'.[142] Matthew and his brother David became ardent Chartists and were joined by Morgan Williams an intellectual and idealistic weaver, son of a trustee of the chapel at Twynyrodyn. The transportation of the leading insurgents and the desertion of the town by those fearful of victimisation had left a vacuum of working-class leadership. In a bold and uncharacteristic display of ambition it was Williams from Penyrheolgerrig who emerged as the leader of the largest gathering of Chartists in Wales.

---

[142] Williams, 'The Merthyr Election...', p. 364; *Rising*, p. 154.

7

In A Righteous Cause

...seditious ragamuffins, demagogues, and spouters of treason.

Merthyr Guardian, 21 April 1848

Morgan Williams, articulate in Welsh and English, autodidact, intense idealist, accomplished mathematician, had been a rising star in the fierce controversies that characterised Merthyr politics in the 1830s. In 1830, aged twenty-two, he attended the Political Union debates. In 1833 he was arguing in the radical *Hereford Times* for the abolition of stamp duty on newspapers, the 'taxes on knowledge'. In 1834 with the scholarly musician and fellow Unitarian, John Thomas (*Ieun Ddu*), he produced the small bilingual monthly *Y Gweithiwr/The Workman*, a journal that in May praised the Tolpuddle labourers who in March had been sentenced to transportation for swearing 'illegal oaths' (two years later they were given a free pardon). Bruce, the stipendiary magistrate, sent a copy to the Home Office regarding it as an illegal and seditious publication. By the end of the year Williams was well known enough for letters in the *Merthyr Guardian* to refer to him sarcastically, as 'the mountain Solomon'. [143]

In the general election of 1835 when Josiah John Guest was opposed by William Meyrick, Crawshay's solicitor and a Tory, Williams played a key role. On 6 January with John Jones the

[143] *MG*, 13 and 20 December 1834.

Unitarian minister who had succeeded Tomos Glyn Cothi at *Hen Dy Cwrdd*, Trecynon, he persuaded thousands of workers meeting on the mountain above Penyrheolgerrig to issue a statement that left Meyrick no option but to pull out of the contest. The workmen of Merthyr would withdraw their custom from any tradesman who voted 'contrary to the opinions and welfare of the people'. This declaration of exclusive dealing, probably the first in Wales, with its eloquent and carefully argued statement of representative democracy surely was drafted by Morgan Williams.[144]

At Guest's victory dinner he took the initiative of offering a toast to 'the working classes' and declared

> They are a class of people who have been foully calumniated and I stand forward as their humble representative ...their only desire is the calm and peaceable possession of their political rights, rights which have long and unjustly been withheld from them, and which thanks to the irresistible diffusion of knowledge must soon be within their grasp.[145]

In January 1836, to show that his mind had not been entirely taken up with politics he found time to marry Elizabeth Humphreys, aged twenty-one. One of the two witnesses was a John Jones; assuredly John Jones of Trecynon.

---

[144] The statement appeared in the *Hereford Times*, *The Cambrian*, and *The Cardiff and Merthyr Guardian* 10 January 1835. In an editorial in its 17 January edition *The Cardiff and Merthyr Guardian* wrote of elections 'present and future' ruled by 'Mob Law' which 'will eventually terminate in grape-shot sweeping the streets of Merthyr'.

[145] *The Cambrian*, 17 January 1835. The report has been changed to direct speech.

But in 1837 the alliance between Guest and his middle class supporters, and Morgan Williams and his working class supporters, broke down. Guest in April, to the dismay of his wife, became chairman of Merthyr's Poor Law Guardians. She confided to her journal: 'I would on no account have liked his taking such a disagreeable situation... it will be turned greatly to his disadvantage'.[146] Indeed it was. In the general election of that July a mass meeting of workmen decided to support the Tory candidate, and Guest had to issue a statement that he too was opposed to some of the clauses which workmen considered most obnoxious in the poor laws.[147] Guest won, but Morgan Williams played only a marginal role in the campaign. Instead he contributed to the radical *Merthyr and Cardiff Chronicle* which, in a sign of things to come, carried a statement on 30 September from the Working Men's Association of London addressed to 'Fellow Labourers in the pursuit of Knowledge and Liberty' exhorting the benefits of forming local Working Men's Associations.

Nothing happened for a year as there was a curious attempt to bring middle and working class intellectuals together in a Literary and Scientific Institution, an acknowledged successor to the Cyfarthfa Philosophical Society. Taliesin Williams, the schoolmaster, and Edward Lewis Richards, a London barrister with Merthyr connections were prominent in promoting the idea. On 14 October in the *Chronicle* Morgan Williams addressed an open letter to 'Friends and Fellow-Workmen' ('*Gyfeillion a Chydweithwyr*') urging them to participate. They did not, Morgan Williams declined to become 'curator', and despite Guest becoming President and rooms being made

---

[146] The Earl of Bessborough (ed.), *Lady Charlotte Guest: Extracts from her Journal 1833-1852* (1950), p. 46.

[147] *MG*, 15, 22, and 29 July1837; Bessborough, pp. 49-50.

available, the Society fizzled out. [148] The times were too fevered for a debating society. It was not until October 1838 that the Merthyr branch of the Working Men's Association (WMA) appeared with Morgan Williams as its secretary and leading spokesman. Branches of the WMA had already been established in Newtown, Llanidloes, Welshpool, Carmarthen, Swansea, Llanelli, Pontypool and Newport. Merthyr soon made up for lost time.

On Christmas Day 1838 thousands marched in procession to Penyrheolgerrig, flying their tricolour banner of green, white and blue symbolising earth, sun and sky. It was the largest Chartist demonstration in Wales up to that time. The national petition in support of the Charter had been circulated in both languages and the chief speaker was Hugh Williams, the Carmarthen lawyer, honorary member of the London Working Men's Association, and soon to be legal defender of the Rebecca Rioters. Afterwards 200 sat down to a celebratory dinner confident that the Merthyr working class had joined a national crusade. The nervous Merthyr magistrates asked the commander of troops at Brecon to be prepared to send them to Merthyr if required.[149] They were not.

With 1831 in mind the magistrates' alarm was understandable. *The People's Charter* published by the London Working Men's Association was a revolutionary document and regarded as such by the authorities. Its demands for universal male suffrage, annual parliaments, secret ballots, equal electoral districts, payment for Members of Parliament, and the abolition

---

[148] *Merthyr and Cardiff Chronicle*, 2, 23, 30 September; 7, 14, 21, 28 October; 9 December 1837. Kevin Littlewood, *From Reform to the Charter: Merthyr Tydfil 1832-1838* (Merthyr Tydfil, 1990), pp. 18-19.

[149] David Williams, *John Frost*, p. 119. Bessborough, Vol 1, p. 85.

of property qualifications for voters were not new.[150] But if in the 1830s the Charter's six points had been achieved they would have turned society upside down. Thousands in Britain's industrial areas flocked to its support and the Home Office marshalled magistrates, police forces, spies, and troops to deal with this 'enemy within'.

The Events of 1839

The year 1839 was one of ceaseless activity in Merthyr and the coalfield towns and villages of Glamorgan and Monmouthshire: publicising the Charter, enrolling members, holding demonstrations and gathering signatures for the National Petition signed by 14,700 Merthyr people, nearly three times the number who signed from Newport. Morgan Williams attended the National Convention at which the right to bear arms and the right of just resistance to tyranny were enshrined in its Manifesto. 'Peacefully if we may – forcibly if we must' became the slogan of the movement. In April/May there were disturbances at Llanidloes, arrests of Chartists in London, and the detention of the popular Chartist orator Henry Vincent in Monmouth gaol. There were rumours of arms clubs, of gun traders and of pikes being made in the smithies of the ironworks. Troops were sent into Newport, Abergavenny and Monmouth. On Whit Monday, 20 May, thousands, including most of Crawshay's workmen and some from Dowlais, attended a rally at Blackwood which adopted proposals agreed at the National Convention. Gatherings of 5,000 or more were held

---

[150] Their lineage has been explored in E. P. Thompson, *The Making of the English Working Class* (Gollancz, 1963); Gareth Stedman Jones, *Languages of Class: Studies in English Working Class History 1832-1982* (Cambridge, 1983), Chap. 3, 'Rethinking Chartism'; Malcolm Chase, *Chartism: A New History* (Manchester, 2007).

in the summer at locations near Merthyr – Rhymney, Hirwaun and Penyrheolgerrig – with John Frost, William Jones, and Morgan Williams as the principal speakers. Henry Hetherington spoke at Dowlais on 25 May. A Defence Fund for Vincent and other Chartist prisoners received £100 from Merthyr. Local tradesmen who refused to contribute were ostracised by female shoppers.

On 12 July, the House of Commons refused by 235 votes to 46 to consider the first Chartist petition. There was riot and arson in Birmingham on the fifteenth, armed Chartists repeatedly firing guns in the air at Bury on the seventeenth, and on the twentieth in Newcastle running battles with damage to a bank and the offices of an anti-Chartist newspaper. Arms were openly being manufactured in a number of midland and northern towns and special constables were sworn. Troops continued to flood into South Wales.[151]

Alarmed by these events the *Merthyr Guardian* became hysterical. On 27 July it warned local Chartists that if they assembled in numbers the following should happen:

> troops should be called in and when 'the Civil Force is unequal to the quelling of the tumult' then 'opposition to the military power will be met with the word of command – FIRE! And that word of command will neither convey the meaning that blank cartridges are to be used, nor that the firing is to be over the heads of the people: but *at the mob*, and if possible, at those who are evidently *leaders of the mob*'. [Capitals and italics in the original].

The paper added: 'Ten or a dozen lives may be sacrificed; but those ten or dozen may save the lives of hundreds'. This was

[151] Chase, *Chartism*, pp. 95-6; Jones, *The Last Rising*, pp. 83-98.

published when there had been no Chartist violence whatsoever in Merthyr.

On 2 August Vincent was jailed for twelve months. On 12 August a monster assembly at Dukestown, near Tredegar, called upon the Queen to dissolve Parliament and release Vincent from gaol. At this time of national disaffection, state repression, and middle class panic the Merthyr Chartists in their thousands made a move. They held a church parade. It was part of what has been called a nation-wide confrontation 'with the social elitism of the Church of England ...and its integral relationship with the political establishment'.[152] A first-hand account appears in a letter dated 18 August 1839 written to Lord Bute by William Thomas, Tory magistrate, popular after dinner speaker and major local landowner:

> On this day at the usual hour of the morning service the Church became unusually filled with workmen and women very decently draped and a good many of them (the greater number) distinguished by the Chartist Badge viz blue ribbon attached to the button hole and flannel waistcoat of a peculiar pattern. – their leader here in point of literary talent is Morgan Williams a weaver, who no doubt has suggested the flannel waistcoat badge for his own benefit – the church was filled to suffocation – it is computed that about 2,000 were inside the church and that 1,000 remained outside – not the slightest disturbance took place – on the contrary all appeared to pay the most solemn attention to the service and there never was a more orderly or more attentive congregation. Mr Gill as well as myself was in attendance ...The weaver in question is occasionally having meetings held near his home on Aberdare Hill but there is nothing connected with them to excite any fear tho' he is

[152] Chase, *Chartism*, p. 97.

> occasionally assisted by a person (probably not unknown to your Lordship) of the name of Dr. Price Nantgarw near Cardiff a fit subject in the opinion of most for a Lunatic Asylum...[153]

This peaceful show of strength was all the more impressive in the face of a provocative sermon, preached by the Reverend T. Williams, the text for which was especially chosen for this event and came from chapter two of Peter's first epistle, verses 13 to 17. The Rev Williams argued that the verses showed that Government was appointed by God, whatever form it might take, and that it was Man's duty to obey that Government, first by submitting to the King as God's earthly representative, and then to all authorities under him; and although the administrator of the laws might be personally objectionable, it was incumbent on man to respect him for the sake of those laws.[154]

The Attack on Newport

By contrast with the thousands at the church few Merthyr people took part in the calamitous attack on the Westgate Hotel, Newport, on 4 November. One of those killed carried a Merthyr WMA membership card and two of those arrested were from Dowlais. Unquestionably there were others (George Morgan was one) but their presence was minimal. Charlotte Guest recorded on 4 November 'Our Works began as usual and have gone on steadily ever since ...Our own men are good and true and stick to their work gallantly'.[155] The Home Office was informed that the very few that came from Merthyr were

---

[153] Cardiff Central Library, Bute Papers XX. Item 20.

[154] *MG*, 24 August 1839.

[155] The Earl of Bessborough (ed.), *Lady Charlotte Guest: Extracts from her Journal 1833-1852* (London, 1950), 99 and 102.

probably tramps.[156] There is no other information as to what Merthyr's alleged membership of 7,000 Chartists were doing that night.

There have been various theories largely based on rumours. Perhaps they did not know the details of what was to happen. That there was going to be a rising was widely anticipated, but no Merthyr delegate was at the crucial meeting in the Coach and Horses at Blackwood on Friday, 1 November, when the final decisions were made. A representative from Dowlais was there and some Dowlais men joined the march. Did Dowlais fail to communicate with Merthyr? Secrecy was such that there were Monmouthshire men marching that Sunday night who themselves did not know what to expect.[157] Or were the Merthyr men being held back to seize the arms of the soldiers stationed in Brecon? This however depended upon success in Newport, as did another possibility which was, *The Times* reported, to take the town of Merthyr itself. So confusing and secretive was the planning of this uprising that we cannot rule out such suggestions: particularly if Newport *had* been taken. That would have taken South Wales and Britain into a wholly different situation.

As it was, tension was high. The Guests sent their five children with their three nurses away under cover of darkness. Many people stopped work. The magistrates met in the Castle Inn as they had eight years earlier and over the next two days swore in 500 special constables, obtained the assistance of 60 armed pensioners, sent to Cardiff for help from the Glamorgan Militia, and issued a proclamation banning mass assemblies. The town remained tense. Resentment over the killings in Newport fuelled demonstrations throughout November, there

---

156 David Wiliams, 'Chartism in Wales', in Asa Briggs (ed.), *Chartist Studies* (London, 1959), p. 238.

157 David Jones, *Rising*, p. 111.

were constant rumours that violence was about to erupt in Merthyr, and on 23 November, troops were urgently sent for and a company of the 45th Regiment came up from Cardiff and was given temporary accommodation in the Dowlais stables, just as in 1831.[158]

Amidst the rumour and speculation two facts stand out. First, despite the magistrates' proclamation, a mass meeting *was* held at Penyrheolgerrig on the Tuesday following the march where a motion to 'strike while the iron is hot' was defeated and a decision taken overwhelmingly to return to work the next day. Secondly, Morgan Williams, a personal friend of John Frost and the recipient of one of the few letters written by Frost from the convict ship *Mandarin*, had chosen to go to London at this time, ostensibly to buy a printing press, and on the day of the attack was returning in a coach. The reason for him being absent from Merthyr at that time can be endlessly speculated. But the striking fact is that he did not lose face by it, neither with Frost nor with the mass of Merthyr Chartists. He continued to be their trusted leader.

Merthyr the Centre of Chartism

The failure of the march on Newport discredited the use of force and gave the authorities the opportunity to flood the coalfield with more troops and to lock away many active Chartists. It also led to an outburst of vilification against Chartism. The Reverend Evan Jenkins of Dowlais published a lengthy sermon in which he claimed that the first Chartist was the Devil, poverty 'the result of the everlasting purpose and appointment of a Sovereign God', and voting by ballot 'nothing but a cloak

[158] These paragraphs are based upon David Jones, *The Last Rising*, pp. 161-6.

for dishonesty, insincerity, hypocrisy and lies!'[159] Guest refused to buy it or distribute it among his workmen and his nephew and fellow ironmaster Edward Hutchins gave instructions that a parcel containing the pamphlet should be committed 'to the flames'.[160]

The *Merthyr Guardian* referred to 'the treasonable and seditious band of Chartists, in which Morgan Williams of Penyrheolgerrig has signed his name as "Honorary Secretary"' and described it as 'that illegal association'.[161] Morgan Williams responded that the Merthyr WMA was no more illegal than the Glamorgan Conservative Association; the only difference being that the one was composed of workers living honestly by their labour, while the other was composed of idlers, pensioners, sinecurists, pluralist parsons, lying newspaper editors, county squires, bull-frog farmers, and other fools of the same stamp.[162]

The 1839 disaster confirmed Merthyr as the major centre of Chartist activity in Wales with an unsurpassed level of organisation. Now part of the National Charter Association (NCA) by late 1842 it had ten wards, the strongest at Georgetown with thirteen discussion classes. Each ward had a collector who sent money to the central treasurer. In a vain attempt to keep out spies, admission to branch meetings was by membership card only.[163] Every Christmas Day there was a festival to commemorate their first great demonstration. Huge numbers signed petitions for the pardon of John Frost, William Jones and Zephania Williams, the leaders of the Newport attack. One, in December 1839, received 15,786 signatures, and a

[159] Rev. Edward Jenkins, *Chartism Unmasked,* (Merthyr, 1840).

[160] Bessborough, p. 106; Elsas, p. 211.

[161] *MG,* 7 December 1839.

[162] D. Williams, *John Frost*, pp. 331-2 quoting the *Northern Star*, 14 December 1839.

[163] David Jones, 'Chartism at Merthyr', p. 233.

second petition was signed by almost 11,000 women. The wives and children of Zephania Williams and William Jones were living in Merthyr and in January 1841 they attended a meeting where 5,000 turned out. In 1844 a petition calling for the Charter and a pardon for Frost, Williams and Jones received 10,640 signatures. Close analysis of Welsh Chartist leaders and speakers reveals that approaching 40 per cent came from Merthyr with additional 'large numbers' coming from Aberdare, Dowlais and the surrounding district.[164]

At the centre of this activity were Morgan Williams and David John (jr.) In the cause of 'enlightenment of the people' Williams and John published Welsh translations of Chartist pamphlets and in March 1840 they launched from Glebeland Street the bilingual fortnightly *Udgorn Cymru*: *The Trumpet of Wales* in which they supported the six points, repudiated violence, advocated temperance and attacked tithes and church rates. In July in response to demand they brought out an English language monthly, *The Advocate and Merthyr Free Press* 'to instruct ...the honest and industrious working man'. But a major aim was to place 'our political views, before many belonging to the Middle and Higher Classes, who are at the present time, in the most lamentable ignorance of the complaints, discontent, and wishes of the Working People'.[165] The combined circulation of these papers at one time reached 1,500 a month; even greater numbers heard them read aloud. Both papers were unstamped and consequently threatened with shutdown by the authorities if they published news. The pamphlet translations, the publication of *Udgorn Cymru* and the earlier *Y Gweithiwr*, were important pioneering initiatives to publicise Chartist ideas through the Welsh language.

---

[164] Angela V. John, 'The Chartist Endurance. Industrial South Wales 1840-1868', *Morgannwg*, (1971).

[165] *The Advocate; And Merthyr Free Press*, July 1840.

The Events of 1842

1842 was a crucial year for Merthyr Chartism, as it was nationally. It began with the economy in recession, severe unemployment, falling wages, and families in hunger. Despite families leaving for America, the Merthyr Board of Guardians estimated a ten-fold increase in able-bodied pauperism.[166] The middle class once again feared 'mob violence'. An activist from Nottingham, George Black, was said to be trading 'vast quantities of arms' in the Merthyr area. Troops were stationed in Dowlais. In April 1842 Morgan Williams went to the Chartist Convention in London to supervise the preparation of a second national petition, taking with him the signatures of 36,000 people from Merthyr, Tredegar, Aberdare and Pontypridd (nearly 22,000 from Merthyr alone). At the Convention he praised Frost as one regarded with the deepest reverence by 'man woman and child who all bore testimony that he ever took the part of the poor man against that of the rich oppressor'. Large crowds saw him off at the station, and on his return more than 5,000 greeted him. Speaking from a cart ('obtained for the purpose') Williams said he had attended the Commons debate on the Petition, which had been rejected by 287 votes to 49. The sight of MPs half drunk and lying full length on the green benches had disgusted him. Justice could not be expected from that unreformed House he told the crowd.[167]

A strike wave that began in June and rolled through the Potteries, Lancashire, the West Riding, the Midlands, and Scotland reached Merthyr in August, the only district in the

[166] Tydfil Thomas, *Poor Relief in Merthyr Tydfil Union in Victorian Times* (Cardiff, 1992), 28-30.

[167] John, 'Chartist Endurance', 26; *MG*, 14 May 1842.

South Wales coalfield to strike.[168] The widespread nature of these strikes known as the 'plug riots' because some strikers pulled the plugs out of boilers and flooded their workplaces, caused alarm and brought out large numbers of troops and police. The causes of the strike were high food prices, low wages and real hunger, but achieving the Charter was seen as the remedy and strike meetings often ended with three cheers given for the exiled Frost, Jones and Zephania Williams. The NCA executive belatedly gave the strike official support in August when it was already fading. Along the way there had been arrests and serious violence between strikers and soldiers – at Halifax 'cavalry cleared the streets'.[169] In the Potteries alone 56 men were transported and 121 men and women imprisoned.[170] In Merthyr there was no violence and no arrests.

The strike in Merthyr was short-lived. The men were influenced by events in England and joined the drift back to work, also accepting the argument that the state of trade ruled out any wage increase.[171] But Chartism in Merthyr was dealt three severe blows. Nineteen activists in the Cyfarthfa works

---

[168] The decision to strike was taken in a meeting at which Enoch Williams a miner, 'stated that he had received £1. 15s.7d. a month for the last two months, and had a wife and four children to maintain', *M.G.* 20 August 1842. Enoch was one of my great-great-grandfathers.

[169] Chase, *Chartism*, p. 218.

[170] Robert Fyson, 'Late Chartism in the Potteries, 1848-1858', *Labour History Review*, 74, 1, April 2009.

[171] *MG*, 27 August 1842. Heather Jordan, *The 1842 General Strike in South Wales* (Our History Pamphlet 75, London, n.d.), stresses the appalling social conditions in Merthyr and middle-class fears of armed insurrection but notes that the strike 'was throughout peaceful' with no evidence of violence 'due to the Strikers' determinedly peaceful conduct', pp. 13-14.

were sacked and 'all who favoured Chartist principles' in the Dowlais works were dismissed. Others were turned out at Penydarren and Plymouth and altogether around one hundred workers lost their jobs. Some begged in the streets with placards in their hats: 'In England, a free and Christian country, we are turned out to starve, for being Chartists'.[172] Secondly, the sales of *Udgorn Cymru* which had been struggling under harassment by the authorities became insufficient to carry on and after 22 October 1842 it ceased publication.[173] But that was also linked to the fact that before the end of the year Morgan Williams disappeared from Merthyr and was not seen there for the next three years.

Spies at the Three Horse Shoes

The rejection of the 1842 Petition and failure of the strike movement turned thoughts again to what might be achieved by force. Desperate times increased its notional appeal just as they aroused middle-class fears. From meetings held at the Three Horse Shoes pub, spies reported much strong rhetoric and talk of arms. On 2 and 3 October 1842 Matthew John advised that everyone should 'have a good riffle piece in their house for that was the only thing that would gain them liberty for it was no use to maintain a set of Idlers on their back any longer, such as the Queen the Bloody Bitch having her £300,000 a year'. David Ellis, a weaver, complained that the Queen was pregnant again and 'was going to fill the country with idlers...' William Miles, miner, a strike leader recently sacked by Crawshay, and a member of the General Council of the National Charter Association, stated that: 'the last argument with a King was a

[172] *MG*, 10 September 1842.

[173] R. D. Rees, 'Glamorgan Newspapers under the Stamp Acts', *Morgannwg*, vol. III, (1959).

Cannon and now that you see moral force is no good, that ought to be your last argument, and every one ought to learn how to use a gun and everyone ought to have one in his possession.' David John (jr.) spoke in the same fashion.[174] Members were exhorted to pay into arms clubs that posed as benefit societies. Feelings were such that Feargus O'Connor, the national leader of Chartism, wrote to them in November warning them against another premature Newport affair.[175] In 1843 when the horse belonging to Merthyr's superintendent of police was shot, the culprit was congratulated as being 'A good hearty fellow' and hints made that the superintendent himself might be next in line. It all came to nothing. Despite attendance at these branch meetings of 250-300 and public meetings in 1843 attracting crowds of over 1,000 the movement across the land was losing supporters as petitions, armed affrays and strikes were all defeated.

In 1845 Feargus O'Connor raised the issue of land ownership. His idea was that the NCA would buy land and allocate small farms to Chartist land-fund subscribers through a lottery. The idea was enthusiastically supported in Merthyr where thousands were just one generation away from the land. Merthyr soon had three branches and all subscribers in Wales were listed under the 'Merthyr District' whose secretary in 1847 was David Morgan, a Merthyr stonemason. In 1848 over £178 was subscribed from Wales in shares and expenses with Merthyr alone providing almost £76. Merthyr branches studied farm management, soil chemistry, and visited Chartist settlements. There was even talk of a settlement just outside the town. Several Merthyr men were allotted smallholdings in

[174] Details of the meetings are in Home Office (HO) 40/57, 45/265, and 45/453. See David Jones, 'Chartism at Merthyr' and A. V. John 'The Chartist Endurance'.

[175] Jones, *The Last Rising*, p. 220.

England. But the National Land Company was never finally legalised and had to be wound up in the early 1850s.[176] Its chief value was providing a focus for Chartist organisation when as a mass movement it was dwindling away.

A revival came in 1848, the year of revolutions in Europe that brought memories of 1830. In February the French monarchy was overthrown. Before the end of March successful revolutions had taken place in Bavaria, Berlin, Vienna, Hungary and Italy. 'France has the Republic, England shall have the Charter' became the cry. Signatures for a third national petition were already being collected but the revolutions gave them fresh impetus. A national Convention was called for 4 April with the petition to be presented to parliament on 10 April. In Merthyr Reform feelings ran high at a succession of meetings. In the Market Square on 20 March David Thomas, a cooper, was chosen to attend the London Convention, the only delegate from Wales. Once there he declared that although his constituents 'were moral force men now they would soon be converted to physical force men'. Once again special constables were sworn in, spies attended the public meetings and the military were put on standby. The *Merthyr Guardian* on 21 April in 'The Chartist Leaders' was at its most hysterical referring to the 'ravings', the 'cloven hoof', and 'the general character of the seditious ragamuffins, demagogues, and spouters of treason' who advocated the Charter. [177] This third and final petition with almost two million signatures again made no progress.

[176] Angela V. John, 'The Chartist Endurance', pp. 31-2.

[177] *MG,* 21 April 1848.

Who were the 'Ragamuffins'?

'Independent tradesmen and professional men were an important element in the Chartist movement' noted the historian Dorothy Thompson but she added, 'They did not, in the main, make up the leadership...'[178] In Merthyr Tydfil they did. Morgan Williams was a self-employed weaver. David John (jr.) came from a family of blacksmiths and founders, the father also a teacher and Unitarian minister. Matthew John, who retained much of the verbal militancy of his youth, developed the family smithy with his other brother Richard, into a successful engineering business based at the commodious Vulcan House in Bethesda Street.[179] William Gould, a prolific platform speaker for thirty years started his working life as an errand boy and boot-black at Cyfarthfa Castle in the service of William Crawshay II, became a rollerman in the Works, and then kept a grocery shop at Taffs Well on Brecon Road. He invented several ballot boxes – none of which worked but they can be seen in Cyfarthfa Museum – and was said to hoist a flag annually to commemorate the taking of the Bastille. When he died in 1875 he owned a total of nineteen houses.[180]

Other prominent activists included Thomas Davies the minister at High Street Baptist chapel, Benjamin Harvard a grocer and elder at Cefn Coed Ebenezer Independent chapel, Henry Thomas, cooper, George Morgan, stone cutter and deacon of High Street Baptist Church, (who had been in the march on Newport and afterwards went to America until matters cooled down), and John W. James, a surgeon educated at Paris and Berlin and proprietor of the *Merthyr Star*. Process

[178] Dorothy Thompson, *The Chartists*, p. 172.

[179] Lyndon Harris, 'Vulcan House – A Chartist's Home', *Merthyr Historian*, Vol. 12 (2001).

[180] Will, proved 17 November 1875.

workers in the ironworks are noticeably absent. Elizabeth, Morgan Williams' wife, tried to form a Female Association although its success is not known.[181] Undoubtedly the promotion of Chartist ideas in Merthyr benefitted from the fact that the prominent leaders were self-employed, and could not therefore be dismissed for their activities.

With the votes of their considerable following they held national roles that linked Merthyr Chartists with the national mainstream. David John (jr.) represented Merthyr, Aberdare, Pontypridd, Newport and Pontypool at the conference in Manchester in July 1840 out of which the National Charter Association (NCA) was born. In 1841 and 1842 Morgan Williams was elected to the NCA five-man National Executive. Gould served on the General Council of the NCA in June 1842 and February 1844. In the June 1841 General Election Morgan Williams stood as Parliamentary candidate against Guest and at the open-air hustings where speeches were made and votes taken on a show of hands, won. Having made his point he withdrew from the poll, as practically all his supporters would not have been eligible to vote.

Chartism in Merthyr continued with some vigour into the 1850s. A new branch was formed in 1856 and in December 1857 John Frost, back from exile, spoke at Merthyr and said he would stand for Merthyr in a Parliamentary election. He never did.[182] Even when Chartism ceased as a national movement meetings were organised locally. John W. James, Morgan Williams, Gould, and Matthew John all lectured on various topics at the subscription library and elsewhere.

They were political activists concerned with a wide range of issues – taxes on knowledge, civil and religious liberty, shorter

---

[181] *The Advocate; and Merthyr Free Press*, July 1840.

[182] Angela V. John, 'The Chartist Endurance' p. 35.

working hours, unemployment, poverty, land reform, emigration, repeal of the Act of Union between England and Ireland. They were troubled by the Crimean War, and supported the northern states in the American civil war. In 1862 Henry Vincent addressed meetings in Merthyr on slavery and in February 1863 at an anti-slavery meeting in the Temperance Hall, organised by Morgan Williams, W. A. Jackson an escaped slave spoke. In November 1866 a crowd of 1,500 in Market Square heard Morgan Williams and Matthew John speak for electoral reform.

Although their numbers dwindled, Merthyr Chartists punched above their weight. The topics they debated were secular rather than religious and that was significant in an age when the questions that dominated Welsh politics were the relations between religion and education, and the disestablishment of the Church of England. They kept alive a radicalism that fed into Liberalism and sustained the vision of a more politically equitable society. It was natural that in 1868 they supported and voted for Henry Richard, a Welsh-speaking pacifist Liberal who claimed to support the Charter. After 1868 William Gould, who had initially opposed the application of the Public Health Act, was a vociferous member of the local Board of Health, the Burial Board and a Poor Law Guardian.

The Whole Hog

The leaders of Merthyr Chartism naturally opposed the 'rascally' New Poor Law of 1834. In its early days they were strongly opposed to the introduction of a police force, David John (jr.) referring to police at a meeting on 20 February 1841 as a 'tyrannical body'. But their most notable characteristic was determination to achieve the Charter and nothing less. On two issues, the introduction to Merthyr of the 1848 Public Health Act and the setting up of a town council, their refusal to compromise on voting rights caused them to oppose middle class reformers and ally themselves with the ironmasters. David John (jr.) and David Ellis were both in favour of repealing the Corn Laws, while Morgan Williams was not, but the achievement of the Charter always received greater priority in discussions. When, in 1849 Joseph Hume produced a 'Little Charter' the Merthyr response was: 'Nothing short of the whole hog, bristles and all will satisfy us ...several attempts within the last four or five months to introduce a 3-legged animal to us ...found us determined to manfully oppose the trash'. And three years later they declared, 'we are determined never to agitate for nor countenance a less measure of reform than the People's Charter'.[183] As the years went by and attitudes changed, the ageing Chartist spokesmen became isolated platform performers, objects of a condescending tolerance.[184]

What happened to Morgan Williams?

The trajectory of Morgan Williams' achievement of local and then national leadership seems unfaltering until 1842 when his actions attracted criticism both from workmen and from the police. Criticised for not speaking at strike meetings he apologised on 26 September at The Three Horseshoes for his recent absence, explaining that if he had been amongst them

---

[183] *Northern Star*, 2 June 1849, 17 January 1852; quoted by John, 'The Chartist Endurance', p. 34.

[184] David Evans, a supporter of incorporation expressed 'a desire to see Mr. Gould and Mr. Matthew John elected aldermen, a remark which created some amount of laughter, and elicited a serious assurance from Mr. Evans that his wish was not advanced in any frivolous manner, for he believed there were no two persons in Merthyr more highly respected than those he had named. (Hear, hear)': *The Merthyr Telegraph*, 27 June 1873.

'he would certainly have been now in the hands of the tyrants for the police had a strong force here in order to get hold of me'. In this he was correct. In August Bute had considered having him arrested. On 6 September Captain Napier, chief constable of Glamorgan, reported to Bute:

> ... Morgan Williams is the sole director of Chartist movements in South Wales, and so long as he continues at large, Merthyr can expect no peace. During the late outbreak he remained within doors and spoke but seldom: his principle occupation consisted in deciphering letters from Birmingham, Manchester, Leeds and issuing directions to those under him to keep up agitation, what subjects should be disrupted, and how they were to proceed... Morgan Williams is so intimately connected with many of the inhabitants that whilst at Merthyr I find myself closely watched: his brother in law is Post Master, and he is nearly related to the High Constable of Merthyr. I do not apprehend any attempt at a rising unless preceded by one in the North, but by holding constant meetings, I fear the system of agitation will be carried on during the winter to the great injury of trade at Merthyr.[185].

By September fellow members of the NCA Executive had been arrested leaving him the only one free. In October he was asked to go to London to advise on the affairs of the Association but made his excuses and disappeared from Merthyr. What actually happened was told in later years to Charles Wilkins by Williams. It was extraordinary but typical of Merthyr. He had received a tip-off from the magistrate William Thomas, that 'proud aborigine' of Merthyr, that a warrant for his arrest was imminent. He slipped away, significantly to Newtown a centre of both weaving and

[185] Cardiff Library, Bute Papers, XXII item 20.

Chartism, where he worked as a weaver and second-hand book seller.[186] It may also have been the home district of his wife, for Humphreys was a name common to that area. He evidently maintained radical activity for on 27 February 1845 'the operatives of Newtown' presented him with a brass inkstand (it is in the Cyfarthfa Museum). By then David John (jr.) had died from tuberculosis in 1844, aged thirty-two. The disappearance in the early 1840s of these two intellectual leaders and activists was a serious blow to Merthyr Chartism at a critical time.

In November 1845 Elizabeth, Morgan Williams' wife, also died from tuberculosis and in 1846 he was back in Merthyr. It seems certain that the loss of his young wife, leaving him with three small children, adversely affected him and for a while he dropped out of political activity. Despite his swift ascent into local leadership one doubts that personal ambition had been the driver. He retained his radicalism and frequently spoke at public meetings in later years; but never exerted the same authority: his unwillingness to go to prison for the cause may have told against him. He moved socially closer to the middle class activists, to whom he was linked by marriage and in 1853 Williams entered public service as parish registrar for marriages.

He died on 17 October 1883. Much of his substantial book collection he left to the establishment of a Merthyr Free Library, his portrait of Lincoln to 'my old friend William Gould', and his copy of the American Declaration of Independence to Henry Thomas. His obituary noted: 'He was ...deeply imbued with the conviction that he was engaged in a righteous cause ...and bound in the nature of things to result in final triumph if pressed with unflagging resolution to the goal'.[187]

---

[186] Charles Wilkins, 'Merthyr Boys who Became Notable Men: Morgan Williams', *Merthyr Express*, 3 March 1900.

[187] *ME*, 20 October 1883; Joe England, 'Morgan Williams: Merthyr's Forgotten leader', *Merthyr Historian,* 2014, pp. 137-149.

8

An Oasis of Calm

> ...a more civil, obliging, good-humoured, quick-witted, and intelligent population, is not to be found among the working-classes of Great Britain.
>
> H. A. Bruce[188]

> Every working class has a system imposed on it by the powerful, and the members of that class must make of this system what they can, for their own protection and advancement.
>
> Alan Fox[189]

As a would-be politician – within a year he had succeeded J. J. Guest as Merthyr's MP – Bruce knew how to flatter his audience but as Stipendiary Magistrate for Merthyr he was well acquainted with its violent history. His father J. B. Bruce, Merthyr's first Stipendiary, had read the Riot Act outside the Castle Inn in 1831. Criminality, argued Henry Bruce, was not inherent in Merthyr people. Three-quarters of those facing indictable offences were strangers, vagrants, and 'the lower class of Irish, who swarm in the worst parts of the town'. As to 'those very foolish and unmeaning, but savage and disgraceful

---

[188] *'Merthyr Tydfil in 1852'. A lecture delivered to the Young Men's Mutual Improvement Society* (Merthyr Tydfil, 1852).

[189] Alan Fox, 'Corporatism and Industrial Democracy', *Industrial Democracy: International Views* (SSRC Industrial Relations Research Unit, Warwick University, 1978), p. 27.

affairs, the riots in 1816 and 1831 ...which make the very name of Merthyr a sound of terror' it was 'in the highest degree improbable' that such events could be repeated because of 'the increased intelligence and improved education of the great mass of our people'.

Mid-Victorian Merthyr was very different from its fraught 1830s. The throngs passing through the market on a Saturday night – 'dressed in their Sunday clothing, clean, warm and comfortable'[190] – its flourishing friendly societies with their ressuring respectable parades, the increasing numbers experiencing the world outside Merthyr through organised trips to the 1851 Great Exhibition and excursions by train to the seaside, the national reputation of the Cyfarthfa Band, (experiencing disappointment and triumph in 1860 at the Crystal Palace), the diversity of its more than fifty chapels, seven Mormon meeting places, two Catholic churches and synagogue, its Temperance Hall opened in 1852 that held 1,200 people, the police taming of China, all were signs of a maturing society.

The days of violent protest were over; a remarkable contrast with the first third of the century. Strikes in the form of 'downers' or groups of workmen briefly staging a protest no doubt continued (strike statistics were not collected until 1888) but significant disputes were rare and none involved violence. Historians have called Merthyr Tydfil 'the undisputed capital of the disturbed districts' of south Wales that were 'in a state of constant civil unrest and violence'[191]. That was true of the 1830s but Merthyr's iron industry in the 1840s and 1850s was an oasis of industrial calm. It was in the coal valleys a few

---

[190] Ginswick, p.50.

[191] Louise Miskell, *Intelligent Town: An Urban History of Swansea, 1780-1855* (Cardiff, 2006), pp. 99-101; Ivor Wilks, *South Wales and the Rising of 1839* (1984), p. 73.

miles to the east and west that strikes predominated. During the years 1840-53 at least thirty-four strikes in South Wales involved colliers.

> On six occasions virtually every sale-coal working in Monmouthshire was stopped; in one strike both the Rhondda and Aberdare valleys were idle; at another period every collier in the Aberdare valley struck; and in 1843 the sale-coal colliers of both Monmouthshire and Glamorgan seem to have stopped work.[192]

At Aberdare in 1850 colliers struck for four months against a wage reduction and one man was killed by a bomb thrown into his bedroom after he had been warned not to blackleg. Iron-workers and colliers in Merthyr carried on working. In 1857-58 the colliers in Monmouthshire and the Aberdare and Rhondda valleys struck against a 15 per cent cut in wages, there was much bitterness before they eventually went back to work on the owners' terms. Merthyr colliers very briefly came out of work and then went back. The iron workers remained in work. George Clark at Dowlais commented upon the forbearance of his workers in times of distress, contrasting that with Aberdare where machinery had been smashed.[193]

Apart from the few days of the 1842 strike, part of the Chartist rolling strike, and the few days in December 1857, there are only two other reported strikes in Merthyr in the 1840s and 1850s and in neither was there any violence. In 1844 colliers at Penydarren and Dowlais briefly struck for a wage increase. At Dowlais in 1853 a significant six-week strike, occurring a year after Sir John's death, arose partly from Lady

---

[192] E. W. Evans, *The Miners of South Wales* (Cardiff, 1961), p. 63 and Appendix 1.

[193] *Merthyr Telegraph*, 5 December 1857.

Charlotte's inexperience and her desire to demonstrate that she was now in charge, and partly the vacillations of the other Merthyr ironmasters.[194] In 1847 there were strikes in Monmouthshire works, mainly at Ebbw Vale and Nantyglo, arising from wage cuts and high food costs. The Merthyr ironmasters agreed to co-operate with the Monmouthshire masters and not to employ any strikers. Dowlais supplied two of the companies affected with iron.[195] But there was no industrial action at Dowlais or Merthyr.

The transformation from insurgency in 1831 to the 'temperate reformism of the 1860s', although not unique in the middle decades of the nineteenth century, was 'singularly sharp' in Merthyr.[196] What had happened? The rejection of the third Chartist petition in April 1848 was followed nationally by a time of lowered tensions, growing prosperity and calm at home and abroad. Yet the more historians examine this mid-Victorian 'equipoise' the more it is clear that there are considerable local variations.[197] The repeal of the Corn Laws, the improving economy, the conservative behaviour of skilled workers – the 'labour aristocrats' – the paternalism of large employers have all been suggested as reasons. In Merthyr Tydfil the change in working-class behaviour came well before 1848. It came in 1839.

---

[194] Elizabeth Havill, 'The Respectful Strike', *Morgannwg* Vol. 24 (1980); Edgar Jones, *A History of GKN*, Vol. 1, pp.276-280; Guest and John, pp. 177-185.

[195] Elsas, pp. 44-46; Daunton, *WHR* Vol. 6, No. 1 (June 1972), pp. 636-40.

[196] Chris Evans, *The Labyrinth*, p. 3.

[197] Neville Kirk, *The Growth of Working Class Reformism* (1985) chapter 4 provides an introduction to the debates.

What happened in 1839?

Where on that wet November night when Chartists from the valleys marched on Newport were the workmen of Merthyr Tydfil, a town with a reputation for violence and the largest number of Chartists in Wales? Some marched, but they were relatively few. Was the decision to avoid armed conflict influenced by the memory of the dead and wounded lying in the gutters of Merthyr eight years earlier? It is hard to believe that such a traumatic event — not just the massacre, for such it was, but the totality of that experience with its violence and courage, fear and intimidation, ferocious arguments and inevitable surrender – did not leave deep scars in the minds of all caught up in it. The men of Monmouthshire had been told the soldiers would lay down their arms when attacked.[198] The men of Merthyr knew differently.

The victory of the masters in 1831 and the subsequent supressing of trade unions in 1831 and 1834 meant that the masters had weathered the storm and the political context had changed severely. State power stood firmly behind the masters not simply through the law and the courts but with an enhanced resident police force and troops in barracks at Dowlais. The magistrates had a tighter grip on law and order, unlike 1831 when a turning point in its breakdown came when three thousand stormed the Bush inn and released two prisoners with impunity.

The leaders of 1831 had disappeared. Those involved in assault and redistributing goods – Lewis Lewis, David Hughes, Thomas Vaughan, David Thomas and John Phelps – had all been transported. Richard Lewis (Dic Penderyn) had been hanged. But where were those who had drilled the rioters in army fashion, and who had led the attacks on soldiery coming from Brecon and

---

[198] David Jones, *The Last Rising*, pp. 94-5.

Swansea? We know that in the aftermath of the insurrection there was an exodus from the town amounting to thousands. Among them surely were those who feared arrest or at the very least victimisation.[199] This reality cast its shadow over Chartism in Merthyr. It is startling in the light of events elsewhere that no Merthyr Chartist appears to have been transported, and apparently only two, the Dowlais men at Newport, tried.

The balance of political power was not the only change. The Merthyr economy had changed too. Compared with 1831 employment in 1839 was booming and wages, instead of being cut, were at an all-time high. Debt was neither as widespread nor as desperately pressing. The Court of Requests no longer existed. There were no truck shops in Merthyr. Cyfarthfa and Plymouth had never had them, and those at Dowlais and Penydarren had been closed down. The contrast with social conditions in the sale-coal villages of eastern Monmouthshire is illuminating. The wages of iron workers in 1839 were significantly higher and more secure than sale-coal colliers who were often laid off or put on short time due to seasonal fluctuations in the demand for coal, or adverse weather affecting the availability of ships. The national earnings of heads of households in mining fell from £66 in 1831-5 to £42.73 in 1836-40 and Monmouthshire would hardly have escaped this trend. This was particularly so as the population of the sale-coal area at the centre of the 1839 March more than doubled.[200] In Merthyr well over a third of those employed in the ironworks were regarded as 'skilled'

[199] Williams, *The Merthyr Rising*, p. 64, n.5. So many Irish left, the town was without a Catholic priest for three years. Paul O'Leary, *Immigration and Integration: The Irish in Wales 1798-1922* (Cardiff, 2000), p.57.

[200] See John Elliott, *The Industrial Development of the Ebbw Valleys 1780-1914* (Cardiff, 2004), pp.179-80.

men with relatively high wages, and in employment. In Monmouthshire company shops with their high prices and system of 'long pay' were promoted by the independent coal-owners. Families in the coal villages were in constant debt and food prices were 10 to 15 per cent dearer than in Merthyr,

The hated workhouses appeared in the 1830s at Abergavenny, Newport, Pontypool and Tredegar whereas Merthyr's did not open until 1853. In Merthyr a population approaching 34,000 was setting down roots, its size creating a need for shops, pubs, preachers, teachers, doctors, lawyers; a small but influential middle class had developed, the ironmasters and their agents were familiar presences. In the Monmouthshire northern valleys the coal-owners were largely absent from the isolated villages, and company shops prevented the growth of a shopocracy. It was out of that distressed, debt-ridden and vulnerable society – 'the Black Domain' – that the "Scotch Cattle" emerged, basically a pre-industrial mode of enforcing justice and solidarity that under the local conditions resorted to violence. It was rare for them to appear in Merthyr, although in 1834 they issued threats against the employment of Irish at Hirwaun and Dowlais.[201]

A Town of Opportunity

It is significant that Chartism developed and flourished in Merthyr during the prosperous 'railway boom' phase. As early as 1829 Penydarren received the contract for rails on the Liverpool and Manchester Railway. In 1836 Dowlais produced 20,000 tons of rails.[202] Thereafter the Merthyr works concentrated on producing rails and iron furniture for railway companies at home

[201] Ursula Masson, p. 81.

[202] John A. Owen, *The History of the Dowlais Iron Works 1759-1970* (Risca, 1977), p. 156.

and abroad. At Cyfarthfa in 1837 there were seven furnaces in blast and the furnaces at Ynysfach had been doubled from two to four. At Dowlais in 1839 there were fourteen furnaces in blast and a further four under construction. It was in 1839 that the Ivor Works was built to cope with expanding production. From 1834 up to 1848 almost every year at Dowlais was highly profitable. The other works shared in this expansion of investment, output and employment.[203] The following table shows the tons of iron produced at the four great works. The first four columns show the quantities actually sent to Cardiff for export. The column for 1846 contains the entire produce of each works, of which 184,608 tons were sent to Cardiff, the remainder being consumed locally. Between 1830 and 1846 the production of iron in Merthyr grew by almost 300 per cent.

Table 8.1

	1796	**1820**	**1830**	**1840**	**1846**
Dowlais	2,800	11,115	27,647	45,218	87,251
Cyfarthfa	7,204	19,010	19,892	35,507	56,278
Plymouth	2,200	7,941	12,177	12,922	35,198
Penydarren	4,100	8,690	11,744	16,130	25,612
Total	16,304	46,756	71,460	109,777	204,339

Source: H. A. Bruce, 'Merthyr in 1852'.

Just as significant as the thousands of jobs is the fact that they

[203] J. H. Clapham, *An Economic History of Modern Britain: The Early Railway Age 1820-1850* (Cambridge, 1950), pp. 382-3, 429; Edgar Jones, *A History of GKN: Innovation and Enterprise 1759-1918* (London, 1987), pp. 62-66, 103-05; Atkinson and Baber, *The Growth and Decline of the South Wales Iron Industry 1760-1880* (Cardiff, 1987), pp. 10-11.

had been created on upland sites *without destroying pre-existing skills or crafts*. Nor was there in those rural hills a pre-existing tradition of strong trade unionism as practised in eighteenth century urban centres by carpenters, printers, tailors, hatters, tailors, wool-combers and weavers.[204] A telling illustration is the contrast between Merthyr, the fastest growing town in Wales, and the fastest growing town in England in the 1830s and 1840s, Bradford. The expansion of Bradford as the centre of worsted manufacture *did* come at the expense of pre-existing crafts. Handloom weavers and wool-combers accustomed to setting their own rhythm of work and who enjoyed the status that came with independence, lost through mechanisation both their independence and a cherished superior status. They rapidly descended into abject poverty. The resultant festering bitterness had a major impact upon social relations in the north of England. Bradford was a centre of physical force Chartism, with the dispossessed prominent in its leadership. When an armed rising was aborted there in January 1840 seven out of the ten men jailed were wool-combers. The technologically obsolete hand-loom weavers of Yorkshire and Lancashire were prominent advocates of physical force.[205]

The rhetoric in The Three Horse Shoes in 1842-43 underlines this aspect of Merthyr Chartism. In the midst of a slump that had brought severe poverty, and when many had been victimised for their Chartist beliefs, there was no actual or even

---

[204] John Rule, *The Experience of Labour in Eighteenth Century Industry* (1981), pp. 147-171.

[205] Dorothy Thompson, *The Chartists: Popular Politics in the Industrial Revolution* (1984), pp. 209-233. The plight of the wool-combers is dealt with by the Bradford Wool-combers Report of 1845 reprinted, with a valuable introduction by J. A. Jowitt, in *Mechanization and Misery*, (Bradford, 1991). See also, D. G. Wright, *The Chartist Risings in Bradford,* (Bradford, 1987).

rhetorical attack upon the ironmasters or against capitalist exploitation. The targets were the monarchy and the aristocracy; there was much mention of 'tyranny' and 'rich idlers'. Charlotte Guest in 1840 had confided to her diary that at a meeting held in Merthyr to petition the Government to release Frost, 'the speeches were entirely political (of the usual tenor) without any local or personal allusions'.[206] Morgan Williams, who saw labour as the source of all wealth, seems never to have attacked the capitalist system. On the contrary his close ally David John (jr.) recognised Merthyr's economic advantage when he told the delegate meeting in Manchester in 1840: 'We are not so poor in Merthyr Tydfil as you are in many parts of England, but that is no reason why we should not have our rights'.[207] It was the growth of the local economy, the expansion of employment, the significant increase in skilled workers and in earnings after 1834 which helped to reconcile workers to the new capitalist order. When in full employment workers in Merthyr could earn three to six times the wages of labourers in west Wales.[208] These political and economic aspects go far to explain the political temper of Merthyr's workmen after 1834. They provide the context for peaceful acceptance of the nascent sliding-scale which tied earnings to the price of iron. Nothing better illustrates the change in temper than the contrast between the insult flung at the Crawshay family in 1831: 'There go the devils'; and the 1844 workers' testimonial to William Crawshay II that begins: 'Most Worthy and Respected Master.'

---

[206] Lady Charlotte Guest, *Journal*, 27 August 1840.

[207] David Jones, 'Chartism in Welsh communities', p. 250. *Northern* Star, 14 March 1840.The quotation has been turned into direct speech.

[208] Williams, *The Rising*, p. 48.

Hoping for Better Times

Within that context changes in the price of bar iron between the peaks and troughs of the trade cycle caused severe wage fluctuations.

Fluctuations in Wages

Date	Miners	Colliers	Puddlers
1837	19s.7d [95.58p]	22s.6d [110.25p]	30s.0d [150p]
1839	21s.3d [105.25p]	27s.0d [135p]	35s.0d [175p]
1844	10s.6d [50.25p]	13s.0d [65p]	23s.7d [115.58p]

Source: A. H. John, *The Industrial Development of South Wales*, p. 84.

In this table earnings in 1837 reflect the gradual recovery from the low level of the early 1830s, a recovery that continued into 1839 before the severe depression of 1842-3 produced the earnings seen in 1844, although by then the economy was beginning to recover and 1846-47 were good years. Then in 1848 came another downturn so that by 1849-50 earnings were reported to be as much as 40 per cent lower than two or three years earlier. A Penydarren roller told the *Morning Chronicle* correspondent:

> In the good times I earned sometimes as much as £3 15s [£3.75p] a week. That was in 1846, working rails. I now earn from 25s [125p] to 30s [150p] a week; never more because we have no rail-work, only merchants' bars. Since then there have been three reductions in wages. The first was a fall of 4s [20p] – the second 2s 6d [10.5p] – and the third 2s [10p] in the pound.

These substantial cuts in skilled men's earnings caused the *Chronicle* correspondent to comment that the men's understanding of the reasons for the cuts – a commercial depression, the ending of the domestic railway boom and the check to exports caused by revolutions in Europe – had made them 'patient under the reverse, still hoping for better times'.[209]

Hope was based on experience. For the past fifty years bad times had been followed by good. In May 1844 crowds of cheering workmen greeted the announcement that there was to be an 'advance' at Dowlais. Two meetings were held shortly afterwards by Cyfarthfa workmen in praise of William Crawshay II. An address to him, unanimously agreed, began 'Most Worthy and Respected Master' and went on to refer to

> the magnanimity which you have evinced by standing forward as the chief mover in the present advancement in the scales of wages ...we feel satisfactorily assured, that to you, and you alone, belongs the principal merit on the occasion – therefore, the laurels of liberality which have always so deservedly adorned your brow shall never willingly be planted by us upon any other.[210]

Within a week, when it was learned that Sir John had arrived in Dowlais, a crowd of 2,000 gathered. The chairman, a miner named William Evans, spoke of the price of labour being 'dependent on causes which are perfectly out of the control of both master and workmen' and praised Sir John for his personal 'bounty' in relieving during the winter of 1841 'the sufferings of the poor of Dowlais, who, I trust, will never forget their

[209] Ginswick, pp. 45-6.

[210] *MG* 1, 15, 22, 29 June 1844.

benefactor. (Loud cheering.) '. A collier, Watkin Williams, in a revealing speech said:

> There was time when, if a reduction in wages took place we (the workmen) always laid the blame upon our employers, and attributed the fall in prices to their desire to oppress their workmen and enrich themselves. Recent events have brought conviction to every reflective mind, that our employers are not only subject to the same depressing influences as ourselves, but they have done more; they have taught us that there is a point beyond which reductions cannot go; and we have seen our employers, rather than attempt such reduction, sacrificing a portion of their capital in paying more for a ton of iron than it could be sold for in the market.

He also mentioned 'contention' regarding 'who first made known the advance of wages in South Wales. All I wish to say on the subject is that the workmen of Dowlais can congratulate themselves upon being the *first* in South Wales to enjoy the *fruits* of that advance.'

He was followed by John Thomas, a master puddler, who spoke of the 'excellent feelings' in Dowlais between the employer and those employed. In this, Dowlais was an example to the surrounding ironworks for when Chartism was 'deluding the working men ...the men of Dowlais stood firm and uncompromising to their duties, and to their own and their employers' interest.'

> What is it that has caused the existence of an armed force among us? Why is it that soldiers and policemen walk our streets? Because of our own errors, our own imprudence, our own turbulence. Let us then strive to retrace our steps, to reform our habits and labour, to intention excellence by the

> cultivation of our moral and intellectual faculties. Let every man faithfully serve and promote the interest of his employer, and endeavour to make that interest his own; for any injury done to the one will ultimately and surely recoil upon the other.[211]

Eleven years later in 1855, 600 workmen at the Plymouth works fired cannons, displayed flags, and presented an address to Anthony Hill praising him for increasing wages weeks before the other works and expressing their 'warm and fervent attachment to you as our Employer, and to tender our grateful acknowledgements for the humanity and unvarying kindness which has ever distinguished you…'.[212]

Labour Aristocrats

What does this behaviour mean? First, it signals relief. Although generations of workers had been through the same learning process – that wage cuts during recessions would be followed by an increase in better times – they did not know *when* that would happen. The rudimentary sliding-scale that tied wages to the price of iron was neither formal nor automatic. The decision *when* to grant an increase lay firmly in the masters' hands and objections to that power had been surrendered. The puddlers were no longer the militants of the past but willing collaborators. Percentage wage reductions had the advantage for the puddlers and other skilled process workers of maintaining existing pay differentials and thereby their status above other workers. It also left untouched their property rights in the job and their control over the labour process. Like the Mid-Victorian craft unions, they were content to collaborate

---

[211] *MG* 1, 15, 22, 29 June 1844.

[212] *MG*, 6 October 1855.

provided the employers did not attack this control.[213] It was an attitude that could only be maintained as long as technological change did not take their control away. Change was on the way but not in the 1840s.

Historians have debated at length whether skilled workers contributed to the mid-century harmony between employers and workers and the apparent coming to terms with capitalist industrialisation. Hobsbawm's seminal article on the 'labour aristocracy' stimulated a range of studies and from these it is clear that the technology of different industries in varying local societies produced different economic and political outcomes, both in the timing of the accommodation to capitalism and in the reasons for it. [214] The general consensus is that the labour aristocracy was not a significant factor.

But in the iron industry the technical processes of iron-making gave the master workman an authority acknowledged by both men and masters. This status had been strengthened

---

[213] Richard Price, *Labour in British Society* (1986), chapter 4.

[214] E. J. Hobsbawm, 'The Labour Aristocracy in Nineteenth-century Britain' in J. Saville (ed.); *Democracy and the Labour Movement* (1954) and reprinted in E. J. Hobsbawm; *Labouring Men: Studies in the History of Labour* (1964); J. Foster, *Class Struggle and the Industrial Revolution: Early Industrial Capitalism in Three English Towns* (1974); P. Joyce, *Work, Society and Politics: The Culture of the Factory in Later Victorian England* (Brighton, 1980); Neville Kirk, *The Growth of Working Class Reformism in Mid-Victorian England* (1985); R. Q. Gray, *The Labour Aristocracy in Victorian Edinburgh* (Oxford, 1976); G. Crossick, *An Artisan Elite in Victorian Society* (1978); Henry Pelling, *Popular Politics and Society in Late Victorian Britain* (London, 1968); pp. 272-315. The most approachable reviews of the debate are Robert Gray, *The Aristocracy of Labour in Nineteenth-century Britain c. 1850-1914* (1981), and Joan Allen, Alan Campbell, John McIlroy (eds.), *Histories of Labour: National and International Perspectives* (Pontypool, 2010), pp. 75-79.

by the dramatic technological and market changes after 1790 that propelled the industry to new significance in the national economy. Richard Crawshay hoped by introducing Cort's process in the 1790s to make a complete break with the existing power of forgemen which ironmasters found so disturbing to their own authority.[215] Instead, the new technology gave birth to puddlers, rollers and other skilled process workers who enjoyed high earnings while continuing to control the way work was done. The master workman in the iron industry differed therefore in significant ways from other examples of labour aristocrats. Puddlers and rollermen were not a 'new upper stratum' of the labour force that appeared in the 1840s, as Foster has argued was the case for piecemasters in engineering, spinners in cotton and checkweighmen in mining. Nor was this 'upper stratum' called into being by the employers as a deliberate tactic to divide the working class.[216] On the contrary they were a product of the technology and for a generation puddlers had been a thorn in the flesh of the masters. But by the 1840s the puddlers no longer disputed that earnings would be determined by the price of iron. They were important to this evolutionary acceptance of the employer's authority both because they had been the militants and because rates for puddlers were, by virtue of their skills and physical endurance, a guide for earnings throughout the works.[217]

Was their behaviour *the* determining factor in the general acceptance? Probably not: workers beyond the influence of puddlers, such as miners and colliers employed by the ironworks also accepted this form of wage determination. The resolution of power relations post-1834, the effect of the

[215] Chris Evans, *The Labyrinth*, pp. 96-100.

[216] Foster, p. 227.

[217] Alan Birch, *The Economic History of the British Iron and Steel Industry* (Manchester, 1967), p. 263.

railway boom upon the local economy, and the insecurities of the iron trade provided the context within which the rise and fall of earnings could be accepted, if workers' experience showed it was a system that 'worked' and they could see no alternative.

The advantages to the masters of a selling-price sliding scale are clear. It brought industrial peace by taking argument out of pay determination and avoided the danger of set-piece confrontations. Best of all, profit margins were largely protected. Labour costs, affected by the numbers employed, and workers' earnings, went down as the selling price of iron fell. Intellectual respectability was added by the prevailing wage fund doctrine that attempts by workers to increase wages were futile as the fund available for wages at any one time was fixed in size. Wage increases that threatened profits and capital accumulation could only have the effect of reducing the amount available for distribution in wages and so were counterproductive.

The dominance of the ironmasters was such that in 1863 William Crawshay II gave a reason for delaying an increase even though trade had picked up. He argued that workers

> have not any justifiable expectation for any advance of wages until their masters *have* enjoyed the benefit of an advance in the price of the production of their labour ...in common justice they ought to allow 2 or 3 months for the working off of orders taken for the purpose of affording them work and wages.[218]

There was even an occasion in 1850 when wage cuts were made as trade improved. Asked about this Anthony Hill told the *Morning Chronicle* correspondent:

---

[218] Addis, p. 119.

> What are the masters to do? They are as considerate as they can be. But for the past year, the trade has been carried on actually at a loss; this must be recovered, and the present seems the best time for the purpose. As the trade improves the men will know from former experience we shall not be backward in giving them their share of the benefit.[219]

Hill's explanation puts a cultural gloss on the market realities. If workers – skilled workers – stayed with employers through the bad times the masters would look after them in the good times. The relationship suggested is not only one between wage awards and the state of trade (including an appreciation by workmen of the financial costs to the employer) but one of dependent workers and benevolent patriarchal employers. The proper response of workers to the generosity of a benevolent employer in this relationship should be one of gratitude.

The workers' comments also contain strong assertions about which employer was first to increase wages. This is works chauvinism heightened by a competitive spirit. In modern sporting parlance: Who had the bragging rights? Despite the fact that workers moved between works, pride in and attachment to their place of work was strong in substantial elements of the Merthyr workforce. It is a reminder that still in mid-nineteenth century the evolving town of 'Merthyr Tydfil' was composed of immigrants drawn from many different sources. Geographically it was a collection of separate communities clustered around four major places of employment. Pride in work and in the place of work helped to bind together people from different places of origin. And the works were themselves large communities with cultures of their own. In 1847 the four large ironworks at Merthyr and

[219] Ginswick, p. 46.

Dowlais were compared to religious parishes or medieval manors because

> just as when parishes were first instituted, it was every man's interest to think what parish he belonged to, because his rights of relief, employment, and redress were all parochial or manorial, so now does the same interest make him think of these or those works, and not at all, or very remotely of the parish. In the works is his sick fund, sometimes his benefit society; in the works is his hope of employment; in the works (by a tolerated system of fining), is his ordinary court of justice'.[220]

The Merthyr works indeed had features reminiscent of medieval estates. They were family owned, had a dominant master in a large house, ownership passed from one family generation to the next. Each of the four works had been built on a green-field site and the sole reason for the communities clustered around them was their dependence upon the work that the ironworks provided. The works, in varying degrees, provided schools, housing, medical services and places of worship. What was the reality of this apparent paternalism?

---

[220] R. W. Lingen, *Inquiry into the State of Education in the Counties of Carmarthen, Glamorgan and Pembroke*, (1847), p. 20.

9

The New Paternalism

> I assert, deliberately and advisedly, that, in my opinion the workmen of Merthyr would have amply repaid more care and consideration, and a more liberal treatment than they have experienced.
>
> **H.A. Bruce**[221]

> Paternalism was not only a role for authority but its justification.
>
> **A.P. Thornton**[222]

The Crawshays were known as 'Iron Kings' with good reason. For three generations they were outstanding in their chosen trade and from their castle they surveyed their 'kingdom' spread over the urban villages of Georgetown, Penyrheolgerrig, Cefn Coed, Brecon Road and Caepantywyll. The Hill family was supreme at Abercanaid and Pentrebach, the Homfrays, Thompsons and Formans at Penydarren. It was these settlements, huddled near the ironworks along the banks of the Taff and on the hillsides that, with the old village clustered around St. Tydfil's church, constituted Merthyr Tydfil. Josiah John Guest, the greatest ironmaster in the world in the 1840s presided over Dowlais, a town apart. When in 1801 industrial Merthyr Tydfil was

---

[221] H.A. Bruce, *Merthyr Tydfil in 1852* (Merthyr Tydfil, 1852), p. 16.

[222] A.P. Thornton, *The Habit of Authority: Paternalism in British History* (1966), pp. 172-3.

revealed as the largest town in Wales it was neither a planned company town like New Lanark, Saltaire or Bourneville, nor even a town. The traveller from Cardiff was told that after passing the Plymouth ironworks 'you appear to be entering upon an extended suburb of a large town; but the town itself is nowhere visible; it is without form or order...'[223] The ruthless tipping of cinders and slag over farms, houses and fields was not the laying out of a town, but the desecration of a landscape.

It was done in the service of making iron, and the Iron Kings had the life-giving power of providing work. The families in these settlements experienced each day that power and its accompaniments: the conditions and terms of employment, landlordism, the level of rents, the lack of clean water, the rise and fall of employment and earnings. The masters assumed and exercised these powers in the late eighteenth and early nineteenth centuries when the state was dismantling the centuries-old paternal protections of workers' living standards. Trade unions were banned by the Combination Acts of 1799-1800. The clauses of the Elizabethan Statute of Artificers (1563), which enforced apprenticeship in many trades and provided for the settlement of wages by justices of the peace, were repealed in 1813-14; the arrangements for relief of poverty, dating from Elizabethan times, were under an attack that culminated in the 1834 Poor Law Amendment Act. The less government the better was the doctrine of the day; legislative protection of industries or of individuals was unnecessary. The pursuit of self interest, *laissez-faire*, would result in the common good.

It was a doctrine the ironmasters were happy to accept. Self-interest required that skilled men, without whom iron could not

---

[223] *The Cambrian Tourist or Post Chaise Companion through Wales* (6th edition, 1828) quoted by Neil Evans in Trevor Herbert and G.E. Jones (eds.), *People and Protest Wales, 1815-1880* (Cardiff, 1988).

be made, should be looked after. They were comparatively well-paid, were found houses, received medical care, and their sons employed. At Pentrebach, Williamstown and Georgetown, in Penydarren and in Dowlais houses were built and rented to skilled workers. As production accelerated in the early 1800s the need for accommodation for skilled men and their families grew. By 1813 there was terraced housing in Pentrebach. The early houses had two, sometimes three rooms. This was not paternalism. It made hard business sense, as did holding on to these workers in depressions. Richard Crawshay in the aftermath of the 1816 riots commanded 'Do not even hold out reduction of the men, employ them if they behave quietly...Bad and ruinous as the trade now is, we must lose rather than starve the labourer'.[224] On at least one occasion Crawshay employed men on half-pay 'when his works was on a stand' to clear the ground of stones.[225]

The great expansion of iron production between 1830 and 1840 brought increased house building. William Crawshay II began the two-up two-down terraced cottages known as Williamstown within the environs of the Cyfarthfa Works in 1836 and from 1840, the year after the Chartist march on Newport, he built the fifty four room double-fronted houses known as Cyfarthfa Row in Georgetown.[226] The description given by the *Morning Chronicle* of the interior furnishing of some of these houses with their mahogany chests of drawers, eight-day clocks, portraits and books, confirms that they were occupied by the better-paid workmen.[227] The houses later

---

[224] Pollard, p. 206.

[225] Evans, *The Labyrinth*, p.83.

[226] J.B. Lowe, *Welsh Industrial Workers' Housing 1775-1875* (Cardiff, 1977), p.36.

[227] Ginswick, pp. 51-54. For confirmation of the quality of housing provided for skilled workers by Crawshay see the letter signed by William Gould and three others in *ME* 14 November 1874.

known as The Triangle at Pentrebach were built by Anthony Hill between 1840 and 1852.[228]

Crawshay introduced medical care and employed a doctor, the men contributing to the cost, a provision soon followed by the other works. Houses and medical care were part of an employment relationship where the skilled worker accepted discipline and achieved the necessary work performance. The unskilled labourers, arriving daily in their hundreds, whether employed by contractors or by the works received nothing beyond a subsistence daily wage. Accommodation they found for themselves in shanties, lodging houses, and jerry-built terraces put up by speculators. On 2 August 1845 the *Merthyr Guardian* baldly stated 'The Hamlet of Garth,' [to the north-east of Merthyr town and mainly inhabited by Dowlais workers] '...contains upwards of 1500 houses, but a great many of them – probably one-fifth – are merely huts and quite unfit for the residence of human beings.'

In 1834 a discussion between Merthyr's great and good about how to improve civic amenities had resulted in no more than a market house in private ownership so that

> A very handsome yearly income, which might have been appropriated to the draining, cleansing, and lighting of this dark, unsewered and filthy town, have been for ever alienated, or are only redeemable at a cost which would not make them worth the purchasing.[229]

[228] J.B. Lowe, p. 51.

[229] Ginswick, p. 49; *MG* 3 Feb 1844.

Towards a New Moral Order

The general harshness of the regime shocked those sent to investigate. In the wake of the 1839 attack on Newport the government inspector Seymour Tremenheere, noted, 'The whole district and population partake of the iron character of its produce; everything centres in and ministers to the idolatry of profit...' and in his memoirs recorded, 'Nearly the whole body of employers acted on Bentham's theory that the masters had no responsibility beyond paying the men their wages; everything else that they wanted the men had to do for themselves'.[230] Seven years later R.W. Lingen, a Fellow of Balliol sent to enquire into the state of education in South Wales and confronted by a society he struggled to understand, compared the great Merthyr ironworks to medieval parishes yet also commented on the linguistic divide between the Welsh-speaking workers and their masters:

> His superiors are content, for the most part, simply to ignore his existence in all its moral relations. He is left to live in an underworld of his own, and the march of society goes so completely over his head, that he is never heard of, excepting when the strange and abnormal features of a Revival, or a Rebecca or Chartist outbreak, call attention to a phase of society which could produce anything so contrary to all that we elsewhere experience.[231]

Lingen's comments were part of the report on the state of education in Wales that outraged Welsh opinion in 1847

[230] E.L. and O.P. Edmonds (eds.), *I was there: the Memoirs of H.S. Tremenheere* (Eton, 1965), p. 24. Quoted in Jones, *The Last Rising*, p. 24.

[231] *Inquiry into the State of Education*, p. 4.

because of its attacks on the alleged inadequacies of the Welsh language and uncritical reporting of comments on the morality of Welsh women and men. Most of the report about the state of education was factual and informative but the less than ten pages devoted to moral issues caused it to be known as *Brad y Llyfrau Gleision* (The Treachery of the Blue Books).[232]

Lingen wrote in an intellectual climate reacting to the attack on Newport, the rolling strikes of 1842, and the sustained Chartist arguments for equality and democracy. In his *Chartism*, published in 1840, Carlyle had condemned *laissez-faire* as an abandonment of leadership, responsibility and ruling class guidance. In 1845 J. S. Mill had discerned, but condemned as outdated, a move towards 'a new moral order, or an old order revived, in which possesors of property are to resume their place as the paternal guardians of those less fortunate'.[233] Apprehension about Chartist activities combined with the profits produced by the railroad boom of the 1840s stimulated a willingness to incur extra expenses to gain workers' loyalty.

In Merthyr this current of opinion was belatedly echoed by two of its leading citizens. On 12 December 1849 the Rector of Merthyr Tydfil, J.C. Campbell, spoke to the members of the Merthyr Library on 'The Social State of the Mineral Districts'. Avoiding direct description of the situation in Merthyr, Campbell spoke admiringly of the way in which the Consett Ironworks had provided rent-free houses to 'colliers, miners, puddlers, and iron workers' with a garden of a quarter of an acre, established eight day schools in six different buildings, a library and reading room, and treated the workmen with 'that kindness and openness which is due from man to man'. Campbell's description was a direct quote from the evidence

[232] John Davies, *A History of Wales*, pp. 390-392.

[233] John Stuart Mill, 'Claims of Labour', in G.L. Williams (ed.), *John Stuart Mill on Politics and Society* (1976).

provided to the Home Office by Seymour Tremenhere who had in 1840 made scathing remarks upon the situation in the South Wales iron district. Campbell invited his audience to 'apply my general observations, as far as they are applicable, to our own position'. The next day Campbell's brother-in-law Henry Bruce, delivering judgement as stipendiary magistrate in Aberdare on a case concerning labour contracts, made a point of asserting that the cause of strikes was 'the ignorance of the men' and that strikes would not occur if men were properly educated 'and the means of education are in the masters' hands – if sober and temperate habits of thought were cultivated, these strikes would not occur as they do now'. He went on to argue that:

> If masters would show their men that they were anxious to treat them with strict fairness, would sympathise with them and interest themselves in their welfare in every sort of way, the men would be far less likely to engage in any objectionable courses.[234]

He too referred to employer paternalism in the north of England. Bruce, who would shortly become a trustee of the Dowlais works, was well aware that the situation at Dowlais was substantially different from that in Aberdare or Merthyr.

Schools and Churches

At the beginning of the century the view had been that education for working people was both unnecessary and dangerous, making them discontented with their lot. By the 1840s Campbell and Bruce were expressing an opinion about education that had become common: ignorance amongst the 'lower orders' was deemed to be a cause of strikes and rioting.

[234] *MG*, 15, 22 December 1849.

A view had developed that the better people were educated the better citizens they would become. There was of course, no national system of education. Schools were private enterprises charging fees to those who could afford them, a mixture of 'dame schools', sometimes held in the kitchen of a private house, and larger more reputable ones like Taliesin Williams' or the Tydfil School established at Courtland Terrace in 1859. Teaching, occasionally bilingual, was usually through the medium of English. The most important source of education for Welsh children and adults was their Welsh-medium Sunday schools. In 1843 the National Society for Promoting the Education of the Poor, an Anglican charity, opened a school in Georgetown and another in Merthyr high street in 1845. They were not favoured by Nonconformists.

The provision of education by ironworks was not an idea new to South Wales. The Blaenavon and Neath Abbey works had each set up schools in 1816. Francis Crawshay had established one at Hirwaun in 1820 and J.J. Guest had opened schools in Dowlais in 1828. By 1840 there were eleven such schools in South Wales and a further fifteen were established between 1840 and 1852 following Tremenheere's report.[235] The Merthyr ironmasters were late in the day with their schools. Robert Crawshay started a school on the Brecon Road in 1848 and schools for boys and girls at Cefn in 1861. They were financed, as was customary, by compulsory stoppages from the men's wages and by a fee of a penny a week per child. Very little is known about the attitude of the owners of the Penydarren works but, doubtless influenced by the example set by Dowlais and Cyfarthfa, the Penydarren works school was opened in 1852 with departments for boys and girls and an average attendance of 200.

---

[235] Leslie Wynne Evans, *Education in Industrial Wales 1700-1900* (Cardiff, 1971), pp. 30-32.

Anthony Hill was the slowest to take action. Respected as a Tory gentleman, the pensions he paid to elderly and disabled workmen and to the widows of workmen were acts of personal charity not part of a paternalism that sought to intervene in the lives of workers outside the workplace. For most of his life he made no attempt to do so and only toward the end built a church and schools. It was not until 1855 when he was seventy-one that the Plymouth Works schools finally opened. In his will, however, Hill made provision for the fabric and maintenance of the schools, for the salaries of the headteachers (Boys, Girls, Infants), and for the continuance of education for his workers and their children if 'the existing school should for any reason cease'.[236] If a desire to break down the perceived ignorance of the working classes was a motive in setting up works schools there was also the need as the works expanded for clerks and office workers, people competent in the 3Rs. The schools became a production line for these future employees, teaching them discipline, respect for authority and the rewards that came from hard work.

Religion could play a similar role. Major employers in the English cotton towns considered the building of churches as part of their duty to their town 'and its operative population'[237] In Wales, however, most workers who did attend religious sevices were Nonconformist, not Anglican. Until 1847 there were only two churches in the whole of the Merthyr parish, St. Tydfil's the parish church and St. John's in Dowlais, built by J.J. Guest in 1827. In 1847 St. David's church in Merthyr high street largely became a church for the English-speaking middle class. Both Hill and Guest hesitated

[236] Len Deas, 'Anthony Hill and the School within his Works', in Huw Williams (ed.), *Merthyr Tydfil: Drawn from Life* (Merthyr Tydfil, 1981); Anthony Hill obituary, *Merthyr Telegraph*, 9 August 1862.
[237] Patrick Joyce, *Work, Society, Politics*, p. 174.

over contributing towards the building of St. David's on the grounds that they could not appoint the architect. Eventually Hill contributed £200.[238]

Hill and Robert Crawshay both built churches in the 1850s. Hill paid for the Church of St. John at Pontyrhun, consecrated in January 1853, and Robert Crawshay gave land for Christ Church, Georgetown, completed in 1857. In addition he rebuilt the dilapidated church of St. Gwynno at Vaynor at a cost of £1,368 in 1870 and ensured that the £700 already collected toward its cost went towards building a new church at Cefn Coed, St. John's (1874). All three ironmasters chose to be buried at local churches they had built: Guest inside St. John's at Dowlais, and Hill inside St. John's at Pontyrhun. Robert Crawshay, however, chose not to be buried at Georgetown but in the churchyard of St. Gwynno under a five ton block of granite bearing the famous epitaph.

Robert Crawshay

Robert Crawshay, appointed manager at Cyfarthfa in 1839, was much more personally involved with his workmen than Anthony Hill at Pentrebach and if, by comparison with some other employers his paternalism was limited, his influence was felt everywhere. The twenty-two-year-old was high-spirited and attractive, he had grown up around the Works and was on first-name terms with many of the workmen. Accounts of him trying his hand at various tasks in the works are persistent enough to suggest that he probably knew more about the practical details of iron-making than any Crawshay since his great-grandfather Richard.[239]

He knew the skilled men would repay fostering. Each year he

238 E.T. Davies, *Religion*, p. 29.

239 *Journal of Iron and Steel*, 1879, pp. 328-9.

paid for, and joined in excursions by the Cyfarthfa Fireman's Club, probably the successor of the Cyfarthfa Friendly Society registered in 1796. Sometimes they went to beauty spots in Breconshire, sometimes by train to Cardiff or Swansea. A typical day out, described in 1851, involved assembling at the Lamb and Flag on Brecon Road at 6.30 on Saturday morning, then, preceded by the Cyfarthfa Band, they marched to the railway station where a special train was waiting to take them to Cardiff. On arrival they marched through the Cardiff streets 'headed as before by the brass band' and arrived at the station of the South Wales Railway where another train took them to Chepstow. There they again marched in procession to a field 'kindly lent for the occasion by Mr. Baker of the George Hotel.' Within the field were

> several hampers, each containing a sufficient quantity of bread and beef for a party of 27 or 30 persons, and small casks, containing as many quarts of beer – the club allowance being a loaf of bread, one and a half pounds of beef, and one quart of beer for each man. By previous arrangement each member knew which hamper contained his allowance, and it was amusing to witness the hitherto regular procession divide, at a given signal, and, in a moment, scattered, in groups of about 27 or 30, around the respective hampers. The office of carving was allotted to the agents of the work, one of whom was to be seen at each hamper. The band struck up the tune of 'The Roast Beef of Old England' and that was the signal for the playing [sic] of knives and forks...Two of the groups were teetotallers, and instead of ale they were plentifully supplied with ginger-beer.

The members were then free to spend the next six hours exploring Chepstow (and no doubt its pubs) before making the return journey and arriving in Merthyr 'at eight o'clock, where thousands had assembled to await their arrival.'[240]

The excursion to Swansea in 1854 involved more than 700 who travelled on a special train on the Vale of Neath railway. Thousands lined the streets to see the procession on its way to the station, led by the Cyfarthfa band and Robert Crawshay with his principal agents. The *Merthyr Guardian* assured its middle class readers:

> And truly the sight was well calculated to afford gratification; for the way in which the working men of the place turn out on such occasions, the cleanness of their appearance and the neatness with which they dress, is highly creditable; and what is true of Merthyr workmen generally is more especially so of the Cyfarthfa clubs... A new feature also appeared on this occasion, and we are happy to note the fact, — the wives of the men accompanied them on their excursion, and shared with their husbands the pleasure of the trip.[241]

In 1857 900 marched to 'divine service at the new Cyfarthfa church', 'the firemen led by the brass band, and the colliers by the juvenile fife band', a careful distinction.[242] By then Crawshay had extended his association with friendly societies to the Oddfellows. In 1855 he joined the 3,600 Merthyr members in an excursion to Swansea where they were met by members of the Swansea branches and processed through the main streets. This became an annual event accompanied by the Cyfarthfa Brass Band.[243]

---

[240] *MG*, 9 August 1851.

[241] *MG*, 28 July 1854.

[242] *MG*, 27 August 1857.

[243] Paul O'Leary, *Claiming the Streets*, p. 63.

The Band was Robert Crawshay's pet project which, although initially recruited from among the workmen was not conceived as a works band but for the entertainment of himself and his guests. He designed the band's uniform, bought the instruments from Vienna (the bandsmen reimbursing him by instalments), and during the 1840s recruited the best brass musicians that could be found, providing them with jobs in the works. The band rehearsed in the Lamb and Flag on the Brecon Road where the Cyfarthfa Firemen met and where Crawshay had an account for the band's drinks. They were no more than two dozen but their repertoire was extensive and sophisticated. Among the more than 350 pieces of handwritten music that survive are several symphonies and extracts from Italian operas along with many contemporary dance tunes. It is believed to be the first British brass band to play a Beethoven symphony.[244]

When, in May 1846 Robert married Rose Mary Yeates, Cyfarthfa workmen went down the valley to Troedyrhiw, took the horses out of the carriage bringing Robert Crawshay and his new bride to Merthyr, and with ropes around their waists pulled the carriage to Cyfarthfa Castle amidst cheering crowds in the Merthyr streets.[245] Paul O'Leary has commented that uncoupling the horses and pulling the carriage, a common practice at election times,

> was an act of profound symbolic importance in the nineteenth century, and it could be read in a variety of ways. It could denote the brute force of working people who were being

---

[244] Trevor Herbert, 'The Virtuosi of Merthyr', *Llafur*, Vol. 5, No. 1 (1988); Trevor Herbert, 'The repertory of a Victorian provincial brass band', *Popular Music*, Vol. 9, No. 1 (1990); Trevor Herbert, 'A Softening Influence: R.T. Crawshay and the Cyfarthfa Band', *Merthyr Historian*, Vol. 5 (1992).

[245] *MG*, 23 May 1846.

> substituted for the physical power of the horses, and the resulting submission of those people to the service of their social betters. However, the act of taking the place of the horses was open to be interpreted in other ways, too. Drawing an employer's carriage could be seen as yoking workers to the employer in a way that implied reciprocal responsibilities and duties (as it could in elections when unfranchised men yoked themselves to the candidate).[246]

Wedding celebrations continued for weeks and during the winter William Crawshay II, living at Caversham but still a dominant figure, arranged a series of balls in honour of the young couple. A wagon shed at the works was converted into a ballroom, no room at the Castle being large enough. The transformation was so splendid, with a polished wooden floor, shrubs down each side of the shed, draperies, flags, and gas-fired chandeliers that workmen longed to see it and 200 puddlers were allowed to enter on condition they left their boots outside.[247]

With a young hostess at the Castle – she was eighteen and he was twenty-nine – Robert entered fully into his social responsibilities serving as chairman of the Board of Guardians and member of the local Board of Health, hosting celebrity dinners at the Castle, allowing the Band to play at various functions, enabling workmen to attend the 1851 Great Exhibition at the Crystal Palace, associating his prestige with the friendly society movement and in 1856 becoming president of the new Merthyr Poultry and Flower Show which, 'will have

[246] O'Leary, *Claiming the Streets*, p. 60. In 1887 when Gladstone visited Wales he avoided Merthyr because he feared the enthusiastic crowds would take charge of the carriage. *WHR*, 2013.

[247] Margaret Stewart Taylor, *The Crawshays at Cyfarthfa Castle* (1967), pp. 81-9.

a direct and strong tendency' commented the *Merthyr Guardian* 'to encourage the growth of the domestic virtues...'[248] He gave £1,000 towards the cost of a Town Hall, proposing a site in Castle Street.

Rose Mary Crawshay

Rose Mary Crawshay was a formidable person in her own right. As mistress of Cyfarthfa she conventionally dispensed charity. For thirty-three years three times a week, until she became a widow and left the Castle, she ensured that soup was provided for the local poor. But her local activities went well beyond that. When in February 1862 an explosion at Crawshay's Gethin pit killed forty-nine men she visited every bereaved family. She encouraged local women to learn dress-making. She had a room at the works where penny readings, songs and recitations were held, and out of her own money established and personally paid for seven free libraries in Merthyr and Cefn Coed. They were heated, well stocked with books and, unusually, open on Sundays. After the 1870 Education Act she won election to the Merthyr school board, one woman among ten men. She also chaired the Vaynor school board; the only woman then to sit simultaneously on two school boards.

The marriage was unhappy and, unlike Charlotte Guest, she never immersed herself in her husband's business or appeared to take much interest in the Welsh language or customs. Her interests were wider and more radical. Not surprisingly, she favoured marriage reform. She argued that women should be allowed to be medical doctors. She signed the first women's Suffrage Petition of 1866 and was friends with Elizabeth Garrett and her sister Millicent Fawcett. Both, at her invitation,

---

[248] *MG*, 22 August 1857.

spoke in Merthyr on women's rights. She prominently supported the establishment of Swansea Training College in 1872 which for the first time enabled women to train as teachers within Wales. Despite her support for women's rights and interest in education she did not ensure that her daughters received an adequate education. She spent much time in London leaving her daughters with Robert. His favourite daughter Rose Harriette he summoned with a dog whistle and obsessively photographed her in a variety of poses.

In London, and at the Castle where she entertained, Rose Mary mixed with the literary and scientific elite of the day including Robert Browning, Thomas Huxley, Herbert Spencer, Henry Irving, Ralph Waldo Emerson and Charles Darwin. In 1873 she was Vice-President of the Bristol and West of England National Society for Women's Suffrage. She was a founder member of the Council of the Cremation Society of England, formed in 1874 and once suggested to Robert's horror that when she died her body should be thrown into one of the Cyfarthfa furnaces. At the Social Science Congress of 1874 she presented her paper on 'Domestic Service for Gentlewomen' and opened a 'Lady Help' registry office in the West End of London where prospective 'lady helps' could take cookery lessons as well as find jobs. She supported euthanasia and favoured decimal coinage on the grounds that it was easier for children to understand than pounds, shillings and pence. She died on 2 June 1907 and was cremated at Golders Green. The literary prize for women which she founded in 1882 continues, administered by the British Academy.

The Soft Face of Power

After the suppression of trades unions in 1834 and the surge of employment brought by the railway mania Merthyr's ironmasters were largely unchallenged even at the height of Chartist influence. Through their membership of the Guardians and the Board of Health they determined the public life of Merthyr; Hill and Crawshay most potently over the supply of water and aspirations for incorporation. If needed, the masters had at their disposal the 'hard' option of the new police force and the troops still stationed at Dowlais. But 'soft' measures consolidated their position. For Robert Crawshay in particular, schools, churches, a pension list, railway excursions, dinners, the incorporation of friendly societies into a paternalistic ethos, band concerts, libraries and penny readings all played a part in making pervasive a culture encompassing Cyfarthfa works and Crawshay benevolence. These events, it was noted, 'are replete with pleasure and gratification to himself, as well as to the workmen in his employ, while they tend to establish and strengthen that sympathy and kind feeling which should ever exist between employer and employed'.[249] They were also an antidote to trade unions, a potential alternative focus for loyalty.

A belief in the common interests of masters and men could be found in most British towns during the 1850s. In Merthyr and Dowlais the fortunes of the local ironworks dominated men's thoughts and hopes. They and their masters were 'all in it together' as indeed, in a one-industry town, they were. A cloud hovered over the renewal of the Cyfarthfa lease. Although it did not fall due until 1864 discussions about a settlement were the subject of negotiations for the thirty years beforehand. The fears of the Cyfarthfa workmen over its renewal were expressed in a letter to William Crawshay II in 1859.

> ...these large works may within a very few years cease to exist, that the ties which have hitherto bound us together may shortly

[249] *MG*, 28 July 1854.

> be severed, never perhaps to be reunited, and that we with the families dependent upon us, amounting in all to upwards of six thousand persons may be scattered abroad and compelled to seek our daily bread in other places or perhaps in other countries and other climes.[250]

When in 1860 the Cyfarthfa lease was successfully renewed a carnival was held with fireworks, flags, huge crowds in the streets, six brass bands and a specially written song that began 'Cyfarthfa Lease being now renewed Let Merthyr shout for joy!'[251]

The Crawshay Aura

Yet deferential statements expressing loyalty and gratitude for wage increases were far removed from workmen's statements in 1831, 1842 or from what would happen in 1874. The many faces of the power exercised by the masters would always find a response in deference. The everyday use of the term 'master' was itself an acknowledgment of subordination. But it was known that agricultural workers might touch their forelocks to their 'betters' while simultaneously raising two fingers to them behind their backs. Deference can exist alongside alienation. A great deal of deferential behaviour may be no more than 'the necessary pose of the powerless'. [252] *Droit de seigneur* was a brutal display of employer power confirming the dominance of work over people's lives,

The aura of Crawshay power and *bonhomie*, strong and pervasive for the first twenty years or more of Robert

---

[250] *MG*, 6 August 1859.

[251] Addis, pp. 128-9.

[252] Howard Newby, *The Deferential Worker* (1977), pp. 112, 110-11.

Crawshay's rule, always had to compete with the influence of the chapels and their democratic forms of organisation, the Merthyr tradition of radical politics, latent but waiting to re-emerge in 1868, the impact of technological changes and the fluctuations of the product and labour markets. Behind the processions and flag-waving mid-Victorian social relations were a fragile compromise.

The aura did not last. It was undermined by the urge for franchise reform, the flowering of newspaper readership and debate, the increase in the number of colliers in the labour force, the 1867 Reform Act that gave workers the vote and the 1868 rejection of Bruce the ironmasters' candidate, followed by a resurgence of trade unionism. The stroke that Robert suffered in January 1860 certainly contributed. It not only made him severely deaf it also affected his personality. His deafness isolated him from the workmen, his outbursts of anger grew, his hypochondria increased as his capacity to cope with the works declined. He became sensitive to slights, real and imagined, cutting all connection with the Flower Show after one such incident although he had been its chief supporter.[253] His decline was a personal tragedy. Years that began in youth and strength ended in infirmity and paralysis. Years that began in popularity ended with him closing the works and locking-out the workers. Cyfarthfa, once a leader in the industry became technologically obsolete.

The Crawshay letters at the National Library, Aberystwyth, reveal the decline. The early Crawshays write about the business. Robert's letters are increasingly less about the business and more about shooting, fishing, ordering wine (after his death 15,541 bottles of wines and spirits were found in the Castle's cellars) and the dividends he is receiving from share

[253] Taylor, *The Crawshays of Cyfarthfa Castle*, p. 147.

holdings. The family motto was *Perseverance* but although he liked the idea of being head of Cyfarthfa he lacked the moral strength and all-consuming drive that characterised the first three generations of the family. They were not easy times. The local iron ores had run out, the works faced new and significant competition from the north-east of England, Scotland and the USA, and expensive capital investment was necessary to change to steel production, but these were problems the Dowlais Iron Company largely surmounted in the second half of the century by investing in plant and technology and training managers.

Robert, like his forefathers entered into Merthyr mythology. The Crawshays were seen as 'characters' and had a common appeal that the solemn Guests never achieved. Most of the stories about Robert concerned his lechery but not all. A persistent one is that when the priest at Cyfarthfa Church unwisely chose the St. Matthew text 'It is easier for a camel to go through the eye of a needle than for a rich man to enter into the kingdom of God' Robert banged his stick upon the ground, exclaimed 'It's a damn lie', left the church and swore to tip waste from the works over the church. The story goes that only the lock-out and shutdown of the works in 1874 saved the church.[254] It is noticeable that he chose not to be buried there.

The lock-out ended Cyfarthfa paternalism. For Robert the fact that 'his' workers joined a trade union was a betrayal. Their loyalty should have been to the Cyfarthfa ironworks and to him personally, not to an external force coming between him and

---

[254] A.Trystan Edwards, *Merthyr, Rhondda and 'The Valleys'* (1958) pp. 54-56 has examples of stories about the Crawshays as does Wilkins in his *History* and other writings. Margaret Stewart Taylor throws cold water upon the Cyfarthfa Church story in *The Crawshays*, p. 150. The story was told to me by my grandfather born in 1871 who heard it from numerous family members who played in the Cyfarthfa Band and in the church.

them. The workers, in turn, felt betrayed by his insistence upon a wage cut twice the level of that imposed by the other employers and by his stubborn closure of the works. It was the end of highly personalised workplace relations at Cyfarthfa.

10

Dowlais: Company Town[255]

> Paternalism was a paying proposition, not least, to one degree or another, because it was paid for out of the low wages and long hours of those who were its beneficiaries.
>
> **Patrick Joyce[256]**

> The manager of a great Welsh ironwork is in a position not very unlike that of the governor of a colony without a legislature.
>
> **J.C. Fowler[257]**

In 1845 the Dowlais Iron Company (DIC) was the largest ironworks, probably the largest capitalist enterprise, in the world. Around it since its foundation in 1759 had grown a community distinct from the town of Merthyr Tydfil, and proud to be so. 'We are a separate town' declared Thomas Jones a

---

[255] Three unpublished theses provide much detail on Dowlais. K.T. Weetch, 'The Dowlais Ironworks and Its Industrial Community 1760-1850', M.Sc. Econ. thesis, London University, 1963; G.P. Smith, 'Social Control and Industrial Relations at the Dowlais Iron Company c.1850-1890', M.Sc. thesis, University of Wales, Aberystwyth, 1981; M.J. Lewis, 'G.T. Clark and the Dowlais Iron Company: An Entrepreneurial Study', M.Sc. thesis, University of Wales, Aberystwyth 1983.

[256] Patrick Joyce, *Work, Society & Politics* (Brighton, 1980), p. 146.

[257] John Coke Fowler, *The Characteristics and Civilization of South Wales* (Neath, 1873), p. 12. He explicitly had Dowlais in mind.

Dowlais grocer in 1876. 'We have our own market house, two churches, and 16 or 18 chapels, some of them capable of holding 2,000 persons. We have our own rector, an infirmary, and a library and a reading room at the Memorial Hall'.[258] Dowlais Eccelesiastical District created in 1834 had by 1861 a population of 15,588 of whom over 40 per cent were directly employed by the Company. In 1865 Menelaus, the general manager, reported the number as 7,827. These employees, their dependents, the shops and other services in Dowlais depended for their sustenance upon the DIC on its forty acre site.

Initially the structure of dependence emerged through the dispensation of work, the building of houses for key workers, the provision of a doctor and a sick fund financed by compulsory deductions from wages, the truck shop, DIC ownership of the market house and the absence of another major employer. It became embedded by the personal rule of the Guest family from 1767 when John Guest was appointed manager of the original furnace. For much of the nineteenth century the Dowlais Iron Company was ruled by just two men: Josiah John Guest, in charge from 1814 to 1852, knighted as Sir John in 1838, and George T. Clark, trustee and managing director from 1856 to 1892. Guest's widow, Lady Charlotte, was in charge from 1852 to 1855.

The fear in 1847-8 that a dispute over the ground and mineral leases would lead to the closure of the works (it almost did) emphasised the community's dependency. During the autumn of 1847 and the following spring, negotiations with the Marquess of Bute were on the brink of failure.[259] On 21 December 1847 Lady Charlotte confided to her Journal, 'I knew it to be my last day at Dowlais, at Dowlais in its glory ...I knew

---

[258] ME, 6 January 1877.

[259] John Davies, 'The Dowlais Lease, 1748-1900', *Morgannwg*, vol. 12, 1968.

that I would never see them in their old activity again.' By February 1848 three of the furnaces had been blown out and workers were being made redundant. The *Mining Journal* reported that 'The hitherto thriving mining town of Dowlais ... will be, I fear, ere long marked by little else, than a heap of deserted ruins'. Six weeks before the lease was due to expire Lord Bute collapsed and died at Cardiff Castle. A settlement was reached on 21 April 1848 ten days before the expiry date.[260]

Dowlais erupted.

> Publicans did more business on Monday, than they had done for the preceding three weeks, flags waved above the highest buildings, bands of musicians paraded the streets ...the taverns were all full, and one half the adults in Dowlais were said to be labouring under the effects of unbounded joyfulness.[261]

Thousands turned out in a procession over a mile long to greet Sir John and Lady Charlotte when they returned to Dowlais. The procession included over a thousand members of eighteen friendly societies, the Cyfarthfa Band, gentry, tradesmen and the police.[262]

Josiah John Guest

The Memorial Hall, mentioned at the 1876 Inquiry, had been designed by Sir Charles Barry and erected to the memory of Sir John Guest, (1785-1852), Merthyr's first MP and grandson of John Guest. Sir John, ambitious and single-minded was one of

---

260 Guest and John, pp. 172-74.

261 *MG*, 29 April 1848.

262 O'Leary, *Claiming the Streets*, pp. 60-3.

the great mid-Victorian industrialists. Born in Dowlais, Guest died in Dowlais and is buried in St. John's Anglican Church there. *The Times* in his obituary portrayed him as a man to whom 'this country owes so much of her wealth and prosperity'.[263] Ambition and a sense of public duty took him into Parliament where he spent twenty-five years as an MP, first entering public life aged thirty-one as MP for Honiton, Devon, (1825-31). He lost the Honiton seat because he favoured parliamentary reform, for which he consistently voted. When Merthyr Tydfil was made a parliamentary constituency in 1832 he became MP and held the seat until his death twenty years later. Initially of radical sentiments he favoured free trade, repeal of the Corn Laws, the secret ballot, and civil and religious liberties – voting for Catholic emancipation and repeal of the Test and Corporation Act that discriminated against Dissenters. (He was, after all, from a Methodist family.) However, he was firmly against the Chartist programme and trade unions. A Philosophical Radical and stolid parliamentary performer he moved in the 1840s in the highest circles of Whig society, regularly dining with Lord Melbourne and Lord John Russell.[264]

His considerable contribution to the development of South Wales included the creation of the Taff Vale Railway and parliamentary support for the Marquess of Bute's docks at Cardiff, even though they quarrelled bitterly over politics and the Dowlais lease. The railway and its branch lines facilitated the export of coal from the Taff, Cynon and Rhondda valleys through Bute's docks and made Cardiff a major port. A reputation for solemnity was shaken when at forty-eight he had what can only be called 'a whirlwind romance' with Lady Charlotte Bertie, the remarkable daughter of the Earl of Lindsey.

---

[263] Guest and John, p. 171.

[264] Christopher Gillham, 'The Politics of Sir John Guest 1825-1852', M.A. Dissertation, University of Wales, 1971.

They met on 17 June 1833 and were married forty-two days later on 29 July at St. George's, Hanover Square. She was twenty-one and his second wife. His first, Maria Rankin had died in 1818 leaving him childless. When in 1838 Josiah received a baronetcy for political services Charlotte, disappointed, called it 'a paltry distinction'.

Josiah had been introduced to Charlotte by Mary Anne, wife of his partner Wyndham Lewis. After Wyndham Lewis died Mary Anne married Benjamin Disraeli. This marriage by all accounts a happy one provided Disraeli, thanks to wealth accumulated at Dowlais, the opportunity to pay off some of his debts and pursue his political career — not the least of the many unforeseen consequences that resulted from the establishment of that solitary furnace in 1759. It was Disraeli who recommended Ivor, the Guests' eldest son, to the peerage as Lord Wimborne and it was Mary Anne who introduced Ivor to the woman he married, Lady Cornelia Churchill.

In 1833 Guest was the major shareholder in the works and since 1814 had been the sole manager. In that year he had discussed plans for opening a school for his workmen's children although it is not clear whether he succeeded in persuading William Taitt of its desirability. Taitt died in 1815 and by 1820 Guest had established a purpose-built school for boys and girls. Everyday running costs and the salary of the schoolmaster were met by a monthly stoppage of twopence in the £ from wages and a contribution of one penny a week from parents of attending children. A new girls' school followed in 1828. More than Hill, Crawshay or Foreman he felt that wealth carried obligations. He had, after all, been born in Dowlais and after the early death of his mother been nursed by 'Marie Aberteifi' from whom he had an understanding of Welsh. Although brought up as a Wesleyan he built in 1823 a chapel of ease for Dowlais people and followed that in 1827 by paying for the building of the church of St. John the Baptist specifically for the workmen, managers and their wives.[265] In 1836 he was the prime mover in setting up the Merthyr Savings Bank. The Tory *Merthyr Guardian* paid him tribute and commented 'How is it, we ask, that in all the proceedings by which the place, and the labouring population are to be benefited, he stands alone?'[266] A major purpose of the Bank was to hold the surplus funds of Friendly Societies, which Guest saw as a working class alternative to Chartism. On Christmas Day 1838 a march by 400 Oddfellows in Dowlais diverted attention from the greater Chartist celebrations in Merthyr. One of the Oddfellows lodges in Dowlais was named The Lady Charlotte.

It took time for Lady Charlotte to become involved in Guest's educational schemes. For the best part of a decade she was engaged with translating into English *The Mabinogion* (after she had learned medieval Welsh) and then its publication. There were also the cares and demands of motherhood. She had ten children in thirteen years and a miscarriage between her second and third child, A turning point came in 1842 when she and Guest visited the German mining districts and were impressed by the Prussian education system where schooling was compulsory between six and fourteen. Enthusiastically she joined in the planning and reorganisation of their ironworks schools. In 1844 the number of school places was increased with upper and lower classes for boys and for girls, and the then unusual introduction of separate classrooms for different age groups. Qualified teachers were employed, a fully equipped laboratory for science classes provided, and schools for infants introduced. Subjects included the 3 Rs, chemistry and model drawing. When the Inquiry into Education reported in 1847 the

[265] Huw Williams, *A History of the Church in the Parish of Dowlais* (Dowlais, 1977)

[266] *MG*, 16 April 1836.

Guest schools were praised.[267] These initiatives were accompanied by the opening in 1845 of the Dowlais Tradesmen's and Workmen's Library paid for by the Company. Initially there was a subscription of 1s. 6d (20.5p) but in 1853 it became a free library.

Education and Rational Entertainment

From 1848 Charlotte's 'maternalism' became more evident.[268] The lease issue had been resolved, attention could once again be given to Dowlais and praise for the Guest schools in the 1847 report was welcomed as an opportunity for further improvement. But it was the massive Chartist demonstration on Kennington Common on 10 April 1848 and the government and middle class fears that surrounded it that made her think anew about the relations between rich and poor. The day after the demonstration she wrote in her journal: 'Something must be done for our unemployed, the events of yesterday must not lull us into security and make us overlook this duty, this necessity'. And three days after it she wrote of 'the necessity of educating, of humanising, the lower grade.'[269]

By the autumn she had introduced evening schools for men and women, probably the first non-religious classes for adults in Wales. The school for women was free and attended on the first night in October by 177 women workers, servants and the daughters of workmen. Only twenty could read and write and most found English a difficult language. The subjects included

---

[267] Guest and John, p. 247; Leslie Wynne Evans, *Education in Industrial Wales 1700-1900* (Cardiff, 1971), chapter four.

[268] Angela V. John, 'Beyond Paternalism: The Ironmaster's Wife in the Industrial Community' in Angela V. John, *Our Mothers' Land: Chapters in Welsh Women's History 1830-1939* (2011).

[269] Guest and John, p. 59.

the three Rs, history, geography and needlework. The adult male classes were for youths and men employed by the Dowlais Company. A class for men studying higher mathematics was held in the reading room. The classes were a success and were in the minds of J.C. Campbell and Henry Bruce in December 1849 when they urged Merthyr and Aberdare employers to educate their workers.[270]

Her desire to 'educate and humanise' found other outlets. In the autumn and winter of 1850 she developed an idea proposed by her husband and Henry Bruce to hold evening parties for 'steady workmen' – the skilled men who had put down roots. A series of evening 'rational' entertainments were provided, Lady Charlotte believing that 'by mutually agreeing to come together thus, we shall be better enabled to carry out the ends of our creation and eradicate all unseemly and rough edges from our minds'. Henry Layard, Charlotte's cousin, spoke of his discovery of Ninevah, music was played, Handel choruses sung, sandwiches and tea provided.[271] The numbers attending were considerable, 500 to 600. In that year also she promoted the Dowlais Band, following Robert Crawshay's example. [272] On 21 July 1851 the Dowlais Workmen's Exhibition Club made the train journey to London to see the Great Exhibition, a trip which included visits to the British Museum and the Houses of Parliament and a huge picnic on the lawns of the Guest's estate at Canford in Dorset. In 1852 a cricket field for healthy activity was opened at Dowlais.[273]

The culmination of these schemes came on 11 September 1855 with the formal opening of the new £20,000 Dowlais

---

[270] Guest and John, pp. 73-9; Leslie Wynne Evans, pp. 95-120.

[271] *MG*, 19 October, 7 December 1850.

[272] *MG*, 9 November 1850.

[273] *MG*, 24 July 1852.

central schools designed by Sir Charles Barry who had also designed the 1844 improvements. On that day 642 boys and girls were enrolled. In addition new schools for Roman catholics were supported by the DIC and schools built at the villages of Pant and Pengarnddu. From 1856 the schools were publically inspected and their high standard recognised throughout the educational world. In 1892 when the schools were finally transferred to the Merthyr School Board the total number of pupils was 2,492. The number attending the evening classes was separate and additional.

By 1855 Sir John was dead and Charlotte had left Dowlais. She made a special journey to attend the opening of the new schools. For three years after Sir John died on 26 November 1852 Charlotte, as sole trustee, was in charge of the DIC until she forfeited her rights as a trustee by marrying Charles Schreiber on 10 April 1855. New trustees were then appointed, G.T. Clark, Edward Divett and Henry Bruce. Clark became the resident trustee, in effect managing director and driving force for the next thirty years. Broadly the Guests had left him a two-part legacy, the first of which was a paternal regime in which economic and moral purposes had combined to produce a largely quiescent labour force.

The Screw

In 1831 the Dowlais workmen had kept clear of the Rising. In 1834 and always afterwards trade union members were victimised. In 1842 Guest had dismissed Chartist supporters while giving generously to the needy. Key workmen, puddlers and rollers, had been courted. Most important of all, from their earliest days in infant school Dowlais children were immersed in the Dowlais Iron Company's benevolent sphere of influence. The Guests' belief in the value of education was genuine but their schools, as all ironworks schools, were training grounds for the next generation of workmen, clerks and technicians. Along with their quality education they learned to be punctual, loyal and diligent. The vast works, visible and audible throughout Dowlais, was both benefactor and beneficiary.

Dowlais was a Guest fiefdom and it followed naturally that those who had a vote would vote in ways approved by the Company. Freeholders who held mining or haulage contracts with the Company understood, or were made to understand, what was expected of them. As early as 1807 William Taitt wrote to his nephew Josiah Guest concerning a Glamorgan parliamentary election: 'I wish you to ask Dick of the Wayne & all those you know who have Votes to give them to Mr. Llewellyn ...'. [274] 'Influence politics' was widespread in the manufacturing districts and known more colloquially to the Victorians as 'the screw'. Pro-employer voting was both understood and expected.[275] Not everyone, however, could be taken for granted. On 7 April 1853 John Jones, a Dowlais grocer, wrote to the General Board of Health in Whitehall concerning the election to the Local Board of Health:

> I can not rest happy under the flagrant abuse of authority we suffer in this place without making our complaint known to you, as a higher power ...Will you be so kind so as to inform me whether it is legal for Iron Masters or any other party to send their agents to follow the deliveries of the voting papers dictating to the voters how to fill them – and not only that but to fill them for them, — and cross the names of the other candidates out, — the abuse here has been very great plenty of evidence to prove it – ready and willing – your kind instructions

[274] Evans, *The Labyrinth*, p. 136.

[275] Joyce, pp. 218-221.

on the subject will oblige your humble Servt and hundreds of voters.

Your most obedt
Servt John Jones
Grocer

Please to turn over

I enclose you a paper that has been written by some I know not that was intended to be sent to our Chairman at Merthyr. You will see by it what the General feeling is here.

The paper read as follows:

Sirs, the next time you send your Voting Papers to Dowlais, please to leave them all at the Dowlais Office, for it will spare you and them a great deal of trouble. For the Man that was distributing this time could not find out the Voters residence because he was a Stranger in the place. Then the Dowlais Agents had to call at every house to tell the voter who he was to vote for.

So the easiest way is the best way to accomplish everything that will answer the same purpose in the end. Therefore I beg to call your attention to the above plan, for it will answer the same purpose, and save a great deal of useless bodyly exercise to both parties, and time spent without doing any good, Which the late renowned Benjamin Franklyn said was Money.

Wishing you success in your endeavours, I remain yours truly A Voter. [276]

---

[276] A. H. Williams (ed.), *Public Health in Mid-Victorian Wales* (Aberystwyth, 1983), p. 125.

What happened to Jones as a result of this spirited independence we do not know but, as his letter illustrates, the Dowlais screw was well organised. In the 1868 general election 58 per cent of the votes cast in the Merthyr area for Bruce, a Dowlais trustee, came from Dowlais and neighbouring Penydarren.[277] This inheritance of paternalism and influence George Clark welcomed and built upon, but first he had to deal with the second part of his inheritance.

Saving the Works

The Dowlais Iron Company was in difficulties. In 1856 it made a loss of £52, 907. Iron prices were falling, competition from new works in Scotland and the north-east of England had increased substantially and anxieties over the renewal of the lease meant that investment in the works had suffered in the years up to 1848. More than that, capital reserves were low. Guest and his partners had withdrawn more than a million pounds from the works, an average of £64,000 per annum, between 1830 and 1848. During the 1840s Sir John used £335,000 of profits to purchase and improve the Canford estate in Dorset. Although improvements to the Works were made after the lease was renewed, little was spent in the two years after Guest's death.

The Company required 'despotic management' Clark said, and he supplied it.[278] His strategy had four elements. He used revenue to invest in new technology, foregoing short run profits for long-term gain; he entered the coal market to offset falling profits from the sale of iron, opening new pits at Fochriw and buying the Penydarren coal reserves; he bought English ores

[277] *ME*, 21 November 1868.

[278] L.J. Williams, 'Clark the Ironmaster' in B. Ll. James (ed.), *G.T. Clark: Scholar Ironmaster in the Victorian Age* (Cardiff, 1998).

instead of the depleting Welsh and then bought cheaper Spanish ore instead of English; and continued the old policy of making and stockpiling iron in a depression until prices rose whilst at the same time reducing wages. In the year ending March 1858 a 20 per cent reduction in wages saw a corresponding reduction of 12.5 per cent in total costs.

In all this he received formidable assistance from William Menelaus (1818–1882) who he appointed general manager after securing the retirement of John Evans the long-serving works manager. Menelaus was a disciplinarian who insisted on weekly reports from each department on its financial and physical state of health. It was Menelaus who produced landmark reports, one in 1857 on the state of the Company and then in 1861 on the case for Dowlais to enter the coal trade. In the early 1870s he helped negotiate the deal for cheap Spanish ore which resulted in the Orcenario Iron Ore Company jointly owned by Dowlais, Consett and Krupps. (The general manager at Consett was William Jenkins, a Dowlais 'old boy'.) In 1882 the extremely capable Dowlais-born E.P. Martin (1844-1910) succeeded Menelaus as General Manager and supervised the erection of the new Dowlais works at East Moors, Cardiff, in 1902.

The first fruits of Clark's strategy of investment in new technology resulted in the Goat Mill, the most powerful rolling mill in Britain, which from 1859 handled the longest and heaviest rails then being made and increased efficient use of the company's pig iron. The increase in rolling capacity, however, required an increase in puddling furnaces. In 1848 there had been 109. By 1870 there were 160. Puddlers were both expensive and occupied a powerful and independent position in the production process. Despite this the work was so arduous that the supply of men willing to undertake the work barely kept up with the jobs available. Schooling meant that educated boys were aspiring to 'something better'. The logical response by the Company, as for the industry as a whole, was to find a way of mechanising the puddling process. Various methods were tried without success until the Bessemer process of making steel seemed to offer an alternative. Experiments with the Bessemer process began at Dowlais in 1856 but, due to the high levels of phosphorus and sulphur in the pig iron fed into the early converters, the metal produced was liable to crack. When the first steel rail was rolled at Dowlais in 1858 it broke while still hot 'to the undisguised rejoicing of the assembled puddlers'.[279]

Clark and Menelaus, recognising the future, persevered with the Bessemer process. In July 1865 steel bars were successfully rolled into rails. Steel production began the next year and in 1871 Dowlais installed a second steel mill. From 1870 experiments began at Dowlais with the Siemens-Martin method of steel-making and in 1871 the works produced 581 tons of Siemens ingots. Bessemer steel was more suitable for rail production, and steel rails, tougher and more reliable, steadily took the place of wrought iron rails. On 6 November 1876 Clark wrote to Ivor B. Guest '...so far as we can see, no great railway company will again lay down iron rails ...The iron rail trade is a thing of the past'.[280] So was puddling. By 1885 the number of puddling forges at Dowlais was 19, there had once been 255.[281]

---

[279] Edgar Jones, 'The transition from wrought iron to steel technology at the Dowlais Iron Company, 1850-1890' in Jonathan Liebenau (ed.), *The Challenge of New Technology: Innovation in British Business since 1850* (Aldershot, 1988).

[280] Lewis, p. 250.

[281] Owen, pp. 81-2. For a pen picture of 'a man of considerable importance in his day' see 'Welsh Character Sketches: The Old Puddler', in Charles Wilkins (ed.), *The Red Dragon: the National Magazine of Wales* (Cardiff, 1883), Vol. 3, pp. 443ff.

A foretaste of the future came in 1888 when work began on building a new 'Dowlais' works on waste moorlands near Cardiff docks, an acceptance that a coastal site was more economical for both the import of ore and the export of finished products. Iron was first produced there in February 1891 and in September 1895 steel production commenced, the finished product being steel plates for ships. Steel production also continued at Dowlais.

The Turn to Coal

When in 1859 the Penydarren mineral rights and pits (but not the iron-making plant) were bought by Dowlais for £59,875 they provided easily worked good quality coal above the amount required for iron-making. The result was reduced production costs at Dowlais and large contracts for coal deliveries to Cardiff, Swansea, Liverpool, London, Hereford, and Shrewsbury. This was just the beginning. Work on sinking two new pits at Fochriw had begun in 1857 as part of the modernisation of the works recommended by Menelaus and these began to produce coal in 1863 and 1866. By then Menelaus had convinced Clark that Dowlais should unhesitatingly enter the sale-coal trade. He calculated that there would be a surplus of 1,000 tons a day for sale. There would be a further advantage. The opening of sea-coal collieries would reduce the bargaining power of colliers who supplied the ironworks. He wrote:

> Colliers have been at all times difficult men to manage and have become worse owing to the great demand for men in Aberdare and the adjoining districts. They are ever ready to take advantage of the masters on the slightest pretext. When an ironworks only raises sufficient coal for daily use in iron-making

> the men have always the power to inflict grievous loss upon the master by simply idling, keeping the Furnaces and Forges short of coal. In good times if the master refuses to accede to the demands of the colliers, which are frequently most unreasonable, they attempt to gain their ends by keeping the works short of coal preventing the master making quantity when he would be able to realize large profits. If we produce more than we need only a general strike can interfere with our make – as we can send sale coal to the works.[282]

Investment in new pits followed. Work began on sinking a colliery at Bedlinog in 1874 and in 1881 No. 1 pit was opened, followed in 1883 by No. 2. In 1890 the company started work on a new colliery at Abercynon. The total numbers employed grew as investment in the pits paid off and profits grew substantially after 1863. From 1872 the company made more profit from steel than from iron; and from 1884 profits fron the sale of coal were greater than the profits from steel.[283] By 1902 those employed in the collieries alone numbered 5,197.

Moulding the Labour Force

Clark enthusiastically embraced power and the opportunity it gave him to guide and mould 'his' workers. Good and careful workers were essential for the success of the works and he introduced a variety of measures designed to increase labour efficiency and commitment to the DIC. The company schools were an essential element in this aim for Clark had a moral mission. He enthusiastically backed the expansion of the schools envisaged by Charlotte Guest culminating in the opening of the

---

[282] Morris and Williams, p. 88; Lewis, p. 160.

[283] Lewis, Appendix A.

Central Schools in 1855. A prime purpose of this education was to assist in the moral improvement of the workforce. In an address to the workforce on 7 March 1857 he stated: 'The continual, recurring, enduring question is not do we make good iron at a profitable rate, but what do we make of colliers, our puddlers, our millmen.'[284] Wherever possible he employed workers who had been educated in the Company schools. The journey from childhood to the world of work was guided by the beneficence and morality of the DIC. As at Cyfarthfa the development of a loyal labour force was enhanced by recruitment from the families of trustworthy workers already employed.

The medical scheme initiated by Guest was supplemented in 1872 by Mrs. Clark's hospital on Dowlais high street where P.R. Cresswell the Company doctor supervised eight beds. Clark took a particular interest in the four separate sick funds for colliers, forgemen, millmen and furnacemen, believing that they encouraged self-reliance and thrift among the workmen. They were financed, however, by a compulsory deduction of 2d. in the pound from the men's wages and subject to company oversight, which could be heavy-handed. In September 1866 a dispute erupted over the medical funds. The men alleged unfairness in the way the scheme was run and wished to have more control over the services provided. Characteristically Clark threatened to abolish the whole scheme and the men withdrew their complaints.

Excessive drinking continued to cause concern. Employees operating beer shops from Company-owned premises were dismissed. Clark changed the method of wage payment, paying in coin rather than notes so that workers did not need to go to a pub to get change. He opposed, not always with success,

[284] Smith, p. 63.

applications for licensed premises in Dowlais and continued to provide lectures and musical evenings as alternatives to the attractions of the public house. The voluntary savings bank scheme established by Guest in 1852 naturally received his commendation and the deduction from wages of the rent for company houses was emphasised as a lesson in prudence and foresight. He applauded the substantial local membership of Friendly Societies, regretting that their chief meeting places were in public houses.

When in 1859 there was national alarm over the warlike ambitions of Napoleon III Palmerston encouraged the setting up of a form of Home Guard known as the Volunteers, Clark set one up at Dowlais which replicated the Company power structure. Clark was the commander-in-chief, with Menelaus and George Martin captains, and departmental managers as lieutenants over the rank-and-file members drawn from their own departments, usually skilled men. The numbers involved were few compared to the total employed and Clark appears to have had an obsession with extensive parade ground drilling.[285]

In the context of then current new paternalism Clark's concern to mould his labour force and instil the virtues of industry and thrift was not unusual. He was building on solid foundations laid down by Sir John and like Sir John he lived in Dowlais House cheek by jowl to the Works and not, like Crawshay, in a medieval fantasy surrounded by parkland behind a high wall. In his actions he was more thorough than Crawshay or Hill, possessing a moral fervour that Robert Crawshay could not pretend. And, unlike Crawshay's Kingdom spread over several urban villages, Dowlais was a single discrete community without an area like Georgetown with its tradition of

[285] Joyce, *Work, Society and Politics*, p. 169 notes that in industrial towns 'the Volunteers went far to reproducing the world of the factory on the parade ground'.

philosophical inquiry, Unitarian and Chartist networks and a public house, The Three Horseshoes that had been the headquarters of 1831 rioters and 1842 Chartists. Clark's grip upon Dowlais was much more secure.

'My own Men are like my own children'

Part of that grip, and compatible with his moral concerns, was the disciplinary framework laid down by Guest: the written rules, the disciplinary fines, the discharge notes that identified malcontents, the prosecutions for breach of contract. The Guest policy of rejection of trade unions continued. Arbitration in disputes Clark regarded as decisions by 'imported strangers'. Paternalism required one focus of authority, the firm and its master who was head of a family that encompassed all workers. In evidence to the 1867 Royal Commission on Trade Unions he explained:

> My own men are like my children and I should as soon think of refusing to listen to my own children as of refusing to listen to any man who came from the works to talk to me on any matter because I think it of equal importance that my men and I should be on good terms as that I should be on good terms with my own family.[286]

And in relation to South Wales he declared:

> A very kindly feeling has always subsisted, I believe, between masters and men there. The masters live among the men, and the men have access to them at all times, their difficulties come to the surface, and I conceive that that is not only a good thing

[286] P.P. Royal Commission on Trade Unions, 1867-68, C. 3980, Fifth Report, Q. 10,074.

> socially, but also, speaking as a manufacturer, I conceive it to be an excellent thing, and I think that if I could not meet my own men, and if a person who represented, not my men alone, but the whole district, came to me to discuss questions, that feeling would be broken into, and I do not think that we should settle matters so advantageously to both parties.[287]

There were elements of truth in this account but it ignored the labour protests of 1831 and 1834, the 1839 march on Newport, the six-week strike at Dowlais in 1853, the many strikes by colliers in the valleys surrounding Merthyr and Dowlais and the flirtation in 1864 by Dowlais puddlers with John Kane's ironworkers' union based at Gateshead. It ignored too the power relations that brought those disputes to an end. If there was an element of self-deception in his account, it arose from the same conception of authority relations that caused Robert Crawshay to react to trade unionism by shutting Cyfarthfa in 1874. When that issue arose in Dowlais Clark dealt with it differently, but just as ruthlessly.

There were limits to loyalty as Clark well knew. He told the Commisioners it was the younger men 'who have saved nothing' who were the most likely to strike or migrate whereas 'the older and more steady men, who have saved money, and in a large number of cases are cottage owners, are like the masters and for the same reasons by no means prompt to act, but are willing to wait on market forces'. In 1864 with buoyant demand for iron and faced by a threatened strike by puddlers the ironmasters had unwillingly given them an increase. In 1866 a proposed cut to colliers' wages had been withdrawn when colliers threatened to migrate to better paying areas. The Irish, of whom there were over 2,000 in Dowlais, were a problem too

[287] Ibid, Q. 10,124. Smith, p. 38.

for, unlike the Welsh, Clark grumbled, they did not follow the laid down grievance procedure and take their complaints to the office but went without notice, to the magistrates. This was tantamount to airing a family quarrel in public. But they were not part of the family. Clark had not sought to bind them to the Company, employing them in unskilled tasks only.

Ever present behind the processions and manifestations of joy when pay rises were given, leases renewed, company outings enjoyed were the booms and slumps of the market. Clark was content that the price of iron regulated the level of wages, urging thrift in the good times as a bulwark against the bad. Dowlais, however, was not a closed world. Migration to Australia, America or the expanding Rhondda coalfield offered an alternative to what under Menelaus had become a harsh regime. He had a reputation as an austere man and his contemporary Charles Wilkins was uncharacteristically blunt:

> The sympathies and sentiments of life affected him not, and he had begun to regard men as so much animated mechanism. They were the cogs of the wheels. Inefficient men were like an ill-made crank or defective piston, to be put aside. iron-making was a trade that admitted of no other consideration than capacity on the part of the labourer. It was the schoolmaster's duty to look after the education of the mind, the priest's after the welfare of the soul: his care was to obtain efficiency at its market value, and with this his relations with his men began and ended.[288]

Housing increasingly became a problem. In the eighteenth century the Company had provided houses for skilled workers and in the 1840s railway boom had built a number of cottages.

---

[288] 'Notable Men of Wales: William Menelaus', *Red Dragon* vol. 1(Cardiff, 1882), p. 390.

By the 1860s the Company's policy was to lease land for 99 years to workers who wished to build for themselves. Clark, as chairman of the Board of Guardians from 1859, approved of this display of thrift and self-reliance. Leasing also gave the Company through the terms of the lease some control over the use of dwellings. But building now lagged behind demand. By 1866 the DIC had 8,500 employees. Between 1866 and 1875 the number of houses in the whole Merthyr area only increased by 212.[289] In Dowlais colliers who sought accommodation ended up as lodgers. Houses built half-a-century before were deteriorating through lack of investment. Poor housing, overcrowding, and inadequate sanitation was an issue in Dowlais as it was in Merthyr. It was another reason to seek new pastures.

In November 1874 when the DIC was in a bitter dispute with its workers a letter from the Company to the local board of health discussed the company's policy of rents and house building in Dowlais and contained the statement:

> ...the Dowlais Company does not accept any responsibility further than the finding of work and fair wages for their workpeople. In these days of fair trade and independence, the Dowlais Company holds that it ought not to interfere with the unfettered action of those it employs. Working men are perfectly able to look after, and to take care of their own interests in all matters of business...[290]

Paternalism had given way to the market.

---

[289] Smith, p. 35

[290] *ME*, 21 November 1874.

11

The Old Order Changeth

A Revolution is coming on in the Iron Trade, which will shake Wales to the very roots...

William Crawshay II[291]

In the political history of the nineteenth century the 1860s were the decade of most momentous change in Wales.

Ieuan Gwynedd Jones[292]

In 1868 the electors of Merthyr Tydfil dismissed Henry Austen Bruce their MP for the previous sixteen years. In a three horse race for two General Election seats he ended bottom of the poll behind Henry Richard and Richard Fothergill. For twenty-one years, ever since his appointment as the stipendiary magistrate in 1847, a post his father had held before him, Bruce had been intimately connected with the constituency. He was a senior trustee of the Dowlais works, a Poor Law Guardian and campaigner on behalf of orphan children, a strong advocate of education for workers, and a friend of Gladstone. His dismissal shocked the political world. Since 1862 he had been Under-Secretary of State for the Home Department and his standing within the Liberal Party such that when Gladstone became prime minister after the election he found a parliamentary seat for

291 Addis, p. 132.

292 Ieaun Gwynedd Jones, *Mid-Victorian Wales: The Observers and the Observed* (Cardiff, 1992), p. 103.

Bruce in Renfrewshire and made him Home Secretary. No MP or former MP for Merthyr has held such high office. As Lord Aberdare he chaired the 1880 inquiry into higher education in Wales and Monmouthshire that boldly reformed Welsh secondary and higher education. When in 1859 William Crawshay had warned of an impending 'revolution' he was predicting a decline in the South Wales iron trade, but the dismissal of Bruce in 1868 throws a searchlight upon wider economic and political developments that were changing Wales forever.[293]

Reform Agitation

By the 1860s, a full generation after the 1832 Act, the case for further franchise reforms was becoming unanswerable. The population of England and Wales had grown to over five million yet the number of electors was under one million. Five out of six adult males were not eligible to vote. In the Merthyr Boroughs constituency where the population was overwhelmingly working class only one man in fifty-seven had the vote. In Brecon there was one MP to 6,000 people, in neighbouring Merthyr it was one to 63,000.[294]

Fear of 'the mob', of Chartist revolution, had largely disappeared. Mid-Victorian harmony found Gladstone in 1864 declaring in a much quoted speech that 'every man who is not

---

[293] The election of 1868 has been carefully analysed by Ieaun Gwynedd Jones in the following: 'The Election of 1868 in Merthyr Tydfil', in *Explorations and Explanations: Essays in the Social History of Victorian Wales* (Llandysul, 1981); 'The Politics of Religion: Dr. Thomas Price and the Election of 1868' in *Communities: Essays in the Social History of Victorian Wales* (Llandysul, 1987); '1848 and 1868: Brad y Llyfrau Gleision and Welsh Politics' in *Mid-Victorian Wales: The Observers and the Observed* (Cardiff, 1992).

[294] I. G. Jones, *Explorations and Explanations*, p. 273.

presumably incapacitated by some consideration of personal unfitness or of political danger, is morally entitled to come within the pale of the constitution'. The National Reform Union campaigned for reform from 1864 and in 1865 the more radical Reform League, backed by the trade unions, argued for manhood suffrage and the secret ballot. At Merthyr the League brought together ageing Chartists and middle class reformers – Morgan Williams, Matthew John, William Gould, C. H. James, J. W. James, W.L. Daniel, Peter Williams, T. W. Goodfellow and a number of Nonconformists ministers – an alliance that mirrored the national picture where within the League middle-class social reformers were sympathising with and campaigning for the political aspirations of labour.[295] In November 1867 large public meetings in Merthyr's market square and in the new Drill Hall were addressed by George Mantle of the League.[296]

A leading advocate of reform was John Kane the leader of the Ironworkers' Union based in Darlington but soon to make an impact in South Wales. In an article in the *Ironworkers' Journal*, which he edited, Kane analysed the composition of the unreformed House of Commons:

> In the present Parliament there are ...204 members who are directly related to peers, who chiefly represent the counties: in addition to 63 baronets and sons of baronets there are 50 professional men and 100 naval and military, and, above all, 30 directly representing the iron and coal trades. All interests and classes are represented except labour. There is not a singly working-man in Parliament...[297]

[295] Margot C. Finn, *After Chartism: Class and Nation in English radical politics, 1848-1874* (Cambridge, 1993), pp. 237-54.
[296] *ME*, 22 and 29 September, 24 November 1866.
[297] Arthur Pugh, *Men of Steel by One of Them* (1951), p. 34.

The campaign gained enormously from the abolition of the 'taxes on knowledge'. The ending of Stamp Duty in 1855 and the duty on paper in 1861 had produced an explosive rise in newspaper circulations and the birth of new papers and journals. *The Daily Telegraph* relaunched in 1855 as a voice of liberal opinion rapidly achieved a circulation far in excess of *The Times*. In Wales by 1860 there were twenty-five newspapers and over the next twenty years the number rose to sixty-one, thirteen of them in the Welsh language. A number were the journals of nonconformist denominations, others supported the cause of labour. Printing flourished at Merthyr where the *Merthyr Express* began its long history in 1864. *The Merthyr Star* enjoyed a revival in its intermittent existence. *Y Fellten* ran from 1868 to 1876 and in 1873 came the bilingual newspaper *The Workman's advocate: Amddiffynydd y gweithiwr*. Aberdare too had become a lively centre of journals that gave voice to nonconformist views but also covered industrial issues giving space to the workers' point of view. Principal among these were *Y Gwron* (The Hero), *Y Gwladgarwr* (The Patriot) and *Y Gweithiwr* (The Worker). Later, the influential *Tarian y Gweithiwr* (The Worker's Shield) that ran from 1875-1934 was also published at Aberdare. In 1861 the English language *Aberdare Times* appeared. From 1869 the Conservative *Western Mail* established as a daily and based in Cardiff, circulated throughout South Wales presenting its views to the newly enfranchised workers. The letter pages of newspapers and journals across Wales opened up debates on a whole range of issues – franchise reform, temperance, slavery, land reform, Nonconformist grievances and disestablishment of the Church.

The Liberation Society, originally formed as the Anti-Church-State Association in 1844, and renamed the Society for Liberating the Church from the State in 1853 significantly increased its activities in Wales during the 1860s. It argued that Wales should be represented in Parliament by those who would present the grievances of Welsh Nonconformists. A key figure in this growing movement was Henry Richard who in his *Letters on the Social and Political Condition of the Principality of Wales* published in London in 1866, and in his eloquent speeches was developing a political vision for the Welsh people.[298] Gladstone's determination to break the connection between the Church in Ireland and the state was a central issue in the 1868 general election, a question of principle supported in Nonconformist Wales despite misgivings about the possible consequent growth in strength of the Catholic Church in Ireland. Disestablishment of the Church in Wales, however, was an issue not resolved until 1920.

The End of Iron

These national concerns were subjects of fierce debate in Merthyr Tydfil where fundamental changes were already occuring. The great days of the iron trade were over. Penydarren and Hirwaun works had closed by 1859, and only after great uncertainty had the Cyfarthfa lease been renewed in 1862. In that year Anthony Hill died and in 1863 the Plymouth works were sold to the Aberdare Iron Company principally owned by Richard Fothergill. By the 1870s its output had been drastically reduced and it closed in 1875. William Crawshay II died in 1867 and Robert Crawshay, increasingly infirm and inept, sought to sell Cyfarthfa.[299] By the middle of the 1870s the works at Hirwaun, Penydarren, Plymouth, Abernant, Gadlys, Nantyglo, Treforest, Beaufort and Abercarn had all closed.

---

298 I. G. Jones, *Mid-Victorian Wales*, pp. 157-165

299 Addis, *Crawshay Dynasty*, pp. 133-6, 145-6.

These closures were the result of increasing competition from ironworks in Scotland, the north-east of England and north Yorkshire that enjoyed the availability of high quality iron ores at a time when the best of the Welsh ore had largely been worked out. Even when the Welsh works imported ore from Cleveland and Whitehaven they incurred transport costs the English works did not. From the late 1850s competition came too from ironworks in France and Belgium.

The future of Merthyr's economy lay with the exploitation of another of its natural resources, coal. It happened in two ways. First, the ironworks began to sell coal rather than mine it solely for iron-making. It was not a decision agreed jointly, for each works had its own reasons for the timing of its entry into the trade. Anthony Hill at Plymouth had seen the opportunity in the early 1850s. Possibly influenced by the example of Lucy Thomas' pit at neighbouring Waun Wyllt he was by 1859 selling 200,000 tons a year and making a profit of £10,000. Similar developments at Dowlais, already described, were under way by the 1860s. The Crawshays had long maintained, in opposition to the view of their landlords, that they were free to sell coal, but it was only after the lease had been renewed that Cyfarthfa felt it safe to enter the coal trade and sunk the Castle Pit in order to do so.[300]

The exploitation of the previously untapped coal reserves of the southern end of the parish was a separate development. John Nixon, a north of England mining engineer, already a substantial colliery owner at Mountain Ash, began in 1864 to sink a deep colliery at Merthyr Vale. In 1873 F. W. Harris and company began sinking an even deeper pit, appropriately named Deep Navigation, at a place that became known as

[300] The preceding paragraphs are based upon Morris and Williams, *Coal Industry*, pp. 83-91; Edgar Jones, *GKN*, *vol.1*, pp. 249-251, 314-5.

Treharris. Its first coal came up in 1878-9. Its two shafts, one to a depth of 593 metres and the other to 690 metres, were the deepest in the South Wales coalfield at the time. These investments were a direct result of the growth of steam shipping and Nixon's success in opening the French market to imports of Welsh steam coal, including the adoption of Welsh coal by the French navy. He also had a part in the successful British Admiralty trials of Welsh coal.[301]

The result was a significant geographical shift of population and rateable values in the borough. The new townships at Merthyr Vale and Treharris did not have the squalid housing of Merthyr's early years and benefitted from the public health reforms of clean water and mains sewerage. They attracted workers from Wales and England who came to work in the pits rather than in ironworks. By 1881 Merthyr Vale had 500 houses and a population of 3,000 and coal production in the borough was over 1.3 million tons. The demise of the Iron District and the development of collieries in the north and south of the Borough altered Merthyr's status. No longer the centre of an industry but now part of the wider South Wales coalfield, the Merthyr brand signified quality. Of the 14 Rhondda firms on the Admiralty list for the supply of steam coal to the Royal Navy in 1914, ten had the word 'Merthyr' in their title. These developments were more than equalled in the short-term by what had happened in Aberdare, a part of the parliamentary constituency since 1832.

[301] Morris and Williams, pp. 18-19, 31-43; Brian Davies, 'John Nixon and the Welsh Coal Trade to France', *Merthyr Historian* vol. 25, (2013), pp. 251-6.

Aberdare: A New Voice

In 1831 Aberdare's population had been 3,961 compared with Merthyr's 22,083 with only one-fifth of the Merthyr electorate. By 1871 the population of the Aberdare parish had grown to 40,305 while Merthyr's stood at 54,741 and the proportion of Aberdare voters to Merthyr voters in the 1868 Election approached equality: 11,446 voted in Aberdare and 13,329 voted in Merthyr. Aberdare had become a major industrial centre in its own right, like Merthyr predominantly working-class with its own Chartist tradition, newspapers, journals, a Temperance Hall larger than Merthyr's and influential Nonconfomist chapels. The twelve Baptist chapels were the best organised, with Dr. Thomas Price the minister at Calfaria, enthusiastic supporter of the Liberation Society and editor of the widely read *Seren Cymru*, the dominant personality. Although the number of Methodist chapels was almost as numerous as the Baptists, Dissent of the older variety was predominant for in addition to the Baptists there were Independent chapels and the influential Unitarians at Hen dy Cwrdd.

Commercial and business links between Merthyr and its youthful neighbour were close. H.A. Bruce had been born on the family estate at Duffryn, Aberdare, whose coal royalties underpinned his fortune. Richard Fothergill owned the Plymouth and Aberdare ironworks with their associated pits. C. H. James had a solicitor's practice in Aberdare and Thomas Dyke and other Merthyr people were active in the Aberdare Freemasons lodge. But Aberdare had flourished in the past thirty years through the exploitation of steam coal seams in the Cynon valley. The pioneers were the Wayne family. Matthew Wayne, who had been a furnace manager at Cyfarthfa, bought the Gadlys ironworks in 1827 and in June 1837, prompted by his son Thomas, formed a company to exploit the Aberdare four foot seam. When, in November, at a depth of sixty yards they hit the seam it was 'a momentous day in the history of Aberdare'.[302] Between 1840 and 1853 sixteen steam-coal pits were opened in the Cynon valley and the output of coal from the Aberdare parish rose from 177,000 tons in 1844 to over 2,000,000 tons by 1864.[303] Two other Merthyr entrepreneurs opened pits in the valley – Lucy Thomas opened the Lletty Shenkin pit in 1843 and Samuel Thomas, a successful Merthyr grocer, sank the Ysgubor-wen pit the forerunner of the Cambrian Combine in mid-Rhondda. The major developer of the Cynon valley, however, was Thomas Powell. He laid the foundations for the Powell Duffryn Company that by 1869 owned ten of the thirty collieries in the valley. More and more colliers from Merthyr found work and then settled in the Cynon valley where wages were 15 per cent above those in Merthyr.

The Consequences of Reform

The 1867 Reform Act, thanks to Disraeli's audacious determination to outflank the Liberals, was far more radical than had been anticipated. It made male occupiers of houses, including lodgers of twelve months residence, electors. The impact upon Merthyr Boroughs was huge: the number eligible to vote rocketed from under 1,400 to well over 14,000 (1,387

[302] Wilf Owen, 'Matthew Wayne (1780-1853)', *Merthyr Historian, Vol. 26* (2014), pp. 151-160. Despite generously funding St. Mary's Church, Aberdare, Matthew Wayne and his wife were regular worshippers at the Unitarian *Hen-dy-Cwrdd*, Cefn Coed, and are buried there.

[303] Colin Baber and L.J. Williams (eds.), *Modern South Wales: Essays in Economic History* (Cardiff, 1986), p.35. John Williams, *Digest of Welsh Statistics*, Vol. 1 (Cardiff, 1985), p. 341.

to 14,577). Overnight Merthyr Boroughs became in electoral numbers the most democratic constituency in Wales. The Act gave the constituency a second Member of Parliament because of its increased population.There was more to the change than the sheer increase in the number of electors. A large number were colliers who, and especially the Aberdare colliers, brought a history and a voice distinctly more radical than Merthyr's ironworkers. As more and larger pits opened, the number of voters who were colliers steadily increased.

The Aberdare colliers had differences with Bruce that went back to their strikes of 1850 and 1857. The strike from December 1849 to April 1850 had seen the return of Scotch Cattle tactics and a fatal home-made bomb attack upon John Thomas a 'turncoat' who had ignored warnings. The vast majority of colliers had disassociated themselves from the attack but Bruce as stipendiary magistrate had ordered to Cwmbach a detachment of the 13th Regiment at Dowlais Barracks to protect English miners brought in as blacklegs.[304] The strike had collapsed as a result of the successful employment of these outsiders.

In the post-Crimean-war slump of 1857-8 the demand from America for rails had fallen away and the Indian Mutiny meant 'a total cessation of exports to India'. A 20 per cent cut in wages for Merthyr ironworkers and colliers was accepted. In the Aberdare and Rhondda valleys the colliers struck in November 1857 against a 15 per cent reduction and were soon followed by the colliers in Monmouthshire. The strike began in good humour amongst some colliers who

> ...in a state of perfect nudity, were amusing themselves by running races directly in front of the house of one of the masters.

---

[304] *MG*, 12 January to 13 April 1850; Mark Curthoys, *Governments, labour and the Law in Mid-Victorian Britain: The Trade Union Legislation of the 1870s* (Oxford, 2004), p. 150.

> Would it have been believed that such barbarism existed in enlightened Britain in the middle of the nineteenth century?[305]

However, fears that collieries would be flooded led to a detachment of the 22nd Foot being briefly quartered in Aberdare. Bruce as the local MP intervened, had the troops withdrawn to Cardiff and persuaded the Mountain Ash men to return to work. He then addressed a mass meeting of colliers in Aberdare Market Hall and in the second of two speeches attacked the colliers for asking more than the industry could afford, and more than they should expect to receive. It was perfectly possible for them to live on less than they were demanding. He then proceeded to denounce the futility of strikes. The result was that Bruce was identified as an employers' man and the strike continued. The miners eventually went back to work before the beginning of February 1858 on the employers' terms.[306] Throughout all this the Merthyr works continued working.

Ten years later those events were remembered with bitterness during the 1868 election campaign. Some remembered that as a junior minister at the Home Office Bruce had opposed relaxing the law on picketing. And in 1867-8 in the middle of a depression the miners were again at odds with their employers, this time over the emotional issues of safety and working methods. The increasing number of mines being sunk to ever deeper levels raised urgent issues of safety, working conditions, ventilation, inspection and compensation for injuries. Since 1849 nearly 300 men and boys had died in Merthyr and Aberdare collieries from accidents and explosions. Both men and masters were considering ways to improve safety when, on the afternoon of 8 November 1867 an explosion at No. 1

---

[305] *MG*, 5 December 1857.

[306] I. G. Jones, *Communities*, pp. 286-8; Morris and Williams, pp. 252-3.

Ferndale Colliery in Rhondda Fach killed 131 men and boys outright with a final death toll of 178. The horror was compounded in Aberdare and Merthyr for men and boys had moved from those towns to work in the Ferndale pit. Thomas Halliday, soon to be president of the nascent Amalgamated Association of Miners, attended the inquest and spoke afterwards at meetings in the Rhondda on the need for trade union organisation.

John Nixon, chairman of the coalowners' association, major coalowner in the Cynon valley and at Merthyr Vale, was an advocate of the double-shift system which he argued would save lives. The men were adamantly opposed.[307] It was the detailed nature of the colliers' response, and the determined organisation they brought to it, that was significant. They set up a committee that took soundings across the whole coalfield and by May had produced two petitions, one on safety the other on double-shift working, which they gave to Bruce to present to parliament. In the subsequent debate Bruce opposed the miners' recommendations on safety and was inaccurately reported as favouring the employers' views on the double-shift. Despite his explanations the miners decided they would not elect him. For them the age of deference was over.

For the past twenty years they had collaborated with the colliers of Monmouthshire and Rhondda, and steps towards formal trade union membership had been made from time to time. The Cwmbach Co-operative Society had been born out of the 1857 strike, and it was in the Cynon valley that this aspect of independent working-class action flourished.[308] When a

[307] I.G. Jones, *Explorations and Explanations*, pp. 203-11; Morris and Williams, pp. 260-2.

[308] Alun Burge, 'From Cwmbach to Tower: 150 years of collective entrepreneurship in the Cynon Valley, 1860-2010' *Llafur* Vol. 11, No. 1 (2012), pp. 129-148.

seemingly strong and militant trade union came recruiting they signed up in droves. The ironworkers did the same.

In retrospect it is not surprising that Bruce lost his seat. He had succeeded Guest as the choice of the ironmasters and in fifteen years had only faced one contest, when in 1859 he had easily disposed of E.M. Elderton a London solicitor and fellow Liberal. The appearance in 1868 of three candidates for two seats meant that a very different electorate had real choices to make. Against the sitting member old resentments surfaced. The colliers' grievances were the most significant but in Merthyr the influential James faction remembered with bitterness the way their candidate W.M. James had been pushed aside in 1852. Chartists seized on Bruce's continuing opposition to the secret ballot.

George Clark at Dowlais issued a statement that he was voting for Richard and Bruce and consequently not for Fothergill. This created such a controversy that another statement followed in which it was made clear that the Dowlais management wished to 'disabuse the minds of the electors in the employ of the Works from any erroneous impression that undue influence would be exercised over them in favour or against either of the candidates'. At Cyfarthfa Crawshay similarly sought to turn 'the screw' by backing Bruce and requiring his agents to ask each Cyfarthfa voter 'if he does not wish to show some acknowledgement of kind feeling towards his employer' by voting in line with Crawshay's wish.[309] Despite these attempts the increase in the electorate meant that there were too many to be coerced even though there was no secret ballot (voting continued to be a public act until the Ballot Act in 1872).

Richard Fothergill had a foot in both Merthyr and Aberdare.

---

[309] Ieaun Gwynedd Jones, 'Clark and Politics' in Brian Ll. James (ed), *G.T. Clark: Scholar Ironmaster in the Victorian Age* (Cardiff,1998).

He employed some 5,000 workers at his Plymouth and Aberdare ironworks and the mines associated with them. His ownership of the derelict Penydarren works gave hope to some that he was a potential provider of future work. He was for the ballot and the abolition of church rates, and described himself as an ardent Gladstonian. He entered the contest early and many assumed that he and Bruce would be the winners. The commercial middle classes favoured his nomination as a sound Liberal and his Aberdare supporters included the influential Baptist minister, Dr. Thomas Price.

Henry Richard (1812-1888), the outsider, swiftly established himself as the leading contender. His credentials were distinctive: secretary of the Peace Society and leading advocate of international arbitration, a Welsh-speaking Welshman, a former Congregationalist minister who voiced the grievances of Welsh Nonconformity with authority, a believer in the secret ballot and other Chartist aims. He was invited to stand by a Representation Committee to which were affiliated eighty-one Nonconformist congregations in the two valleys, which had at its head C.H. James and whose four secretaries comprised three Unitarians and a Baptist. Large and enthusiastic crowds came to hear his fluent and challenging rhetoric.

> The people who speak this language [Welsh], who read this literature, who own this history, who inherit these traditions, who venerate these names, who created and sustain these marvellous religious institutions, the people forming three fourths of the people of Wales – have they not a right to say to this small propertied class [the landed gentry] ...We are the Welsh people and not you?[310]

[310] *Aberdare Times*, 14 November 1868. Quoted by Kenneth O. Morgan, *Wales in British Politics 1868-1922* (Cardiff, 1963), p. v.

The Chartists too were for Richard. On 22 August 1868, 2,000 to 3,000 working men attended an open-air meeting at which J.W. James, William Gould and George Morgan spoke. Morgan eloquently reminded the audience that Richard was a Nonconformist, an advocate for peace and a Welshman who had mass support. There were influences working against working men

> no doubt mighty influences, but strength was on their side – the waters could be dammed for a time but the flood would increase and bear down all resistance. They would in their triumph raise an animating shout before which tyranny and oppression would fall ...never to rise again.[311]

The voting figures in the election were: Henry Richard 11,683; Richard Fothergill 7,439; H.A. Bruce 5,776. In Merthyr, Fothergill's majority over Bruce was only 236 in a poll of 13,613 but in Aberdare it was 1,427 in a poll of 11,285. The Aberdare miners had made the difference.[312] The result confirmed Merthyr Boroughs as one of the safest Liberal seats in Britain, a centre of radical Nonconformity with Henry Richard as the voice of Welsh national sentiment. From it emerged a more confident working class ready once again to join together in organised trade unionism.

---

[311] Angela V. John, 'The Chartists of Industrial South Wales', M.A. thesis, University of Wales, 1970, pp. 210-11.

[312] *ME*, 21 November 1868. The voting figures for Bruce and Fothergill given here differ from those in I. G. Jones, *Communities*, p. 312.

12

Trade Unions: A False Dawn

> In all parts, even as close to this district as Pontypridd, men are stirring and the principle of "union", which in plain English means opposition to the master, is advocated; but hitherto our district has been free. A charmed circle surrounds us.
>
> **Cardiff and Merthyr Guardian**[313]

The 'charmed circle' was about to break. The largest and most industrialised town in Wales could not be immune from "union". The next five years would see Merthyr at the centre of large-scale strikes and lock-outs, an upsurge of trade unionism in many different trades, police reinforcements and threats of military intervention, a prolonged closure of the great Cyfarthfa works and the collapse of attempts at conciliation and collective bargaining in both coal mining and iron and steel making. Merthyr's former MP, Henry Bruce, as Home Secretary stood centre stage in negotiations with the newly-formed Trades Union Congress and in taking labour legislation through Parliament.

Signs of disaffection among Merthyr ironworkers and colliers could be seen from the mid-1860s. Heavy emigration, often a sign of discontent, threatened to bring more than one pit to a standstill.[314] In 1869 the Dowlais Company in the face of a

---

[313] *MG*, 25 September 1869.

[314] *ME*, 28 April 1865, 17 March 1866.

strike threat accepted the principle of men paying for a checkweighman to ensure that colliers' earnings were properly calculated. Although the appointment of checkweighmen had been sanctioned by the 1860 Coal Mines Regulation Act the South Wales employers strongly resisted it and the Dowlais decision caused general concern. In December 1870 the *Merthyr Guardian* acknowledged that 'the determination to set up a union in the south [of Wales] is very strong'.[315] In fact branches of the Amalgamated Association of Mineworkers (AAM) were already in the area and the workmen of Merthyr were vigorously breaking through the 'charmed circle'. Isaac Connick of Troedyrhiw was the AAM agent for the Merthyr district.

By 1874 Merthyr miners, colliers, ironworkers, smiths and their strikers, engineers, printers, tailors, weavers, skinners, and shoemakers were all in union branches. Delegates from Merthyr and Aberdare attended the foundation conference of the Amalgamated Society of Railway Servants (ASRS) in 1872. In February 1874 it was reported that even unskilled labourers had formed a Merthyr branch of the West of England and South Wales Amalgamated Labourers' Union. In April the printers at the *Merthyr Express, Merthyr Telegraph* and *Y Fellten* came out on strike seeking union recognition. In June 1874 a Merthyr Tydfil Trades Council was formed to provide mutual support and a forum for the different local unions.[316] John Thomas Morgan, printer, publisher and editor of the initially bilingual *Workman's Advertiser* was its founding secretary.[317] In September 1874 skilled men from Cyfarthfa and Dowlais met in the Musical Hall public house in Penydarren to join the

---

[315] *MG,* 25 September 1869, 4 December 1870.

[316] *Workman's Advocate,* 14, 28, February, 4, 11 April, 13 June 1874.

[317] *ME*, 17 July 1875.

Amalgamated Society of Engineers. Thomas Davies Matthias, the energetic and radical Baptist pastor at Bethel, Merthyr, spoke on numerous platforms in these years in support of the miners and ironworkers and in March 1874 was elected to the Merthyr school board as a 'Working-Man's Candidate' displacing Rose Mary Crawshay.[318]

The Unions and the Law

This surge of membership and activity was part of a general growth of British trade unionism in the late 1860s and early 1870s when unemployment was exceptionally low. Until then trade unions existed in small pockets of locally based crafts such as glass and bottle making, coach building, printing and bookbinding, tailoring and cabinet making, or in the large centrally organised Amalgamated Society of Engineers founded in 1851 or the Amalgamated Society of Carpenters and Joiners formed in 1860. Persistent attempts by ironworkers in the north-east and midlands of England to form unions and resist wage cuts resulted in strikes and lock-outs from 1862 onwards. Violent attacks in Sheffield in 1866 upon non-members in the localised metal trades attracted great publicity and caused the Government to set up in 1867 a Royal Commission on Trade Unions. Now in the early 1870s railwaymen, seamen, gas workers, cab-drivers, weavers, elementary school teachers, boot and shoe makers, agricultural labourers, box-makers, coal trimmers and builders' labourers were all forming or joining unions. The reform agitation of the 1860s culminating in the 1867 Reform Act had intensified and strengthened working men's interest in political reforms. The Trades Union Congress,

[318] Aled Jones and John Saville, 'Thomas Davies Matthias (1823-1904), Christian Radical', in Joyce Bellamy and John Saville (eds.), *Dictionary of Labour Biography*, Vol. 7 (1984), pp. 178-82.

first held in Manchester in June 1868, became a political pressure group for organised labour, determined to influence the Liberal government's proposed labour legislation following the Royal Commission's 1869 Report.

Henry Bruce, the Home Secretary, was their target. Bruce's 1871 Trade Union Act gave protection to trade union funds, enabled unions to register as Friendly Societies, and laid down in law that they were not in restraint of trade. It gave the unions much that they wanted but Bruce was uncompromising on the need to punish offences 'which they all knew were sometimes committed by trades unionists'.[319] His 1871 Criminal Law Amendment Act which made 'molestation and obstruction' illegal, and did not contain any exemption for 'peaceful persuasion' by pickets as had the 1859 Molestation of Workmen Act, opened the door to judge-made interpretations that could in effect make picketing illegal. The TUC was bitterly opposed to it, seeing it as class legislation, which Bruce denied. In 1872 and 1873 a series of court judgements confirmed TUC fears. In one case heard at Merthyr magistrate's court seven women were gaoled for a week for 'shouting'. The women had no legal advisor and the man said to have been intimidated did not bring the prosecution.[320]

After Gladstone lost the 1874 election the Disraeli government introduced the Conspiracy and Protection of Property Act 1875 which repealed the Criminal Law Amendment Act, thereby making peaceful picketing legal; and also the 1875 Employer and Workmen Act that made breach of contract a civil rather than a criminal offence. By these Acts the unions were acknowledged to have a legitimate role in society.

---

[319] Quoted by Mark Curthoys, *Governments, Labour and the Law in Mid-Victorian Britain: the Trade Union Legislation of the 1870s* (Oxford, 2004), p. 151.

[320] George Howell, *Labour Legislation, Labour Movements and Labour Leaders* (1904 edition), pp. 205-6.

Colliers Organise

That was the situation in law but the ironmasters and coalowners in South Wales continued to oppose the existence of trade unions. For more than twenty years the colliers had been seeking 'a better understanding between master and man'. On Hirwaun Common in March 1850 during the Aberdare strike assembled workmen heard that The Glamorganshire Union of Colliers had been formed. Evan Miles, a collier, spoke eloquently of using 'the weapons of reason and rational argument'.

> Workmen did not complain of their station in life as they knew that different gradations must necessarily exist; but they complained of tyranny to them as a generation of workmen ... everybody has a right to live by his property; but the workmen had no property except their hands which they had the right to live by and to dispose of in the most advantageous way possible. They had been sent into the world and they had a claim to live in it; they had a right to breathe the pure air of heaven and to obtain by fair and peaceable means the best market price for their labour.[321]

Little came of this 'Glamorganshire Union' but the speech by Miles and similar ones by leaders of the 1857 strike illustrate the miners' conciliatory but determined leadership. Unity among South Wales colliers, and indeed among the coalowners, was retarded by the coalfield's division into valleys separated by 'mountains' which hampered communications, the existence of three types of coal – anthracite, bituminous and steam – each with its own markets and labour issues, and the increasing

[321] *MG*, 16 March 1850.

number of colliers employed by the ironworks on lower wages than those not employed by ironworks. Tension between the coalowners and colliers was heightened during strikes by the frequent importation of labour to replace the strikers, a tactic that contributed to the defeat of the strikers but also led to violence and bitterness.

In August 1869 the Amalgamated Association of Miners (AAM), was founded in Lancashire and a month later at Pontypridd began to recruit in South Wales where Thomas Halliday its President had contacts forged in the aftermath of the Ferndale colliery explosion. It was this initiative that the *Merthyr Guardian* had referred to on 29 September. In the boom of 1871 came the first of three large-scale strikes. It was triggered when the ironmasters gave an increase to their colliers and the Rhondda and Aberdare colliers in response sought a 5 per cent pay increase. Their employers, despite the rising price of coal, insisted upon a wage cut in order to bring the wages of their colliers closer to those in the employ of the ironworks. The colliers came out on a strike that lasted for twelve weeks during which the AAM gave financial assistance to those, members and non-members, who were not working. The strike was resolved by the coalowners agreeing to an arbitration which resulted in a 2.5 per cent increase to the colliers. It also stipulated that in future wages at sea-coal pits should be determined by changes in the rates paid to all employees at the ironworks. While this took arbitrary decision-making on pay away from the coalowners it also meant that pay rates in the sea-coal industry would depend upon the fluctuations in the iron trade and the decisions of the ironmasters. It was an agreement that could not be sustained.

The AAM emerged with a much strengthened reputation in South Wales. By the early summer of 1871 it had 5,300 members within the Merthyr Borough constituency – 3,000 in and around Aberdare, 1,300 in nine lodges at Mountain Ash, and a further 1,000 in nine lodges at Merthyr. By June its combined membership in the Rhondda and Aberdare valleys was 9,000.[322] In October its annual conference was held at Merthyr.

It was during this strike that David Morgan, born in Cefn Coed in 1840, addressed a crowd of over 7,000 on the need for arbitration and was selected as one of the colliers' representatives at the talks that settled the strike.[323] Brought up in Merthyr he attended the Unitarian Sunday school in Twynyrodyn and illegally started work at seven-years-old as an air-door keeper at Cyfarthfa colliery. In 1858 he had moved to the Aberdare valley to work underground in the Navigation Colliery. A tall imposing figure with a strong tenor voice he was generally known as *Dai o'r Nant*, a reference to his parents who had kept the Full Moon pub in Nantygwenith, Merthyr Tydfil. In 1872 he became a member of the union's executive committee.

Ironworkers Organise

Meanwhile, amidst the spread of trade union ideas and the initial success of Halliday's organisation, skilled ironworkers were increasingly apprehensive of the change from iron to steel-making with its threat to the jobs of puddlers and other process workers. In addition, there was resentment that Welsh wages were lower than those in north-east England and Staffordshire. Since 1869 there had existed the Board of Conciliation and Arbitration for the Manufactured Iron Trade of the North of

---

[322] Eric Evans, *The Miners*, pp. 101-3.

[323] David A. Pretty, 'David Morgan ('Dai o'r Nant), Miners' Agent: A portrait of leadership in the South Wales Coalfield', *Welsh History Review* Vol.20, no. 3 (June 2001).

England which the ironmasters and the National Amalgamated Association of Malleable Ironworkers led by John Kane (1819-1876) had established to end the exhausting strikes of the 1860s.[324] There was no recent militant history in Merthyr but Kane's union, whose members were puddlers, rollermen, shinglers and other skilled workers, was attractive to Welsh ironworkers threatened by technological change. By 1872 the union's membership in South Wales numbered 1,800. Kane, one of the founders of the TUC was a frequent speaker in Merthyr during 1872-75 at conferences and mass meetings.

In late 1872 a temporary depression in the iron industry caused the ironmasters to announce a 10 per cent reduction in wages. Under the terms of the 1871 arbitration award the sea-coal colliers would also be affected even though the price of coal was rising. Colliers and ironworkers employed by the ironworks resisted the proposed cut and a strike began on 1 January 1873. The sea-coal colliers remained in work during the strike, awaiting its outcome. Once again the AAM gave financial assistance to the ironworks colliers on strike. The Amalgamated Ironworkers union imposed a shilling levy upon its members in work, raised £9,777 by this means and paid over £10,000 to some 1,700 members who were locked out, mainly at Dowlais, Cyfarthfa and Plymouth. The strike/lock-out lasted eleven weeks creating considerable hardship. A strike aid committee set up in early 1873 included T.D. Matthias along with Halliday, Isaac Connick and Henry Thomas the agent for the Aberdare district.

Soup kitchens were set up at Blaina, Nantyglo, Brynmawr, Treforest, and at Merthyr where 500 quarts of soup and 500

[324] N.P. Howard, 'The Strikes and Lockouts in the Iron Industry and the Formation of the Ironworkers' Unions, 1862-1869', *International Review of Social History*, Vol. 18, No. 3 (December 1973), pp. 396-427.

slices of bread were distributed daily.[325] Many Merthyr colliers employed by the ironworks found work in the Rhondda sea-sale collieries. In mid-March an improvement in the iron trade helped to bring about a settlement; the men accepting a token reduction in pay of 5 per cent for five days. During this bitter eleven-week struggle the AAM increased its membership in South Wales to over 45,000.[326] It now brought together sea-coal miners in the Rhondda, Cynon, Taff and Monmouthshire valleys along with colliers who worked for the ironworks.

The strike also enabled the Amalgamated Ironworkers to make a major breakthrough in the unionisation of ironworkers in South Wales, its membership spectacularly increasing to 15,491 in 110 lodges.[327] A demonstration held by the Merthyr and Dowlais Districts of the union in September 1873 illustrates the buoyant mood. It culminated in Penydarren Park, Merthyr Tydfil, 'kindly lent' by R. Fothergill, MP.

> The lodges in the upper portion of the district marched down through the principal street, preceded by the 12th Glamorgan Rifle Volunteers' band and the Penydarren Fife and Drum Band. At the lower end of the town several other lodges joined the procession, and on returning through the High-street presented a very creditable and imposing appearance; a party of Christy's Minstrels in the rear causing some amusement.

Some 2,000 ironworkers marched, all wearing white rosettes. A resolution was passed 'believing that the interests of [capital and labour] are mutual and reciprocal' and calling for 'the formation of a board of conciliation and of arbitration, to settle

---

[325] *ME*, 8 February 1873.

[326] Evans, *The Miners*, p. 108.

[327] Arthur Pugh, *Men of Steel*, pp. 11 and 48.

all disputes and disagreements between the employers and employed'.[328] This was an attempt to replicate the Conciliation Board in the north of England, essentially a device to avoid strikes. The advantage to ironworkers would be the acceptance of their union as part of the Board's procedures and, although a sliding-scale based on the price of iron would largely determine the level of wages, the decisions on wage cuts and advances would no longer rest solely in the hands of the masters.

Changing Attitudes

Neither Robert Crawshay at Cyfarthfa nor George Clark at Dowlais would stomach such a deal.[329] Cyfarthfa and Dowlais lived on as family-owned firms where personal rule still mattered, where Clark's dominant personality was widely recognised and where Robert Crawshay, like his forbears, was still referred to as 'the Iron King'. The other works in the once 'iron district' had either gone out of business or were now joint-stock companies. The entry of Cyfarthfa and Dowlais into the sale-coal market meant however that they could not ignore the growing strength of Halliday's Associated Mineworkers union and the realisation pressed home by the 1873 strike that the coalowners needed to present a united front against that union. Reluctantly, therefore, Crawshay and Clark joined the Monmouthshire and South Wales Coalowners Association established in 1873 which brought together 85 companies owning 222 pits and included ironmasters as well as sale-coal owners.

By 1873 colliers and ironworkers in South Wales, through

---

[328] *Workman's Advocate,* 13 September 1873.

[329] *ME,* 1 February 1873.

exposure to the more sophisticated arguments prevalent in the English-dominated unions, had undergone a fundamental shift of attitude. They were asking a new question. They remained in favour of conciliation and arbitration rather than brute trials of strength through strikes and lock-outs – despite the growth in union membership the financial cost of strikes was crippling both to the men and to the unions – but it was no longer enough for the masters to demonstrate a fall in the price of iron or coal as a reason for a wage cut. The new question was: what profits were being made? As *The Times* pointed out: 'They want to know whether they have a fair share in the returns of business, and they begin to doubt whether, even if the price of iron has fallen, the Masters can fairly reduce their wages.' For the first time in more than eighty years the proportion between wages and profits was being questioned.

> The immediate issue, therefore on which the strike turns is not so much the rate of wages as whether the Masters shall be the sole judges of that rate. The Masters are ready to submit the facts of the trade to independent inquiry, but reserve the inferences to themselves. The Men ask that both facts and inferences shall be submitted to Arbitration.[330]

The stage was set for the next confrontation. That came in 1874-5 when the economic tide turned and coal and iron prices fell. The AAM's finances had been undermined by the support it had given to disputes in 1873 so, when in May 1874 and again in August wage reductions of 10 per cent were announced, the colliers were advised to accept them. The owners refused to provide information about the actual cost of coal production and when a further reduction of 10 per cent

[330] *The Times*, 11 January 1873.

was announced in December a strike inevitably followed. A number of the colliers and miners in the ironworks accepted the reduction and returned to work, whereupon the Coalowners Association pointed out that this breach of their united policy opened the possibility of men in work financing those on strike. As a result a general lock-out, including ironworks, began on 1 February 1875.

Cyfarthfa Lock-out

In Merthyr disaster had already struck. Fothergill's Aberdare Iron Company was in financial difficulties. In 1865 it had bought the Penydarren works but the furnaces were never relit. Financial problems accumulated during the troublesome 1870s and by 1875 both the Plymouth and Gadlys works had closed. These events were minor, however, compared to what was happening at Cyfarthfa. Robert Crawshay in failing health and faced with trade union demands that offended his tradition of direct dealing with 'his' men, had since 1872 been trying to sell the Cyfarthfa works for £1 million.[331] Then, on 9 May 1874 Crawshay announced that he had no orders and that he could no longer continue stockpiling iron. All employment contracts would be terminated and only renewed if those manufacturing iron accepted a 20 per cent cut in wages. For day-wage men there would be a 10 per cut. 'If they did not like to work at that rate the furnaces would be blown out and the works closed'.[332] Three weeks later the other South Wales ironworks announced a ten per cut which was accepted. The Cyfarthfa men refused the 20 per cent cut.[333] In July a 20 per cent cut was imposed at Dowlais.

[331] Addis, pp. 145-7.

[332] *Merthyr Telegraph*, 8 May 1874.

[333] *Workman's Advocate*, 6 June 1874.

There was then a move to return to work by some of the Cyfarthfa men and then a decision not to. Robert Crawshay stood his ground and one by one the furnaces at Cyfarthfa were blown out, the last in March 1875.

Hundreds of men travelled to other districts for work, returning to their families at weekends, while others left for America and Australia. Hundreds more accepted parish relief in return for stone-breaking. Wives begged for food from door-to-door. An appeal for funds to feed the children was launched by the Rector. Donations from the rest of Britain, from Germany, France and from an Indian judge poured in and daily for fifteen weeks from the beginning of March an average of 4,000 children were fed at the soup kitchens in Merthyr, Dowlais, Cefn Coed, Abercanaid and Troedyrhiw.[334] (The Poor Law Guardians aided the ironmasters and coalowners by refusing relief to strikers, a story told in chapter 16.) The general lock-out ended with an agreement signed on 28 May 1874 that colliers' wages would be reduced by 12.5 per cent for three months and thereafter would be determined by a joint committee composed of six employers and six men's representatives. This committee would negotiate the details of a sliding scale linked to the average price of coal, not iron, that would regulate colliers' wages.

The AAM, bankrupted by this prolonged and rancorous conflict, collapsed entirely and was succeeded in South Wales by district unions which elected representatives to the Sliding Scale Committee.[335] The dominant personality on the union side

[334] Dr. Dyke, *Eleventh Annual Report on the Sanitary Condition of Merthyr Tydfil Being that for the Year 1875,* pp. 13-14.

[335] J.H. Morris and L.J. Williams, 'The South Wales Sliding Scale, 1876-79: An Experiment in Industrial Relations' in W.E. Minchinton (ed.), *Industrial South Wales 1750-1914* (1969); Evans, *The Miners*, pp. 110-113.

was the charismatic William Abraham (Mabon), brilliant orator in English and Welsh, a Methodist and enthusiastic *eisteddfodwr*. A firm believer that the interests of employers and workers were essentially the same he became full-time agent in 1877 for the Rhondda Cambrian Miners' Association and was elected MP for the Rhondda in 1885, the first of the remarkably talented trade union leaders and politicians to emerge from the South Wales coalfield over the next fifty years. The owners' chief representative was W.T. Lewis, later Lord Merthyr. The principle and details of the agreement carried a number of disadvantages to the men, some of which only became apparent after several years experience.[336] But a form of mining trade unionism, albeit much weakened, survived in South Wales and for seventeen years the sliding scale largely eliminated large-scale strikes in the South Wales coal industry although, 'with changing geological conditions making for a fruitful source of disputes at individual pits', 'unofficial' and 'illegal' stoppages of work continued.[337]

Cyfarthfa

The Cyfarthfa works did not reopen in May 1875. Robert Crawshay no longer took pleasure in the works. His daughter Trotty had noted the year before: 'The works and men are a great bother to him. I fear he is getting sour and hardened'.[338] In February 1876 a written petition from the Cyfarthfa men asked for the works to be re-opened. They expressed their sincere regret that they had

---

[336] Evans, *The Miners*, pp. 117-123.

[337] John Williams, 'Miners and the Law of Contract, 1875-1914', *Llafur,* vol.4, no. 2 (1985), pp. 36-51.

[338] Quoted by Margaret Stewart Taylor, *The Crawshays of Cyfarthfa Castle* (1967), p.154.

> committed the blunder they did in the spring of 1874 ...They had lived to see it was a grievous mistake, but having abandoned all forms of union, they threw themselves upon his kind consideration, and begged him to do something for them by reopening the works.

Robert Crawshay responded that the closure had saved him 'an immense sum of money' but he was glad they had 'taken a reasonable view of things at last; the difficulty now was to get any orders at all' and 'whether the workmen would be willing to accept such rates as he could afford to give, provided he could get any orders. The deputation said they would.'[339] The works remained silent. Further pleas were made but the works were still closed when Robert Crawshay died on 10 May 1879.

Robert's three sons, William Thompson, Robert Thompson, and Richard Frederick Crawshay carried on the business under the name of Crawshay Brothers and Company. When production restarted in the first week of November 1879, Merthyr's High Constable, David Williams, gave away 600 quarts of home brew to the Cyfarthfa workmen, 'so that they might exhibit their joy in the restarting of these important works'. And 'an influential tradesman' claimed to have 'changed more £5 notes on Saturday than he has done for five years'.[340] The brothers spent £150,000 to convert Cyfarthfa to steel production. The strain on their finances compelled them in 1890 to seek incorporation as a limited liability company.

---

[339] *ME*, 19 February 1876.

[340] *Colliery Guardian*, 14, 21 November 1879. For the re-opening see *Merthyr Telegraph*, 31 October, 7, 14, 21 November 1879.

Red Dragon Unions

After 1875 the Welsh branches of the Ironworkers' Union ceased to exist altogether and for more than a decade nothing took their place. But behind the defeat of the miners' and ironworkers' unions in the great strike/lock-out of 1875 there lay a particular reason for their collapse in South Wales. Both unions were criticised and deserted by hundreds of their South Wales members who were suspicious of the use made of the central funds and the level of 'unnecessary' expenditure on officers. A letter from 'A Cwm Rhondda Collier' in the *Merthyr Express*, 14 November 1874, claimed:

> There was too much of our money going to England, and too much spent in ways we didn't approve. Hundreds of pounds were spent by officers riding about for their own pleasure, though they managed to put in some sort of a show of work for the union.

The correspondence rumbled on. In July 1875 a writer asked of Halliday, 'What has he done, and what can he do, except to spend the workman's money and drive the bread and cheese from South Wales up to England to give them plenty while we starve'?[341] In part this attitude was a reflection of the prevailing localism in British trade unionism, evident in the separate English county mining organisations, the fragmented district organisation of the Amalgamated Society of Railway Servants, the separatism of Scottish unions, and, co-terminous with the disaffection in South Wales, a similar rebellion in the Forest of Dean against the leaders of the AAM and their centrally-determined actions.

[341] *ME*, 10 and 17 July 1875.

There was more, however, to the opposition in Wales than an inadequate understanding of the necessity for unity and central co-ordination of decision-making in major strikes. A distinct strain of nationalism appeared in the arguments used. The *Merthyr Telegraph* whilst welcoming trade union organisation in both the north and south of Wales, supported disaffection with the England-based unions, referring to men no longer willing 'to submit to foreign domination' and the days of 'alien agitators' being numbered.[342] Similar arguments appeared in the *South Wales Daily News*. There was, of course, potential for a variety of misunderstandings between the headquarters in England and the Welsh membership as within both the mining and ironworkers' unions many members were solely Welsh-speaking. In the AAM three-quarters of the Welsh membership were said not to understand English.[343]

There was a move to set up Welsh unions where all business would be conducted through the medium of Welsh. Branches would have Welsh names. A lively debate, for and against the new unions blossomed in the local Welsh language newspapers. 'What is the old union ...?' inquired one writer in Welsh. 'Answer: worship of the English, waste and tyranny.'[344] The decisions to form breakaway Welsh unions were taken in Merthyr. Members of the AAM met at the Corner House Hotel in Merthyr on Saturday, 20 June 1874 and resolved to establish a new miners' union with the title 'Y Ddraig Goch/The Red Dragon'. Also in June 1874 there were calls for a breakaway ironworkers' union with the main voices coming from Rhymney,

342 *Merthyr Telegraph*, 7 August, 27 November 1874.

343 Richard Burton Archive, Swansea University, 1874 AAM Conference Report. SWCC/MNB/PP/1; 1-3.

344 *Y Gwladgarwr*, 1 August 1874, quoted in Aled Jones, 'Trade Unions and the Press: Journalism and the Red Dragon Revolt of 1874', *WHR*, vol. 12, (December 1984).

Dowlais and Tredegar. Within a few weeks of a meeting in the Cross Keys Inn at Merthyr on 4 July thousands of ironworkers had joined a new union called the Ironworkers' Association for South Wales and Monmouthshire. Neither breakaway union lasted long. After briefly flourishing, both fell apart in the face of employer repression, as had the nation-wide English-based miners' and ironworkers' unions.

Low unemployment between 1868 and 1874 had helped trade union membership in Britain to rise to around one million. In the prolonged depression after 1874 many of these members were lost. Unions that had recruited unskilled workers largely disappeared. But there were survivors from the wreckage. The unions of the skilled – engineers, boilermakers, printers, carpenters – grew nationally, and branches continued in Merthyr although they were not recognised at Cyfarthfa or Dowlais. New unions – teachers, railwaymen, boot and shoe workers – survived and grew. By 1897 a Merthyr man, Richard Bell, had become General Secretary of the Amalgamated Society of Railway Servants. The miners' district unions in South Wales survived in an emasculated form to fight again another day. And when they did come together it was as a South Wales organisation based not on national feeling but because South Wales differed in nature from other coalfields. It was an exporting coalfield with a variety of coals and difficult geological conditions that largely ruled out mechanisation. Coal-getting came down to men wielding picks and shovels. But trade unionism took a back seat until 1898. It is time to examine the nature and ambitions of the small but extremely significant Merthyr middle class.

13

Unitarians, Freemasons, Radicals

> In the ...process ...which was fusing village and ironworks settlements into a new urban community ...the crucial role was played by that social group which has largely been an absentee from our social history, the town middle class.
>
> **Gwyn A. Williams[345]**

> 'The masters were masters, and the rest of us simply their serfs ...The middle classes are ignored'.
>
> **David Evans[346]**

When David Evans, an auctioneer, gave a public lecture in October 1874 and spoke of 'the undue influence exercised by the ironmasters over our local affairs', he added: 'I do not believe that the ironmasters pay that proportion of the rates which a more equitable adjustment of the rateable value would produce'.[347] The level of rates, who should pay them and in what proportion lay at the heart of local politics. Three Acts of Parliament – the Poor Law Amendment Act 1834, the Municipal Corporation Act 1835 and the Public Health Act

---

345 Williams, *The Merthyr Rising*, 55.

346 *ME*, 23 December 1876. See also the attack by Rev. Charles White, minister of High Street Baptist chapel, upon the ironmasters and references to 'sycophantic twaddle' in his letter 'A Park for Merthyr' in *The Merthyr Telegraph*, 23 June 1866.

347 *The Merthyr Telegraph*, 23 October 1874.

1848 – and their local application became battlegrounds fought over by the ironmasters, the workers and the middle class. But who in Merthyr Tydfil could be called 'middle class'?

The general opinion among contemporaries, echoed later by historians, was that early nineteenth century Merthyr did not possess a middle class. The town was so grimy, its proletarian character so unmistakeable, its social structure so simple, divided between masters and workers. Unquestionably, despite the town's growth, 'the middling classes' in Merthyr compared with other towns remained relatively and absolutely few. Out of a population of over 22,000 in 1832 the number of householders who were rated at £10 per year, and thereby qualified for the vote, was around 450 (some fifty of the electorate of 502 lived in Aberdare). Merthyr and York had populations of roughly the same size in 1841. But 22 per cent of the York population was in the top socio-economic groups 1 and 2 compared with 6.2 per cent at Merthyr.[348] By 1860, when Merthyr was still the largest town in Wales, one in six adult males in Cardiff paid income tax, in Swansea one in seven. In Merthyr it was one in fifteen.[349]

The problem was not merely numbers. There was a lack of 'quality'. The notion of 'quality' arose from a conception of the middle class as leisured gentry. Traditionally, where the gentry established residence in towns they took the lead in voluntary civic duties, acted as magistrates and patrons of the arts, performed good works, set standards of refined taste. No-one in Merthyr, it was said, was of independent means and position, resident in the town but above the interests of industry and

---

[348] Harold Carter and Sandra Wheatley, *Merthyr Tydfil in 1851* (Cardiff, 1982), pp. 13, 18.

[349] W. D. Rubinstein, 'The size and distribution of the English middle classes in 1860', *Historical Research,* 61 (February, 1988).

commerce.[350] This was largely, if not entirely, true. Merthyr Tydfil, an explosion of industry and urban squalor certainly did not have gentry.

Who was Middle Class?

Who then in Merthyr were of the middling orders? Their economic position was defined by their sources of income: rent, trading profits, and fees. The ironmasters, of course, in the context of the British class system were middle class. But in the context of Merthyr they were potentates: their power and authority universal. We must leave them to one side. In pre-industrial Merthyr the tiny middle class consisted largely of freehold landowners, independent weavers, Church of England clergy, carriers, shopkeepers and innkeepers. From the last quarter of the eighteenth century onwards, these rural occupations were augmented by wholesale traders, brewers, small manufacturers, company agents, schoolteachers, auctioneers, nonconformist ministers of religion, pharmacists – added to which there was a smattering of those traditionally recognized as being of middle-class status; gentlemen with independent incomes, lawyers, surgeons, former naval and military officers.

Altogether few in number they were self-consciously a distinct class and they were not without talent. Shopkeepers with their business acumen and eye for financial detail made those with civic ambition obvious choices for offices such as overseer of the poor, surveyor of highways, churchwarden. Throughout the nineteenth century the politically minded middle class members

---

350 G. T. Clark, 'Iron manufacture in south Wales' *Westminster Review* (1848); T. W. Rammell, *Report to the General Board of Health... into... the sanitary condition of Merthyr Tydfil* (1850); William Kay, *Report of the sanitary condition of Merthyr Tydfil* (Merthyr Tydfil, 1854).

sought and gained election to the plethora of local committees; the select vestry, the Board of Guardians, the local board of health, the school board, the burial board, the urban district council. Merthyr's chief civic office, the antiquarian and largely pointless High Constable of the Hundred of Upper Senghenydd, was theirs throughout the period.[351]

Some enjoyed considerable income. Among the most comfortable was William Thomas (1794-1858) of The Court; magistrate, substantial landowner, Anglican, and proud to be 'an aborigine of the place'. A trained doctor who had married into money, his taste for racy jokes and his attachment to all things Merthyr made him a popular character. Much less popular was William Meyrick the parish solicitor. Son of a Neath publican he had grown wealthy acting for William Crawshay in legal disputes. When Crawshay moved out of Gwaelodygarth House, and into Cyfarthfa Castle, Meyrick bought it from him for £2,500. In 1835 he briefly challenged Josiah Guest for the parliamentary seat.[352] Another influential person was J.B. Bruce the first stipendiary magistrate who owned mineral-rich lands in the Cynon valley. All three were Tories and not typical of Merthyr's growing middle class.

For economics did not alone define this group. The local families carried a radical tradition that stretched back to the Civil War. They believed that freedom of worship was the foundation of all freedoms. From the 1780s as Merthyr burgeoned, opportunities for trade increased and immigrants with their own history of Nonconformist thought reinforced the local radicalism.[353] Prominent among these was the formidably

---

[351] Wilkins, *History*, pp. 360–2.

[352] Williams, *The Rising*, p. 58.

[353] See the account of one family's radical connections: Caroline E. Williams, *A Welsh Family from the beginning of the Eighteenth Century* (1885).

intelligent and handsome James family from Whitchurch. Unitarian in faith and largely composed of astute businessmen and lawyers this family was to be a force in Merthyr politics throughout the nineteenth and into the twentieth century.

Unitarians were the civic leaders in early nineteenth century Merthyr. Certainly fewer than a hundred, their political influence as in Manchester, Birmingham, Leeds, Liverpool and Newcastle was out of all proportion to their number.[354] They were the left wing of a radicalism that attacked the old order of Church and Aristocracy on grounds of liberty of conscience, justice and equality. They were for the secret ballot, male suffrage, and the incorporation of towns; and against trade unions, the Corn Laws and 'taxes on knowledge'. Naturally they were against the Established Church with its bishops, rents and tithes.

An active core of the middle class, largely though not exclusively Nonconformist, linked by networks of family and marriage, business interests, religious and voluntary associations, fought political battles in key areas – public health, municipal incorporation, civic amenities including a town hall – that reinforced their consciousness of sharing interests separate from those of the Anglican ironmasters or the turbulent lower classes. Before Merthyr's workers achieved a coherent political stance a nucleus of its middle class already possessed a radical tradition and around this gathered others who wished for reform. The fact is that the Merthyr middle class sought to play a political role during the nineteenth century no different from that played by middle-class elites in other British towns

[354] Tristram Hunt, *Building Jerusalem*, pp. 140–45; Asa Briggs, *Victorian Cities* (Harmondsworth, 1977), ch. 5; John Seed, 'Unitarianism, political economy and the antinomies of liberal culture in Manchester, 1830–50', *Social History*, 7 (1) (1982).

at the time.[355] That role has been obscured by the emphasis placed upon 'Merthyr's working class tradition'. Despite the perception that Gwyn A. Williams was 'a people's remembrancer', an historian of the working class, as indeed he was, he did more than anyone to illuminate the significance of the middle class in early nineteenth century Merthyr and uncover the roots and flowering of its radicalism.

Yet small numbers did bring limitations. Merthyr never had the numbers, ambition, or range of scientific interests of those who founded the Swansea Scientific Society in 1835 and gave that town an intellectual and cultural life which was at the centre of *its* urban identity.[356] In 1807 with the formation of a Philosophical Society, in 1837 with attempts at a Literary Society, and in 1846 with the founding of a subscription library, the Merthyr middle class sought to promote debate and promulgate scientific and literary knowledge. But for too many, and to the exclusion of other interests, Merthyr was both a place to make money and one in which it was a daily struggle to survive.

In the aftermath of the 1831 upheaval the middle-class radicals did achieve two significant successes. At local level they

[355] R. J. Morris, *Class, Sect and Party. The Making of the British Middle Class, Leeds, 1820–1850* (Manchester, 1990); T. Koditschek, *Class Formation and Urban-Industrial Society: Bradford, 1750–1850* (Cambridge, 1990); J. Smith, 'Urban elites c.1830–1930 and urban history', *Urban History*, 27,2 (2000). For Cardiff, Martin J. Daunton, *Coal Metropolis: Cardiff 1870–1914* (Cardiff, 1977); For Denbigh, J.W. Pritchard, '"Fit and proper persons": Councillors of Denbigh, their status and position, 1835-1894', *WHR* 17, No. 2 (1994); for Swansea, Louise Miskell, *'Intelligent Town': An Urban History of Swansea, 1780–1855* (Cardiff, 2006). For Pontypool and Bridgend, Julie Light, 'The Middle Classes as Urban Elites in Nineteenth Century South Wales', *Urban History*, 32, 1 (2005)

[356] Miskell, *Intelligent Town*, pp. 158ff.

secured control of the select vestry where twelve attempts in three years to levy a church rate were voted down and where they replaced Meyrick the Tory parish solicitor with the workers' advocate William Perkins. Then in 1836 they gained a majority of the Merthyr seats on the new Board of Guardians. But this was only half their success. Josiah John Guest, the master of Dowlais, had captured the Merthyr seat with the support of the James faction. He favoured local public health reforms and advocated municipal incorporation for Merthyr. On these substantial issues he was aligned with the local radicals and in opposition to the views of his fellow ironmasters.

The Loyal Cambrian Lodge

Just as the working class through benefit societies and attempts to form trade unions built alliances that provided mutual assistance and reinforced their class identity, so the middle class recognized a similar need. For them, marriage, business partnerships, sectarian beliefs and cultural networks were key institutions. One of the latter was Freemasonry. A striking number of the radicals that supported Guest in the 1830s were Freemasons – members of the Loyal Cambrian Lodge founded in Merthyr in 1810. Nor was this accidental: membership of the fraternity is by invitation.[357] In its early years the Lodge struggled to survive, being largely a meeting place for commercial travellers and by the winter of 1827–8 was almost defunct. It was resuscitated partly through the efforts of Thomas Burnell, chandler, member of the select vestry and church warden, who in 1831 gave evidence in support of Dic

[357] Unless otherwise noted, all references to Freemasonry and Freemasons in Merthyr are from J. Fraser, *An Illustrated History of the Loyal Cambrian Lodge, Merthyr Tydfil, 1810–1914* (Merthyr Tydfil, 1914).

Penderyn. It may or may not be significant that in January 1828 the initiation took place of William Aubery, who twenty-one years earlier had been a founder of the Cyfarthfa Philosophical Society. But the initiation of Rhys Davis (1797–1847), draper and postmaster, in January 1830 was certainly so. A friend of Iolo Morgannwg and supporter of Guest in the fevered politics of the 1830s his family connections make him a pivotal figure in middle-class politics. From the beginning of 1831 there was a compelling surge of radicals into the Lodge. The influence here may have been Guest himself. He had been initiated into Freemasonry at the Glamorgan Lodge on 5 April 1810 and in 1836 he was appointed Provincial Grand Master for South Wales, a position he held until 1848. Not until July 1840, however, did he join the Loyal Cambrian Lodge becoming Worshipful Master of the lodge in the next month.

A more likely candidate as the organizer of what amounted to a take over of the lodge is Edward Hutchins who was initiated on 3 February 1831. Hutchins was Guest's 22-year-old nephew, educated at Charterhouse and St. John's, Cambridge, and holder of two shares in the Dowlais enterprise.[358] Politically aware and at this time more radical than his uncle, Hutchins was in the thick of reform movements. On 23 December 1830 he spoke at the mass meeting in the parish church that drew up a petition calling for annual parliaments, the abolition of rotten boroughs, the ballot, members of parliament for large towns, a vote for all who contributed directly, or indirectly, to national or local taxation and the dismissal of placemen from the Commons.[359] In the

[358] Hutchins was the son of Edward Hutchins of Briton Ferry and Sarah Guest, Josiah John's sister. He was MP for Penryn and Falmouth 1840–41 and for Lymington 1850–57. He sold his Dowlais shares in 1851 to Sir John for £58,000, thus enabling Guest to become the sole owner.

spring of 1831 he, with other of the town's radicals, supported the Reform Bill and agitated for Merthyr's claim to a parliamentary seat. In the aftermath of the June insurrection he served on the select vestry, losing no opportunity to rally support for radical causes and the political advancement of his uncle. He was installed as Worshipful Master of the Loyal Cambrian Lodge on 20 December 1832 and again the following year. There followed a steady recruitment of Guest supporters into the lodge.

The recruits fall into two groups: the known radicals; and those who were employees of the Dowlais works or tradesmen from that community who were subject to Guest's influence. The radicals included some of the most experienced activists. Roland (or Rowland) Hopkins, brewer, was initiated on 1 December 1831. Prominent in local politics he was elected to the first Board of Guardians in 1836 when the radicals and Guest's supporters overwhelmed the opposition in the Merthyr parish of the Union. William Purnell, Dowlais grocer and radical was initiated on 2 February 1832. Like Hopkins, he too was elected to the first Board of Guardians. Thomas Darker, leading publicist for the Guest cause was initiated on 16 February 1832. He had served as churchwarden, overseer of the poor and since 1822 as select vestryman. The first man in Merthyr to use gas by illuminating his grocery and drapery store, the furnishings of his house ostentatiously proclaimed his middle-class status. It was 'stocked with very superior mahogany, a superior piano and an elegant organ, "big enough for a chapel"'. In case of thieves, he slept with two large pistols loaded with swan shot at his pillow. In the 1835 election campaign he was the Merthyr correspondent for the *Hereford Times*.[360]Another

[359] Williams, *The Rising,* pp. 95–6.

[360] Williams, *The Rising*, p. 53; idem. '1835 election'.

experienced local politician was William Teague, keeper of the Swan inn at Dowlais who was initiated in July 1832. Appointed a parish overseer in March 1831 he was a member of the reform committee set up to investigate parish administration. Upon initiation, he took an active part in the lodge, holding 'Lodges of instruction' on Sundays at his house. It is likely that he was the object of the *Merthyr Guardian*'s sneer that, if there were a Corporation, 'What forbids that every office in the Corporation shall be filled by mere ten pound voters? The radical Beer-house keepers of Dowlais.'[361]

Along with these members of the shopocracy the Lodge enrolled the two leading radical lawyers. In April 1833 Edward Lewis Richards, son of the keeper of the Greyhound pub, and former student at Gray's Inn, became an Honorary Member of the lodge. He was to become in 1842 the first County Court Judge in Flintshire, and subsequently Chairman of Flintshire Quarter Sessions. A strong radical and admirer of Cobbett, he had ferociously attacked Guest in 1830 for running a truck shop but had subsequently become a firm supporter. (Guest gave up the truck shop on becoming MP for Merthyr.) In November 1831 he had proposed that 'the upper class of workmen' should be sworn as special constables.[362] Richards presented to the lodge a 'loving cup' which, filled with Madeira was used on ceremonial occasions (and apparently still is). In May 1833 William Perkins, solicitor, workers' legal advocate, and ally with Guest in attempts at conciliation during the 1831 uprising, was initiated.

In addition to these known radicals, eleven initiates from Dowlais were recruited between October 1831 and March

---

[361] *MG*, 22 April 1837. Suspicion about the favours he received was voiced in 1829; see the reference to Billy Teague in the letter from John Warateg [sic] to J. J. Guest in Elsas, p. 79.

[362] Williams, *The Rising*, pp. 57, 92–3; Elsas, p. 218.

1840. They included four company agents, two company cashiers, three Dowlais tradesmen and, significantly, in 1837 John Evans, general manager of the Works and Guest's right-hand man. The list of lodge Worshipful Masters from 1832 onwards is a roll call of prominent Guest supporters: E. J. Hutchins, 1832–34; Roland Hopkins, 1834–36; Rhys Davis, 1836; William Teague, 1837; Roland Hopkins again in 1838; J. C. Wolridge (Dowlais cashier) 1839; Guest himself in 1840.

It was during Hutchins's period as Worshipful Master that 'A custom crept into the working of the Lodge ...of passing and raising candidates by resolution, and it continued for many years'.[363] This 'custom' may account for the fact that, from 1832 until August 1840, no-one explicitly associated with Cyfarthfa appears to have been recruited. Then, Thomas Shepherd, cashier at Cyfarthfa, was initiated on 13 August 1840. He was a member of the first Board of Guardians and well known to the radicals. Guest's supporters had consolidated their home base. After Guest's death in 1852 there is no further evidence of political bias in the membership of the lodge beyond the fact that the majority of the Merthyr middle class were of Liberal persuasion.[364]

The Rising Generation

While members of this early nineteenth-century political elite were embedding themselves into institutions of power and influence – the select vestry, the Board of Guardians, the Freemasons – the next generation was being prepared at the

---

[363] Fraser, *An Illustrated* History, p. 68.

[364] The membership of the Loyal Cambrian Lodge was firmly middle class. For comparison see Roger Burt, 'Industrial relations in the British non-ferrous mining industry in the nineteenth century', *Labour History Review*, 71 (1) (2006).

school established in 1816 by Iolo Morgannwg's son, Taliesin Williams. Here were sent 'the children of the most respectable tradesmen of the town and district'.[365] Some entered the wider world, as did William Milbourne James, later to be knighted, marry a daughter of the bishop of Chichester and become judge of the Court of Appeal and a Privy Counsellor; Walter Morgan, who was also to be knighted and made Chief Justice of the Supreme Court at Agra; and John Petherick, the Nile explorer and Consul to the Sudan. Others from those school days made their mark in Merthyr. These included Morgan Williams and his fellow Chartist Matthew John; Thomas Dyke, future medical officer for the town, exemplary public servant and a reforming influence from the 1830s until the end of the century.[366] Charles Herbert James, who became partner to the radical solicitor Perkins, and in 1880 was elected Liberal MP for Merthyr; Frank James, solicitor, and clerk to the Guardians, and his brother, J. W. James, who produced his own Chartist newspaper *The Merthyr Star*, both of them cousins to Charles Herbert James; Rees Lewis, the future printer; John Howells, stationer and bookseller, who became a Freemason in October 1833; John Bryant of the Board of Guardians; and George Overton, solicitor, coroner for Merthyr, and Deputy Lieutenant for Breconshire.[367] Not all became reformers. Also among Taliesin's pupils was W. T. Lewis, later Lord Merthyr, coalowner and scourge of trade unions.

---

[365] Charles Herbert James, *What I remember about Myself and Old Merthyr* (Merthyr, 1892: written in 1881), p. 8.

[366] Barbara A. Frampton, 'The Role of Dr. Dyke in the Public Health Administration of Merthyr Tydfil 1865–1900', M.A. thesis, University of Wales, 1968.

[367] C. H. James, *What I Remember.* On Overton, *The Brecon County Times*, 5 May 1888; on J. W. James, *The Merthyr Express*, 12 October 1895. Taliesin Williams married Petherick's sister.

As the population increased by leaps and bounds, immigrant shopkeepers and professionals reinforced this new middle class generation. William Wilkins moved his bookselling business to Merthyr in the 1830s, later becoming head postmaster. His son Charles, who in 1846 was librarian of the subscription library at the age of sixteen, lived until 1913 and throughout the century chronicled developments in Merthyr and South Wales industries. Thomas Stephens, the Unitarian pharmacist internationally known as Wales's leading literary critic, arrived in 1835; James Ward Russell, a solicitor proud to have been at Eton at the same time as Gladstone, the first clerk to the local Board of Health, Chairman of the directors of the Merthyr Gas Company and four times Worshipful Master of the Cambrian Lodge, arrived around the same time; David Williams, senior partner in the Taff Vale brewery, supporter of incorporation, a Poor Law Guardian and member of the local board of health came to Merthyr in the early 1840s. Thomas Wilson Goodfellow, grocer and rate collector, Methodist lay preacher and agitator for incorporation also came in the 1840s; in 1844 James Colquhoun Campbell, educated at Cambridge, arrived as Rector and left in 1859 when he was elected Bishop of Bangor; Campbell's wife was the sister of Henry Austin Bruce; Peter Williams, outspoken editor of the *Merthyr Telegraph* who was once horsewhipped in the bar of The Bush came in 1849. He too was a Freemason.[368]

Walter Smyth, chemist and no respecter of persons, arrived in 1852 with the reputation of being the only Tory in Merthyr although, 'in local affairs he was as forward and progressive a man as the most thorough going Radical'.[369] William Simons, solicitor, authority on mining law, Freemason, 'an uncompromising radical' with 'a commanding presence' also

[368] Obituary, *ME*, 19 October 1895.

[369] *ME*, 17 November 1894.

arrived in 1852.[370] In 1853 J. C. Fowler, educated at Rugby and Pembroke College, Oxford, took up the post of resident stipendiary magistrate vacated by H. A. Bruce on his election to Parliament. Solicitors who came at this time were Robertson Smith and John Plews, both active in civic politics. Of these mid-century arrivals, probably the most influential was Harry Southey, who arrived in 1857 and within a few years was editor and subsequently proprietor of the *Merthyr Express*. Southey, a Freemason, was an ardent supporter of incorporation and a pioneer of secondary education in Merthyr advocating these causes both through the columns of the *Express* and in private. [371]

Intermarriage played a part in bringing some of these native and immigrant families together and creating, when the ramifications of the James family are taken into account, a closely meshed civic elite in which Unitarians were prominent. Morgan Williams's eldest sister, Gwenllian, married Rhys Davis, the postmaster and Freemason. Morgan Williams was therefore brother-in-law to Rhys Davis (and worked in the post office with him). In turn, Rhys Davis and Gwenllian had three daughters, Mary, Gwenllian, and Margaret Elizabeth, who, consequently, were Morgan Williams's nieces. One of them, Margaret Elizabeth, married Thomas Stephens. Known principally as the author of *The Literature of the Kymru* and other critical works, Stephens took an active part in Merthyr's civic politics, was briefly an investor and director of the *Merthyr Express*, helped to create a cemetery at Cefn Coed for 'non Christians', assisted the building of the Temperance Hall, and in 1858 was High Constable.

Rhys Davis also had a son, Richard Rhys Davis. After qualifying as a chemist Richard Rhys Davis worked as an

[370] *ME*, 28 October 1893.

[371] *Webster's Directory* (1865) lists names and addresses of public office holders and businessmen.

assistant to his brother-in-law Thomas Stephens and when Stephens died continued the chemist's business in partnership with his sister Mrs. Stephens. He was initiated into the Loyal Cambrian lodge in October 1878. Thus, Morgan Williams, the leader of Merthyr's thousands of Chartists in the early 1840s and characterized by Napier, the chief constable of Glamorgan as being so dangerous that 'so long as he continues at large, Merthyr can expect no peace', was brother to the wife of the town's postmaster and uncle to their children, who included Thomas Stephens's wife and brother-in-law. No wonder Napier complained (without irony) at the height of Chartist agitation in September 1842 that when in Merthyr he found himself closely watched.

Eliza, one of the daughters of John Evans, the general manager at Dowlais and Guest's *confidante*, married Thomas J. Dyke. Another, Clara Maria, married the doughty William Simons. Consequently, two of the most gifted members of the Merthyr middle class were brothers-in-law, both in favour of public health reform and incorporation, both Freemasons and with a powerful father-in-law who was also a Freemason but whose allegiance was to the fortunes of the Dowlais Iron Company. There was no issue from Dyke's marriage. But William Simons had six daughters and four sons – one of whom, Charles, qualified as a doctor and went into practice with his uncle, Dyke. Another son, Sydney, a Freemason and solicitor worked hard to achieve incorporation in 1905 and in 1906 was Mayor of Merthyr. By mid-century the small but influential group around Guest was being reinforced and gradually replaced by new talented people who, like the original group, were linked by kinship and marriage, left-wing Nonconformity, Freemasonry, business associations, and political experience. Some had lived in English incorporated towns and brought a fresh eye to Merthyr Tydfil. [372]

Despite this the James faction overplayed its hand in 1852. Immediately upon the death of Guest posters went up around the town announcing that William Milbourne James, barrister, and son of Christopher James would be a candidate for the vacant parliamentary seat. He was proclaimed as an advocate of free trade, parliamentary and franchise reform and the secret ballot. The insensitivity of this move affronted many and he withdrew from the race a few days later when H. A. Bruce was backed by the ironmasters. James, as a representative of 'that Independent Party which had in parochial matters successfully opposed the Iron Masters' was not acceptable to the Masters and therefore had no chance of winning. He and Bruce eighteen years later, in different roles, combined to solve a difficult Merthyr problem.

Meanwhile, residential segregation began. In the elevated Thomastown area where between 1849 and 1865 villas and 'genteel residences' were built for the first time on a gridiron pattern, shopkeepers and professionals moved out of the High Street and into Thomas Street, Church Street, Union Terrace, Courtland Terrace, Upper Thomas Street, and Newcastle Street. This was 'the first exclusively residential area to be created by those at the top stratum of Merthyr's population'.[373]

The *Merthyr Express* was launched in 1864 by a group that

---

[372] The reminiscences of Charles Russell James which were published in the *Merthyr Express* in 1922 provide valuable insight into middle-class life in Mid-Victorian Merthyr Tydfil. They were collected and republished by T.F. Holley, 'Charles Russell James' Childhood', *Merthyr Historian*, Vol. 13, (2001).

[373] Harold Carter and Sandra Wheatley, *Merthyr Tydfil In 1851*, p. 34. See also Wilf Owen, *Doctor Thomas of the Court, Squire of Merthyr Tydfil: His life, his family and his times 1794–1858* (Merthyr Tydfil, 2006), pp. 66–73.

included C. H. James, Thomas Stephens, Frank James, T. W. Goodfellow and Thomas Williams, the principal mover in Merthyr's Liberal Association after 1868.[374] In 1878 the shopocracy organized the Merthyr Chamber of Trade with the objects of safeguarding the interests of commerce and suggesting local reforms. The initial members comprised familiar names including David Williams, Dr. J. W. James, Peter Williams of the *Merthyr Telegraph*, Southey of the *Merthyr Express*, Dr Dyke, Frank James and the outspoken auctioneer David Evans.[375]

Raymond Grant, referring to the 1850 local board of health election, noted that '[s]hopkeepers and professional people in a comparatively new town like Merthyr Tydfil had not yet developed a sense of community of interest or purpose; the town had no corporate institutions such as a town council through which they could have developed political consciousness'[376]. In fact they lacked neither a sense of purpose nor political consciousness. Nor did they lack organisation. Seventeen years before 1850, they were calling for a town council, believing that they could dominate it. Their goal was power; a desire that Andy Croll overlooks when he comments that: 'As long as Merthyr remained a place to make – and take – money from, rather than a town in which to live, there was little reason to develop a machinery of local government that could temper the worst excesses of urban growth.'[377] The 'worst excesses' were not an issue when in 1833 the middle-class

---

[374] W.R. Lambert, 'Thomas Williams, JP, Gwaelodygarth (1823–1903)', *Glamorgan Historian*, 11 (1975).

[375] *Merthyr Telegraph*, 16 August 1878.

[376] Raymond K. J. Grant, 'Merthyr Tydfil in the Mid-Nineteenth Century: The Struggle for Public Health', *Welsh History Review*, 14 (4) (1989), republished Cowbridge, 1993.

[377] Croll, *Civilizing the Urban*, p. 18.

radicals sought a town council even while the eventual Municipal Corporations Act 1835 was still at the Bill stage. The fundamental issue was one of power and at the heart of that were the economic interests of the ironmasters.

The constant theme of the middle-class reformers, sometimes overt sometimes implicit, is resentment at the power of the ironmasters. It comes out in references to the masters' opposition to having a local board of health; in the many references to the ways in which they manipulated voting and committees; in references to the way that they allowed workmen's houses to descend into squalor; in references to their opposition to incorporation. Sometimes it finds direct expression as with David Evans who declared the nature of government in Merthyr to be 'autocratic'. On public health the middle class reformers achieved an important victory; on incorporation they failed until after Victoria's reign. Both cases illustrate the middle-class elite's strengths and weaknesses.

14

A Great and Urgent Necessity

> Merthyr Tydfil, with Pen y Daran and Dowlais ... a large cottage town, without any public care for supply of water, drainage or cleansing ...sun and air saving its population from still greater evils than those to which they are now exposed from the filth so abundant in it.
>
> **Sir H. T. De La Beche**[378]

In his *Portrait of an Age* G.M. Young in a striking phrase wrote of 'the filth and horror which had crawled over the early Victorian towns'.[379] Nowhere was this more evident than in the streets of Merthyr Tydfil. Visitors were shocked that this town with its river, hilly location and plentiful rainfall was as foul as the worst parts of the worst cities in Britain. Dr. Holland wrote on 15 December 1853 to the General Board of Health, Whitehall: ' ...with the worst parts of London and Manchester I am familiar, that extremely dirty City of Bristol I have recently examined but never did I see anything which could compare with Merthyr'. The 'physical rottenness' in Merthyr was graphically set out by Dr. Holland.

---

[378] *Second Report of The Commissioners for Inquiry into the State of Large Towns and Populous Districts*, Vol.1, 1845, pp. 316-328.
[379] G. M. Young, *Victorian England: Portrait of an Age* (Oxford Paperbacks, 1960) p. 57.

> ...*everywhere*, even along roads and paths constantly frequented are visible indications of the absence of those places of accommodation [lavatories] generally thought indispensable. So universal is the presence of this filthiest of filth that it requires constant watchfulness to avoid treading in it.'[380] [Italics in original.]

Holland's report was so damning that Whitehall asked for a second opinion from Dr. William Kay, temporarily employed as Merthyr's Officer of Health. He responded: 'As regards the dirtiness of Merthyr generally, it would be difficult, I think, to speak of it in the language of exaggeration.' 'The presence of unseemly deposits almost everywhere, but too plainly evidences the extremely limited extent of the accommodations essential to decency'. Without a regular organized system of drainage and an adequate supply of water, it was utterly out of the question that Merthyr could approach sanitary health

The more than doubling of the population between 1831 and 1851 had swamped the original inadequate facilities. The result in mid-century was that typhus, smallpox, tuberculosis, diarrhoeal diseases, measles and scarlet fever were ever-present among the population, sometimes erupting in epidemics. One in nine persons died of typhus, one in six of tuberculosis. Cholera killed at least 1,600 in 1832, a further 1,416 between May and September 1849, and called again in 1854 and 1866. Between 1847 and 1852 the average mortality rate in Merthyr was higher than any other town or district in Wales. It 'was 29 per 1,000 without cholera, 34.7 with cholera' compared with the accepted average norm of 20 per 1,000. The 1848 Public Health Act could be applied to districts where the mortality rate exceeded 23 per 1,000. The average age at death in Merthyr

---

[380] A. H. Williams (ed.), *Public Health in Mid-Victorian Wales* (Aberystwyth, 1983), Vol. 2, 125/10.

in 1852 was estimated by Dr. Kay to be 17.6 years. But the average age at death varied considerably between classes. For the 'gentry' and better-off middle class in Merthyr it was 35, for 'tradesmen' (shopkeepers) it was 22 and for 'mechanics' it was 15. Like Liverpool the worst town in Britain and only marginally worse than Merthyr, the main reason for the low average was the appalling level of infant mortality. 'More than half the funerals that take place in Merthyr are those of children under 5 years of age; and more than one-fourth of infants under 1 year'. [381]

Human excrement, animal dung and urine mingled in the streets, courts and alleyways and sluggishly drained into the river Taff from which people took their drinking water. The Taff if captured above the town would have been a source of clean water but the Cyfarthfa and Ynysfach works used it to supply steam engines and turn water wheels – the largest turning about 40 tons a minute in the wet season. It was then channelled to the Plymouth works where it was the main source of power. Crawshay and Hill therefore regarded the Taff as for their private use, as it had been for 80 years. In Dowlais the Dulais brook passed through the works, joined the Morlais brook and proceeded black and dirty to the Penydarren works where it was again used before emptying into the Taff. On the hills above Cyfarthfa and Dowlais drains collected water into ponds as a largely free power resource for the ironworks.

The water people used for washing, cooking, drinking came in ways which are distressing to learn. Least objectionable was rainwater collected in casks and butts. Next, from distant springs or 'spouts', women undertook the laborious, heavy, and time-consuming task by night and day of carefully gathering

[381] William Kay, M.D., *Report on the Sanitary Condition of Merthyr Tydfil drawn up at the request of the local board of Health*, (Merthyr Tydfil, 1854). I.G. Jones, *Communities*, pp. 246-8

water in pitchers and kettles, bottles and buckets. The Rector of Dowlais, the Rev. Evan Jenkins explained the process:

> During winter, there are from 6 to 8 spouts, some half a mile, some a mile distant from the houses, but in summer they are reduced to three, the remainder being dried up ...I have seen 50, 80 and as many as 100 people waiting for their turn, and then some obliged to go away without any water at all. They have been obliged to wait up all of the night. In the case of women having a young family, they are left at home at these times to take care of themselves. Instances have occurred of children being burned to death while their mothers are waiting at the spouts. They have no other supply of water whatever fit to drink in summer time, and have no alternative but to wait.[382]

Families that could afford to do so employed an extra servant solely to carry water. Desperate necessity caused people to beg for it, to pay owners of wells – too often dug near slaughter houses and crowded cemeteries – for a bucketful of it, or to gather it from stagnant pools and polluted tips. Worst of all they took it from the Taff. H. A. Bruce told of his regular crossing the river on horseback.

> I scarcely ever pass without seeing people close to me, on the right and left, easing themselves, whilst only a few yards off women and girls are filling their pitchers with water. The air is poisoned for a considerable distance around this place, and the exposure of person is most indecent.

The stench from the river was matched by that from the refuse in the streets, the rancid slaughter houses and tanneries, the

382 Rammell, pp. 37-8

rat-haunted fetid courts and alleyways. Hill, Guest and Crawshay had each provided superior housing for their skilled workers at Pentrebach, Dowlais, Georgetown and Williamstown but at Tydfil's Well, Pontystorehouse, Caedraw, Pedwranfach, Ynysgau, and Atkins Row at Dowlais there were labyrinths of miserable tenements, cellars and filth that ranked with the worst in Britain. The sixty overcrowded common lodging houses were breeding grounds for contagious diseases. There were twenty-one separate burial grounds.

Yet, amidst these appalling conditions, more than one observer noted the glowing interiors where women kept their domain. Dr. Carte, a local practitioner, said he did not blame the people for the filth that surrounded them. 'I think they are naturally the cleanest people I ever saw. They are constantly washing their houses. A Welshwoman does not cease scrubbing from one day to another.'[383] The men and boys returning from work stripped each day and washed thoroughly in front of the fire, a custom that scandalised some observers.[384]

A Call to Action

It was the shopocracy that first determined on action. The unlikely agency was the Merthyr subscription library, an institution opened at Wilkins's Temperance Room on 1 December 1846 with 227 subscribers. Prominent on its committee were: Charles Herbert James, Thomas Dyke, James Russell, Frank James, Morgan Williams, Francis Carlyle (Congregationalist cousin of Thomas Carlyle), the Rev Owen Evans (Unitarian minister at Cefn Coed), and the Rev Thomas

[383] Rammell, p. 29.

[384] When in 1935 Jack Jones chose to open his novel *Black Parade* with such a scene there were calls for the novel to be banned.

Davies (Baptist minister and Chartist supporter).[385] The secretary was Thomas Stephens. At the first annual meeting in 1847 it was proposed by Stephens, seconded by Morgan Williams, and agreed that funds should be set aside for obtaining lecturers.[386]

The founders of this institution had, no doubt, a variety of motives including belief in the value of rational knowledge, the virtues of voluntary action, and a desire to civilize the lower orders. For the Chartists among them it was a means by which books and lectures would promote adult education.[387] It also marked the reintegration of Morgan Williams into public life after his years in Newtown. The library was initiated in a climate of social concern. Edwin Chadwick's 1842 *Report on the Sanitary Condition of the Labouring Population* and the reports of the Royal Commission on the State of Large Towns (1844) had revealed the horrors of the new industrial towns. A national debate was raging over whether the state should be involved in an issue – the health of towns – that many argued was a matter for each locality. Sir Henry De La Beche had visited Merthyr Tydfil in 1844 on behalf of the Royal Commission and D. W. James and James Russell had been among those who contributed evidence. James' view was that only by compulsory means 'enacted by the Legislature' could Merthyr's problems be remedied.[388]

---

[385] For Owen Evans, see Tom Lewis, *The History of the Hen Dy Cwrdd Cefn Coed Y Cymmer*, (Llandysul, n.d.), pp. 82–92; Thomas Davies left Merthyr in 1856 to become Principal of Haverfordwest Baptist College.

[386] *MG*, 6 November 1847.

[387] For the autodidactic culture of Chartism, see Angela V. John, 'The Chartists of Industrial South Wales'.

[388] *Second Report of The Commissioners for inquiring into the State of Large Towns and Populous Districts*, Vol. 1 (London, 1845), pp. 316–28.

In the spring and early summer of 1847 typhus, a disease spread by the faeces of lice, reached epidemic proportions in over-crowded Merthyr. In February 1848 there came a serious outbreak of smallpox and by September there were intimations that cholera was again on its way. It was a terrifying prospect. At the beginning of October a 'meeting of the most respectable inhabitants of the town' – including Guest (but no other ironmaster), H. A. Bruce, Frank James, D. W. James, William Thomas of the Court, J. L. White, T. J. Dyke, Overton and J. W. Russell – discussed the need to clean up areas of the town, particularly Quarry Row and the cellars at Pontystorehouse, Colliers Row, Pedwranfach, River side, Caedraw, Ynysgau, and Atkins Houses and Brecon Street, Dowlais. The Nuisances Removal and Diseases Prevention Act 1848 had just become law and inhabitants were urged to report 'nuisances' to the Poor Law Guardians who would issue notices for the offending areas to be cleansed. The *Merthyr Guardian* explained: 'Everything, therefore, must depend upon the activity and courage of the householders of Merthyr. To them will accrue the credit of successful exertion; on them will remain the guilt of permitting their town to be ravaged by a most terrific disease'.[389]

Such *laissez-faire* attitudes were inadequate in the eyes of the library committee. Within ten days Dyke introduced a discussion at a meeting of the library 'on the influence upon the public health of the sanitary condition of towns'. As a result, the library committee decided to hold a public meeting and press for the application to Merthyr of the new Public Health Act. This provided that a local health board could be set up to deal with problems if a petition from 10 per cent of the inhabitants of a district, or from places where the death-rate

[389] *MG*, 7 October 1848.

was above 23 per 1,000, was received in Whitehall.[390] A few days later 'a heavily attended meeting' chaired by D. W. James as chairman of the Poor Law Guardians, heard Robert Jones, grocer, member of the library and later, High Sheriff of London, eloquently propose the following motion: 'That this meeting, taking into consideration the great want of sewers, drains, and public conveniences in Merthyr Tydfil, deems it expedient that the town should be placed under the provisions of the Public Health Act.' The kernel of his argument was the:

> great and urgent necessity which exists for some interference with respect to our sanitary condition ...Merthyr Tydfil ...exists in its present magnitude and importance without any local act of Parliament, or control of any local authority, to manage its affairs and to insure proper sanitary regulations within its limits ...The result of having no regulations compulsory on the town has been just what might be expected; what has not been enforced by law has not been done by voluntary effort. Neither the owners of property nor the inhabitants in general have exerted themselves to provide for the cleanliness of the town.

He then set out the facts. It was probably the first occasion when an influential Merthyr audience was urged to take action on the issue:

> Here we are in the nineteenth century – the age of progress and era of reform with a disgraceful spectacle immediately before us – namely, a large and populous town without any sewers, public supply of water, or ash pits, and, in the vast majority of cases, without any drains whatever or privies attached to the dwelling houses, and hence the lodgement of putrid matter and

[390] *MG*, 21 October 1848. On 23 and 30 September 1848 the *Merthyr Guardian* carried summaries of the Public Health Act.

> gaseous and poisonous liquids in our streets, the accumulations of ash heaps and dung hills in our thoroughfares, and the most indecent exposure of persons in almost every secluded corner and byway in and near the town.

'The great question for us to decide', he concluded, 'is not so much the extent of the evil as the mode of meeting it with an efficient and speedy remedy'. Walter Thompson seconded the resolution and Dyke supported it with statistics.

Anthony Hill then rose. In a speech that might fall into the category of 'the rule of unmitigated selfishness and penny wisdom under the specious mask of local liberty'[391] he did not doubt the accuracy of Dyke's statement but

> it must not be forgotten that after all the question is one of pounds, shillings and pence [laughter]. If some generous personage would drain and otherwise improve the town for us, then such things would be very desirable; but as no liberal gentleman will supply us with the means, we must not blind ourselves to the expense, [that] would be entailed upon us.

Numerous clerks, inspectors and surveyors would have to be paid for by ratepayers. Moreover, there would be unnecessary central control: 'We have of late been giving up the power we had in our hands a great deal too freely ...once placed under the board of health we shall be bound to move as they direct; and if once you place the tremendous machinery of this Act in operation I know not where it will end.'

---

[391] Tom Taylor, secretary of the Local Government Act Office, referring to local authority attempts to resist the public health acts. Quoted in Christopher Hamlin, 'Muddling in Bumbledom: On the Enormity of Large Sanitary Improvements in Four British Towns, 1855–1885', *Victorian Studies* (Autumn 1988).

Hill also raised the issue of local cottage owners who did not pay rates yet were the ones responsible for the miserable housing. His remedy for 'the undoubted ills', was for them to be dealt with through a local Act of Parliament. Bruce supported Hill's recommendation, as did the chairman D. W. James. Robert Jones' motion was then withdrawn on condition that a committee was set up immediately to frame a local Act. The committee included Bruce, prominent members of the subscription library and ironmasters from the four works with Hill as chairman.[392]

But at a meeting a week later, William Crawshay reported that it would not be possible to provide the required notice, plans and specifications in time to apply for a local Act. Why this was so is not clear. However, Hill's committee promptly dissolved itself. In response the members of the library determined to push ahead with their original plan and instantly prepared a petition which stated:

> That there is a total want of Sewerage Drainage and Supply of Water in the said Town and Parish and That the State of the Burial Grounds therein is such as to be injurious to the health of the Inhabitants generally.
>
> That the average number of deaths according to the Registrar General's last Return upon the population of 1841 is Thirty in a Thousand for the last Seven years in the [Poor Law] Union of Merthyr Tydfil which includes a large healthy agricultural area and therefore that the average must be higher in the town itself.

It went on to request the General Board of Health in London to direct 'a Superintending Inspector' to make the necessary inquiry and report, preparatory to bringing the parish and town of Merthyr Tydfil under the Public Health Act.

[392] *MG*, 4 November 1848.

Dyke, Thomas Stephens and friends collected 169 signatures, considerably more than the required one-tenth of ratepayers in the parish. The petition was sent to the General Board on 8 November 1848 by Frank James, Clerk to the Poor Law Guardians. At the head of the list of names was the Rector, the Reverend James C. Campbell. Those immediately following were D. W. James, Chairman of the Board of Guardians, Frank James, solicitor, John Thomas, Thomas Montgomery, tea dealer, W. Thomson, banker, J. W. Russell, solicitor, T. J. Dyke, surgeon, Thomas Stephens, chemist. It was this petition that brought Thomas Webster Rammell, superintendent inspector, to the town. It was a victory for the concerned, rational, middle-class reformers who called for the implementation of the Act, unlike middle-class ratepayers in many other towns who opposed the Act because it might bring higher rates. [393] The *Merthyr Guardian* took the latter view on 14 April 1849, referring to 'That most dangerous and insidious of centralising schemes – the Public Health Act'.

[393] *MG*, 4, 18 November 1848. The obituary of Dyke in the *Merthyr Express*, 27 January 1900 based on Dyke's reminiscences to Charles Wilkins contains a number of errors concerning these events. The same errors appear in Wilkins's *History*. Although submitted by Frank James, clerk to the Board of Guardians, the Minutes give no indication that it was discussed at Board of Guardians meetings on 4, 11, and 18 November.

15

Clearing up the Mess

> The virtue of the Act of 1848 lay less in its immediate results than in the large opportunities it gave for local initiative and scientific intelligence to work together.
>
> G.M. Young[394]

Rammell finally arrived on 15 May 1849 to conduct his inquiry. He found a noisy vestry room crowded with workmen 'who had been called together by misrepresentations purposely to oppose' implementation of the Public Health Act.[395] Frank James, Clerk to the local Board of Guardians, acted as Welsh interpreter. Soon the room was so crowded and hot, the meeting so confused, that everyone adjourned to the front of the Market Place, a favourite place for large meetings, where a crowd of over 600 gathered. 'An animated discussion of some length' then took place and 'at the end of these somewhat boisterous proceedings,' Rammell managed to impose order by dividing the town into five districts, each of which would send four delegates in favour of the proposal and four against, to confer

---

394 G.M. Young, *Victorian England: Portrait of an Age* (Oxford Paperbacks, 1960), p. 57.

395 All quotations in the following section are taken from T.W. Rammell, *Report to the General Board of Health on a Preliminary Inquiry into the Sewerage, Drainage, and Supply of Water, and the Sanitary Condition of the Inhabitants of the town of Merthyr Tydfil* (London, 1850).

with him. The five districts were based upon the four ironworks plus the town area.

The arguments basically broke down into four. The concerned middle class spoke about the filth and the lack of water and called for the Act to be applied to Merthyr. The Rector of Dowlais, the Reverend Evan Jenkins, supported this at length and upon the suggestion of Thomas Stephens his statement was translated into Welsh. Owners of cottages, a number of whom were workmen, objected to the imposition of the Act because it would lead to an increase in the Poor Law rate which would fall upon them. They also openly declared that any increase in the local rate would be passed on to their tenants through a rent increase.

The third argument came from workmen who said the fundamental problem was poverty. An increase in the rates would be passed on to tenants through a rent increase and they could not afford to pay more. Rammell quoted a spokesman who argued that the high rate of mortality was caused by working underground 'and by want of sufficiency of food, and not by the want of sanitary laws. What they wanted was more meat.' It was a straightforward argument about undernourishment. John Williams of Caepantywyll, a miner and owner of three cottages, bluntly stated: '...people have not enough to buy food, and have nothing to spare for water; and that it costs them nothing to fetch water. The wives of many being barefoot, there is no expense of shoe-leather.' The Chartists Matthew John and William Gould had a fourth argument. They opposed implementation of the Act, partly because there would be an increase in rents but also on the grounds that the property qualification required before people could vote for a local board of health would, by the working-class nature of the town (and as Rammell calculated), exclude over 70 per cent of the population.

Rammell was shocked by what he saw, yet he had been told that such an effort had been made to clear up the town before his visit that it was like 'the west end of London, compared with what it was'. His Report published in the spring of 1850 was a turning point in the development of Merthyr. Accidentally it was distributed free of charge by the local stationer who should have charged a shilling for each one. Frank James informed Whitehall and received *gratis* a further fifty copies. Rammell's scathing conclusions included the following:

> that the town of Merthyr Tydfil is almost entirely destitute of drainage; that there are few or no privies in Merthyr, and those which exist are for the most part in a filthy condition, full to overflowing; that there is utter want of proper provision for supplying the town with water, either for public or private purposes; that there are a very large number of cases of epidemic, endemic and contagious diseases; that there is no local Act for the paving, lighting, or cleansing of the town of Merthyr, nor for supplying it with water, nor any governing body connected with the place having authority for such purposes.

He therefore recommended that the Public Health Act 1848 be applied to the town and parish of Merthyr Tydfil and that a local board of health be elected. Finally, he emphasised the two tasks 'which should be immediately undertaken': the provision of a water supply and the provision of drains and sewers.

Ten days after Rammell's arrival cholera broke out and between then and the end of September a total of 1389 died of the disease and another 41 died of diarrhoea. Altogether in four months 1430 died.[396] There were so many bodies that a new cemetery was opened at Pant, the first burial on 18 July 1849.

---

[396] Ieuan Gwynedd Jones, 'Merthyr Tydfil: The Politics of Survival' *Llafur*, Vol. 2 (Spring 1976). Raymond K.J. Grant, 'Merthyr Tydfil in the Mid-Nineteenth Century: The struggle for Public Health' *WHR*, Vol. 14, 4 (December, 1989) records that 3,248 cases were reported and 1,416 died.

The Local Board of Health

The ironmasters were, with the exception of Guest who died in 1852, against having a local board of health. That was why they had enabled workmen to pack the initial meeting with Rammell. They could not however, faced with the cholera outbreak and Rammell's recommendations, resist having one but they strongly influenced, or impeded, the Board's proceedings, especially after Guest died and Robert Crawshay became chairman.

The members of the first board elected in October 1850 were: Guest as chairman, Anthony Hill and Robert Crawshay, Benjamin Martin of the Penydarren Iron Company and John Evans of the Dowlais Iron Company, William Thomas of the Court House, Walter Thompson and David Evans, local bankers, D. W. James and Lewis Lewis, merchants, Edward Morgan, landowner, William Meyrick and James Ward Russell, solicitors, Edward Purchase, farmer and Samuel Thomas, coal merchant. J. W. Russell resigned in November to become clerk to the Board and C. H. James, solicitor, was elected to fill the vacancy. Initial progress was extremely slow. A letter to the General Board of Health in London, dated 24 November 1852, from James Benest, appointed surveyor to the board in March 1851, suggests a reason:

> In the exercise of my duties as Surveyor under the Health of Towns Act – I have incurred the enmity of two members of the Local Board – and as they are rather powerful and exercise a great influence in the Board I am led to expect great opposition may be offered to any measures I may bring forward for the improvement of this town – if such a thing should occur have I a resource in appealing to the General Board for protection.[397]

[397] A.H. Williams, (ed.) *Public Health*, 125/7, ii.

The local board took three years to appoint a medical officer, William Kay, and then only on a temporary basis. The two matters that Rammell had singled out as needing immediate attention – the provision of water and drainage – were not tackled until ten years after the board was elected.

The major issue was how to provide clean water. Initially, seeing a chance of profit, the ironmasters proposed a scheme for a private joint stock company to supply water to the town in which they would be the principal shareholders. The General Board in Whitehall rejected this on the grounds that experience had shown that such schemes provided water only to those who could afford what the company charged, while those in poorer districts did not receive water. The local board itself as a public body in June 1852 therefore secured a private Act of Parliament 'for supplying the Inhabitants of the town of Merthyr Tydfil and Adjacent Places with water'. But no action followed. Charlotte Guest in October 1853, in charge at Dowlais after her husband's death, offered to supply Dowlais with water from the Works and find the funds to do so but her offer was not followed up.[398]

The Minutes of the local board and press reports over the period make clear that indecision and interminable arguments between the members of the board partly came from fear of making a mistake where large sums of money were involved. Merthyr was not alone in this.[399] But the major reason for delay was that Robert Crawshay and Anthony Hill, regarded the waters of the Taff as 'theirs' (they claimed to be 'the riparian owners') and wanted to be protected by an Act of Parliament before allowing the river to be used to supply the town. They argued that if, as engineers proposed, the Taff should be used to supply

---

[398] Guest and John, p. 81.

[399] Christopher Hamlin, 'Muddling in Bumbledom: On the Enormity of Large Sanitary Improvements in Four British Towns, 1855-1885', *Victorian Studies*, Autumn 1988.

water to the town then they wanted compensation for any loss of water power. There were numerous delays arising from their objections. On 2 March 1855, five years after Rammell's Report, the Merthyr solicitor William Simons wrote to Sir Benjamin Hall, MP, President of the General Board of Health, absolving both Lady Charlotte and the Penydarren company from the 'hostility' to decency which he attributed to Crawshay and Hill.

> ...During the whole of the long frost, which has just left us, the sufferings of the poor, from want of water, were intense; and in dry summers hundreds sit up all night, waiting their turn at the little rills about the town.
>
> There is so great a dread of the ironmasters in this place, and their powers so extensive, and so sure to be hostilily [sic] applied; that public duty and Christian obligations are alike forgotten. Disease sweeps away its thousands, without an effort to control the agencies that induce it; and the sufferings of the poor, induced by the want of water, occasion less dread than the powers of an Ironmaster.
>
> ...Shame, and conscientious obligations, have no influence with the powers of this place. Nothing moves them but force. The only remedy for the ills I have pointed out is to put the compulsory powers of your office into operation. The object of the resisting Ironmasters is evident. They seek some enormous compensation for that which is of little value to them, or else, they desire to delay operations until the local act expires; which is due in June next. They would thus, avoid paying their share of the cost of improvements; and would also preserve what they call their vested rights in streams, bestowed by Heaven on all regardless of the sacrifice of life thereby occasioned. I trust your exertions may save the town from both disasters. [400]

---

[400] A.H.Williams (ed.) *Public Health*, 125/16, i.

His letter was referred to the local board of health and a denial issued concerning the attitude of Crawshay in particular. But arguments continued to revolve around Crawshay and Hill until in May 1857 they stated that they did not want financial compensation but a storage reservoir, specially built, from which they could draw water. This was agreed by the local board of health, not without wrangling, and in November 1857 a parish meeting voted by twenty votes to four that a joint-stock company be formed to carry out the work. But after learning that only £4,000 had been subscribed and £50,000 was required (Crawshay had declined to invest on grounds of difficult times), it was decided to proceed no further with a private company.

Once again the board procured a local Waterworks Act (1858) that safeguarded the water rights of Cyfarthfa and Plymouth ironworks and the Glamorganshire Canal. Crawshay and Hill agreed that water could be made available to the town in advance of the completion of 'their' reservoir. For them the Taff Fechan was dammed near Dolygaer, creating the Pentwyn reservoir. Cyfarthfa and Plymouth works had first call, but it was agreed that in unusual drought conditions the water would also be available for the town. It was completed in February 1863, although leakages and repairs to the dam were a major issue until in 1927 the river was dammed at Ponsticill to create the Taff Fechan reservoir.

Meanwhile, in the hot summer and drought of 1859 women queued for hours for water, beginning as early as 2 or 3am. One dropped dead while waiting. The *Merthyr Guardian* commented that it was 'a very sad reflection that the large population of this locality should be wholly dependent upon a few small waterspouts for the supply of this first necessity of life'.[401]

[401] *MG*, 16 July 1859.

Eventually by creating a reservoir at Penybryn clean water finally became available in the town in December 1860 from 12 standpipes, the Board of Health members enjoying a glass of 'the limpid sparkling element' at their January meeting.[402] By November 1862 almost 5,000 houses in Penydarren, Dowlais and Merthyr had running water. Troedyrhiw had water from the mains in 1863 and Abercanaid in 1864. By 1866, 9,570 houses in Merthyr and district were receiving good quality water at the rate of almost a million gallons a day. Perversely, the plentiful availability of water made more serious the other matter that Rammell had insisted a decade earlier needed 'immediate' attention: the lack of drains and sewers.

Thomas Dyke and George Clark

Two men were central to tackling the parish's public health problems. Thomas Dyke, who had been instrumental in bringing Rammell to make his inspection, made a huge contribution over many years.[403] Born in Merthyr in 1816, a graduate of St. Thomas' Hospital, a qualified apothecary in 1837, a member of the Royal College of Surgeons in 1838, he returned to practise in Merthyr in January 1839. In 1865, fifteen years after Rammell's Report he became the full-time Medical Officer to the local board of health and set about his task with humanity and vigour. As an active Freemason and member of the subscription library he knew well the realities of the town's politics, as well as its public health needs. He had served at various times as parish surgeon to the upper district of Merthyr and then the lower district, as surgeon to the

[402] *Merthyr Telegraph*, 19 January 1861.

[403] Barbara Frampton, 'The Role of Dr. Dyke in the Public Health Administration of Merthyr Tydfil 1865-1900', M.A. thesis, University of Wales, Swansea, 1968.

Dowlais Iron Company for ten years in the Penydarren district and then for four years in lower Dowlais. In 1849 he contracted cholera while tending the sick but had survived.

His approach to public health was based upon the 'miasma' theory, adopted by Chadwick, that diseases were caused by poisonous vapours in the air that could be detected by their foul smell. The theory gained credence by the fact that as refuse was removed and clean water and improved drainage achieved, foul smells diminished, levels of disease fell and life expectancy increased; the result, of course, of removing bacteria, the real cause of infections. Dyke was also aware of the effect of poverty upon health and the importance of the worker earning enough to buy nutritious food. His annual reports from 1865 to 1879 deliberately set out the price of staple foods and the level of wages. He knew too from his meticulously kept records that in prosperous times excessive drinking led to increases in heart and liver disease and that in severe economic circumstances 'fewer persons induced sicknesses by over indulgence in intoxicating drinks' and fewer deaths occurred.[404]

The second key person was George Thomas Clark (1809-1898). A man of exceptional energy and diverse talents – a surgeon, a railway engineer, a genealogist, an author of books on medieval castles, and a former superintendent inspector for the General Board of Health who had written over forty reports on the public health of cities and towns in England and Wales.[405] He joined the local health board in 1852 after the death of Sir John Guest. By Sir John's will he had been made a Dowlais trustee and became in effect managing director of the Dowlais Company after Lady Charlotte remarried. The arguments in the local health board and behind the scenes over

[404] Medical Officer of Health, *Eleventh Annual Report... 1875*, p. 15.

[405] For his multi-faceted achievements see B. Ll. James (ed.), *G.T. Clark : Scholar Ironmaster in the Victorian Age* (Cardiff, 1998).

the provision of water were largely played out between Crawshay and Hill on one side and Clark, a strong personality, on the other. In 1862 Clark became chairman of the board and it was he who appointed Dyke. Clark was determined to press on with the next phase of the board's work – providing drains and a sewerage system. In June 1864 he drew attention to the district's continuing high mortality rate and attributed it to the lack of house drains and street sewers. To obtain water, he wrote, 'the town had to buy off the opposition of wealthy and powerful opponents; to sewage no one can be opposed'.[406] He was wrong.

Completing the Task

In September 1864 the Board instructed its surveyor, Samuel Harpur, to prepare plans and estimates for the laying of sewers in Merthyr Tydfil, Dowlais, Abercanaid, Pentrebach and Troedyrhiw. Harpur submitted his detailed plans in July 1865 which included discharging the sewage into the Taff. In August the Board borrowed £27,000 from the Atlas Assurance Society to finance the sewerage scheme and when cholera appeared a year later ten miles of brick sewers had been constructed and nineteen miles of sewage pipes were in place. By October 1868 fifty-five miles of sewers had been completed with the discharge entering the Taff, about half-a-mile below Troedyrhiw. Already heavily polluted, the Taff now became an open sewer.

It was a nuisance at Common Law to discharge sewage into a river. It could not have been a surprise therefore when in 1869 an injunction was issued against the board to prevent it from polluting the river. Clark, who had put his full weight behind the scheme as a means of saving lives, had been warned

---

[406] Grant, 'Water and Sanitation...' p. 27.

of that likelihood in July 1865. Injunctions to prevent pollution of rivers existed at Cheltenham, Leamington Spa, Tunbridge Wells and other English towns. The interim injunction, enforced by the Court of Chancery, was obtained by the coalmining firm of Nixon, Taylor and Correy which was sinking a mine about a mile below the outlet of the sewage. The Company claimed that in eight or nine years some 5,000 people would be living in the vicinity of their colliery. The injunction prevented any further connection of houses to the sewer and required the Board to prevent raw sewerage entering the river. At the same time the Company promoted a petition asking for the setting up of a new Health District to be known as Merthyr Vale. It was clear that the new body would be under the control of Nixon and company and that an attempt was being made to escape paying public health rates to Merthyr. A public inquiry was held in August 1869 and in November Arnold Taylor, the Government inspector, rejected this request as unnecessary.[407]

In response to the injunction the local board of health pressed ahead with constructing a sewage irrigation farm but various objections from landowners resulted in slow progress and the Chancery Court in November 1869 issued a sequestration order against the local board. However, if a satisfactory plan for abating the nuisance was proposed, the court would grant reasonable time for its completion. Harpur then proposed a scheme that he felt would satisfy the Court. Its success depended upon acquiring additional land in the vicinity of Troedyrhiw and Pontypridd for sewerage irrigation and cleansing. There were objections again from landowners and on 27 April 1870 a public inquiry was held to determine whether the Board should be allowed to purchase the land compulsorily.

At this point the board decided to send a deputation to seek

---

407 A.H. Williams (ed.), *Public Health*, 125/25, i-ix.

the help of the Home Secretary, H. A. Bruce, who knew more about the circumstances of Merthyr Tydfil than any Home Secretary before or since. Bruce received them 'with evident interest' and gave them 'much good advice'. The deputation also met with others (whom they were not in a position to name) who were concerned with the sewage issue and the deputation returned to Merthyr with 'reason to believe their visit [had been] a profitable one.'[408] A few days later the Inspector, once again Arnold Taylor, reported in favour of the board's request to purchase land, so that 'the sewage of the District may be relieved by that process from noxious or offensive ingredients'.[409]

The final act came when another Merthyr 'old boy' Lord Justice James,[410] head of the Chancery Court (perhaps one the deputation discreetly did not name) directed that John Bailey Denton, civil engineer, should pursue at Merthyr the system for the treatment of sewage suggested by the eminent chemist Edward Frankland. This, the first occasion on which this had been tried on a large scale, was a complete success. On 10 June 1871 Dr. Frankland reported 'the water entering the Taff from the Merthyr intermittent filters was considerably purer than the Thames water, which we are often compelled to drink in London.'[411]

[408] *Merthyr Telegraph*, 21 May 1870.

[409] A. H. Williams (ed.) *Public Health*, 125/30, i-ix.

[410] William Milbourne James (1807-1881) was born in Merthyr a son of Christopher James and cousin to C. H. James. It was his name that had been put forward in 1852 as a Parliamentary candidate when Guest died, and just as swiftly withdrawn when it was clear the ironmasters were opposed to him and favoured Bruce.

[411] Thomas Jones Dyke, *The Health History of Merthyr Tydfil* (Merthyr Tydfil, 1885).

The Cost of Health

The cleansing of nineteenth-century Britain, the world's greatest industrial and imperial power, was a crusade initiated by Edwin Chadwick and carried forward in Whitehall by John Simon. In the towns of Britain conscientious and humane officials pursued the ideal. Merthyr was fortunate in having Thomas Dyke who both initiated the debate about public health and as medical officer unremittingly sought improvements. His appointment in 1865 came earlier than similar appointments in Leeds, Manchester or Birmingham. Despite its appalling initial condition public health in Merthyr improved spectacularly. The death rate from cholera dropped from 26.7 per 1,000 in 1849 to 8.3 in 1854 and to 2.0 per 1,000 in 1866 when clean water was available. By 1894 the average death rate from all causes was 19.8 per 1,000, 'the lowest recorded during the 29 years I have been your medical officer'. The average age at death was 25 compared with 17.5 years 'in the dark days of Merthyr'. [412]

Dyke and the Rev. John Griffith – 'the brusque, genial, fearless old rector' – together with the Rev. Thomas West (Wesleyan minister) and the Rev. D. Jones (Congregational minister) became the trustees of a children's hospital opened in 1877. The success of this hospital and the lack of facilities for adults that followed the closure of Mrs. Clark's hospital in Dowlais led eventually to the charitable funding and opening of the General Hospital in October 1888 in which W.T. Lewis played a leading role.[413]

---

[412] Medical Officer of Health, Dr. Thomas Dyke, *Thirtieth Annual Report*, January 1895, pp. 4-5.

[413] A full account of the history and opening ceremony of the hospital appears in *ME* 6 October 1888. The involvement of middle-class men and women in fund-raising and managing this initiative is apparent.

In a presentation to the British Medical Association at Cardiff in 1885 Dyke reported that the cost of the works for the water supply was £155,000, the works for sewers, sewage irrigation and the purchase of lands came to £260,000, and a further £240,000 should be added for scavenging, gas lighting, paving and interest on money borrowed. Against that the annual district rate for the past ten years had been 3s. 8d. in the £ and rents and profits from sewage farming amounted to an annual income of £8,920. The properties of the local board – water works, freehold lands, and houses – were estimated to be worth £300,000. He drew a conclusion that reflected in large measure his life's work. Sanitary works 'well planned, well executed, and thoroughly worked' bring better health, a longer life, and become a source of profitable income to communities.[414]

[414] Dyke, *The Health History of Merthyr Tydfil.*

16

Seeking Civic Power

> Men were so engrossed in building mills that towns were left to build themselves.
>
> J. L. and Barbara Hammond[415]

> In a word, for all intents and purposes of civic government, Merthyr Tydfil is as destitute as the smallest rural village in the empire.
>
> T.W. Rammell[416]

On 3 July 1838 Richard Cobden wrote to his publisher in Edinburgh explaining that for six months he had been campaigning for the incorporation of the city of Manchester. Success had been achieved, he wrote, by 'exposing the trickery of the Tories' and by rallying the support of the £10 householders who had been given the vote by the 1832 Reform Act, and who now favoured municipal reform. Jubilantly Cobden wrote: 'the *shopocracy* has been successful'.[417] In just three years after the passing of the 1834 Municipal Corporations Act Manchester had achieved its charter, which

---

[415] J. L. And Barbara Hammond, *The Town Labourer 1760-1830: The New Civilisation* (1925), p. 44

[416] T. W. Rammell, *Report*, p. 12.

[417] Richard Cobden to W. Taitt, 3 July 1838; quoted in John Morley, *The Life of Richard Cobden* (London, 1906), pp. 123-124: italics in the original.

meant it could have a town council. It was a process that took the Merthyr shopocracy seventy years. In fact, the debate about whether Merthyr should have a town council began before the Municipal Corporations Bill had been presented to Parliament and outlasted the whole of Victoria's reign.

Yet for the greater part of the nineteenth century Merthyr was the largest town in Wales, only the addition of new boundaries enabling Cardiff marginally to overtake it at the 1871 census.[418] It was also reputed to be the dirtiest, the least healthy, the most crime-ridden, and the least possessed of civic amenities of all the towns in Wales. An inspector of the General Board of Health observed in 1853: 'Merthyr Tydfil presents one of the most strongly marked cases of the evil ...of allowing a village to grow into a town without providing the means of civic organization.'[419] Why then did half a century elapse after that comment before the town achieved incorporation? Altogether the issue was discussed in 1833, 1834, 1837, 1857, in the late 1860s, again in 1873-76, in 1880, in 1896-97 and finally in 1901-5.

To that question there is a short answer. Those who agitated for reform were comparatively few in number and had no firm power base. They were opposed by men of vast wealth who were determined to resist any move that threatened that wealth or challenged their power. The journey from beginning to end concerned the exercise of power – who would lose and who would gain; and for which ends would wealth and power be exercised? Behind the personalities there was an ideological conflict between private interests and what were increasingly seen as public needs.

---

[418] John Williams, *Digest of Welsh Historical Statistics, Vol. 1*, (Cardiff, 1985), p. 63.

[419] A. H. Williams, *Public Health, Vol 2* , 125/10, pp. 1019-1024, P.H. Holland, 15 December 1853.

This is true but the whole truth is more complicated. Private property was the cornerstone of the entire society; private gain was seen as contributing to public good. The ebb and flow of immigration and emigration and the constant circulation through the town of young males, said to number 10,000-11,000 in the 1840s vitiated any sense of belonging or civic pride. For workmen without a vote and whose livelihood depended upon the fluctuations in the iron trade the benefits of civic reform were not self-evident, while at the same time their masters portrayed it as an unnecessary and expensive diversion. The result was powerful but unexpected alliances against incorporation. The topography of the parish of Merthyr Tydfil and the raw exploitation of its mineral resources also became increasingly relevant. In the arena that was Merthyr Tydfil the interaction between class and power was nakedly exposed.

Taking Control

Despite its growth into a large town Merthyr retained until 1836 the traditional rural parish form of self-government. Magistrates were appointed by the Lord Lieutenant of Glamorgan, and a rate to look after the poor was fixed quarterly by ratepayers meeting as a 'vestry': a system totally unsuitable for the new industrial world. When the long-term voracious demand for labour was interrupted by short-term falls in the demand for iron, hundreds of unemployed and destitute workers sought parish relief. The result was that the level of the poor rate, and who was to pay it, became the major issue in local politics from the late eighteenth century onwards. The parishioners wanted to shift the burden of paying for paupers and their dependents onto the shoulders of the ironmasters who were responsible for attracting this ever-growing population and who were making handsome profits. Almost unwillingly, the ironmasters became embroiled in local politics as they sought to avoid paying higher rates and a higher proportion of the rates.

They began by agreeing in September 1795 that they would make a voluntary additional contribution to the parish funds of £20 per furnace per annum. But when in April 1797 the parishioners proposed a new rate assessment that the ironmasters considered 'enormous' they appealed against it and during 1797-8 went on the offensive. The parishioners' demands were rebuffed and the ironmasters emerged totally victorious. For the next decade the parishioners concerned themselves with law and order; establishing a rudimentary gaol — 'the black hole', a court of requests to recover small debts and in June 1811 extra payment for constables.[420]

The growth of the population, the 'disorderly' conduct of the people, the demands upon the rates of paupers and the appearance in the town of more ambitious traders and businessmen led in 1822 to the creation of a Select Vestry, dominated by the ironworks' interests but in which the James family and their associates played an increasingly prominent role. Until the formation of the Board of Guardians in 1836 the Select Vestry with its twenty members governed the town. But these were years of economic distress, industrial strife and demands for Reform. By 1830 the parish was £660 in debt. A cross-party alliance of Anthony Hill and William Thomas, both Tories, William Crawshay II who was in his radical phase, and the reforming James interest, set up in March 1831 a standing committee to reform parish administration. Apart from the ironmasters and William Thomas, every member 'was a Unitarian or a Unitarian's kinsman. Three were members of the

[420] Evans, *The Labyrinth*, pp. 188 ff.

James family'.[421] The Select Vestry, the standing committee, and ironmasters acting as magistrates while absorbed in the fortunes of their ironworks, were inadequate instruments to maintain law and order in the turbulent frontier town that was Merthyr Tydfil. In 1827 leading citizens petitioned the Home Secretary that the appointment of a resident Stipendiary Magistrate was 'absolutely necessary' and Melbourne in 1829 appointed J. B. Bruce to the office. This was how Merthyr with a population approaching 30,000 was governed when the Municipal Corporations Act was passed in 1835.

The significance of the Act was that for boroughs, traditionally governed in a variety of ways, it created a town council; a body of councillors elected by all male householders who paid the poor rate and who had been in residence for three years. This had two implications: the council could be called to account by local ratepayers through regular elections; and it was a recipe for an expansion of the power of the rate-paying middle classes. When in February 1833 it was announced that such a Bill would be introduced it was also intimated that large unincorporated towns like Merthyr that had been granted an MP under the 1832 Reform Act should, by a separate measure, also be made corporate boroughs with a town council. [422]

Drawing the Battle Lines

These proposals from the reformed Parliament, in themselves 'considered to be of great political and party significance',[423]

---

[421] Williams, *Rising*, pp. 61–4.

[422] Sidney and Beatrice Webb, *English Local Government From The Revolution to the Municipal Corporations Act: The Manor and the Borough, Part Two*, (London, 1924), p.710.

[423] G.B.A.M. Finlayson, 'The Politics of Municipal Reform, 1835' *The English Historical Review*, Vol. 81, No. 321. (October, 1966).

came when political controversy in Merthyr was intense. In the aftermath of the 1831 armed insurrection, the 1832 election of Josiah John Guest as the town's first MP and radical cries for more reform, William Crawshay who had been an outspoken democrat in 1831 moved to the right and the Marquess of Bute, President of the Glamorgan Tories, financed the *Merthyr Guardian* in November 1832 specifically to oppose Guest and the radicals.[424] Anthony Hill and Alderman Thompson respectively of the Plymouth and Penydarren works were strong proponents of *laisser-faire* and opposed to every concession of power to the people.[425] It is no surprise therefore to find a fierce debate breaking out in Merthyr when the Bill that would introduce municipal government to towns favoured by the Reform Act was presented to Parliament by Lord Brougham on 22 August 1833. Edward Lewis Richards, barrister and admirer of Cobbett, raised the issue on 3 September at the end of a meeting convened to discuss the improvement of postal services to Merthyr. Guest and J.B. Bruce, the stipendiary magistrate, decided the matter was of such importance that a separate meeting was required. Accordingly, a notice appeared in the *Merthyr Guardian* calling for a public meeting on 4 October to discuss the Bill and to consider 'erecting a Town Hall and such other buildings as may be found useful in regulating the affairs of the said borough'. In addition to Guest and Bruce the signatories included Dr. William Thomas of the Court Estate, E. L. Richards, Thomas Darker, Christopher James and his cousins William Jones and Henry Jones.[426]

Guest, for reasons that are not clear, did not turn up. The meeting of 4 October was postponed to 25 October and again,

---

[424] R.D. Rees, 'Glamorgan Newspapers under the Stamp Acts', *Morgannwg*, Vol. 3, 1959.

[425] H.W. Southey in Wilkins, *History*, p. 538.

[426] *MG*, 7 September 1833.

despite 'nearly all the most respectable and influential gentlemen of the borough' 'waiting a considerable time' he did not turn up.[427] The meeting was therefore adjourned to 7 November at the Castle inn. Again Guest did not attend. The crowded meeting went ahead with William Crawshay voted into the chair in Guest's absence. The main speakers were Anthony Hill and William Meyrick, Crawshay's solicitor, who had briefed the prosecution case against Dic Penderyn. Meyrick concentrated on the alleged costs that incorporation would bring: £1,000 for a Recorder; £300 for a town clerk; £200 for a deputy town clerk; £100 for a treasurer. These and other costs would result in a bill of £2,300 per annum. Worse, the Bill would empower 'a Corporation to go to any expenses, to form any estimates, to levy any sums they choose to estimate on the parishes of Merthyr, Aberdare and Vaynor, without any appeal'.

Anthony Hill, who spoke first, argued that Merthyr was not ready for such a Bill. The town had no resident landed gentry. Those gentlemen who were resident in Merthyr were fully engaged in business. The town already had an experienced and impartial stipendiary magistrate. In a dig at the shopocracy he declared: ' I hope that no glittering visions of fancied glories, no fond anticipations of civic honours, have made any of our neighbours imagine they are elevated in the path of honour, by rising in civic power'.

The application of the Bill to Merthyr would

> bring among us envy, malice, and all uncharitableness. It will set brother against brother, friend against friend, neighbour against neighbour, in the constant animosity of contested elections. It will bring, if not corruption into the seat of

[427] *MG*, 2 November 1833.

> judgement, at least the suspicion of it, which is almost as pernicious.[428]

Resolutions against incorporation were carried with acclamation and unanimity.

In this first debate on incorporation we hear the three main arguments against that were to be repeated throughout the century: the open-ended cost; the satisfactory nature of the existing system; and the alleged desire of the middle class to aggrandise themselves through civic power.

In fact Brougham's Bill was dropped, but the local debate was revived in dramatic fashion a few months later in January 1834. The government had appointed a Royal Commission in July 1833 to inquire into the state of municipal corporations in England and Wales in order to prepare the ground for the proposed Municipal Corporations Bill.[429] On 13 January two Commissioners appeared in Merthyr unannounced (Guest denied any previous knowledge of their appearance, a statement difficult to accept), spent the day dividing the parliamentary borough into six wards (of which Aberdare would comprise two), and had a meeting with Guest. He then issued a handbill inviting electors to meet the next day to consider appointing a deputation to meet with the Commissioners to discuss any objections to incorporation. He proposed the meeting should follow one already arranged to discuss postal improvements!

The highlight of the meeting was Anthony Hill's scathing

---

[428] *MG*, 9 November 1833. These arguments against had already been rehearsed in the *Merthyr Guardian*, 2 November 1833.

[429] For the circumstances surrounding the appointment of the Royal Commission and the nature of its Report see Sidney and Beatrice Webb, *The Manor and the Borough*, Part Two, pp. 712-721; G.B.A.M. Finlayson, 'The Municipal Corporation Commission and Report, 1833-35', *Historical Research*, Vol. 36, (1963).

attack upon Guest, who was in the chair. He argued that no such deputation was needed because the meeting in November had taken a clear decision against incorporation.

> What! Was the honourable gentleman, so lately elected without one dissentient voice by the inhabitants, so unfit for his station, was he so imbecile of mind, so incapable of the duties devolving upon him, so destitute of language in which to assert our sentiments, as to require this assistance. If it were so, he for one would tell him to his face that he was not fit to be our member, and that the sooner he resigned that station the better. (Hear. Hear). But he entertained no such opinion of him ...

Despite this verbal assault and a supporting speech from Meyrick, a proposal by D.W. James to send a deputation was passed by 22 votes to 12. The deputation selected consisted of Guest and his radical supporters: William Perkins, Walter Morgan, D.W. James, Henry Jones, William Bryant, and Joseph Coffin.[430] Such an outcome was not surprising for, as the *Merthyr Guardian* pointed out, in a room that would only hold forty 'by a wonderful concurrence of chances the 22 who, it seems, out of 500 voters are favourable to the bill, are assembled in the room!'[431]

The discussions on incorporation brought a heightened sense of civic responsibilities among the middle class activists, of both political camps. Meetings in October and November 1834 discussed the need to provide a town hall, a market place, and a savings bank.[432] Guest almost single-handedly promoted the bank, the market place was achieved, but as a private enterprise

[430] *MG*, 18 January 1834.

[431] *MG*, 25 January 1834.

[432] *MG*, 1, 15 November 1834.

rather than as a public facility, and as for the town hall, that story is almost as long as that for incorporation. Discussion began in 1833 and the town hall was finally completed in May 1896. Arguments went on for years about where to build it, about the cost of the building and whether there was really any need for one.

When in 1835 the Municipal Corporations Bill passed into law Merthyr, like Manchester, was no longer a town that could automatically receive charter borough status. To achieve that, a Royal Charter of Incorporation would have to be obtained by petitioning the Crown through the Privy Council which would then set up an Inquiry. Petitions calling for incorporation had to be large enough to demonstrate that a substantial number of the town's rate-paying inhabitants were in favour of incorporation.

Guest and the radicals attempted this in 1837. The immediate excuse was an attempt to get rid of Bruce the stipendiary magistrate but the meeting, chaired by Guest on 31 March, turned into one calling for a petition for the incorporation of the borough. Scornfully the *Merthyr Guardian* pointed out the dangers. 'Once give a Corporation the right of taxation and ...who can define the limits of Merthyr vanity and ambition ...What forbids that every office in the Corporation shall be filled by mere ten pound voters? The radical Beer-house keepers of Dowlais'.[433]

Once again the opponents argued that the costs of incorporation could only be met by raising rates against which there could be no appeal; that there were no gentry resident in the town capable of filling the various civic offices; that a Corporation would embroil friends and neighbours in contention for civic honours and foment bad feeling; that the

433 *MG*, 22 April 1837.

Court of Requests had been a cause of the 1831 riot because the people in charge of it had abused their power, a fact proven by Parliamentary inquiry; and that all Merthyr really required was a renewal of the Act granting Merthyr a stipendiary magistrate. The reference to the Court of Requests was a shrewd blow aimed at Joseph Coffin, Chairman of the Court of Requests and a leading member of the middle class reformers.

Those favouring incorporation argued that the town was the first in population, wealth and commercial importance within the Principality. Although Parliament had granted it an MP no provision had been made for the 'local wants' arising from the growth of population and that this population having only a parish vestry and constables was without 'any institutions for the quiet and good government of their town'. The granting of a borough charter together with an efficient Recorder and a borough court would deal with all problems. The meeting was told that Guest's purse 'was open to assist in furthering their views' and the petition was adopted with only one person voting against. But a warning came in a letter from William Crawshay: 'he could not fully enter into their views, until he had conferred with Messrs Guest, Thompson and Hill'.[434] The opposition of Crawshay, Thompson and Hill killed off the hopes of the small group of radicals and the question of incorporation did not resurface for another twenty years.

Instead, new institutions of local government appeared that superseded the Select Vestry and became the focus for local politics. The 1834 Poor Law Amendment Act required the election of a Board of Guardians to deal with the poor. The voting system linked the right to vote to property ownership and to wealth. The owners and occupiers of the larger

[434] *MG*, 22 April, 13, 27 May 1837. In a satirical article 'A little story for the People of Merthyr Tydfil' the *Merthyr Chronicle*, 26 August 1837, argued the benefits of 'local government'.

properties received extra votes. When the other institution of local government arrived in 1850 — a local board of health — that too was elected on a franchise tied to wealth. The ironmasters ensured that they or their agents were well represented upon these bodies. The problems of pauperism and public health took priority over incorporation.

The Temperance Hall Meetings

The delays in providing clean water to the citizens of Merthyr and Dowlais go to the heart of Merthyr politics in the mid-nineteenth century. In 1857 Crawshay and Hill, on the local board of health, were still obstructing the provision of water to the town seven years after Rammell's report. The middle class, more numerous, more confident, more clearly defined as a 'middle' class standing between the ironmasters and the lower orders, campaigned once again for incorporation. Although the immediate stimulus for resuscitating calls for incorporation arose from comments by Fowler, the stipendiary magistrate and George Overton, the coroner, on the need for local bye-laws, the focus of the middle-class attack was upon the general lack of civic amenities in Merthyr and the failure of the local board of health to provide water. A deputation canvassed the ironmasters seeking signatures for a petition calling upon the High Constable to convene a public meeting. Amongst the 126 signatures were Robert Thompson Crawshay, George Thomas Clark, and William Menelaus. None of these, however, attended the meeting held in the Temperance Hall on 23 September 1857. The tone was set by the chairman Walter Smyth, chemist and High Constable:

> was Merthyr 'so far behind the rest of the country as not to merit what others considered a boon and a privilege? Were the

> tradesmen of Merthyr Tydfil inferior to those of other towns and were they afraid to trust to them the interests and local government of the town? (cheers)'.[435]

In the following debate the heavy-weights of the Merthyr middle class all spoke in favour. T.W. Goodfellow, grocer and former High Constable, moved the resolution for a petition urging incorporation. 'Merthyr is not what it ought to be' he said, 'it does not possess the common necessities belonging to towns of similar size, and which we feel justified in demanding'. Nuisances existed that ought to be removed. The Board of Health had 'treated with slight and neglect the greatest of all wants – the want of water (applause)'. 'Merthyr is not a small village, and ought not to be treated as one. It is a large town and justly demands the rights of a town'.[436] Thomas Stephens, seconded, and was supported by Frank James, clerk to the Board of Guardians, George Overton, coroner for the district, and William Simons, solicitor and authority on mining law, with a 'commanding presence, a fine cultured voice,' and an eye that could 'terrorise a witness by its flashing indignation and scorn'.[437] The meeting overwhelmingly resolved that a petition for a Charter should be sent to the Privy Council.

Upon hearing the outcome of the September meeting sixty-nine year old William Crawshay II immediately descended upon Merthyr from his estate in Caversham and organised the signatures of 121 ratepayers calling for another public meeting. Boldly, Walter Smyth the High Constable refused to call it on the grounds that William Crawshay, Anthony Hill, Forman of Penydarren, and all the other signatories had had proper notice

[435] *MG*, 26 September 1857.

[436] *MG*, 26 September 1857.

[437] Obituary, *Merthyr Express*, 28 October 1893.

of the previous meeting and should have turned up to that one. Undeterred, Crawshay called a meeting anyway on 14 October, and the Temperance Hall was crowded as workers from Plymouth and Cyfarthfa were released from work to attend. In fact neither William nor Robert Crawshay were able to attend due to ill-health and a number of those in favour of incorporation attended this open meeting.

As he had done twenty years earlier Anthony Hill moved a resolution against incorporation, arguing 'that the town and parish of Merthyr Tydfil are in possession of all the requirements for the government of their affairs, and for all the needful benefits, and for the protection of life and property, and for the comfort and well-being of the inhabitants...' and consequently 'any application made to Her Majesty for a Charter of Incorporation to be unnecessary and improper, especially as there is not a jot of property of any sort attached to the parish or town requiring the perpetuation of funds, such perpetuation of property being the main use and object of a Charter of Incorporation.'

W. Robinson Smith, solicitor, then moved an amendment arguing for incorporation. It would not cost more than the current arrangements; Aberdare was shaming Merthyr by going ahead with the building of a town hall; nuisances of so foul a nature existed in Merthyr that its name was infamously known throughout the kingdom. In support of the amendment the doughty William Simons declared 'It is only necessary for Mr. Crawshay to hold up his little finger, and the water will be forthcoming as if the rock had been touched by Moses' rod'. To say that everything in Merthyr was unalterably good was surely absurd. G.T. Clark praised incorporation in principle but stated that it remained to be seen whether the majority wanted it. Furthermore, he declared that 'he would not feel it safe' to trust the security of the Dowlais works in the hands of a town council police force.

It was while George Overton was speaking in favour of incorporation that the meeting was told it was running an hour over time and that the Hall was needed for a concert. In the confusion that followed, a member of the concert party turned the gas off at the meter, plunging the Hall into total darkness and chaos. Despite this 'laughable fiasco' as Harry Southey described it, the expressed opposition of the ironmasters combined with 600 signatures on their petition put an end to ideas of incorporation for the time being. [438]

By mid-century the Merthyr middle class though larger than twenty years earlier was still a much smaller group than existed in towns of comparable size and nature.[439] Nonetheless, their speeches exude a new found confidence. Despite this and their expertise they could not prevail against the ironmasters. In no small measure this was because the working class was also against them. These were the years when a belief in the mutuality of interest between employer and worker was generally accepted. But working class opposition to incorporation was based on more than that.

The principal reason was economic. Workers believed that incorporation would increase the rates and so lead to an increase in rents. It was a message that for the past twenty-four years their employers had hammered home and it was a risk that workers were not willing to take. Most workers in Merthyr did not directly pay rates but had them included in their rents. This had two consequences: under the prevailing property franchise it excluded the vast majority of working men from participating in parliamentary and local elections; and landlords who did pay rates merely passed the cost on to working people

---

[438] *MG*, 17 and 24 October 1857.

[439] W.D. Rubenstein, 'The Size and Distribution of the English Middle Classes in 1860', *Historical Research*, Vol. 61 (February 1988).

by increasing their rents.[440] Consequently, workmen were suspicious of schemes coming from the middle class (a number of whom were English and open to suspicion on that account alone) and regarded with hostility any proposal that could entail increased expenditure.

And understandably so: ironworkers and colliers were only too conscious of the trade cycle and the fluctuations in wages and employment that plunged families into poverty. Material circumstances determine survival. Both the workmen and Dyke, in their different ways, understood that. It has been argued that it is necessary to go beyond 'narrow Chadwickian environmentalism' to recognise that 'the history of struggles over wages and hours ...cannot be left out of the history of public health'.[441] The same economic realities applied in Merthyr to the issue of incorporation.

We are also in the realm of nineteenth-century 'influence politics', at which the iron companies excelled.[442] Company agents were instructed to take petitions against incorporation around to tradesmen and contractors who supplied the works, and also to those employees who were ratepayers. Coercion and patronage ensured that company nominees sat on the select

---

440 Rammell, *Report*, pp. 19-20. This system of 'compounding' was also administratively more convenient than having to collect hundreds of small sums.

441 Michael Sigsworth and Michael Worboys, 'The public's view of public health in mid-Victorian Britain', *Urban History*, Vol. 21 (2) (October 1994).

442 See the letter dated 7 April 1853 from John Jones, Dowlais grocer, to the General Board of Health in Williams (ed.) *Public Health*, 125/9. On forms of influence generally, see Patrick Joyce, *Work, Society and Politics* (Brighton, 1980) and Dianne K. Drummond, *Crewe: Railway Town, Company and People 1840–1914* (Aldershot, 1995).

vestry, the poor law guardians, the local board of health and, when it came in 1894, the urban district council. Company clerks filled in ballot papers for the men who were at work.[443] Workmen were encouraged to intimidate waverers. In addition, a substantial number of the middle class and skilled workmen were cottage owners. Therefore an alliance existed between the ironmasters, the landlords of small cottages who foresaw problems in recouping increased rents, and the leading Merthyr Chartists — Morgan Williams, Matthew John and William Gould — who although they strongly pressed the economic argument also objected to the property qualifications for municipal voters and office holders, standing firm for universal male suffrage and the secret ballot. William Simons called this alliance between the ironmasters and Chartists 'an ugly compact'.[444] Once again the shopocracy retreated and it was not until 1873 that another serious attempt was made. By then much had changed.

The First Inquiry

In June 1873 a lengthy discussion at the Bush Hotel resulted in a committee of fifty to carry matters forward and a public meeting was arranged at the Temperance Hall for 14 August 1873 at 3 p.m., a time deliberately inconvenient for workmen to attend. But two days before it was due to be held, the committee learned that workmen would be released from the Cyfarthfa and Plymouth works to pack the meeting. When the town crier announced to the milling crowd that the meeting had been called off, hundreds gathered in frustration in the market-

---

[443] Thomas Stephens referred to the 'mode of election' to the local board of health as 'vicious'; *MG*, 26 September 1857. See also evidence of George Overton and William Simons to Inquiry, *ME*, 23 December 1876.

[444] *MG*, 17 October 1857.

square where Morgan Williams, Gould, and other opponents of incorporation addressed them from a wagon.[445] Over a year passed before another attempt was made. In October and November 1874 public lectures making the case for incorporation were given in the Temperance Hall, and meetings aimed at getting the support of working people were held in Merthyr, Troedyrhiw, Abercanaid, Dowlais and Georgetown.[446]

Eventually a petition with 3,600 signatures representing a rateable value of £30,000 was sent to the Privy Council. But three petitions against were also sent: one from the Dowlais Company; another from 4,062 inhabitants representing a rateable value of £16,000; and the third from people in the Merthyr Vale district. In addition there was a resolution against from a meeting of ratepayers in Dowlais.[447] The Privy Council decided that the case should be heard and the first inquiry into the proposed incorporation of Merthyr took place in December 1876. It lasted four days.

Representations from Dowlais and Merthyr Vale now brought the topography of the parish into play. With the Plymouth and Cyfarthfa works closed and 2,000 to 3,000 women and children a day being fed by soup kitchens, the northern and southern parts of the parish declared their wish to be independent. Behind both these demands lay the interests of the major employers – the Dowlais Company, and Nixon, Taylor and Cory of the Merthyr Vale colliery. The attempt by Nixon seven years earlier to take Merthyr Vale out of the jurisdiction of the local board of health was still remembered: 'If any local authority were hereafter formed there, it would be completely

[445] Southey in Wilkins, *History*; *Merthyr Telegraph*, 15 and 22 August 1873; *Merthyr Express*, 16 August 1873.

[446] *Merthyr Telegraph*, 23, 30 October, 13, 27 November, 1874; *Merthyr Express*, 7, 28 November 1874.

[447] Report of Inquiry, *Merthyr Express*, 16 December 1876.

under the influence and direction of [Nixon, Taylor and Cory]'.[448] As for Dowlais, G. T. Clark made the definitive statement: 'I have not a word to say against what the ratepayers of Merthyr may propose to do — as a neighbour I shall be glad to do all I can to aid them; but I do not think that the town of Dowlais should be included in the proposed Corporation'.[449]

Fourteen months after the Inquiry the Privy Council ruled that incorporation could not be granted 'for the present'. It was a huge disappointment although the words 'for the present' gave the promoters some hope. Despite his association with Cobden, Henry Richard gave little support to moves for incorporation. Indeed, married to a wealthy wife and living all his adult life in London, Richard's contact with Merthyr and its aspirations was minimal.[450] In 1881, spurred by the election of a Liberal administration, the Privy Council was asked to look at the issue again but refused after so short an interval.

The next attempt did not come for another 16 years. As Harry Southey who was intimately involved in the campaign remarked: 'the most courageous of Incorporationists were disheartened by the failure of their efforts.'[451] But in 1896 another campaign succeeded in achieving an Inquiry in 1897. It was held at the new Town Hall opened in May 1896. The promoters entered that Inquiry with high hopes and came out of it with high hopes too. Although a new 'Dowlais' works had started production at Cardiff, prosperity had returned to the parish. Cyfarthfa had followed Dowlais in converting to steel production, both companies were exploiting to the full their coal

[448] Ieuan Gwynedd Jones, *Communities: Essays in the Social History of Victorian Wales* (Llandysul, 1987), pp. 142-3.

[449] Report of Inquiry, *Merthyr Express*, 6 January 1877.

[450] Gwyn Griffiths, *Henry Richard: Apostle of Peace and Welsh Patriot* (2012).

[451] Wilkins, *History*, p. 545.

reserves, and the collieries at Merthyr Vale and Treharris were in full production. Indeed the coal industry now dominated with 40 per cent of all employed men in the parish classified as miners. House building and rateable values were rising and the population was once again increasing.[452]

Moreover, the politics of the situation had changed. The Local Government Act of 1888 had enfranchised all ratepayers, set up county councils and replaced local boards of health with district councils. Merthyr Tydfil now had an Urban District Council within Glamorgan County Council. There were eighteen urban district councillors, three from each of the six wards — Dowlais, Penydarren, Cyfarthfa, Town, Plymouth and Merthyr Vale. In addition, incorporated boroughs with more than 50,000 inhabitants could become County Boroughs with all the powers of a County. That was the prize that gave the reformers a fresh incentive to seek incorporation. Once again the driving force in this new campaign was the shopocracy now working through the Merthyr Chamber of Trade founded in 1878 and backed, significantly, by the Dowlais Chamber founded in 1894. An application for a Charter in Victoria's jubilee year seemed appropriate.[453]

However, one thing that had not changed was the influence of the employers. The new Urban District Council played an inglorious role. In February it decided by one vote to submit a petition in favour. The petition was submitted. On 4 August on the motion of Councillor H. Gray, the general manager of Nixon's collieries, it voted to rescind that decision. At the next meeting on 18 August it rescinded the rescission. It was a battle between those on the Council who represented, or were

[452] Barry Brunt, 'Economic Development in the Merthyr and Rhymney Valleys 1851-1913: A Comparative Study', *Merthyr Historian*, Vol. 4 (1989); Wilkins, *History*, 545-6.

[453] *ME*, 21 November 1896, 6 March 1897.

influenced by, the major employers and those regarded as independent. Decisions depended upon who turned up to meetings.[454]

The Inquiry itself gave hope. Commissioner Cresswell who conducted the Inquiry peremptorily declared that 'My mind is made up, and has been for many years, as to the obvious advantages of a municipal corporation as compared with other forms of administration'. He sternly criticised the antics of the Council as 'absolutely unprecedented' and 'inconsistent with the duty of public men' and uncovered the pressure that Cyfarthfa had exerted upon its workmen to sign the petition against incorporation.[455] But the traditional opposition from Dowlais and Cyfarthfa was now augmented by the railway companies and by Glamorgan County Council, which had an interest in any change to the status of the Urban District. Above all was the almost unanimous opposition from ratepayers in Merthyr Vale and Treharris. The population in Merthyr Vale was now over 11,000 and the colliery companies at Merthyr Vale and Treharris paid one third of all the parish rates. The cry from the lower end of the parish was 'by all means incorporate Merthyr but leave us out of it'. Crucially, the petitioners against were almost double the number in favour and although it was a shock, on reflection it could not have been a surprise that the outcome was once again negative. The century ended with a large industrial borough which sent two Members to the Westminster Parliament being considered not fit to govern its own affairs.

[454] *ME*, 20 February, 7 August 1897.

[455] *ME*, 9, 16 October 1897.

17

The Guardians and the Poor

> ...of those who receive relief, the enormous majority owe their degradation to ...their own improvidence, intemperance and recklessness, or to the evil example of those who have been paupers before them.
>
> **Henry Austen Bruce**[456]

On 10 January 1860 Walter Dukesell, a labourer aged sixty, lodging in Caedraw died 'from exhaustion, consequent on the want of food'. He was buried in an unmarked pauper's grave. Originally from Worcestershire Walter had twice lost a wife and child in Merthyr. In 1839 his twenty-five-year-old wife Mary and eleven-day-old daughter Elizabeth had died within a few days of each other, the likely effects of childbirth. In 1854 his thirty-six-year-old wife Mary and three-year-old son Walter had also died within days of each other, probably from one of the diseases rampant in that year. When the *Merthyr Guardian* reported Walter's death it added that a few weeks earlier there had been a death from starvation in Twynyrodyn and commented, few of 'the wealthier classes of Merthyr' were aware that 'many poor persons ...are suffering the extremities of want.' [457]

---

[456] H.A. Bruce, *The Present Position and Future Prospects of the Working Classes in the Manufacturing Districts of South Wales* (Cardiff, 1851).

[457] *MG*, 14 January 1860. I owe the details of Walter Dukesell's life to Carolyn Jacob.

How many lived in extreme poverty in Victorian Merthyr is not known. One estimate in the distressed early 1840s reckoned that 6,000 to 7,000 people a year received parish relief, well over 10 per cent of the population. By 1850, in the aftermath of the cholera outbreak, approximately 13 per cent were officially paupers.[458] The number of people in dire poverty went up and down with the trade cycle but by definition they were those who received poor relief, the tip of a very large iceberg. Many chose not to apply. To apply for relief and be labelled 'a pauper' was a social disgrace.

Poverty a Moral Fault

The dominant view was that poverty resulted from moral failings. Henry Bruce, concerned for enlightened progress, believed the 'lower classes' needed guidance from above. On 30 April 1851 in a lecture delivered at the Merthyr Subscription Library Bruce set out his views on 'the working classes' of Merthyr and Aberdare:

> The children running wild about the streets till they were old enough to be turned to profit, the men knowing no relaxation from the hours of labour but the society of the public house, the women ignorant of the sacred duties of mothers and wives – conceive this population yearly increasing with enormous rapidity, with little or nothing to remind them of their duties here, of their hopes hereafter – and ask yourselves, what could be expected of them but improvidence, brutality and ignorance?

And reflecting upon the occasions when trade was good and earnings high

---

[458] Keith Strange, *Merthyr Tydfil Iron Metropolis* (Stroud, 2005), p. 72.

> It means that during what are called the good times, the superfluous earnings are misspent in intoxication and debauchery; it means that the workman contracts irregular habits by gaining in three or four days as much as will enable him to live in guilty and riotous pleasures during the remainder of the week. It means that the workman is as little to be trusted with money as the Red Indian with drink...[459]

Poverty, he argued, arose from moral weakness and 'superfluous earnings'.

The logical response to this widely held understanding was to praise the worker who looked after his family within the limits imposed on his earnings by market forces, and to ensure that those receiving welfare had a lower standard of living than the responsible worker, a view enforced by the 1834 Poor Law Amendment Act. Until then the Elizabethan Poor Law of 1601 had made each parish responsible for giving financial assistance ('relief') to the poor of the parish and empowered parishes to raise a rate for that purpose. Those entitled to receive relief had to be 'settled' in a parish; usually by birth, apprenticeship, house ownership or for a woman, marriage to a man of that parish. The destitute who were not 'settled' were sent back to their original parish. By 1834 a jungle of local practices and levels of relief had grown up which the Act was intended to clear away.

The 1834 Act

The framers of the Act believed that too many people were depending upon welfare rather than finding work. The Act

[459] H.A. Bruce, *The Present Position and Future Prospects of the Working Classes in the Manufacturing Districts of South Wales* (Cardiff, 1851).

therefore had two main objectives. The first was to restore the incentive to work. The second was to reduce the poor rate and lift the burden on ratepayers. Men who did not provide for themselves and their family deserved to be punished. To enforce this view an able-bodied man seeking 'relief' would get nothing unless he, and his family, went into a workhouse where the regime would be as unpleasant as possible. This threat would provide the incentive to find work.

Part of the workhouse unpleasantness was the diet which was intended to be both monotonous and meagre (although there were numerous local deviations). For breakfast men were allowed one-and-a-half-pints of thin gruel made of poor quality oatmeal and water. Three times a week on Mondays, Wednesdays and Fridays they were allowed four ounces of cooked meat. Women received three-and-a-half-ounces. On Tuesdays, Thursdays and Saturdays men and women were allowed two ounces of cheese. The quality was poor and the official diet for able-bodied men was less than the 292 ounces of solid food per week allowed to prisoners. It was, however, guaranteed. In the last resort poor relief was designed to prevent starvation not to prevent poverty. More distressing was the harshness with which families were treated. Wives were separated from husbands; children above the age of two were separated from their mothers. The workhouse uniform had to be worn; there were strict rules – up at five a.m. in the summer, up at seven a.m. in winter, bed by eight p.m. at the latest. Able-bodied men worked at stone-breaking, the women worked in the laundry.[460] Inmates lost the right to vote and were shut away from the community.

To administer the Act there were three Poor Law Commissioners in London while around the country parishes

[460] Anne Digby, *British Welfare Policy: Workhouse to Workfare* (1989), pp. 30-2.

were grouped together in Poor Law Unions. The Merthyr Tydfil Union, responsible for a population of about 50,000, included nine parishes covering not only Merthyr but Aberdare, Vaynor, Gelligaer, Penderyn, Rhigos, and much of what is now Rhondda and Caerphilly. These Poor Law Unions were administered by elected 'guardians of the poor'. Only those who had £500 in real property or an income from property of at least £15 a year were eligible to stand for election as a Guardian. Only property owners were eligible to vote and their voting power depended upon the value of their property. Those with property rated at less than £50 had one vote, property worth £50-£100 gave the owner two votes, owners of property with a value of £250 or more had six votes. In the Merthyr Poor Law Union there were twenty-one elected Guardians, only eight of whom were from Merthyr. The ironworks as major ratepayers had *ex officio* as well as elected representatives on the board of the Merthyr Union. But of the eight representatives from Merthyr elected to the first Board in 1836, five were members of the Unitarian faction and Freemasons — D. W. James (the first vice-chairman), Richard Jenkins the auctioneer from Aberfan, William Jones, grocer, William Purnell, Dowlais grocer and Roland Hopkins, brewer. The other three elected members were Benjamin Martin, Penydarren, Thomas Evans, Dowlais, and Thomas Shepherd, Cyfarthfa; all three employed as agents for their works. Josiah Guest was an *ex officio* member and chairman of the first meeting held in the Castle Inn on 3 November 1836.

The Act was flawed from the beginning. It had been designed to deal with the many impoverished agricultural field labourers in the south of England and with the subsidies paid from the rates to those on starvation wages. It did not take account of, or foresee, the poverty that could occur among able-bodied men in the growing industrial towns of the north of England, the Midlands, and in the South Wales 'iron district' where unemployment was of a quite different character. A slump could throw hundreds, even thousands, temporarily out of work but a recovery would find most of them back in employment.

There was huge opposition to the Act. It was seen as part of a concerted assault on 'the lower orders' that included exclusion from the 1832 Reform Act, the new police, and the Tolpuddle repression of trade unions. Dickens' *Oliver Twist* published in 1838 accurately expressed the popular view that it was an instrument of centralised tyranny that gave licence to local corruption and incompetence. In Merthyr the blind balladeer and activist Richard Williams, *Dic Dywyll*, was alleged to have single-handedly delayed by years the building of the local workhouse through his carefully aimed verses. The reality was more substantial. The reformed Parliament, elected without working-class votes, had passed the Act into law just three years after Merthyr's armed insurrection. Troops were still stationed in Dowlais and fear of another uprising gripped the shopocracy throughout the thirties and forties. This fear was fed when from 1839 the Merthyr Chartists became the largest and best organised working-class movement in Wales, all deeply opposed to the New Poor Law and to the building of a workhouse.

Faced with these problems and alive to the local situation the Merthyr Guardians resisted all pressures from the men in Whitehall. Pragmatically they continued to make cash payments to those out of work until the local economy recovered. In effect relief was used as a dole until the return of full-time work. This was entirely against the spirit and intention of the 1834 Act but many industrial areas did the same. [461] An attempt to return to the ethos of the Act came in 1842 with the Outdoor Labour Test Order which said that outdoor relief could be given to able-bodied men and their dependents, if the unemployed men did

---

[461] Geoffrey Best, *Mid-Victorian Britain 1851-1870* (Fontana, 1979), p. 163

tasks such as the breaking of stones. The virtues of the 1834 Act were eloquently championed at the first meeting of the Merthyr Guardians by Assistant Commissioner Clive who had come to give advice and ensure that the Merthyr Guardians understood their responsibilities. A workhouse, he explained, would become a place of refuge and comfort for the old, the helpless and the destitute. 'For the idle and dissolute, it would be a punishment'.[462] It was nineteen years after the passing of the Act before one was built in Merthyr.

Why Build a Workhouse?

With the great majority of the population determined to oppose a workhouse, and the local Guardians resisting pressure from Whitehall, why eventually build one? The explanation lies in that most potent of compulsions: 'Events, dear boy. Events'.[463] The depression of 1842 saw the amounts paid out in relief rise from almost £6,000 in the period April 1840-March 1841 to well over £9,000 in April 1842-April 1843. The depression of 1848-50 resulted in payments rising from £11,400 in April 1848-March 1849 to well over £14,000 in succeeding years.[464] These payments were not solely caused by industrial depressions. The lack of clean water and the filthy condition of the town caused illnesses leading to poverty. Analysis of those who received poor law relief in the 1850s has revealed that illness, which accounted for a third of all cases, was the main cause. Accidents and disease were rife in Merthyr and major

---

[462] *MG*, 12 November 1836.

[463] A phrase popularly attributed to the British Prime Minister Harold Macmillan (1894-1986).

[464] Tydfil Thomas, *Poor Relief in Merthyr Tydfil Union in Victorian Times* (Cardiff, 1992), p. 26. This is a detailed and excellent account of the subject.

epidemics coincided with periods of prolonged economic depression that reduced resistance to disease. Second among recipients were widows and their dependent children and third were the aged infirm, the majority again being women. Together, these three categories account for almost three-quarters of all cases of pauperism.[465] In the absence of a town council, and before there was a local board of health, the responsibility for coping with sick paupers fell upon the Guardians.

The outbreak of typhus in the spring of 1847 caused Dr. Dyke, in representations to the Guardians, to argue that infected paupers, living in filthy cellars or in Merthyr's overcrowded lodging houses, should be moved to somewhere more suitable for human habitation such as a temporary hospital. The *Merthyr Guardian* gave him support.[466] No action was taken. In February 1848 there came a smallpox epidemic; in 1849 cholera arrived. Despite these epidemics and the horrifying stories that accompanied them, the Guardians neither made provision for a hospital nor for a workhouse.

This highlights the dilemmas faced by the Guardians. The desire to keep the rates down was why even a temporary hospital was not provided, despite the terrible condition of sick paupers. But frugality was undermined by the necessity in recessions to provide outdoor relief for hundreds in exchange for stone-breaking or road mending. A fear of rebellion by 'the mob' inhibited the guardians from building a workhouse. On that they were largely agreed, but on other matters they were riven with indecision because they were evenly divided between those who thought something should be done, and those who objected to the cost of any action. On the whole it was those from the rural parishes outside Merthyr and Aberdare who objected to cost.

---

[465] Strange, pp. 64-5.

[466] Tydfil Thomas, *Poor Relief*, pp. 43-9; *MG*, 12 June 1847.

In 1847-8 the crisis at Dowlais over renewing the lease brought an Inspector down from Whitehall to urge the Guardians to build a workhouse. They pointedly replied: How could a workhouse built for 450 accommodate thousands of unemployed? However, Inspector Farnell of the Poor Law Board raised another issue. Because Merthyr did not have a workhouse it was a magnet for tramps and vagrants claiming outdoor relief. Some 10,000 men were reckoned to be roaming the hills looking for work, or dodging the police and not looking for work. Every year that number passed through Merthyr. There were times when as many as 120 to 130 tramps a week were given relief in the town. The Inspector pointed out that to keep a vagrant in a lodging house cost six shillings (30p) a week, whereas it would only cost 3s.2d (15.8p) in a workhouse. Merthyr was open house for vagrants and it was costing a lot of money. The Poor Law Board suggested that a police constable who had knowledge of vagrants should assist the relieving officers. The Guardians accepted this suggestion and the number of vagrants seeking relief fell to fewer than 40.[467]

Suffer the Little Children

If disease and runaway expenditure were not sufficient to move the Guardians to build a workhouse, they had to face a deeply emotive issue. Almost one third of the paupers who received outdoor relief were children. Most were the children of widows, but there were growing numbers of orphans, 'illegitimates', and deserted children. The official policy both in Whitehall and in Merthyr was to pay the minimum relief without taking any interest in the subsequent welfare or education of the child.

[467] Tydfil Thomas, p. 41.

Children who did not have a family member to look after them were farmed out to anyone who would take them together with the small sums paid to look after them. Begging and running wild around the streets, they ended up in the notorious cellars and lodging houses on course to becoming thieves and prostitutes.

In 1847 the Poor Law Commissioners were replaced by a Poor Law Board that favoured taking children out of workhouses and putting them in separate schools where they could learn a trade. In Merthyr, the rector the Rev. J.C. Campbell, took up their cause and wrote to the Guardians in March 1848 proposing that they take over the disused Old Brewery to house the children. When the children were old enough they should be sent to school. He believed the money could be raised through public subscriptions. The Guardians calculated that the children could be housed at a cost of £8 per child per annum, and proposed to investigate the Old Brewery as a suitable place. Extraordinarily they further thought it would be a good idea to house vagrants with the children. Whitehall inspectors were against the plan, the premises were unsuitable, and Henry Bruce, who as stipendiary magistrate was an *ex-officio* member of the Guardians, argued that the only solution would be to build a workhouse and provide a separate school for the children. An inspector further pointed out that the expenditure of the Merthyr Union was increasing, while expenditure in Unions with workhouses was falling.

The issue came to a head at a meeting of the Guardians on 17 June 1848. Bruce proposed 'That the interests of economy and humanity would be equally promoted by the erection of a workhouse'. He appealed to the Guardians to consider the present and eternal welfare of the children against the small number of able-bodied adults who would enter a workhouse, if built. The resolution was seconded by Robert Jones. A tense debate resulted in a tied vote, eleven for and eleven against. D.W. James exercised his right as chairman to have the casting vote and the resolution was carried by twelve votes to eleven.

After, Bruce, with his brother-in-law Campbell, pursued the campaign to have a separate school set up for the children. The *Morning Chronicle* reporter accompanied Campbell to discover how the farmed-out pauper children were living. In one house:

> An old table, two chairs, and a stool formed the only furniture of the main room of this house. The woman was out, and we found four children squatted round a handful of fire which was burning in the grate. The oldest of them might be about nine years of age. There was no fender to protect them from the fire, nor was there anyone in charge of them. The house was filthy and stinking ... the eldest girl ...was barefooted and in rags; her hair was matted, and her hands, face and neck were black with dirt.

She slept with three or four others on a bed of straw.

In another house they found

> ...the corpse of a child in a winding sheet, laid out upon a table ...Though the child had been dead two days, it was unprovided with a coffin. The odour of the house was most insupportable. Before the fire were three or four children; amongst them was a boy Martin B—, eleven years of age, who had been placed there by the parish, the allowance being 2s. (10p) per week. This boy had no shirt; he was barefooted, in rags, his hair bristled up, and he was literally black with filth.[468]

To rescue the children from these conditions was only part of the problem. As the Poor Law Board had recognised,

---

[468] Ginswick, pp. 86-9.

workhouses had a reputation as abodes of vagrants and prostitutes and as being totally unsuitable places in which to bring up children. On 8 June 1850 the *Merthyr Guardian* in an editorial launched a coruscating attack upon the Guardians for contemplating taking the children, and particularly the girls, into the proposed workhouse and not providing a separate school for them.

> [In] the name of commonsense, of humanity, and of Christianity itself, how can the Guardians – reverend gentlemen, experienced magistrates, intelligent tradesmen, and respectable farmers – how can they reconcile it to their consciences to persist in a system fraught with the present and eternal ruin of these wretched victims of misfortune and impolicy! Are the rates paid and spent, are the Guardians selected, in order to furnish the best and cheapest supply of thieves and prostitutes to the large towns in the neighbourhood? ...Better drown them in the deepest pool in the Taff, or shovel them forthwith down the nearest abandoned coal pit, than thus educate them for infamy and wretchedness. It would be cheaper and far more humane.

Bruce and Campbell did not carry the day. When after various delays, the workhouse finally opened in the autumn of 1853 children remained in the workhouse with inadequate schooling. A separate 'industrial school' was set up in Aberdare after 1877.[469]

---

[469] Tydfil Thomas, pp 73-82.

Who were the Inmates?

The workhouse was not meant for 'the poor', no workhouse could hold that many. Indeed, an essential purpose of the workhouse was to keep the great majority of them out. Both for the state and for the poor the workhouse was a place of last resort which only the desperately destitute should enter. The extent of poverty was much greater than the official statistics portrayed. They only reflected the numbers who received relief and thereby accepted the stigma of 'pauper'. Many who did apply were regarded as ineligible because as recent immigrants they had not acquired a right of residence. They were put in carts and 'removed' to their native parish.

People in the workhouse were classified in five ways: children up to age fifteen (but many were sent to work at age nine); able-bodied women; able-bodied men; non able-bodied women; non able-bodied men. The largest single category in the Merthyr workhouse was children. In 1870 a total of 270 children were resident, comprised of 125 orphans, 44 children of unmarried parents and 101 'legitimate' children. The non able-bodied women and men were the aged, unable to work, sick in mind and body, the feeble and epileptic. The able-bodied women were usually widows, or the mothers of young illegitimate children. The able-bodied men, of whom there were few, were usually tramps or men categorized as too lazy to work, the 'idle and worthless'. These were set to work at corn-grinding, and stone-breaking; the women at back-breaking domestic work such as scrubbing or working in the laundry for nine hours a day. Gradually by the beginning of the twentieth century the numbers in the workhouse fell as children were sent to a separate school, the truly insane were sent to asylums, the seriously sick went into hospital. The largest category remaining were the aged and infirm and those classified as 'imbecile', suffering from memory loss but not insane. Yet the workhouse as a destination where one could 'end up', cast its long shadow over generations of working-class families.

How did the great majority of the impoverished avoid the workhouse? Single labourers went tramping, seeking work or begging. For those who had put money into friendly societies it was time to draw money out. The money did not go far, especially in a prolonged recession such as 1842-3 or 1850, or during a strike or lock-out. Those who did not have surplus cash to put into a friendly society had no such resource. Goods were pawned, coal tips were scavenged for fuel, some shopkeepers gave credit (and household debt piled up), family and friends helped if they could. There were charitable soup kitchens for women and children. Many, especially women, went hungry. But when thousands were affected there were two main answers to the threat of destitution. The first was emigration.

Transnational Merthyr

Merthyr was not only a town that people flocked to; from the early years Merthyr people had moved on. They went to France with George Crawshay in the 1830s and to Salt Lake City with the Mormons; to the ironworks and coal mines of Pennsylvania in the 1840s; to California, Australia and British Columbia in the 1850s searching for gold; in the 1860s to the developing collieries in the Cynon and Rhondda valleys where wages were higher than in Merthyr, and to the iron and steel works of the north-east particularly to Middlesborough, Durham and Gateshead; and in the 1870s to the Ukraine with John Hughes.[470] Throughout the century North America attracted the

---

[470] Merthyr Tydfil was a stronghold of Mormonism in Britain in the 1840s and 1850s. See Eira M. Smith, 'Mormonism in Merthyr Tydfil', *Merthyr Tydfil 1500 Years* (Merthyr Tydfil, 1980), pp. 38-47.

majority, emigration agents arranging the passage. The vision of a new life or the anticipated thrill of discovering riches were obvious attractions but it was insecurity, falling wages, unemployment and poverty that were the overwhelming reasons why people left Merthyr (a pattern repeated in the 1930s).[471] Thousands lost their jobs when from 1875 to 1879 the Cyfarthfa Works was locked. Emigration was also an escape for those who resented the dominance and power of the ironmasters. It was an easier option than protest followed by victimisation.[472] Colliers could cut coal anywhere when the labour market outside Merthyr was expanding. Accurate figures for emigration from Merthyr do not exist but it was particularly heavy during the 1860s and 1870s, years of uncertainty and serious industrial disputes. The impact can be seen in the population figures which moved little in thirty years.

Merthyr Tydfil Population

1851	1861	1871	1881
46,378	49,794	51,949	48,861

Source: Census.

A Moral Fable

The second way able-bodied men could avoid the workhouse was to accept outdoor relief in exchange for stone-breaking or road mending. Many were driven to this during prolonged

[471] Bill Jones, 'Inspecting the extraordinary drain: emigration and the urban experience in Merthyr Tydfil in the 1860s' in *Urban History* vol. 32, no. 1 (2005).

[472] A.O. Hirschman, *Exit, Voice and Loyalty: Responses to Decline in Firms, Organizations and States* (Cambridge, Massachusetts, 1970).

depressions or strikes and lock-outs. Before the workhouse was built the local Guardians saw these payments as a means of relieving poverty without complying with the strict form of the 1834 Act. After 1859 when George Clark became chairman of the Merthyr Board of Guardians, the spirit and letter of the Act were increasingly imposed. Less than a year after Clark became chairman, Robert Crawshay suffered a stroke which left him deaf and increasingly unwell. Anthony Hill at seventy-six was ailing. Clark, senior trustee of the Dowlais Iron Company and in reality its managing director was left as the dominant local personality.

A strong supporter of the 1834 Act, he believed that workmen should acquire habits of thrift in good times so that they could survive difficult times. This also meant that the thrifty workman would not ask for poor relief and consequently avoid the stigma of being a pauper. 'Idle and vicious persons' on the other hand should face the consequences of their conduct. 'A Fable' printed at the beginning of Samuel Smiles' *Thrift* expressed his creed:

> A grasshopper, half starved with cold and hunger, came to a well-stored beehive at the approach of winter, and humbly begged the bees to relieve his wants with a few drops of honey.
>
> One of the bees asked him how he had spent his time all the summer, and why he had not laid up a store of food like them.
>
> 'Truly', said he, 'I spent my time very merrily, in drinking, dancing, and singing, and never once thought of winter'.
>
> 'Our plan is very different, ' said the bee; 'we work hard in the summer, to lay by a store of food against the season when we foresee we shall want it; but those who do nothing but drink, and dance, and sing in the summer, must expect to starve in the winter'.

Smiles' self-improving books *Self-Help* (1859) and *Thrift* (1875) were bought in their hundreds of thousands. As precepts they had much to commend them but the ideals glossed over certain realities. They did not take into account the fact that while skilled men in the ironworks were usually kept on in a recession at reduced wages, unskilled workers lost the poorly paid jobs on which they had been scraping by, and had no income at all, except poor relief, in recessions. They did not take into account the number of mouths in a family. Or the effect of sickness and injuries upon earnings; or the wider family responsibilities when children had to look after aged parents. Clark was very firm that they should do so. It was their duty; and it helped to keep the rates down. And the Dowlais works was the largest rate-payer.

Working-class families feared the destitution that would send them into the workhouse. Clark, of course, did not want them to go in. He wanted them to 'stand on their own two feet'. But he also believed that the interests of ratepayers should come before those of paupers. He began to cut costs. In 1866 all healthy women with only one child were ordered into the workhouse instead of receiving out-door relief. Healthy men, temporarily sick, were denied relief. A national tightening up on the provision of relief in the early 1870s, after the national Poor Law Board was replaced by the Local Government Board, was rigorously enforced in Merthyr. Deserted mothers were ordered into the workhouse. After 1878 out-door relief was forbidden to any applicant who, in the opinion of the Guardians, was responsible for their own destitution. In this national 'Crusade against Out-relief' one third of those on outdoor relief in England and Wales were denied relief.[473]

---

[473] Andy Croll, 'Strikers and the Right to Poor Relief in Late Victorian Britain: The Making of the *Merthyr Tydfil* Judgement of 1900', *The Journal of British Studies*, Vol. 52 (January, 2013), pp. 128-152.

The most testing time came when iron and steel workers and coal miners were locked out of work from 30 January to 25 April 1875. How could task-work be found for thousands of able-bodied men so that they could receive relief? How could they be induced to return to work? Clark as head of the Dowlais works and chair of Merthyr Guardians took the opportunity to use the Poor Law to break the strike. The conditions for receiving relief were steadily tightened. A month after the lock-out began the Guardians decided to grant relief only to those breaking stones who were heads of families or single men with families dependent on them. Stones had to be broken so that they could pass through a ring 2.25 inches in diameter. The rings were supplied by the Guardians. Payments were at the rate of one shilling (20p) per cubic yard of limestone, men breaking field and quarry stones received an additional third of a shilling (27p in total). If stones were not available men would be employed in quarries. The Highways Board was asked to find work for men. From 19 February it was decided that all single men without families would only receive relief if they were in the workhouse, so long as there was room. In a deliberate move to force the Guardians' hand on 27 February 900 single men turned up at the workhouse asking for relief. When the workhouse was full the doors were locked. Those left outside went away, those inside disrupted the workhouse routines. By 13 March four policemen were installed in the workhouse to maintain discipline.

The crisis reached a peak three days later when, with the agreement of the Guardians, the Dowlais Company offered work to twenty-five men at its collieries. The men were being offered work at a place from which they had been locked out. If they refused they would receive no poor relief. If they accepted they would betray fellow workers in return for no more than would be 'sufficient to keep them off the rates'. Inspector

Doyle of the Local Government Board agreed with the company's offer. Alexander MacDonald MP wrote to the Amalgamated Association of Miners in conference at Swansea: 'In the history of our country I cannot recollect a parallel to this – workmen degraded to be compelled to seek relief and to be next employed as paupers by those whose wealth they have in large degree contributed to increase.'[474] Dr. J.W. James and William Gould, former Chartists who had been elected Guardians, objected to the Inspector's decision and the refusal to pay relief to men faced with such a choice. The men refused the offer and were told that if they faced starvation that was how the law worked: 12,000 to 15,000 men and their families were affected. George Clark meanwhile had obtained Home Office permission to call in troops if he thought it necessary. On Good Friday seventy-one men in the hospital stoneyard threw down their hammers and said they were going to church. They were dismissed and left without income.

The vice was tightened. On 20 March the Guardians adopted a resolution that 'all relief to able-bodied men whether stones be broken or not should be by way of loan'. William Gould and the Reverend William Davies protested that the men would have to pay twice for money received: once by breaking stones for it, and then, by repaying it when back in work. Their objections were swept aside. Clark was ruthless in the application of his moral logic which, as he explained, was that when the loan was paid back the men could then say they had not been paupers.

> The men of this district have a dread of becoming paupers. If we give relief by loan a time will come round, when the men will be able to report 'I never accepted parish relief myself' … we have no right to make them paupers if the men can get out

[474] Richard Burton Archive, Swansea University, 1875 AAM Conference Report, SWCC/MNB/PP/1; 3-6.

> of it ...by recovering the money will remove what most of the men would consider a great stigma.[475]

The men of Merthyr and Dowlais as in 1834 were denied relief, and facing eventual starvation returned to work with a wage cut of 12.5 per cent. There had been no violence. [476]

In 1889 the first volume of Charles Booth's *Life and Labour of the People in London* appeared. Altogether there were 17 volumes that revealed the extent of poverty which, in London stood at 30.7 per cent of the population. In 1901 Seebohm Rowntree's study of York, *Poverty: A Study of Town Life* found 28 per cent of the population in dire need. These surveys, ambiguous as in some respects they were, awoke Edwardian Britain to the fact that rather than moral turpitude, the causes of poverty were unemployment and poor health, appalling housing and hard work for inadequate wages. The workhouse remained however as 'a Poor Law Institution' until 1930.

---

[475] Minutes, Guardian Board Meeting 3 April 1875, Smith, p. 181.

[476] Tydfil Thomas, pp. 121-9.

18

Chapels and Politics

> Of the institutions of their own creation the largest, most prestigious and most influential were religious ones.
>
> Ieuan Gwynedd Jones[477]

Merthyr Tydfil has never elected a Tory Member of Parliament. The bedrock of Merthyr's post Civil War political radicalism had been religious Dissent, a view of life from outside the established order and at times outside the law. The restoration of King Charles II meant that local Dissenters had to worship in secret at Blaencanaid farmhouse until the Toleration Act of 1689 permitted them to worship in licensed meeting-houses and Baptists, Congregationalists and Presbyterians worshipped together at Cwm-y-Glo until breakaway congregations built chapels at Cefncoed in 1747 and at Trecynon, near Aberdare, in 1749-51; both known as *Yr Hen Dy Cwrdd.* Both congregations gradually moved to Unitarianism. In 1749, close to the river Taff at Merthyr a Welsh Independent chapel at Ynysgau was built. For forty years these remained the local Dissenters' places of worship.

Then, as the ironworks expanded and the Welsh in search of work colonised Merthyr's bare hills in their thousands, chapel building flourished: 1789 Zion, Welsh Baptist; 1793 Ebenezer, Welsh Baptist; also in 1793 Pontmorlais, Welsh Calvinistic

[477] Ieuan Gwynedd Jones, *The Observers and the Observed*, p. 13.

Methodist; 1797 English Wesleyan (built by Homfray for his Yorkshire workmen); 1803 Zoar, Welsh Independent. Altogether, between 1792 and 1836 the bishop's court registered twenty-three Dissenting meeting places in Merthyr and Dowlais. A quarter of them were for Welsh Calvinistic Methodists but most were for Baptists and Independents on the left-wing of Nonconformity, reinforcing the local radical tradition.[478] As more people arrived the number of chapels continued to increase, sometimes through doctrinal or personal differences within congregations.[479] Altogether, sixty-six Nonconformist chapels were built between 1747 and 1911 in the Merthyr town area, Penydarren, Dowlais, Penyrheolgerrig and Cefn Coed. *Taith a Pererin*, the 1688 Welsh translation of *Pilgrim's Progress* increasingly found a place in Merthyr homes. In 1851 the religious census recorded sixty-one places of worship, including a synagogue, a Roman Catholic church, five Mormon churches, seven (including three schoolrooms) for the Church of England, and forty-seven for various Nonconformist denominations.[480] The religious census disclosed something else.

The Godly and the Ungodly

More than half Merthyr people, 52 per cent, did not attend any place of worship, a revelation that seemed to confirm a society divided between *pobol y tafarn* and *pobol y capel*, the 'rough' and the 'respectable' working class. It fitted the widely held view of Merthyr: 'In Merthyr dwelt all the dross and rubbish';

---

[478] Williams, *Merthyr Rising*, p. 80

[479] Steve Brewer, *The Chapels of Merthyr Tydfil: a historical and pictorial guide* (Merthyr Tydfil, 2011).

[480] Ieuan Gwynedd Jones and David Williams (eds.), *The Religious Census of 1851: A Calendar of the Returns relating to Wales. Vol. 1 South Wales* (Cardiff, 1976), pp. 170-183.

'Samaria was the Merthyr Tydfil of the land of Canaan'. Yet it was immigrants who brought their religion with them and largely paid for the construction of the chapels. Religious observance in the English industrial towns was far lower than in Merthyr whose churches and chapels could accommodate 57.9 per cent of the population. Manchester's could hold a mere 31.6 per cent. That Christians were in a minority, particularly in the towns, was not a total surprise. All Nonconformist and Anglican Churches accepted that it was their duty to preach the Gospel to non-believers, to fight the battle against the forces of darkness, drunkenness and lawlessness. The reasons for non-observance, however, were not straightforward.

There were many who could not afford to dress in the required Sunday best; dressing for church or chapel demonstrated financial status as well as respectability. There were those who saw, with some justification, organised religion as a form of social control. Churches were built by the ironmasters. Non-attendance was a protest. Among many families there was simply an indifference to religion, an indifference that grew as the century wore on. The central concerns of the chapels were not the poverty, unemployment, poor health and slum housing of the urban working class. Religion emphasised the life hereafter, rather than the life of today which had not only to be endured but accepted because that was the way that God had arranged things. The popular hymn *All Things Bright and Beautiful* with the verse: 'The rich man in his castle, The poor man at his gate, God made them, high or lowly, And ordered their estate', held a message easily understood but not always welcomed by the workers at Cyfarthfa.

Nor did drink mark an immutable dividing line between the sheep and the goats. Many members of the working and middle classes enjoyed social drinking without embracing drunkenness. Saran, the heroine of Jack Jones' novel *Black Parade* and a regular attender at Zoar, expressed a widely-held view: 'I see no harm in a man having a drop of beer if only he keeps himself tidy'. Before the growth and institutionalisation of the chapels, pubs provided a meeting place for worshippers, Zoar began in the long room of The Crown, and initially pubs were the home for a rich cultural life that only later found a place in chapels and non-alcoholic meeting places. The division became accentuated from the late 1830s when temperance became a social crusade.

Not all church or chapel-goers were true believers. To conform to a way of life – bible-black 'best' clothes, attendance at morning and evening services and at Sunday school (established for adults as well as children), family readings of the Bible – confirmed both a family's respectability and its social status. Nonetheless, the periodic 'revivals', often associated with epidemics and economic depressions, created so many believers that Merthyr, with the rest of Wales, exported Nonconformist preachers to England.

The chapels set the tone for the whole society, condemning the drinking, sports and gambling associated with rural customs. Undoubtedly there were hypocrisies, prudery, a restriction of spirit, a little brief authority given to zealots but nonetheless the hegemony of the chapels was unmistakeable. Despite doctrinal differences and the growth of secularism and commercialised leisure activities they proclaimed a faith and way of life that emphasised personal responsibility, self-discipline, and a moral universe whose influence was felt in Wales well into the twentieth century. It was a world far removed from Lord Melbourne's complaint: 'Things have come to a pretty pass if religion is going to interfere with private life'.[481] But in Wales, religion and particularly Nonconformity, 'was organically a part of society and not something defined from above and imposed from without by force of law'.[482]

Jack Jones in *Black Parade* portrays the dominance of the chapel and the divide between those waiting for the pubs to open and those on their way to church and chapel.

> If the boozers, bouncers, bullies, wife-beaters and children-starvers had had it all their own way the day previous, they certainly did not on the Sabbath, when the nonconformist battalions marched proudly into Nebo, Caersalem, Shiloh, Noddfa, Tabernacle, Beulah, Moriah and scores of other citadels. Even Glyn, son of a stalwart nonconformist though he was, was made to feel unworthy and he wilted as he walked with downcast eyes past his more righteous brethren...[483]

The Welsh Sunday Closing Act of 1881 met little working class opposition, an instance of how the determined minority imposed its will on the majority.

Who were they?

It was largely the skilled and better paid workers who, along with members of the shopocracy, were the backbone of chapel congregations. The deacons and officers of Caersalem Welsh Baptist chapel, Dowlais, included: three colliers, three carpenters, two masons, two weighers, two publicans, and one

---

[481] R.H. Tawney, *Religion and the Rise of Capitalism* (Pelican Books, 1938), p. 18. Geoffrey Best, *Mid-Victorian Britain 1851-70* (Fontana, 1979), p. 194.

[482] Ieaun Gwynedd Jones, *Explorations and Explanations*, p.235.

[483] Jack Jones, *Black Parade* (Parthian Books, Library of Wales, Cardigan, 2009; first published 1935), p. 68.

each of yeoman, foreman bricklayer, puddler, clerk, boot-maker, ironstone miner, shopkeeper, milk vendor, refuse collector, rollerman, and overman. The early Pontmorlais register contains miners, colliers, a shearer, a carpenter, a sadler, a shoemaker and a roller.[484] Some chapels, like Zoar, or the Unitarian chapels at Cefncoed and Twynyrodyn had a higher proportion of middle-class members than most.

Chapel-going involved much more than Sunday observance and the assurance of a moral compass. Chapels were centres of self-government, practical democracy, and sociability. They drew from within their congregations Sunday school teachers, Sunday school superintendents, deacons, treasurers and preachers. The public speaking and administrative experience provided by these roles, the education imparted in Sunday schools where many caught up their knowledge of the three Rs, the sociability of the 'Adult Fellowship' and 'Young People's Fellowship', the Band of Hope, Mothers Union, *Gymanfa Ganu,* choirs, parades and outings enabled self-improvement, self-confidence and a social life with members of the opposite sex that often led to marriage. For newly-arrived immigrants chapels provided a ready-made Welsh language community, a welcoming environment of polished wood and familiar hymns.

It was in the chapels that *Eisteddfodau* flourished, providing opportunities for self-expression and creativity. Out of the *Eisteddfodau* came the choral music that runs as a thread through industrial Merthyr. From the chapels and the temperance societies emerged choral societies built across denominational lines that sang the major anthems and oratorios increasingly available in cheap sol-fa editions. With middle-class

---

[484] J. Ronald Williams and Gwyneth Williams, *History of Caersalem Welsh Baptist Church, Dowlais* (Llandysul, 1967), pp. 89-92; Noel Gibbard, 'Merthyr Nonconformists from c1800-c1850', *Merthyr Historian*, vol. 19, (2008), p. 213.

support the largely working-class choirs of Merthyr and Dowlais won national renown, often amidst tumultuous scenes of bitter rivalry.[485] 'How's the tenors in Dowlais?' was no idle question. The choirs, the conductors and the soloists attracted admiration and support. Money was raised to send gifted locals to music academies. Joseph Parry, a Merthyr man, was a national hero.

Chapel membership offered a way of life, a culture separate from that of the pub and the enveloping iron companies. True, the values of self-responsibility, temperance, and respectability promoted by the chapels were those the ironmasters wished upon their workers, but the chapels by their internal organisation gave these values a democratic expression. They were an arena where men and women could participate not only in worship but in a range of social activities valuable in themselves but also contributing to the influence of the chapel. And, given the grievances and prejudices of Dissent the chapel culture was also and inevitably political. The power of pulpit oratory gave an influential leadership role to preachers whose political views were well-known and accepted. Nonconformist ministers naturally participated in the Liberation Society and the Reform League. It was Nonconformist ministers who issued the invitation to Henry Richard to stand in Merthyr. The chapels, expressions of popular religious Dissent, were at the heart of Merthyr politics.

---

[485] Gareth Williams, '"How's the tenors in Dowlais?": The choral culture of the South Wales Coalfield c. 1880-1930', *Transcriptions of the Honourable Society of the Cymrodorian 2004*, Vol. 11, 2005; idem, 'Citadel of Song – Merthyr's Choral Culture c. 1870-1970', *Merthyr Historian Vol. 20*, 2009. Huw Williams, 'Brass Bands, Jazz Bands,Choirs: Aspects of Music In Merthyr' *Merthyr Historian Vol 3*, 1980; Andy Croll, 'From Bar-stool to Choir-stall: Music and Morality in Late-Victorian Merthyr', *Llafur*, Vol. 6 No. 1 (1992); idem, *Civilizing The Urban: Popular Culture and Public Space In Merthyr, c. 1870-1914* (Cardiff, 2000), pp. 106-136.

Thomas Williams, Gwaelodygarth, President of the Merthyr Liberal Association was a deacon at Zoar chapel from 1862 until his death in 1903 and chapel secretary for thirty-five years. He built up the local Liberal Association using as the nucleus the Nonconformist Election Committee that helped to return Richard in 1868. He regarded the Church of England as 'the rich man's church', attacked 'aristocratic rule', saw the alcohol trade as a system that kept working men in subjugation, and put up the capital for the Gladstone Coffee Tavern in the High Street.[486] At election times chapels such as Zoar became part of an electoral network that stretched throughout the constituency. The coalowner D.A. Thomas, when MP for Merthyr, took care to be 'a generous patron of Merthyr chapels'.[487] In the celebrations for the victory of the two Liberal candidates in 1880 eight ministers were among those who spoke – the Reverends Waldo James, Rowlands, T. Rees, D. Jones, P. Jones, John Davies, R. Evans, and L.P. Humphreys. The celebrations at Dowlais, chaired by the Rev. J. Morris of Zion, included the singing of the *Marseillaise*.[488]

Parliamentary Politics

Until the Reform Act of 1867 most Cabinet posts of importance, including that of Prime Minister, were held by members of the House of Lords. Parliamentary politics was largely the preserve of aristocratic families wealthy enough to pay the food and drink bills that ensured election. The Tory landed aristocracy supported the Anglican Church. The Whig

---

[486] W. R. Lambert, 'Thomas Williams, J.P. Gwaelodygarth (1823-1903)', *Glamorgan Historian*, Vol. 11, (1975).

[487] Kenneth O. Morgan, 'D.A. Thomas: The Industrialist as Politician', *Glamorgan Historian*, Vol. 3 (1966).

[488] *ME*, 10 April 1880.

landed aristocracy, with contacts to commerce and trade, favoured toleration for Nonconformists. Alliances between families were more significant than party programmes and ambitious young men might find parliamentary seats before arriving at mature political opinions. Gladstone began his parliamentary career as a Tory; Disraeli as a Radical. MPs were elected to look after 'interests'. At Merthyr the Crawshays and Hills were confident that the interests of the iron trade were safe in the hands of Guest, Bruce and their own extensive Parliamentary connections. The ironmasters' primary local concern was to control the Board of Poor Law Guardians and its Assessment committee where the rateable charge upon their businesses was determined.

By the 1860s the loosely organised Liberal Party represented a coalition of reforming interests held together by faith in free trade, *laisser-faire*, the liberty of the individual and opposition to Anglicanism and its privileges. Within this coalition Nonconformists found a natural home along with those who argued for equity before the law, freedom of conscience, franchise reform, arbitration and conciliation in industrial and international disputes and non-intervention abroad. Gladstone, by 1865 the party's leader in the Commons, was looked up to by Nonconformists as a God-fearing statesman, his portrait in miners' cottages. By contrast, a cautious and more coherent Tory Party strongly supported the Established Church, religious education in schools, the Empire, the landed aristocracy, and, until abandoned, trade protection. It gained working-class support through its relaxed attitude to the drink trade, gambling and horse racing. Disraeli, with ringlets and embroidered waistcoats, opportunistic, cynical, dazzling in debate, seemingly alien yet a stout defender of the Anglican Church, existed beyond chapel-goers' experience or imagination.

Merthyr was therefore Liberal, influenced by and reflecting

many strands of thought. Sir John Guest spoke for industry and free trade, Thomas Stephens for Welsh literature and the language, Henry Richard for Peace and Wales, the James family and their middle-class supporters spoke for civic virtue, the chapels for Godly righteousness, the working class for political rights and economic security. All cohered in what came to be understood as Welsh Nonconformist Liberalism, cemented by the thousands of Nonconformists able to vote after 1867. Its spokesman was Henry Richard who, as Ieuan Gwynedd Jones has eloquently argued, presented himself as the defender of Welsh Nonconformity against its detractors and the defender of Welsh people against assaults on their intelligence and morality.[489]

Merthyr Tydfil was Liberal and when, in 1868 working-men first exercised their voting power, this was confirmed. The election of Richard and Fothergill in 1868 began a thirty-two-year period of elected Liberal MPs in Merthyr, a time of a growing sense of Welsh national identity. The existence of a national eisteddfod from 1858 onwards, the establishment of the Welsh-speaking settlement in Patagonia in 1865 and the adoption of *Hen Wlad Fy Nhadau* as a national anthem pointed to Welsh cultural separateness. It could be seen in the 1870s resentment against English trade union leaders and 'agitators', in the campaign for temperance that culminated in the Welsh Sunday Closing Act, and in the move to have a Welsh university (Aberystwyth founded 1872), a Welsh system of secondary county schools, and the campaign to keep religion out of schools (Nonconformists said that was provided in Sunday schools). The increasing demand for the disestablishment of the Anglican Church grew into a campaign to disestablish the Church in Wales and in 1887 Welsh disestablishment became Liberal Party policy. But disestablishment was only the most persistent

---

489 Ieaun Gwynedd Jones, *The Observers and the Observed*, p. 164.

of political issues that fed into a sense of Welsh distinctiveness. Land reform and security for tenant farmers was another Welsh cause. At the end of the century the *Cymru Fydd* movement which advocated Home Rule for Wales attracted leading Welsh Liberal politicians, including Lloyd George. In Merthyr Boroughs national politics turned on who would challenge the sitting Liberal representatives and how would the enfranchised workers use their votes in the future?

The 1874 Election

An early answer came in the general election of February 1874 fought amidst a confident trade union surge that included growing parliamentary ambitions. At Morpeth and Stafford respectively the miners' leaders Thomas Burt and Alexander Macdonald were elected with Liberal Party backing. The first workers' representatives in parliament they were known as Lib-Labs. John Kane stood unsuccessfully at Middlesborough. In Merthyr Thomas Halliday was sponsored by the Amalgamated Association of Miners as a working man's representative. He stood on a platform of improved safety conditions in the mines and Home Rule for Ireland. Unlike Burt and Macdonald he was not an official Liberal candidate and therefore challenged the sitting members. He was damaged by the *Merthyr Telegraph's* revelation that he was a Catholic, although it brought him Irish votes, and by his indictment at Manchester Assizes for conspiracy in respect of miners breaking their contracts. The jury disagreed and the case lapsed.

In all the circumstances, including the reputation of the two sitting members, the weakened state of his union's finances, and the fact that he was English and a non-Welsh speaker, his poll of 4,912 votes compared to 7,606 for Henry Richard and 6,908 for Richard Fothergill was more than respectable. It was possibly enhanced through abstentions by disaffected Nonconformists who were unhappy with Forster's 1870 Education Act that allowed religious education in elementary schools. It was certainly helped by the absence of a Tory candidate which meant that he received strong support from the Tory *Western Mail* and Tory 'plumpers' who only cast one vote and that for him. Nationally the Liberals suffered heavy losses and Disraeli was returned to office. In Merthyr the re-election of the sitting members affirmed that class feeling found its expression through Nonconformity.

Tory Challenges

Tory challenges to the Liberal domination of Merthyr Boroughs were rare, only three occurring between 1868 and 1895. The first, and most significant, came in the general election of 1880 which Fothergill did not contest because of financial troubles. His place as Liberal candidate alongside Henry Richard was taken almost inevitably by a member of the James family, the Unitarian solicitor Charles Herbert James (1817-1890), well-known in both Merthyr and Aberdare. Although James owned mineral rights in Glamorgan and Monmouthshire it was the first time that neither of the Liberal candidates had the status of an industrialist. The Liberal *Merthyr Express* noted that although neither of the sitting members was an ironmaster or colliery proprietor 'neither would knowingly inflict a shadow of injury upon the interests of capital ...On the other hand who could represent with greater effect, the advanced Liberal feeling of the borough, the overwhelming preponderance of the labour element, and beyond all the distinct and accentuated Nonconformist character of the constituency.'[490]

[490] *ME*, 20 March 1880.

Their opponent, Merthyr-born William Thomas Lewis (1837-1914) was one of the most prominent industrialists in South Wales, the dominant figure in the South Wales Coal-owners Association. Lewis apprenticed at thirteen as a mechanical engineer at the Plymouth Works, where his father was the chief engineer, had risen to be agent for the Bute Estate and a Rhondda coal-owner in his own right. He stood as an Independent although his connections with the Earl of Bute meant that he was generally viewed as a Tory in disguise. His appeal rested on his local contacts, his image as an experienced and successful businessman (the two Liberal candidates were dismissed as impractical men with 'ideas'), and the support he received from the licensed victuallers of Merthyr and Aberdare opposed to the proposed Sunday Closing Bill. Lewis had a considerable and deserved reputation as a scourge of the unions. In Mountain Ash a crowd smashed the windows of pubs thought to favour the Conservative cause and in Aberdare the police had difficulty in controlling a 'lot of ruffians'.[491] Henry Richard and James were comfortably returned, Lewis' 4,445 votes being fewer than those received by Halliday six years earlier.[492]

The second Tory challenge came in the election of January 1892 when the local Conservatives put forward B. Francis Williams their first official candidate at Merthyr since Meyrick in 1835. Williams, a barrister and Recorder for Cardiff, would

[491] *Merthyr Telegraph*, 16 April 1880.

[492] Lewis was knighted in 1885, became Lord Merthyr in 1896 and was made a Freeman of the Borough in 1908. In 1905 he acquired Sengheneddyd Universal Colliery where 439 colliers were killed in an explosion in October 1913. The fountain at the bottom of Merthyr High Street was a gift by him to the town, commemorating the coal industry and Lucy Thomas to whom his wife was related. He was the major contributor to Merthyr General Hospital.

represent in 1902 the coalowners and in 1906 the Taff Vale Railway in high-profile legal cases against trade unions.[493] At Merthyr in 1892 he received a rough ride. Fights broke out at his meetings and at the Oddfellows Hall in Dowlais a group of the audience tried to rush the stage. D.A. Thomas and Pritchard Morgan, the sitting Liberal MPs, were re-elected with the largest majority in the country. The voting figures were: Thomas 11,948, Morgan 11,756, Williams 2,304. Three years later in July 1895 Herbert Lewis, W. T. Lewis' son, presented a much more formidable challenge. His policies included bringing in old age pensions and an eight-hour working day, his family influence was substantial and the Tories were better organised locally than the Liberals. Thomas and Morgan survived but their majorities were slashed. Lewis achieved 6,525 votes, Morgan 8,554 and Thomas 9,250. A fourth candidate, Edward Upward a journalist, was invited by the miners to stand as a workers' representative. He polled only 659 votes and his appearance at the count was 'received with uproar and hisses'.[494]

Pritchard Morgan the Workers' Choice

The key question in Merthyr Boroughs parliamentary elections after Halliday's defeat in 1874 was: who would the working men vote for? As the *Merthyr Express* clearly saw:

> The constituency is, in the main, a working man's constituency. If the workmen unite upon any question, or candidate, a

[493] Paul Smith, 'Unions "naked and unprotected at the altar of the common law". Inducement of Breach of Contract of Employment: *South Wales Miners' Federation and Others v. Glamorgan Coal Co. and Others* [1905]', *Historical Studies in Industrial Relations* No. 35 (2014).

[494] *Cardiff Times*, 20 July 1895.

> combination of all the other classes in the constituency is powerless to affect the result... There are two interests – labour and capital – but labour has all the votes, and capital must obtain its representation through the votes of labour or not at all.[495]

Halliday lost, but thousands voted for him, a trade union leader who was not an official Liberal candidate. The question remained: for how long would the most working-class electorate in Wales continue to vote for middle-class candidates? In the 1880 celebrations in the Temperance Hall following the success of Richard and James over W.T. Lewis, Frank James, cousin to Charles James the newly elected MP, declared: 'The working men have proved in this election that they know well how to appreciate and make use of the privileges afforded them under the franchise by sending two Liberals to Parliament'.[496]

In the condescending reference to 'privileges afforded' to the workers we see both the assumption and the apprehension of the middle-class oligarchy that ran the Liberal electoral machine. In the elections of 1885 and 1886 Richard and James were returned unopposed but in 1888 Charles James caused a by-election by unexpectedly announcing that he wished to stand down for family reasons. In a realistic assessment of the situation the Merthyr and Aberdare Liberal Associations conceded that the working men of Merthyr Boroughs should nominate their own Liberal candidate.[497] A century and more

[495] *ME*, 30 August 1873.

[496] *ME,* 10 April 1880.

[497] The account that follows is indebted to Gerard Charmley, 'Working Class Solidarity? The Miners and the Merthyr Boroughs By-elections of 1888', *Llafur*, vol. 10, no. 2 (2009); idem 'W. Pritchard Morgan (1844-1924): Adventurer in Politics', *Morgannwg*, Vol. LVIII (2014).

of dominance by the ironmasters had such a grip upon their political sensibilities that the Dowlais branch of the Merthyr Liberal Association wrote to Thomas Merthyr Guest, second son of Sir John, in the hope that they might nominate him. The Abercanaid branch wrote to W.T. Crawshay of Cyfarthfa. Neither was suitable and neither chose to stand. The ironworkers played no further part in the selection.

The Merthyr and Aberdare Miners' Association on the other hand asked the local Liberal Associations to delay considering possible candidates until the colliers had had an opportunity to choose their own nominee. A series of rancorous meetings came close to farce on more than one occasion. At a mass meeting on Saturday 25 February Philip D. Rees of Aberaman volunteered to sing a song whereupon members present shouted that 'this was a meeting called for the transaction of business and not for vocal exercises'. The meeting finally resolved not to nominate a labour candidate and ended in a rush for the exit as Philip Rees got up and sang his song. Subsequent meetings in Merthyr and Cwmaman again failed to agree on a candidate. The obvious choice, David Morgan, *Dai o'r Nant*, local miners' agent since 1882 lacked the necessary gravitas and popularity while David Evan Davies, *Dewi Mabon*, a colliery manager nominated by the miners of Cwmaman turned out to be a full member of Aberdare Conservative Club and not, as he claimed, just 'a drinking member'.

With the failure of the miners to unite behind a candidate the Merthyr Liberal Association chose David Alfred Thomas, Cambridge graduate and coalowner with a reputation as a good employer. Born in Aberdare and the son of Samuel Thomas a former Merthyr shopkeeper, he was duly returned without opposition on 14 March 1888. In fact, he had been quietly nursing the seat for a year in anticipation that Henry Richard, whose health had been deteriorating, would soon retire. Six months later on 21 August Henry Richard died.

The miners now had another opportunity to nominate a candidate. They were encouraged by the Merthyr Liberal Association which agreed that D.A. Thomas as a representative of capital should be joined by a representative of labour. A month went by while the colliers failed to agree and the Liberal Association was finally informed that the working men of Merthyr Boroughs were not ready to put forward a candidate. Meanwhile, four days after Henry Richard's death forty-four-year-old Pritchard Morgan had announced his candidature. An experienced publicist, self-proclaimed barrister, prospector for gold in Australia for eighteen years, and the owner of a gold mine in Merioneth, Pritchard arrived in the constituency and established himself at the Castle Hotel.[498] He presented himself as someone who understood mining and the problems of the working man in a way that the middle class clique of small businessmen, lawyers, doctors, shopkeepers and Nonconformist ministers that ran the Liberal Association could not. He knew what it was to work hard. He favoured Irish Home Rule, non-sectarian education and Welsh Disestablishment.

The Liberal Association ignored him and finally nominated Ffoulkes Griffiths, a former Baptist pastor, a Welsh speaker and a London barrister. Pritchard Morgan refused to withdraw and declared himself an Independent Liberal candidate. The contest became one between Ffoulkes Griffiths supported by D.A. Thomas, and Pritchard Morgan favoured increasingly by working men, particularly Aberdare colliers. There was enormous enthusiasm for Morgan but the contest turned sour, Morgan and Thomas accusing each other of being Tories, of hiring thugs to break up meetings (there were fights and windows smashed in public halls and chapels) and Morgan emerged victor with 7,149 votes to 4,956 for Griffiths.

[498] He had studied at the Australian Bar. When his examiner failed to appear Morgan claimed that he had obviously passed.

The events of 1888 revealed how politically ill-prepared were the working men of Merthyr Boroughs. Despite the evidence that Henry Richard's health was faltering and the readiness of the Liberal Associations to consider a candidate representative of labour, no preparations had been made to find such a successor. The ironworkers were living in the past, the railwaymen were occupied with reviving their branch, the colliers of Merthyr employed by the Cyfarthfa and Dowlais companies let the Aberdare colliers dominate the nomination discussions. Without an acceptable authoritative personality there could be no agreement.

Liberals Unhinged

Pritchard Morgan's victory against the official Liberal candidate unhinged the Liberal Association in Merthyr. It ceased to function and for twenty years was moribund. The Brecon Road Liberal Association in Merthyr had no grasp on constituency affairs, the Liberal Clubs in Aberdare and Merthyr were simply resorts for largely middle-class drinkers. In one way this did not matter. D.A. Thomas was wealthy enough to maintain his own organisation and agents, Pritchard Morgan employed an agent at election times. Morgan and Thomas emerged from 1880 with a strong dislike for each other, a dislike that grew. For the sake of the Party they showed a united front at elections and emerged victorious in 1892 and 1895. But while D.A. Thomas enhanced his reputation as a solid member, Morgan in the aftermath of his 1892 re-election (in which he was an official Liberal candidate described as 'the working man') spent lengthy periods away from the constituency and the Commons. He explored for gold in Ireland, spent six months in Australia in 1895-6 returning with substantial gold mining concessions, spent the first half of 1897 in China and in 1899-1900 was there again acting as Imperial adviser on mining operations in Szechuan province.[499] His continued absences led to a gradual deterioration in his constituency standing.

In its way the election of Pritchard Morgan in 1888 was as significant as the election of Henry Richard twenty years earlier. One had ended the electoral dominance of the ironmasters. The second was a revolt against the clique that had dominated the selection of candidates. When the Liberal Association protested against the violence that had broken out in the election Pritchard Morgan issued handbills reading:

> Pritchard Morgan will be proud to have the Votes of the men the Liberal Association call the SCUM of the place, and the ROUGHS of the Borough.[500]

He had his victory but the price for destroying the Liberal caucus and antagonising D.A. Thomas came twelve years later.

[499] Charmley, 'W. Pritchard Morgan', pp. 34-8.

[500] Charmley, 'W. Pritchard Morgan', p. 27.

19

Labour's New Voice

> Keir Hardie's victory was, to a large extent, a psephological accident and certainly could not be regarded, seriously, as the sign of a socialist breakthrough.
>
> Deian Hopkin[501]

> Hardie's return at Merthyr in 1900 was ...the consummation of a long courtship.
>
> Martin Wright[502]

In the 1895 general election Edward Upward the Radical candidate at Merthyr received 659 votes. Five years later Keir Hardie the Independent Labour candidate who spent hardly any time in the constituency received 5,745 votes and was elected. How did he win one of the safest Liberal constituencies in Britain? The obvious explanation lies in the collapse of local Liberal Party organisation after 1888 and the antagonism between the two sitting Liberal MPs, one of whom, Pritchard Morgan, was frequently absent for long periods. Certainly these

---

[501] Deian Hopkin, 'Labour's Roots in Wales, 1880-1900' in Duncan Tanner, Chris Williams and Deian Hopkin (eds.), *The Labour Party in Wales 1900-2000* (Cardiff, 2000), p. 57.

[502] Martin Wright, 'Wales and Socialism: Political Culture and National Identity c 1880-1914', PhD thesis, Cardiff University, 2011, p. 150.

were the major reasons but they are only part of the story. Hardie brought a message, a way of thinking that was to dominate Merthyr and the South Wales valleys for most of the twentieth century. There was also the appeal of Hardie himself.

Spreading the Message

The message was called 'Socialism'. There was, however, more than one version and each had its messengers. Perhaps the first to reach Merthyr from a London based organisation was Neath-born Sam Mainwaring, a founder-member of the Socialist League. In August 1887 he toured South Wales. John Rees of Alma Street, Dowlais, heard him speak at Pontmorlais and subsequently wrote to the Socialist League:

> ...workers endorse the opinion that we the toiling masses by all common sense and justice ought to be on a higher level than we now are. There was however a reason why workers would not become actively involved in the socialist cause: The fact of the matter to speak plain [is] men are afraid one of the other. I refer to tale-bearing and its consequences. I heartily wish better principles and better feelings could be instilled in them so that we could confide one in the other. I was sorry to find so many walking away without signing their names that night in Merthyr ... as a matter of course, if I signed I thought I might be a marked man ... [503]

The South Wales coalfield with its huge discrepancies in wealth and power was an obvious target for itinerant socialist speakers. The railway trucks of the Powell Duffryn Company carried the

---

[503] Wright, pp. 38-9. For Mainwaring, see Ken John, 'Sam Mainwaring and the Autonomist Tradition', *Llafur*, vol. 4, No. 3, (1986).

initials PD, interpreted locally to stand for Poverty and Death (in the 1930s it was read as Poverty and Dole). The average infant mortality for England and Wales in 1910 was 122 per 1,000 live births. In Aberdare it was almost twice that at 213, while in Rhondda it was 183 and in Merthyr 173.[504] The Social Democratic Federation (SDF) a party dominated by H.M. Hyndman, from which the Socialist League was a break-away body, in 1897 had a branch in Pontypridd. The Aberdare Socialist Society agreed to join but neither the SDF nor the Socialist League, both founded in 1884, left an enduring mark in Wales. William Morris, the leading thinker in the Socialist League, did however find many readers for his utopian vision *News From Nowhere* (1891).

Also in 1884 a group of London intellectuals founded the Fabian Society. By the early 1890s the Society had a Cardiff branch but little, if any, personal contact with Merthyr or Aberdare, although Edmund Stonelake of Aberdare thought the Society's tract *Facts For Socialists* (1887) had 'made more Socialists than any other Socialist work ever printed'.[505] The increasing use of the word 'socialism' can be seen from the 1880s onwards in the correspondence columns of local newspapers. In the 1890s socialist campaigning began to have an impact in Merthyr. The Independent Labour Party (ILP) formed at Bradford in 1893 would be the most important influence but there was also the campaigning group inspired by Robert Blatchford's *Clarion* newspaper (1891) and his best-selling book *Merrie England* (1895).

---

[504] Tanner, Williams, Hopkin (eds.), p. 37.

[505] A. Mor-O'Bren (ed.), *The Autobiography of Edmund Stonelake* (Bridgend, 1981), p. 151.

Blatchford's Clarion

Merrie England, a seductive picture of what life could be, sold three-quarters of a million copies. His message was spread by horse-drawn caravans staffed by full-time volunteers. During August and early September 1897 a *Clarion* van toured right across the South Wales valleys holding the most extensive and sustained series of socialist meetings to take place in Wales up to that date. A bemused description of the van was published in the *Merthyr Express* on 28 August 1897

> The *Clarion* Van is a veritable home on wheels, and is neatly fitted up with sleeping bunks, side benches, with lockers underneath for literature and clothes, a marvellous sliding table which draws out and vanishes mysteriously when it is no longer required, while a cooking stove and patent wash stand, in addition to a food cupboard and clothes press, complete the indispensible furniture. When the Vanners are numerous or the ground permits, a tent is pitched for use as a sleeping place of the men, the van itself being appropriated for the ladies' use ... A feature of the van tour is the amount of free literature which is distributed in all places through which the van passes while actually en route.

There was also a disconcerting reversal of patriarchal roles.

> The Vanners do all their own work themselves, and it is a sight for gods and men to see the woman in charge, a BA in honours of London University – washing the dishes, while prominent men in the Labour Movement, such as Tom Mann, or Bruce Glasier, sit round meekly "drying up" under her direction.[506]

[506] Wright, pp. 116-7.

The Independent Labour Party

Many of Blatchford's supporters were members of the ILP, idealistic enthusiasm being common to both. The ILP first took root in Merthyr Boroughs at Treharris where a branch was established sometime in 1895. Why there is not certain, but an important part of an explanation must have been the energy and enterprise of Oliver Jenkins, a railway signalman, who was the branch secretary. In addition the collieries at Treharris and Merthyr Vale had strong workers' representatives who were interested in the new politics. In 1895 35-year-old Enoch Morrell was checkweighman at Nixon's colliery Merthyr Vale where Rowland Evans and Andrew Wilson would follow him in that position. All three later became Labour councillors and Merthyr mayors. There seems little doubt that they were among the thirty members of the Treharris branch holding weekly debates by March 1896.

Early in December 1895 Oliver Jenkins organised a meeting in the Merthyr Drill Hall with the intention of starting a Merthyr ILP branch. John Owen Jones (*ap Ffarmwr*) the editor of the *Merthyr Times* and a supporter of trades unionism, chaired the meeting, although he remained a Liberal.[507] It was not until July 1896, however, after a meeting addressed by Ben Tillett (who had not been able to attend the previous meeting) that the Merthyr branch was finally formed. Among its founder-members were George McKay, secretary of the Merthyr branch of the Amalgamated Society of Railway Servants, H.T. Hamson a sub-editor on the *Merthyr Express*, William Nathan

---

[507] *ME*, 7 December 1895. On John Jones, see David A. Pretty, *The Rural Revolt That Failed: Farm Workers' Trade Unions in Wales 1889-1950* (Cardiff, 1989) and also 'John Owen Jones ('Ap Ffarmwr') and the Labour Movement in Merthyr Tydfil, 1894-6', *Morgannwg*, Vol. 38 (1994), pp. 101-114.

Scholefield, a commercial traveller and Richard Martin a compositor. The branch met regularly at the Welcome Coffee Tavern, and earnestly discussed among other topics 'Socialism and Love: Are They Separate?'

Branches followed at Dowlais and Penydarren. At Penydarren, the branch met in the Elim Schoolroom and took turns, in the absence of visiting speakers, to read and debate papers on 'Do Socialism and the Bible Agree?', 'The Nationalisation of the Railways' and 'Socialism and Drink'. The unofficial debates took place in the barber shop of Llewellyn Francis, secretary of the branch. The Dowlais branch was formed in 1897 by David Davies from Pant. Davies, a forty-year-old signalman inevitably known as 'Dai Box', was at the heart of trade union and Labour developments in Merthyr.

Earnest debates were characteristic of all these branches. In the summer of 1896 the Treharris branch organised a lecture tour by J. W. Wood, who spoke on the 'Religious Aspect of Socialism'. Meetings in Merthyr Boroughs attracted large crowds, and 10,000 assorted leaflets and copies of the *Labour Leader* and *Clarion* were distributed. Oliver Jenkins claimed in 1897 that over the years he had distributed over 1,000 copies of Blatchford's *Merrie England*. Hard on the heels of the Blatchford van, Bert Alpass and George Belted came from Gloucester and spoke on the Merthyr tips to a crowd said to be 6,000.[508]

It is important to keep all this in perspective. The ILP branches were weak with fluctuating and often tiny membership numbers. The thousands who turned up to open-air meetings (if the numbers claimed can be believed) were not necessarily supporters. The majority came out of curiosity. Some came to jeer. Working men in Merthyr had overwhelmingly supported

[508] Wright, pp. 107-8, 116. Deian Hopkin, 'The Rise of the Labour Party in Wales', *Llafur*, Vol. 6, No. 3 (1994).

and voted for the Liberal Party ever since they received the vote in 1867. As D.A. Thomas pointed out in 1894, Labour and Liberal were almost interchangeable terms in the Merthyr Boroughs.[509] Nevertheless, the meetings and rallies, the books, newspapers and pamphlets spread socialist ideas through the coalfield. From these straws in the wind bricks were eventually made.

The following letter from a Lewis Jones, which appeared in the *Merthyr Express*, on 15 August 1896, is significant in the light of what happened four years later.

> I was one of the many who stood to listen to a Socialist speaker last Sunday evening at Pontmorlais. He is the first Socialist I have heard in Merthyr, and I am glad I heard him, inasmuch as I previously held, as I now know, erroneous ideas on the subject. During his speech he referred to the present state of affairs, and said it was due to individualism, at present prevailing to an awful extent in the country. If he was a Merthyr man, he could name a case in point, namely, the Plymouth Collieries. We Merthyr people all know the misery entailed by the Plymouth workmen during last winter by that lamentable dispute, which was not of their sowing. And to what end was all this misery caused and endured? Was it not so that a certain class of individuals should profit by their labour? I am, or at least was, a Liberal, but when I come to think that one of our MPs is an individual who lives by the life's blood of other men, and the other who promised to do so much for us during the last election, when elected shipped to Australia to prospect for gold, and has recently bought large claims there, I want to know how he is going to look after our interests and rights in Parliament while he is out prospecting and looking after No. 1 in Australia? ...I say that if the Independent

[509] Jon Parry, 'Labour Leaders and Local Politics, 1888-1902: The example of Aberdare', *Welsh History Review*, Vol. 13, No. 3.

> Labour Party brought down here an efficient man and got a few of the sort of the man that spoke last Sunday at Pontmorlais to help him, there's no earthly power to stop them getting a seat in Merthyr in the present state of affairs. [510]

Trade Unions Again

There was another development. Separate from the talk of socialism was a resurgence of trade unionism. A business revival and rising employment enabled national trade union membership to roughly double between 1888 and 1892. Unions that had lain dormant since the 1870s began to recruit members. A Merthyr branch of the Amalgamated Society of Railway Servants reappeared in 1888. In 1889 the London gasworkers strike was followed by the momentous London dock strike. New unions for the unskilled were born, promoting a great surge of unionism among those excluded from the unions of skilled workers. The new unions for Dockers and Gasworkers both added 'and General Labourers' to their titles. In South Wales they initially recruited in port towns but as early as 1890 the Gasworkers began to recruit colliery surface workers in South Wales. Recruitment at brickworks, in local authorities, at steel and tinplate works, laundries, waterworks and tramways followed.[511]

In February 1895 a Merthyr branch of the National Union of Shop Assistants was formed and began to campaign for shorter working hours. In July that year the Typographical Association revived its Merthyr branch. In November there was a strike/lock-out of those working at the Plymouth collieries (referred to in the letter by Lewis Jones above).[512]

---

[510] Wright, pp. 124-5.

[511] Joe England, 'Notes on a Neglected Topic: General Unionism in Wales', *Llafur*, Vol. 9, No. 1 (2004).

[512] *Merthyr Times*, 21, 28 November 1895.

Hairdressers, stone masons, engineers and teachers in the town joined unions.

In August 1898 came a major development. Tom Mann, President of the Dockers' Union and national Secretary of the ILP, had on May Day launched a new general union – the Workers' Union. That August he spoke at an open-air meeting to Cyfarthfa and Dowlais workers. This was followed on 22 August by another meeting at which the main speaker was Charles Duncan, secretary of the Workers' Union. The meeting voted in favour of joining the new union.[513] A boom in the iron and steel trade helped recruitment but so did the uncertainty created by the news on 1 October 1899 that the Dowlais works had merged with the Patent Nut and Bolt Company to create Guest, Keen and Company.

By the end of 1899 there were ten Workers' Union branches in the Merthyr district with a combined membership of 1,300, a quarter of the national membership. The town branches met in the Anchor and Imperial public houses in Merthyr High Street. In March 1902 Merthyr people heard that the share capital of Cyfarthfa had been acquired by the Guest, Keen Company. In the 1904-5 economic depression the Workers' Union membership in Merthyr dwindled away but a core of around 200 remained and the union successfuly fought a number of cases under the Workmens' Compensation Act, 1897; accidents at work being a serious problem at Cyfarthfa and Dowlais.

This general upsurge brought a revival of the Merthyr Trades Council, the prime mover being David Davies who two years earlier had started the ILP branch in Dowlais. The Trades Council provided an industrial forum for delegates from the unions and soon claimed to have 7,000 affiliated members. Key positions were held by trade unionist members of the ILP. A parallel move came in Aberdare with the formation of the Trades Council with Edmund Stonelake as secretary and Charles Stanton, ILP activist and future miners' agent, a prominent member.

[513] *ME*, 20, 27 August 1898.

The 1898 Coal Strike and the Employers' Offensive

At the end of the century two strikes occurred that had major industrial and political consequences in Britain. Both affected Merthyr workers immediately. In August and September 1893 a strike by the hauliers of the coalfield had foreshadowed discontent with the sliding scale agreement that regulated wages. The hauliers' strike fizzled out but in 1898 South Wales' colliers gave notice to end the sliding scale agreement, demanding a ten per cent wage increase and the introduction of a minimum wage. The owners refused these demands, negotiations were sparse and when the existing agreement expired on 9 April 1898 the owners imposed a lock-out, although some men had struck on 1 April. Collieries were closed from April to the first week in September 1898 in a bitter and exhausting struggle.

It ended with a five per cent pay increase but the sliding scale remained, there was no minimum wage and the miners lost 'Mabon's Day', a coalfield holiday taken on the first Monday of each month. The men reacted by abandoning their separate district unions and forming the South Wales Miners' Federation (SWMF) with a view to ending the sliding scale. In 1899 the SWMF joined the larger Miners' Federation of Great Britain (MFGB) and pursued a policy of securing a minimum wage for the whole of the British coal industry. By 1901 the membership of the SWMF stood at 128,000, some 80 per cent of the miners in South Wales.[514]

---

[514] For the background to the 1898 strike Eric Evans, *The Miners of South Wales*, pp. 133-169, and L.J. Williams, 'The Strike of 1898' *Morgannwg*, Vol. 9 (1965), reprinted in John Williams, *Was Wales Industrialised?* (Llandysul, 1995). For Mabon's Day see Andy Croll, 'Mabon's Day: The Rise and Fall of a Lib-Lab Holiday in the South Wales Coalfield, 1888-1898', *Labour History Review,* Vol. 72, No. 1 (April 2007).

The second event was a strike on the Taff Vale railway, whose thousands of trucks took coal from the Merthyr, Cynon and Rhondda valleys to the docks at Cardiff. The strike, not in itself much of a disturbance, began on 20 August 1900 and by the beginning of September had ended. However, a final judgement given by the House of Lords in 1901 on a case arising out of the strike has been described as 'the most celebrated judgement in the history of trade union law.'[515] The Law Lords decided that this action by the union, the ASRS, had damaged the Taff Vale company. The decision undermined the legal status of trade unions established by the Trade Union Act 1871, and the door was now open for trade unions to be liable for heavy damages for actions arising from their activities. The Taff Vale company sued the ASRS, recovered £23,000 and in addition the union lost £19,000 in costs. Further actions against unions followed including £57,562 awarded in damages against the SWMF.

Across Britain employers went on the offensive. In South Wales the coalowners successfully won legal cases against the SWMF over the law of contract and the payment of poor law relief to strikers.[516] The unions drew the logical conclusion. From their point of view the laws needed to be changed and they needed representation in the House of Commons. The Labour Representation Committee founded in February 1900,

---

[515] E.H. Phelps Brown, *The Growth of British Industrial Relations*, (1965), p. 194.

[516] John Williams, 'Miners and the Law of Contract, 1875-1914', *Llafur*, Vol. 4, No. 2 (1985); Andy Croll, 'Strikers and the Right to Poor Relief in late Victorian Britain: The Making of the Merthyr Tydfil Judgement of 1900', *The Journal of British Studies*, Vol. 52, (January 2013); Paul Smith, '"Unions naked and unprotected at the altar of common law". Inducement of Breach of Contract of Employment...' *Historical Studies in Industrial Relations*, No. 35, (2014).

in which Keir Hardie took a leading part, began with 350,000 trade unionists affiliated through 41 unions. By January 1903 nearly 850,000 trade unionists were affiliated.

The 1898 'coal war' and the Taff Vale strike, their outcomes, and the persistent use by South Wales coalowners of the law against their employees, fed a growing sense of injustice. The allegiance of the great majority of workers remained to the Liberal Party — the MFGB did not affiliate to the Labour Party (originally the Labour Representation Committee) until 1909 — but disputes, injustice and unrest were fertile ground for socialist propaganda.

Keir Hardie in Wales

In 1887 Keir Hardie attended his first Trades Union Congress as a delegate from the Ayrshire miners. The meeting was held in Swansea and he famously, if ineffectually, argued for a political party of Labour to which all trade unions should belong. It was then that he first set foot in Merthyr Boroughs when he attended a meeting of Aberdare miners and met David Morgan (*Dai o'r Nant*). It was another nine years before he entered the town of Merthyr Tydfil to speak at an ILP meeting. 'The evening was bitterly cold, the meeting was neither large nor enthusiastic, and the impression I carried away of the place was not of the cheeriest'.[517]

The coal strike of 1898 brought him back. Already a national figure as founder of the Scottish Labour Party and then of the ILP, he had been MP for West Ham, was editor of the ILP's *Socialist Leader* and photographs and cartoons of his distinctive appearance ensured that he was instantly recognised wherever

[517] J. Keir Hardie, 'My Relations with the Merthyr Boroughs', *Souvenir ILP Twentieth Annual Conference* (Merthyr Tydfil, Easter 1912), p. 9.

he went. He was particularly remembered in South Wales for his criticism of the Leader of the Commons for failing to express official sympathy for the relatives of the 260 men and boys killed at the Albion colliery, Cilfynydd, in June 1894. He had lost his West Ham seat in 1895.

At the beginning of the strike in April 1898 he visited the coalfield and returned in June 'to spend a fortnight tramping the hills and valleys ...and speaking to such as cared to listen. It was the best holiday I ever had'. At Troedyrhiw, where he addressed a meeting of 5,000 in late June, the surrounding villages had been decorated with bunting and streamers in anticipation of his visit, and five colliery bands led delegations from Plymouth colliery, Merthyr, Dowlais, Treharris and Merthyr Vale to hear him, despite pouring rain. Most of the meetings attracted audiences of at least 1,000.

Hardie wrote a number of compassionate articles about the strike and returned to the coalfield several times. At the end of July he addressed a meeting of 6,000 at Dowlais, and a meeting in a packed Theatre Royal resulted in over 200 joining the Merthyr ILP branch. In August he preached a number of 'socialistic sermons' on the Penydarren tips to audiences as large as 2,000.[518] Again, attendance has to be taken with a pinch of salt. Curiosity always played a part and when the excitement of the strike was over Merthyr ILP branch membership plummeted from 278 to 24 and Penydarren membership from 110 to 45.[519]

In 1899, however, he undertook a less popular task when, under the auspices of the Stop the War Committee, he addressed a pro-Boer meeting in Bentley's Hall where the audience 'was not more than a hundred'. He later reflected: 'had that meeting

---

[518] Wright, pp. 149-150.

[519] Iain McLean, *Keir Hardie*, (1975), p. 77.

not been held I do not think I would have won the seat in the year following. The number of disciples of Henry Richard who were then uncorrupted, and who were present at the meeting ...gave me their active support twelve months later.'[520]

The 1900 Election

When in September 1900 a General Election was called at the height of Boer War fever the context in Merthyr Boroughs, one of the safest Liberal seats in Britain, was not ideal for the Liberals — the local organisation was in disarray and the two sitting MPs were at loggerheads – but no-one contemplated other than the return of both Liberals. An element of tragic-farce was introduced at the beginning after the Tory candidate failed to arrive in Merthyr in time to register his intention to stand. W.T. Lewis, and his son Herbert had both turned down the opportunity to become candidates. Conservative headquarters then agreed that Arnot Reid, *The Times* correspondent in Singapore but recently arrived in Britain, should be the candidate. Reid, suffering from sunstroke contracted on the voyage confused Merthyr with Morpeth and took the train to Newcastle. Told he should be in South Wales he then took the train to Cardiff which he assumed was Merthyr. He was in Cardiff when the time to register his candidacy closed. His lengthy election address was described by the *Merthyr Express* as 'probably the most extraordinary in the whole Kingdom'.[521] Part of it read:

> I have lived, loved and married, owned children and houses, experienced the world, the flesh and the devil, made and lost;

[520] Hardie, 'My Relations with Merthyr Boroughs', p. 10.

[521] *ME*, 6 October 1900.

> made and explored; mined, distilled, manufactured, built, lent and borrowed, bought and sold with Indians, Chinamen, Japanese, Malay, American, Negro, half-caste, Hindoo, Buddhist, Jew and Christian.

He finally arrived in Merthyr, left the same day, and shortly afterwards died from the effects of sunstroke.

Hardie in 1900 was looking for a parliamentary seat and Merthyr Boroughs and Preston were possibilities. Preston, although less appealing than a mining constituency with a radical history, was held by two Conservatives and offered him the opportunity to pick up Liberal votes. In Merthyr Boroughs, the strength of Liberalism among the miners made his nomination appear doubtful. The Preston ILP branch was eager for him to stand. He was nominated there without difficulty and wrote to Llewellyn Francis in Penydarren on 21 September to say he had accepted Preston. However, ILP members in Merthyr Boroughs, ambitious and determined, were already planning a nomination for Hardie and a selection meeting had been arranged for the next day at Abernant where around 80 delegates attended.

Half the delegates were miners, most of whom wanted the candidate to be William Brace, a leader of the 1898 strike, who would take the Liberal whip as a Lib-Lab. 'Dai Box', secretary of Merthyr Trades Council, aware that the meeting would be split between ILP members and Liberal supporters came prepared. The miners' delegates wanted to vote according to the number of miners they represented, some lodges had thousands of members. The ILP members argued for one vote per delegate, as did representatives from the various small trade union branches. Not all of the miners' delegates had been given authority by their lodge meetings to nominate at this meeting and therefore abstained from voting. The decision was in favour of one delegate one vote. Brace's supporters sensed that they were outnumbered and left the meeting. Enoch Archer, the chairman and an ILP member, insisted that the meeting should nominate a candidate there and then. Hardie was chosen by thirty-two votes to seven and when informed, decided to fight both Preston and Merthyr Boroughs. Constituencies were not then required to poll on the same day (Gladstone had once won two seats in the same election). Preston's polling day was on 1 October and Merthyr's the next day. Hardie at Preston, with nearly 5,000 votes, ended bottom of the poll.[522]

He had made some attempt to campaign in both constituencies. On 27 September he addressed five open-air meetings in Merthyr sandwiched between meetings in Preston the days before and after. But inevitably the campaign in Merthyr Boroughs depended upon the local activists. Prominent in Merthyr were Dai Davies, Llew Francis by then treasurer of the Merthyr Trades Council, the signalman Oliver Jenkins, and the Treharris photographer Dan Osborne. In Aberdare, the key group included C.B. Stanton, Edmund Stonelake, Enoch Archer, John Prowle a checkweigher at Nantmelyn colliery, schoolmaster W.W. Price and James Ray, caretaker of the Cwmaman Working Men's Institute. The army of enthusiasts included English supporters: Joe Burgess, who acted as election agent, George Palmer and Sam Hobson; local miners who saw that Hardie, unlike Pritchard Morgan, was a genuine representative of working-men; supporters of Henry Richard's internationalism, and wives and female supporters who arranged meetings and doorstep canvassed. On polling day it rained. Hardie arrived from Preston in time to tour the polling stations in a motor car which had to be abandoned when it could no longer take the hills.

---

[522] Kenneth O. Fox, 'Labour and Merthyr's Khaki Election of 1900', *WHR,* Vol. 2 (1964-5); Iain McLean, pp. 81-2.

The Election Result

The decisive element was the animosity between D.A. Thomas and Pritchard Morgan. During the 1895 election campaign Thomas had distanced himself from Morgan. In 1900 they openly attacked each other. Morgan with imperial fervour put up posters saying: 'Vote for DA Thomas and Keir Hardie – both pro-Boers'. Thomas exploited Morgan's absences on Asian adventures and claimed that he had said he could mine Chinese coal at a shilling a ton. As China was a market for South Wales coal this was a damaging allegation which enabled Thomas, an enlightened major coalowner, to present himself as looking after Merthyr's, and the miners', major interest. Morgan denied the allegation. Thomas' supporters encouraged people to vote also for Hardie, prominently displaying Hardie's posters in Thomas' campaign rooms. Hardie recommended the voters to vote for himself and Thomas.

The election result was: DA Thomas (Lib) 8,508; Keir Hardie (Ind. Lab) 5,745; Pritchard Morgan (Lib) 4,004. In this two-member constituency electors had two votes. Some voted for Pritchard Morgan and Hardie. Those who voted for Hardie alone, that is 'plumped' to vote only for him, were 867. The combined votes for D.A. Thomas and Hardie were 4,437. Merthyr was not a Labour seat. Some 2,000-3,000 miners had lost their vote by accepting parish relief during the 1898 strike and a number would have voted for Hardie, but that would not have put him top of the poll. Although he kept his seat and increased his votes in 1906 and 1910 Hardie was always outvoted by the Liberal candidate and remained 'the Junior Member'.

The psephological explanation for his success in 1900 is that Hardie was not elected as a socialist but as a workingman's representative by the votes of Liberal working men who were disenchanted with Pritchard Morgan. His victory therefore was not an 'accident' but a logical outcome of local circumstances. Hardie's appeal, however, went far beyond that logic. True, he did not hesitate to remind his working-class voters of his knowledge of the coalfield, its troubles, and the value of having a voice in parliament that spoke for them. In his election address he reminded them of his activities in 1898 and during the hauliers' strike of 1893

> I was among you endeavouring to cheer, encourage and strengthen you in the dark days of your recent great Industrial struggle. Not many years ago, when during the Hauliers' Strike, the Government sent soldiers into your District, it was MY VOICE THAT PROTESTED against this in Parliament, when others upon whom you had more claims were silent.

This was the practical politician. But he also came with an ethical Christian message which struck a chord with radical Nonconformity. Christ the carpenter had been a working man. God the Father meant that all men were brothers. The Sermon on the Mount was at the heart of brotherhood and socialism. Hardie's anti-war rhetoric and advocacy of temperance spoke to the chapel-goers who had revered Henry Richard. Broad-shouldered, sturdy and erect, with a fine head, grey-white beard and resonant voice, Hardie looked the teacher and prophet that he was. Against the persecutions and indignities in the collieries, the insecurities at Cyfarthfa and Dowlais, he proclaimed a message that aimed to give 'the working class a new feeling of hope and confidence in themselves'. Workers, he stressed, were 'the foundation upon which the whole superstructure of Society rests'.[523]

The election of Henry Richard in 1868 had broken the

---

[523] May, 'The Mosaic of Labour Politics' in Tanner, Williams, Hopkins (eds.), pp 62-3.

electoral grip of the ironmasters. Pritchard Morgan's election in 1888 had broken the middle class control over the Liberal vote. The election of Keir Hardie in 1900 was much more significant. It was a triumph for aspiration and hope over experience; a defiant response to the suppression of democratic aspirations in 1816, 1831 and 1839; the crushing of trade unionism in 1831, 1834, 1842, 1874-79 and the defeat of 1898. In the dawn of the new century as the ironmasters' influence crumbled, Merthyr's radical impulse produced Hardie. The mould could be broken and was being remade.

20

Keir Hardie and the Dowlais Rising

> A success from the point of view of numbers, but the environment of the place [Dowlais] was most distressing. With skilled men working for three shillings [15p] a day, the place badly organised, and the men with little courage apparently, it was not heartening to speak to them.
>
> **Ben Tillet**[524]

On 27 June 1912, when George V and Queen Mary visited Dowlais, many feared Britain was on the verge of revolution. There was no sign of that in Merthyr and Dowlais as the crowds cheered the royal couple. In Ireland, then a full part of the United Kingdom, the army was divided, arms were being illegally smuggled and a civil war threatened as Edward Carson said Ulster would fight against Home Rule for Ireland. The campaign for votes for women had reached the stage where suffragettes were chaining themselves to railings. Two days before the King and Queen were in Dowlais, the Prime Minister Asquith had to defend in the House of Commons the practice of force-feeding imprisoned suffragettes on hunger strike. The day after the visit the suffragettes started a campaign of window-smashing at Post Offices and Labour Exchanges.

---

524 Ben Tillet, general secretary of the (London) Dockers' Union reporting back from a meeting at Dowlais on 28 August 1911. General Federation of Trade Unions, management committee, 31 August 1911.

Industrial disputes were at record levels. Nearly eighteen million working days were lost on average each year from 1911 to 1914 through strikes and lock-outs. In South Wales in the summer of 1911 police and troops were out in force. From November 1910 to January 1911, 11,000 miners in the Aberdare district (part of the Merthyr Borough's parliamentary constituency) had been on unofficial strike. Violent and riotous behaviour had caused a company of troops to be stationed in the area. The 'abnormal places' issue in that strike was at the centre of the Cambrian Combine dispute in the Rhondda which had begun in September 1910 and would last a year, during which troops would use 'the gentle persuasion' of fixed bayonets. A national rail strike was in being and at Llanelli on 18 August 1911, when strikers tried to stop a train manned by blacklegs, two bystanders were shot dead by troops, provoking a riot. Keir Hardie, Merthyr's MP, wrote a pamphlet entitled *Killing No Murder!: the Government and the Railway Strike*. In Cardiff the strike of seamen and dockers had turned into a city-wide general strike.[525]

In Dowlais all was quiet. True, at the steelworks forty-four moulders were on strike, but the management, doing what it

---

[525] Martin Barclay, '"The Slaves of the Lamp" – The Aberdare Miners' Strike 1910', *Llafur* 2:3 (1978); D. Smith, 'Tonypandy 1910: Definitions of Community' *Past and Present* 87 (1980); Deian Hopkin, 'The Llanelli Riots, 1911' *Welsh History Review* 2:4 (1983); R. Geary, 'Tonypandy and Llanelli Revisited' *Llafur* 4:4 (1987); J.K. Hardie, *Killing No Murder!: The Government and the Railway Strike. What Caused the Recent Railway Strike? Who Settled It? For What Purpose Were the Troops Called Out?* (National Labour Press, Manchester, 1911); Neil Evans, '"A Tidal Wave of Impatience": The Cardiff General Strike of 1911' in Geraint H. Jenkins and Beverley Smith (eds.), *Politics and Society in Wales, 1840-1922* (Cardiff, 1988).

usually did, had brought in blacklegs, mostly young apprentices from other departments, to do the moulders work. In the midst of a political crisis and what seemed to be a national workers' rebellion no-one took much notice of this peaceful minor dispute. The official history of Guest Keen Nettlefold (GKN) does not mention it.[526] In the light of what happened later, it should have.

By the early 1900s the Dowlais steelworks was notorious for its anti-unionism, low wages and shocking working conditions. Although by 1911 several unions had achieved a smattering of membership without company recognition, its reputation as 'the last great bastion of non-unionism in the iron and steel industry' was well deserved[527]. The South Wales Divisional Officer of the Amalgamated Society of Engineers (ASE) referred to it as 'this powerful Trade Union crushing company'.[528] 'Hell with the lid off' was another description. The general manager was William Evans. 'Dowlais', joked one trade union official, was 'where Evans and Hell meet'. Its reputation went far beyond South Wales.

In February 1907 a by-election occurred in the Parliamentary constituency of Brigg in Lincolnshire. It was considered a safe Liberal seat and the party's candidate was Capt. Freddie Guest, a grandson of Sir John Guest. His Tory opponent was a local and popular landowner. Guest lost. The Liberals were shocked by the loss of this 'safe' seat but the constituency contained the Frodingham steelworks and the steelworkers had made the wages and conditions at Dowlais the major issue in the political campaign, using information supplied directly to them from Dowlais. The steelworkers' union journal reflected on the result:

---

[526] E. Jones, *A History of GKN: Vol. 1, Innovation and Enterprise, 1759-1918* (1987).

[527] Hugh Armstrong Clegg, *A History of British Trade Unions since 1889: Vol.2: 1911-1933* (Oxford, 1985), p. 85.

[528] ASE Monthly Divisional Report, September 1911; A. Pugh, *Men of Steel*, pp. 63-4.

> [T]he working-class section of the Brigg Division had to choose between a candidate who is known as a good landlord and a humane employer ... and a candidate who is a member of a family who are directly responsible for such unfair conditions as have so long existed and still exist at a large industrial centre in South Wales... These conditions have become a byword among the workers in the iron and steel industry.[529]

The same tactic was used in 1910 when Freddie Guest contested and won East Dorset. During the election the Merthyr ILP issued a sensational and possibly libellous pamphlet about slum housing in Dowlais written by its secretary, Dai Davies. In response the Guest family commissioned the Liberal agent in Cardiff – H.G.C. Allgood — to investigate conditions in Dowlais and to find out whether there were grounds for legal action. Allgood paid two visits to Dowlais and interviewed a number of people. He advised against legal proceedings. There was, he said, 'a substrata of truth running through the sensationalism'. 'The workmen are badly paid, the place has been neglected by the Guest family, and the "housing problem" – after ten years work by the Council – is not what it should be'. He also considered that the Company was responsible for pushing up rents: '[It] sticks to its pound of flesh, and actually asks for offers from those who want new leases then presses for more'. Although the Guests had done good things for Dowlais it had been neglected during the last quarter of the nineteenth century and wealth from the town had been spent elsewhere.[530]

---

[529] Pugh, *Men of Steel*, pp. 144-5.

[530] K. Sullivan, '"The Biggest Room in Merthyr": Working-Class Housing in Dowlais 1850-1914', *Welsh History Review* 17:2, (1994), pp. 155-85.

Dismal Dowlais

When George Clark retired in 1892 a regime of strong management, low wages and submissive labour was firmly in place. The closure of the Penydarren and Plymouth works and the lengthy lock-out at Cyfarthfa meant that wage comparisons with adjoining firms had long ceased. In 1901 the ageing Lord Wimborne merged the Dowlais Iron, Steel and Coal Company with the Patent Nut and Bolt Company to form Guest, Keen & Company. In March 1902 this company acquired the share capital of Crawshay Brothers. Three months later in June this new company merged with Nettlefolds, Britain's monopoly producer of screws, to form Guest, Keen and Nettlefolds (GKN) with headquarters in Birmingham. In less than twelve months the Crawshays and Guests had given up the control they had exercised for well over one hundred years. Ownership which had been local and tangible had become distant and unknown. William Evans the manager at Cyfarthfa assumed control of both sites. A former Dowlais man who had learned his trade under Menelaus, Evans continued the established pattern of industrial relations. After GKN took over, more than £250,000 was invested in labour-saving machinery. Skilled men were replaced by machines tended by semi-skilled workers, direct supervision increased, the low-wage policy continued.

Low wages and poor working conditions were not the only distinguishing characteristics of Dowlais. A combination of high rents, low wages and a century of jerry-building had resulted in severe overcrowding and hundreds of houses unfit for human habitation that could not be cleared because there was no alternative cheap accommodation. The Dowlais Company which had built sturdy cottages in the 1840s and owned around one-third of the working-class housing had long ceased to build. Many workers were lodging in already overcrowded houses where rent from lodgers was a vital supplement to household incomes. A phenomenon of the early years of industrialisation and mass migration was being repeated. Some beds never grew cold; as those on night shift got out of them, those returning from the day shift fell into them.

Public health had deteriorated. The Medical Officer's report for 1902 noted that despite efforts by the local board of health the Merthyr district had the highest death rate in Glamorgan, 22.96 per thousand, and possessed 'the unenviable reputation of having the highest death-rate among the seventy-six large towns, Liverpool coming next to it with a death-rate of 22.5'. The greatest contributors to the high death-rate was poor housing and infant rearing.[531] In June 1907 the *Western Mail* ran a series on Dowlais in which the author wrote, 'Some of the great employers of labour whose vast wealth comes from Dowlais would not kennel their dogs as they allow their unfortunate work people to be kennelled'. In 1911 *The Lancet* commented on 'squalid people living in ugly and unwholesome dwellings.'[532] A speaker at the Llandaff Diocesan Conference 1901 who knew Dowlais very well had already summed up the situation: 'in no part of this diocese can you find such miserable hovels in which people are expected to live respectably. And yet millions of money have been dragged out of Dowlais for the aristocracy to build large houses'. As for the homes of the workers, 'Lord Wimborne would not stable his horses in some of them'.[533]

---

[531] *Annual Report, Year ending 1902*, pp. 8-9.

[532] *Western Mail*, 27, 28, 29 June 1907; *Lancet*, 21 January 1911.

[533] E.T. Davies, *Religion in the Industrial Revolution in South Wales*, (Cardiff, 1965), p. 132. Ivor Bertie Guest, Sir John's eldest son, was made Lord Wimborne in 1880.

The Strike

Against this social, industrial and political background it might be thought that a strike at Dowlais in the hot and tempestuous summer of 1911 was inevitable. But the strike had actually begun on 27 March and by August was already almost five months old. It arose, as strikes often do, from a management decision to alter a customary practice. The wages of moulders were so low that overtime had become recognised as part of their regular wages. But in March the management decided to halve the overtime payment to men working after six p.m. When the men protested, the management proposed to pay overtime to married men only. When this was rejected the company gave notice to some and offered overtime to others. The moulders decided there should be work for all, with overtime, or they would go on strike.

The local socialist newspaper *Pioneer* pointed out, 'the men at Dowlais are fighting to retain overtime …because they cannot exist on the day rate'.[534] The day rates they were being paid (there was no uniformity) ranged between 3s.8d. (18.3p) and 2s.11d. (14.6p). The agreed district rate for moulders at Ebbw Vale was 6s. a day (30p). The moulders were probably the only workmen at Dowlais who were all in a union. They were members of the Welsh Ironfounders' Trade Union, a small union formed in February 1889 and later known as the Associated Society of Moulders. Its headquarters was in Swansea. The union executive committee declared the strike official and paid the men dispute benefit of 15s. (75p) a week.[535] The

[534] *Pioneer*, 1 April 1911. The *Pioneer* was a socialist newspaper published in Merthyr from 1911-22. See Deian Hopkin, 'The Merthyr Pioneer', *Llafur* Vol. 2, No. 4 (Spring 1979).

[535] The union was affiliated to the General Federation of Trade Unions which agreed to reimburse 5s (25p) per week to the union's strike costs.

management continued to bring in non-union labour to do the moulders' work. But the strike went on, and the longer it continued the more it became clear that the heart of the matter was not overtime payment but the low wages paid at Dowlais not only to the moulders but to *all* the workers at Dowlais.

At first, reaction to the strike was low key. On May Day 1911 a march and political demonstration organised by the Merthyr Labour Representation Committee attracted more than 4,000 to Cyfarthfa Park where the speakers included Hardie, George Lansbury and Margaret Bondfield. A resolution calling for 'the removal of all property qualifications or sex disabilities connected with citizenship', 'the substitution of arbitration for war', 'a maximum working week of forty-eight hours, and a minimum weekly wage of thirty shillings [£1.50]', taxation on all unearned income, and 'the speedy transfer of land, mines, railways, and the principal industries to the State' was carried with enthusiasm. During his speech Hardie declared that the moulders 'were fighting a good fight' and setting an example to other workmen at Dowlais, that 'dark and dismal' locality.[536]

Support for the strike gradually gathered momentum. New life was breathed into the Workers' Union branch at Dowlais and on 1 June 1911 hundreds paraded through the main streets of Dowlais headed by a fife and drum band and the banner of the Workers' Union. An estimated 6,000 people meeting on the Gellifaelog tip was then addressed by Charles Duncan MP, the union's general secretary, Matt Giles, ILP activist and organiser for the union in south Wales, and John Davies the miners' agent for Dowlais. All three urged support for the moulders and the importance of organisation among Dowlais workers.[537]

Up to then the strike had been seen as a purely industrial

[536] *ME*, 6 May 1911; *Pioneer*, 6 May 1911.

[537] *ME*, 3 June 1911.

matter but on 13 June William Jones, the president of the Welsh Ironfounders, wrote to Edgar Jones (Liberal) and Keir Hardie, Merthyr's two MPs, pointing out that GKN at Dowlais was working on government contracts but failing to observe the terms of the 1909 Fair Wages Resolution of the House of Commons. This required firms engaged on government contracts to observe hours and wages 'not less favourable than those commonly recognised by employers and trade societies (or, in the absence of such recognised wages and hours, those which in practice prevail amongst good employers)'.[538] Failure to observe the standards required was, in legal terms, a breach of commercial contract.

It was Edgar Jones who first raised the issue. On 19 June, he asked the First Lord of the Admiralty whether GKN was on the lists of Admiralty contractors and, if so, whether at Dowlais it was complying with fair wages conditions. He received the reply that as far as the Admiralty was aware there was no Admiralty order with the firm that affected the moulders at Dowlais. The next day, Hardie also raised the matter, pointing out that the moulders had been on strike for the past ten weeks. He received the same answer.

When the strike was over Jones made great play of the fact that he had been the first to ask a Parliamentary question about government work at Dowlais and sought credit for himself and the Liberal Party for so doing. Hardie's supporters were scornful: 'he actually asked a question!' The *Pioneer* was so annoyed by Jones seeking credit that it revealed on 7 October that from 19 June to 17 August Jones had raised the issue twelve times in the Commons. Hardie had done so fifty-two times. In addition Hardie had met the government departments concerned on sixteen occasions, kept in constant touch with the

---

[538] H. A.Clegg, A. Fox and A. F. Thompson, *A History of British Trade Unions since 1889, Vol. 1: 1889-1910* (Oxford, 1964), pp. 404-5.

Dowlais men, and written five articles exposing the low wages and high profits at Dowlais. Jones had not met departments, had not met the moulders, had not written articles and, claimed the *Pioneer*, his questions were often misinformed.

Hardie relentlessly pursued the First Lord of the Admiralty, the Under Secretary of State for India, and the Secretary of State for the Colonies as to what contracts their departments had placed with GKN, what work was being carried out at Dowlais, whether they were aware the moulders were on strike because of a reduction in their pay, and what was being done to ensure that fair wages and conditions were being observed? He also enquired whether self-governing British Dominions were aware that GKN was violating the Fair Wages Resolution while carrying out contracts placed with Dowlais for rails? On 3 July it was established that Dowlais was contracted to supply 19,616 tons of rails and fishplates for the Indian State Railways. The Director-General of Stores was sent to Dowlais to investigate.

On 20 July, Hardie elicited from the Secretary of State for the Colonies that orders for rails and fishplates had been placed with GKN Dowlais on behalf of the Federated Malay States Railway, the Trinidad Railway, and the Southern Nigeria Railway. Hardie wrote to the administrations of all the Crown Colonies, giving his view of the situation but it was not until 31 July that the India Office referred the matter to the Fair-Wages Advisory Committee for an opinion. [539]

---

[539] *Parliamentary Debates* (*Hansard*), 5th Series, vol. 27, 3 July 1911, col. 805; 6 July 1911, cols. 1318-19; vol 28: 12 July 1911, col. 359-60; 20 July 1911, cols. 1267-8; 24 July 1911, cols. 1489-90; 25 July 1911, cols. 1512-13; 27 July 1911, cols. 1884-5; vol. 29, 1 August 1911, col. 172.

The Gates of Hell

The questioning in the Commons was paralleled by open air rallies in Dowlais and by a remarkable series of articles on 'Sweated Dowlais' by Hardie in the *Pioneer* in which he publicised the Fair Wages Resolution, excoriated the low earnings in all departments at Dowlais, and revealed the names of major GKN shareholders.[540] In the middle of July a demonstration organised by Merthyr Trades and Labour Council was addressed by Hardie, Arthur Henderson MP, the Rev. David Pugh of Sunderland ('the fighting parson'), and by Charles Duncan MP, Workers' Union general secretary. Henderson, the Secretary of the Labour Party, spoke with authority as National Organiser of the Friendly Society of Ironfounders. In twenty years he had never come across a case in any part of Great Britain where moulders' wages were as low as those at Dowlais. Hardie announced that the wages of all workers at Dowlais were now being investigated. The wages of labourers, he said, were impossibly low. Dramatically he produced wage dockets that had been handed to him that evening by Davy Evans, secretary of the Amalgamated Society of Engineers, Dowlais branch.

> Here is one for five weeks ...and the total earnings are £2. 2s. 11d [£2.14.6p] for five weeks. Out of that has come 9d [3.75p] for the doctor and the fund, 5s 3d [26.25p] for coal and 14s 6d [72.5p] for rent, leaving the man about 6s [30p] a week to feed, clothe, and to provide for a wife and three children.

After giving other examples Hardie urged his audience to join and back their union:

---

540 *Pioneer*, 29 July, 5, 12 and 19 August, 2 September 1911.

> No progress has ever been made without unity and without strength. Why have you slums in Dowlais? Because of low wages and why have you low wages? Because of the intimidation that has prevailed. And why do you have this intimidation? Because you do not stand together ...Learn the solidarity of the class to which you belong, and if you do that there is no doubt whatever that the future holds better and brighter things than the past has seen'.[541]

On 15 August, both the Colonial Secretary and the Under Secretary of State for India admitted to Hardie, for the first time, that 'on the advice of the Fair-Wages Advisory Committee ...the moulders and steelmakers at Dowlais must be regarded as employed on our contract. The wages at Dowlais appear certainly to be low, but the Committee has not yet given me their advice...'. [542] Two days later, the India and Colonial Offices informed Hardie that the Fair-Wages Advisory Committee had that morning advised that the wages paid at Dowlais were 'not strictly in conformity with the Fair Wages Resolution' and that no further Government orders would be placed 'until this state of affairs has been remedied'. The First Lord of the Admiralty, while continuing to deny that the Dowlais works was doing work for the Admiralty, said: 'I consider that the non-payment of fair wages generally by a firm is a good ground for the non-retention of that firm on the list of Admiralty contractors'.[543] After long delays, victory seemed assured.

That week, adding fuel to the fire, GKN issued its annual report showing profits of £383,008, an increase over 1910,

---

[541] *ME*, 22 July 1911.

[542] *Hansard* 29, 15 August 1911, cols. 1739-42.

[543] *Hansard* 29, 17 August 1911, cols. 2084-8

and recommending a final dividend of 10 per cent on the ordinary shares, and a bonus, amounting to 15 per cent on the ordinary shares, free of income tax.[544] At a mass meeting of Dowlais workers, including railwaymen and colliers, held at the Central School yard on 19 August Hardie explained that the victory meant that labourers getting as little as 1s 10d (9.2p) a day would get at least 3s (15p) a day. Moulders, fitters, engineers, blacksmiths and pattern makers getting from 2s 7d (12.9p) to 3s 8d (18.3p) a day would all have increases up to a minimum of 5s (25p) and possibly 6s 3d (31.25p) a day. 'It will mean this – that although the new conditions will not exactly spell Paradise you will be getting a bit further away from the gates of Hell than you are at present'. But Hardie warned that the Company had not yet agreed to these new rates. It could still delay. Theoretically it could cease taking government contracts and seek business elsewhere. He declared: 'If the firm stands obstinate, there is one remedy left which I will not shrink from – to bring out, not only the men working at Dowlais but wherever GKN have men employed'.[545]

Sitting on a Powder Keg

More weeks went by without a response from GKN. The firm seemed unaware that at Dowlais it was sitting on a powder keg. A government investigation had shown the company to be in breach of the Fair Wages Resolutions; the country was in the midst of unprecedented labour unrest, with serious disturbances at Tonypandy, Llanelli and Cardiff; and Hardie and national political and trade union leaders were urging the notoriously divided workmen at Dowlais to unite. On Sunday

[544] GKN Directors' Report, *ME*, 19 August 1911.

[545] *ME*, 26 August 1911.

17 September, a demonstration in Dowlais was followed by a public meeting addressed by local labour and trade union leaders and Robert Morley, the Workers' Union president, himself a former moulder. Morley successfully moved a resolution that stated:

> That this mass meeting of workers is pleased to hear that the iron and steel workers of Dowlais are coming into line in the trades union movement, and further appeals to all those who have not already joined their respective trades unions to do so at once ...[W]e also desire to draw the attention of the general public to the fact that the moulders are still standing out for better conditions of labour.[546]

The next day the situation blew up. The 200 rail bank labourers, the lowest paid men at the works, had asked some weeks previously for an increase in pay and had been told it would be considered. Nothing had been heard since. That morning the day-shift men asked for an immediate reply and were told 'these things take time'. They walked out. The night-shift did the same. The result was that the Bessemer furnaces were blown out and the Goatmill stopped on Tuesday. The strike escalated. The men working at the small-coal washery came out in sympathy as did the coke oven men. Deputations from various departments met William Evans the general manager on Tuesday but without satisfaction. Unanimously the men decided that no department should return to work until all grievances were settled and –significantly – until there was Company recognition of the unions.

By Wednesday morning more than 2,000 men were on strike and the whole of the Old Works had stopped. Departments in

[546] *ME*, 23 September 1911.

the Ivor Works were still working but a procession of 'a couple of thousand' 'induced their fellows to join in the revolt'. On Thursday morning, after a mass meeting in the Oddfellows Hall addressed by Matt Giles, nearly 2,000 paraded through Dowlais carrying a large and new Workers' Union banner. Blacklegs who had been doing moulders' work joined the strike. So did the chaff cutters at the Dowlais stables which meant that the horses underground in the collieries would not be fed. Before the day was out Evans agreed to meet Giles, who led a committee representing seven different unions.[547]

The next day, Friday 22 September, agreement was reached. It was total victory for the men. The terms of agreement, announced to a mass meeting chaired by Morley in the Oddfellows Hall, Dowlais, were: 'that all unions involved be officially recognised; that no legal proceedings shall be taken on this occasion against any workman or Union in respect of cessation of work without notice; that no man or section of men shall suffer from boycott or victimisation for participation in the dispute; that the company agree that they will raise the rates of all departments to the point prevailing in other works doing similar work, and that they will agree with such advances being retrospective from the time of resumption of work'. GKN officially recognised, for the first time at Dowlais: The Workers' Union; the Steel Smelters' Society; the National Blastfurnacemen; the National Steel Workers' Association; the Welsh Moulders' Society; the Boilermakers' Society; and the Amalgamated Society of Engineers. In five days of mass action, from Monday 18 September to Friday 22 September, everything had been achieved. But the moulders had been on strike since late March.

Remarkably, in the fevered national atmosphere of the time,

[547] *ME,* and *Pioneer*, 23 September 1911.

their strike had been largely peaceful. Picketing was systematic and well-organised. Only two cases of harassing blacklegs came to court, both in June. In the first case two moulders were found guilty of striking blacklegs on their way home. In the second case a number of moulders were bound over to keep the peace after singing and shouting 'blackleg' in various Dowlais streets. Later, on hearing the songs, Hardie commented that they were not nearly as bad as 'Hang old Hardie on a sour apple tree'.[548] The chief constable solemnly complained that

> By far the greatest trouble was with the crowds who would shout and boo intermittingly [*sic*], and a very usual practice would be when near a marked house for one of the crowd to shout out 'Are we down-hearted?' and the crowd would yell 'No' and it was impossible for the Police to find the ring-leader of the shouting.[549]

There was evident sympathy for the strikers. Sir T. Marchant Williams, the Stipendiary Magistrate, commented in the first case:

> I do not blame the strikers for trying to persuade men not to work. Strikers are very angry naturally; they would not go on strike unless they were ...I am satisfied the defendants struck the man. You lost your tempers ...one has to make some allowance for men who are on strike and angry, with children at home, and wives unprovided for. Pay 20s (£1) and costs, and don't do it again.

---

[548] *Pioneer*, 1 July 1911.

[549] Chief Constable's letter to the Mayor, 8 December 1911, HO 144/5491, National Archives.

However, the two defendants had already decided to go to prison rather than pay the fine. As they left for Swansea gaol 'they had a rousing send-off at the station' and a week later, when they returned, they were met by a crowd of thousands with as many as 15,000 later parading through Dowlais.[550]

Not until November, after lengthy negotiations between the unions and the management, was agreement reached on the level of wages to be paid and Hardie was able to write to the Admiralty, the India Office and the Colonial Office on 15 November to say that there was no further reason for government orders to be withheld from the company.[551] Throughout the affair GKN and its local management had behaved with extraordinary arrogance. On 6 June, the moulders had applied to the Board of Trade for assistance in bringing about a settlement, but when a conciliation officer went to Dowlais and spoke to representatives of the Company on 19 July he was treated in a manner that made clear that the government department 'was unable usefully to take any further action in the matter'.[552] Even when found guilty of ignoring the Fair Wages Resolutions, it took no action, and was seemingly contemptuous of the claims of the banksmen. The episode is a classic example of hubris leading to downfall.

Hardie's Open Letter to George V

There was one more act to be played. Despite the agreement, the Company did not take back all the moulders. Seventeen were re-instated and fifteen found work elsewhere. For the

[550] *ME*, 17 and 24 June 1911; *Pioneer*, 17 and 24 June 1911.

[551] *Pioneer*, 18 November 1911.

[552] *Ninth Report of the Board of Trade of Proceedings under the Conciliation (Trade Disputes) Act, 1896*, 1911 (HMSO, 1912), p. 45.

remainder – it was alleged that the company regarded them as the ring leaders of the strike – the company said it would find them work when it could. Months went by and evidence accumulated that the company was obtaining castings from elsewhere and even that overtime was being worked by those in employment. The 'solidarity' of the men at Dowlais was indeed fragile.

Eight months later in June 1912 arrangements were being made for the visit of King George V and Queen Mary to Merthyr and Dowlais. Hardie decided to write an Open Letter to the King. He explained that the town had been exploited by ironmasters, that some moulders were still being denied work, and that the proposed visit to the Dowlais works was an attempt to whitewash the principal share-holders so that they might 'once again be made to appear respectable members of society'.

> Go to Dowlais by all means. See the people and their homes, but shun the works as you would a plague spot ...It is for Your Majesty to decide whether ...you should accept hospitality paid for out of the blood and tear-stained wealth of the creators of Dismal Dowlais.[553]

The King ignored the letter. But it stirred the conscience of the Dowlais unions. The very next day the joint committee of unions at Dowlais met and decided that a fight should be made to get the moulders re-instated. The omnipresent Dai Davies, the committee secretary, wrote to various union organisers and to Hardie, who instantly replied. He promised if nothing was settled within seven days by 22 June he would come down on the eve of the King's visit with three MPs who were also

[553] *Pioneer*, 15 June 1912.

national trade union leaders: John Hodge the General Secretary of the British Steel Smelters Association, Charles Duncan of the Workers' Union, and George Barnes chairman of the Labour Party and former general secretary of the ASE. [554] When the Dowlais management heard this on Friday, 21 June, they telegraphed William Jones, the president of the moulders' union, asking him to come at once. Previously they had refused to meet him. He came that afternoon and a settlement was agreed there and then. The eleven remaining moulders were re-instated and started work on Monday 24 June 1912. Three days later on Thursday 27 June the Royal visit took place.

Fifteen months earlier, on 1 April 1911, the *Pioneer* had referred to Dowlais men 'steeped in oppression'. For over a century the company had broken organised opposition. There were allegations that its attack on the moulders' conditions had been intended to break their union branch. Once the strike began GKN employed non-unionists to do the moulders' work, assuming that the strike would collapse. How could forty four men be a threat to its autocratic rule? Yet the moulders stood firm and their determination was the key to everything that followed. Their straightforward refusal to have their conditions unilaterally worsened, and the official union backing they received, set an example to other workers, threw a spotlight upon the low wages that prevailed throughout the works, and gave Hardie, with his flair for publicity, the time and opportunity to stir up a campaign. His persistent questioning was an object lesson in the value of independent working-class representation in Parliament.

Despite his threat to stop the whole works, Hardie knew it would not be possible unless all workers at Dowlais were united. Hence his constant urging them 'to act as men', and to

[554] *Pioneer*, 29 June 1912.

join their respective trade unions. The moulders' strike was more modest in intention than events in Tonypandy where there emerged in the pamphlet *The Miners' Next Step* a revolutionary challenge to the social order. Yet, the moulders challenged and overthrew a century of company intimidation and domination by acting 'as catalysts in a general explosion of consciousness'.[555] The prospective members of the various steel unions, of the Workers' Union, and of the engineers (ASE) climbed on the backs of the moulders and finally stood up. In his Workers' Union annual report for 1911, Charles Duncan wrote:

> The old days of the absolute despotism and tyranny of the employing section of society are rapidly passing away... [T]he slavish, crawling, sheepish, frightened feeling of the workers is rapidly dying out...'[556]

In 1912 it died in Dowlais.

[555] Hyman, *Workers' Union*, pp. 193-4.

[556] Modern Record Centre, Warwick University. Workers' Union, *Annual Report, 1911*.

21

Days of Hope

> The great hope of our Town Council lies in the future, and it is in the opportunity that lies there that every true citizen of the town hopes that much good to the town and the inhabitants will result.
>
> **A Citizen**[557]

On 6 June 1905 King Edward VII gave Royal Assent to a Charter of Incorporation which created the Municipal Borough of Merthyr Tydfil. After seventy years of coercion and obstruction by powerful vested interests Merthyr's inhabitants were at last citizens. The Charter was exhibited at the Town Hall on Monday, 10 July, and later that day with ceremonial processions at Dowlais, Troedyrhiw, Merthyr Vale and Treharris. In the evening there was a banquet, fireworks and band performances.

With Incorporation finally achieved, the population increasing and the economy thriving a confident optimism reigned. True, the days when Merthyr was the largest town in Wales, the epicentre of a defining Welsh industry had ended. Coal had replaced iron in that role with upstart Rhondda the focus, leaving Merthyr stranded on the north-eastern rim of the coalfield. Yet all was well. Merthyr had its own busy collieries that in 1913 produced three million tons of coal. By contrast with the first one hundred years of industrial development when

[557] *ILP Souvenir Booklet: Twentieth Annual Conference Merthyr Tydfil* (1912), p. 83.

the lower part of the borough was farmland there were thriving colliery settlements at Troedyrhiw, Aberfan, Merthyr Vale and Treharris. Their industrial history is different from the iron towns of Merthyr Tydfil and Dowlais and, because of the elongated shape of the borough their association with those towns has always been uneasy; some would argue that it has never been satisfactorily solved.

But they were an important part of Merthyr's late nineteenth and early twentieth century growth. Both Merthyr Vale and Treharris had well over 8,000 residents each and Troedyrhiw grew from 2,360 in 1880 to 12,951 in 1906.[558] In 1911 only 5 per cent of employed Merthyr men worked in iron and steel but eleven times that number, 55 per cent, were employed in local collieries. These were not just the large mines at Merthyr Vale and Treharris and the Plymouth Collieries but in the collieries developed by Dowlais at Fochriw, Bedlinog, Cwmbargoed, Nantwen and Abercynon.

Every year between 1901 and 1911 the population increased by an average of a thousand moving from 69,228 in 1901 to reach 80,990 in 1911. Yet unemployment stood at less than 2 per cent. Paid work in the borough remained overwhelmingly a man's world. Although in 1911 the total number of females employed, 5,032, was slightly more than the 4,894 employed in 1851, increased schooling meant that females employed over the age of ten had fallen from 23.3 to 18.0 per cent. The two largest occupations were the same as those sixty years earlier. Domestic Offices or Services still employed the largest percentage of women in paid work, 40.5 per cent, an increase of 0.9 per cent. Dressmaking employed 19.3 per cent, a fall from 23.5. But in the more arduous occupations there had been a dramatic decline. The number of females employed in Mines

[558] Andy Croll, *Civilizing The Urban*, pp. 13-14.

and Quarries had fallen from 9.7 per cent to 0.3; those employed in Metals, Machines, etc., were down from 8.7 to 0.2; and female employment in Agriculture had fallen from 2.1 per cent to 0.7. On the other hand, female employment in Food, Drink, Lodging had more than doubled from 5.9 per cent to 13.9 and, most spectacularly, the proportion employed in Professional Occupations had increased to 12.0 per cent compared with 1.7 in 1851.[559]

Unlike the early years of immigration the population was much more indigenous. By 1911 60 per cent of residents had been born in Merthyr.[560] Despite the use of English as a medium for education (Penyrheolgerrig school the only one using Welsh) and its increasing use for business, Welsh remained a language for everyday conversation. In 1901 57 per cent of those over three years of age spoke Welsh and although the percentage declined to 50 per cent in 1911, the actual number of Welsh speakers rose from 36,393 to 37,469. Yet, with the exception of the sea-ports of Cardiff, Swansea and Newport, Merthyr Tydfil was the most cosmopolitan town in Wales. From the early nineteenth century it had held a core of English ironworkers, shopkeepers and professionals, a smattering of Irish, and some 200 Scots, many trading as itinerant drapers.[561] During the 1840s thousands of Irish had arrived. Victims of prejudice and largely confined to labouring jobs, they had their own Catholic churches and schools.

In the late nineteenth century significant numbers attracted by the expanding coal industry came from the agricultural counties of Hereford, Gloucester, Somerset and mid-Wales. Spaniards from

---

559 Williams and Jones, 'Women at Work', Table 2.

560 1911 Census, Report.

561 Huw Williams, 'Merthyr Tydfil and Its Scottish Connections', *Merthyr Historian*, Vol. 10 (1999), pp. 269-282; Nia Campbell, 'The Scottish Experience in South Wales: Respectability and the Public Gaze, 1850-1930', *Llafur*, Vol. 11, No. 2 (2013), pp. 9-26.

Bilbao and its hinterland had for some years been coming over with imported iron ore. During the Boer War (1899-1902) the Dowlais works, short of labour, recruited around sixty Irish workers and also skilled Basque workers. The latter were housed in a row of bungalows officially called Alphonso Street after King Alphonso XIII but known locally as 'Spanish Row'.[562] The Czarist 'pogroms' at the end of the nineteenth century, caused hundreds of Jews to flee from Russia and around 150 settled in Merthyr joining a community that had lived in Merthyr since the 1830s (the first synagogue was built in 1848). Although some found work in the mines,[563] the Blooms, Hamiltons, Fines, Bernsteins and Freedmans became well-known professional Merthyr families. Another stream of migrants, this time escaping poverty, came from the Apennines region in central Italy. By 1911 there were over 800 in the towns and villages of Glamorgan providing 'fast food' in their cafes, icecream parlours and fish and chip shops.[564] Viazinni, Barsi, Basini, Sidoli, Conti became familiar Merthyr names. These newcomers were part of the cultural and physical changes that during the Edwardian years transformed Merthyr, the 'metropolis of the hills', from an overgrown village — really a conglomeration of villages — into a town with modern amenities.

The Urban Villages

It was in those urban villages, the one-time settlements of the 'Inhabitants of the Ironworks' where the character of Merthyr

---

562 Masson, pp. 84-5; Stephen Murray, 'Transnational Labour Recruitment: The Dowlais Iron Works' Basques, 1900', *Llafur*, Vol. 11, No. 2 (2013), pp. 27-39.

563 Harold Pollins, 'Jewish Coal Miners in Wales: A Note', *Llafur*, Vol. 11, No. 2 (2013), pp. 157-162.

564 Colin Hughes, *Lime, Lemon and Sarsaparilla: The Italian Community in South Wales 1881-1945* (Cardiff, 1991).

Tydfil had been forged over more than a hundred years. They had clustered within sight and sound and necessary walking distance of the four ironworks. Now grown into settled communities they still retained their individuality. Dowlais was a separate town: Penydarren, Pentrebach and Abercanaid, distinct communities. The most rural, Cefn Coed, with a population around 2,000 and five chapels was one of several settlements neighbouring the Cyfarthfa works. Others, nearer the works were now seen as part of 'the town' although distinct and separate. Caepantywyll, a settlement east of the Taff below the Brecon Road, with Waterloo Street and King Street suggesting its early nineteenth-century development; Georgetown the largest, with a history of radicalism that caused Gwyn A Williams to characterise it as 'a miniature *Faubourg St Antoine* of the spirit';[565] and Penyrheolgerrig on Aberdare mountain above Georgetown the traditional site of workers' open-air meetings.

It was to these settlements that incomers had turned to kin for accommodation, for help in rearing children, for coping with sickness or money problems. Dowlais had a high proportion of household heads from Cardigan and Carmarthen. North Georgetown in addition to many locally-born also had Carmarthenshire and Pembrokeshire families.[566] Family members and workmates developed relationships that were cemented through gossip, neighbourly acts, the shared experience of weddings and funerals, sickness and accidents, poverty and prosperity.

In these networks women whose lives were a relentless round of work, were central. 'They fed, clothed, kept clean and housed their often large families; and they established and upheld both familial and neighbourhood mores… and operated, with others,

565 Williams, *The Merthyr Rising*, p. 73.

566 Carter and Wheatley, p. 27.

a system of mutual support.'[567] Childbearing and rearing consumed years without respite, clothes were washed by hand, ironing done with the heavy smoothing iron (literally made of iron) heated on the coal fire where all cooking and heating of water was done. Meals and baths for the returning men were required on time, often more than once if fathers and sons or lodgers worked different shifts. There were pit clothes to be mended, and all the time the young children needed attention, a sick or aged relative might be in the house, and there was the nagging fear that one of the men or boys would be stretchered home injured or dead.[568]

Different generations of the same family shared houses or lived in close proximity while sons followed their fathers to furnace or pit, learning their skills. The tie to kin became a tie to a locality and to a neighbourhood that became a community. From such associations the wider Merthyr community grew, as happened in other Victorian towns and neighbourhoods, each relative becoming 'a go-between with other people in the district. His brother's friends are his acquaintances, if not his friends; his grandmother's neighbours so well-known as almost to be his own'.[569] The stories and events that gave colour to their lives and to the growing town were told and retold.

---

567 E. Roberts, *A Woman's Place: An Oral History of Working-Class Women 1890-1940* (Oxford, 1984), p. 1

568 Lady F. Bell, *At The Works*, (1911). Elizabeth Andrews, *A Woman's Work is Never Done* (Dinas Powys, 2006).

569 Michael Young, Peter Willmott, *Family and Kinship in East London* (1957), p. 104. In 1861, 18 members of the England family, originally from Bradford, lived in three houses in Nantygwenith Street, Georgetown. It was a family of blacksmiths and moulders employed at Cyfarthfa. In 1891, 28 of them – husbands and wives, children and grandchildren — lived in five adjoining houses in Cyfarthfa Row and Nantygwenith Street.

Memories of working on the land, serving with Wellington or Nelson, the trauma of 1831, the Saturday night fights around the Iron Bridge, accidents and escapades at work, what the preacher said in chapel, the adventures of friends and relatives in America and Australia, the sayings and rivalries of the Guests and Crawshays. True or false, certainly growing in the telling, the stories cemented through common experience a pride in what it was to live in Merthyr Tydfil.

Building on that pride and reflecting the communal experience was the passion brought to choral singing through the competitive successes of the Dowlais Harmonic Society conducted by Dan Davies, the Merthyr Philharmonic under the same conductor (his move to Merthyr 'the Great Betrayal'), and the combined mixed choir of Dowlais and Merthyr that swept to victory in Llanelli in 1903 conducted by Harry Evans. At Merthyr rail station their return greeted by thousands expressing 'unparalleled enthusiasm'. The National Eisteddfod was hosted in 1881 and 1901; in 1908 the Cyfarthfa Brass Band became the Cyfarthfa and Municipal Band. The cultural experience found expression in other ways in this fruitful period with the appearance of Jimmy Wilde, born in Quakers' Yard in 1892 the greatest of a host of professional Merthyr fighters; Arthur Horner the miners' leader born in Georgetown in 1894; and the pioneers of Anglo-Welsh literature, J.O. Francis born in 1882, Jack Jones born in 1884 and Glyn Jones born in 1905.

For most of the nineteenth century the basic leisure choice had been: pub or chapel? Where people earned their living in back-breaking and dangerous environments, alcohol was a release. Pubs were meeting places, informal labour exchanges, debating chambers. They were also where people got drunk. Merthyr remained rough and unruly; drunks were unpredictable, street fights still common. Nor was it easy for the 'respectable' to avoid the 'rough'. Within a radius of 150 yards of Hermon Chapel, Dowlais, there were thirteen pubs. In Merthyr in the 1890s there were thirty-two pubs within 300 yards of the Parish Church and twenty public houses, seven 'beer retailers' and six chapels in Merthyr High Street.[570] The hymn-singing in Zoar could be heard in the neighbouring pubs.

The 'rough', however, were a minority within the working class; the majority of respectable chapel-goers were working class; and the majority of the working class were neither drunks nor church or chapel-goers. Throughout the nineteenth century in various guises, with their flags, banners, and distinctive dress they had paraded as 1831 rioters, Chartist petitioners, friendly society stalwarts, Sunday school scholars, temperance believers and Cyfarthfa bandsmen. In Corpus Christi processions and as football crowds they had 'claimed the streets' of Merthyr Tydfil, their town.

Not What it Ought to Be

It was a town the middle class had done much to shape. Its members were better educated with wider horizons and experience than almost all members of the working class. They had provided the shops, the legal and administrative services, the newspapers, the medical services, the general hospital and in the subscription library a centre for study and debate. 'Merthyr is not what it ought to be — it does not possess the common necessities belonging to towns of similar size, and which we feel justified in demanding', said T.W. Goodfellow in 1857. It was a demand aimed at the ironmasters and their lack of civic spirit. Of course not all shopkeepers worked for reform. Some put lower rates before civic amenities and were opposed to incorporation. Many were coerced by the threat that the

[570] Andy Croll, *Civilizing the Urban*, pp. 79-87.

major companies would withdraw their custom if they stepped out of line. Nor were all those who worked for the public good entirely altruistic. They wanted incorporation because they believed it would improve trade. They resented the power of the ironmasters and their influence over the workers. They openly admitted that they did want civic power and honours for themselves. But driven by revulsion against squalor, and sharing the Victorian enthusiasm for 'improvement' they dreamt of what a town should be; what Merthyr Tydfil could be. They saw the ironmasters as the chief obstacle, tenaciously maintaining a reactionary grip upon power. From one generation to the next the politically active middle class — now radicals, now disciples of Gladstone — persisted until a municipal Charter was achieved. Not least, that achievement came because Merthyr by the turn of the century was no longer of central concern to the major companies.

Into the Twentieth Century

By then and increasingly in the 1900s new landmark buildings and leisure opportunities provided at last the feeling of being in a town and not an overgrown village. The change came from three sources: increased incomes and shorter working-hours encouraged new ways of spending leisure; a growing and wealthier middle class sought ways to invest its money; and new powers in local government finally unlocked frustrated ambitions. Across Britain increased leisure had brought a surge of sporting activities. In Merthyr, despite a lack of suitable playing pitches, amateur soccer, rugby and hockey teams appeared from the 1870s onwards, associated with workplaces, neighbourhoods, pubs and religious organisations. The Troedyrhiw Stars had the Fox and Hounds as headquarters. The Dowlais Railwaymen was just one of six Dowlais soccer teams.[571] The ILP in 1910 had its own football team. In 1881 Merthyr rugby club was one of the founders of the Welsh Rugby Union. A month earlier T. Aneurin Rees, later Merthyr's first town clerk, played in Wales' first rugby international and twenty years later with other members of the middle class he founded the Morlais Golf Club in 1903. Cilsanws Golf Club followed in 1909. Cycling became a national craze as the cost of machines, new and second-hand, fell.

The significant change, however, had been the commercialisation of sport, the result of national organisations and local investors — solicitors, accountants, building contractors, auctioneers, successful shopkeepers, medical practitioners — looking for money-making opportunities.[572] Unsurprisingly the first moves were made by those who had profited from Merthyr's traditional leisure activity. The Merthyr Licensed Victuallers' Association from the 1870s through to the 1890s organised with considerable commercial success sports days and fetes at Penydarren Park that attracted thousands of spectators. Unlike the travelling circuses, boxing booths and theatre companies that had often passed through Merthyr these were locally organised and regular fixtures.

When these faltered new events took their place. Merthyr became for some years a centre of Northern Union professional rugby. The soccer club, Merthyr Town founded in 1908, flourished at Penydarren Park. Both attracted thousands of spectators who thronged the town on Saturdays. The cost of leasing grounds and building stands emphasised the need to get as many paying customers as possible through the turnstiles. Merthyr Town F.C. became in 1911 a limited liability company and in 1912 was promoted to the First Division of the Southern

---

[571] Croll, *Civilizing The Urban*, pp. 141 ff.

[572] For a general survey of these changes in Britain see W. Hamish Fraser, *The Coming of the Mass Market 1850-1914* (1981).

League. Commercial companies promoted roller-skating rinks, there were three in Merthyr in 1909-10. In 1912 came the Lucania billiard hall. Professional boxing appeared regularly in the Drill Hall. The imposing YMCA building with games rooms, a library, gymnasium and rifle range officially opened in 1911.

Most impressively, in 1894 fifteen local businessmen raised £4,000 by selling 800 £5 shares and built at Pontmorlais the building that became known as the Theatre Royal and Opera House. Altogether it cost some £6,000 and was the largest auditorium in Wales. Moving pictures (not yet with sound), the technical achievement that dominated entertainment in the twentieth century appeared next. In 1910 the Electric Cinema appeared in the High Street a few doors down from Zoar Chapel. Patrons who went in before four o'clock could get tea and biscuits. The Palace Cinema followed in 1912. A visit to 'the pictures' and then the fish-and-chip shop became a weekly part of working-class family life. New ways of living had opened. The chapels, despite the surge produced by the 1904 Revival, were losing to the long-term challenge of these new entertainments and the arguments of those who thought decent housing now was more compelling than the promise of a heavenly afterlife.

A building boom was in progress.[573] The *Merthyr Express* in 1876 had forecast that 'were there building land within easy reach of the town to be let at moderate ground rents, it should not be long before clusters of houses arose superior to anything we now have...'.[574] Twenty years later that was happening. Until the late nineteenth century much of the land owned by the Morgan family in the Bolgoed estate remained farmland but

---

573 T.F. Holley and V.A. Holley, 'Foundations, 1893-1902', *Merthyr Historian*, Vol. 7 (1994); and 'Foundations 1903-1912', *Merthyr Historian*, Vol. 9 (1997).

574 *ME*, 19 February 1876.

in 1892 Stuart Williams Morgan succeeded to the estate and, in addition to leasing land for the building of the Theatre Royal, the YMCA, St. Mary's Catholic Church (1894), the County School (1896), Park Baptist Chapel (1903), and the Masonic Temple (1912), leased land to those who wished to build north of Brecon Road.[575] The names of the development tell the story: The Walk, The Avenue, Park Place, The Grove, West Grove, King Edward Villas. Just as sixty years previously those with money had moved away from the noise and crowds of the central shopping area to Thomastown, so now these brick-built villas were the new area for the growing middle class.

In the older parts of Dowlais and Merthyr the company houses, usually two tiny rooms up and down were often of good quality. But in back-to-backs, in cellars without ventilation, and in cottages built of porous sandstone against the earth of the mountainside, the poorest lived in acknowledged slums. Hundreds of houses built by speculators were in the opinion of the Medical Officer unfit for human habitation, a breeding ground for illness and disease. Jack Jones in *Unfinished Journey* describes the 'bug-ridden hovel' in which he was born. It would take many years to deal with this legacy but in 1902 the urban council built Merthyr's first council houses in prosaically named Council and Urban streets, Penydarren. The borough and county borough councils continued this task and between 1902 and 1912, 294 council houses were built with another 300 under construction in Dowlais, Penydarren, Twynrodyn and Merthyr Vale. Compared with other South Wales authorities Merthyr 'was leading the way'.[576]

In the High Street business confidence was high, riding the depressions of 1904-5 and 1908-9 and even the national coal

[575] Wilf Owen, 'The Morgans of The Grawen and Bolgoed', *Merthyr Historian*, Vol. 27 (2015).

[576] Kate Sullivan, 'The Biggest Room in Merthyr'.

strike of February-April 1912 which ended with the Coal Mines (Minimum Wage) Act 1912 from which thousands of Welsh mineworkers benefitted. Between 1905 and 1914 more than a quarter of million pounds was invested by tradesmen in their High Street premises extending from the Pontmorlais district down to St. Tydfil's parish church. In 1904 a modern Post Office opened opposite the railway station. The passengers on the new open-topped electric trams that linked the town area with Dowlais and Cefn Coed surveyed the thriving shops: butchers, bakers, drapers, ironmongers, grocers, furnishers, chemists, tailors, dressmakers, jewellers and watchmakers, photographers, tobacconists, boot and shoe, musical instruments, cafes, printers and stationers, confectioners, bicycles, even chain stores like Lipton's and the Maypole Dairy along with department stores.[577] Shopping had become an activity far beyond the buying of food. 'The place looked real twentieth century ...The upland metropolis of Wales, the first great outpost of the industrial revolution in Wales, was at last a place fit to live as well as work in.'[578]

Behind the High Street prosperity there was an uglier reality. Shop assistants worked eighty-hour weeks and were required to live on the premises, often in intolerable conditions. The 'living-in' conditions at Manchester House, Merthyr High Street, were heard at the Court of Appeal on 30 November 1912.

> The bedrooms of the shop assistants ...were kept in such a filthy condition that they were infested with fleas and bugs. In the summer of 1911 an attempt was made by the plaintiff's servants to disinfect the beds by pouring paraffin on the

---

[577] Mary Owen, 'Dynamism, Diligence, Energy and Wealth, Trade and Commerce in Merthyr Tydfil 1800-1914', *Merthyr Historian*, Vol, 25 (2013).

[578] Jack Jones, *Unfinished Journey* (New York, 1937), p. 118.

> mattresses, but the attempt was unsuccessful. There is only one water closet for the male assistants, and when the shop is closed this is inaccessible. The water closet for the female assistants gives an offensive smell, and so on. There is only one bathroom available for over twenty assistants, both men and women, and it is infested with rats. In some cases one bed only is provided for two male assistants, and in some cases one bed only for two female assistants.[579]

It took strikes by the staff, including the women, to bring these conditions to an end at Manchester House and at Roger Edwards and Co. Drapers.

Citizens at Last

The final attempt at Incorporation had been launched just one year into the twentieth century and three years after the Privy Council had rejected the previous attempt. The key figure was Sydney Simons, solicitor, member of the Chamber of Trade, Freemason, son of the redoubtable William Simons and a member of the District Council.[580] In October 1901 he moved that the District Council appoint a committee to consider again petitioning the Privy Council. The committee was set up but the Council did not go beyond preparing estimates of the financial gains arising from incorporation. In July 1902 Simons undertook to prepare a petition if the Chamber of Trade would collect signatures. Quietly the Chamber collected the signatures of eighty-eight leading businessmen and professionals not employed by Cyfarthfa or Dowlais, and handed the list to D.A. Thomas MP who then submitted it to the Privy Council. To

[579] P.C. Hoffman, *They Also Serve* (1949), p. 45.

[580] Obituary *ME*, 5 February 1938.

general surprise the Privy Council agreed to consider it. Swiftly a second petition with over 3,000 signatures was submitted to back the first, and the District Council organised and submitted a third. An Inquiry was announced and proceedings began on 28 April 1903.[581]

Just six years previously in 1897 the petitioners against incorporation had outnumbered those in favour by almost two to one. Now everything had changed. There were no petitions against. The District Council was unanimously for incorporation. There was overwhelming support from Merthyr Vale and Treharris. Workers' representatives — checkweighmen from Treharris, the miners' agent from Dowlais, and the Merthyr Trades Council representing fourteen different trades — gave evidence in favour. What had happened?

The urban district council was at odds with Glamorgan County Council over the upkeep of the main road through the town, over repairs to the Cefn Bridge, and firmly believed it was not getting value for money from the county.[582] The 1889 Intermediate Education Act, amended in 1902, held out the prospect that county borough status, which would inevitably follow close behind incorporation, would enable Merthyr to control primary, secondary and technical education and plan accordingly. Elementary education had been transferred from the School Board to the District Council in 1902. In Merthyr Vale and Treharris it was realised separation from Merthyr would mean domination by Pontypridd while control of education would remain with Glamorgan County Council.

Crucially, events had changed workers' opinions. After long maturation a sea change was under way in the Merthyr working class. The assumption of mutual interests between masters and

[581] Southey in Wilkins, *History*, pp. 561-2.

[582] Report of Inquiry, *Merthyr Express*, 9 May 1903.

men had not survived the Coal War of 1898 with its six-month lock-out. The formation of the South Wales Miners' Federation, the numbers of Cyfarthfa and Dowlais men who had joined the Workers' Union, the formation of the Merthyr and Dowlais Trades Council and the election in 1900 of Keir Hardie all pointed to change, nothing more so than in 1902 Cyfarthfa and Dowlais becoming part of Guest, Keen and Nettlefolds Ltd. with headquarters in Birmingham. Whatever sentiment remained about the rule of the Crawshays and Guests it was now clear that they had severed all local connections, retiring to country estates at Caversham and Canford, leaving Cyfarthfa Castle empty and rat-ridden while anonymous shareholders far away gathered their GKN dividends. Workers' representatives at the Inquiry reflected a new confidence and a determination to play a part in governing Merthyr. A borough council would provide an opportunity to take responsibility for local affairs, a desire the exact opposite of the decisions made by the once-mighty local employers.

At a symbolic meeting in Troedyrhiw, A.J.Howfield, President of Merthyr Chamber of Trade, and Enoch Morrell, secretary of the Merthyr Vale colliery lodge and future President of the SWMF shared the platform, both urging incorporation. It was there that Morrell put in a nutshell labour's new awareness:

> The opposition [to incorporation] came from those who were not residents, and whose business in life was simply to make dividends, and not to seek the welfare of the people. Incorporation gave great powers of self-government, being practically home rule on all questions affecting public welfare.[583]

[583] *ME*, 25 April 1903.

Despite the absence of an opposing petition the Inquiry heard arguments against incorporation from GKN, the colliery and railway companies and Glamorgan County Council. But the arguments were stale and out of tune with the times. Calls to exclude Merthyr Vale and Treharris flew in the face of local opinion. The Privy Council recommended that the King should grant a Charter and Sydney Simons was asked to prepare a draft. The Privy Council promoted a Parliamentary Bill to confirm the granting of a Charter and by early March 1905 it had been twice read in the House of Lords and passed to a committee of that House.

There was a final moment of drama. The Nixon Coal Company, the Ocean Coal Company, GKN, Glamorgan County Council and the railway companies signed at this late hour a petition opposing incorporation. The House of Lords committee decided that it would reopen the case and took evidence on 28 March. The next day as lawyers assembled Lord Falkland the chairman announced that the Committee could not hear evidence. He had been advised that the Charter was the prerogative of the Crown and the Privy Council decision could not be the subject of a Parliamentary inquiry. The objectors withdrew.[584] The Merthyr Tydfil Corporation Act passed through Parliament and King Edward V11 gave the Royal Assent.

A Fresh Start

In the election for the new Borough Council's eight wards — Park and Treharris had been added to the defunct Urban Council's six — the Trades and Labour Council fielded candidates and fourteen of the thirty-two councillors elected in

[584] *ME*, 4 March, 1 April 1905.

October were Labour, making it the largest single party group.[585] A link back to Chartism was the election of David John, the son of Matthew John. In the very hour of triumph the shopocracy found their longed-for power slipping away from them. Merthyr's second Borough mayor was Sydney Simons who had done more than anyone in the end to achieve Incorporation. But the first mayor of the new municipality was Enoch Morrell, the checkweigher from Troedyrhiw and founder-member of Merthyr Tydfil Labour Party. Labour's victory, a marker of things to come, was for now short-lived. In November in the by-elections caused by appointing elected members to be aldermen, Labour lost all seven seats contested and control of the Council.[586] That was a set-back for the Labour Party but not for the enthusiasm with which Liberal and Labour councillors worked together to repair the neglect and obstruction of more than a century.

At the 1897 Incorporation Inquiry the Commissioner, Mr. Cresswell, had elucidated that Merthyr had no parks, no libraries, no baths nor wash-houses, no public recreation grounds or public halls other than the recently completed Town Hall, and that the main entrance to the town from the south was congested, dangerous and insanitary.[587] In 1897 C.A. Cripps QC had argued that Incorporation would release a civic spirit absent from the Urban District Council. More to the point he had noted that 'the Urban Council only consisted of 18 members, so that there was not a sufficiently large number to carry out the work of an important district of this kind'.[588] He

---

585 Twelve were candidates of the Trades and Labour Council and another two took the Labour whip.

586 *ME*, 25 November 1905.

587 *ME*, 9 October 1897. See the evidence and interrogation of T.F. Harvey, surveyor of the Urban District Council.

588 *ME*, 9 October 1897.

might also have said that a high proportion of the eighteen members were employed by or represented the major companies whose main objective was to spend as little money as possible. The change to a thirty-member borough council and the entry of the ILP into local politics had swept away these limitations.

Under pressure from the Trades Council the District Council had, since the 1897 Inquiry, made a beginning with building council houses. It had opened a Reading Room (library) in the Town Hall in 1900 and followed that in 1902 with libraries at Penydarren, Abercanaid, Troedyrhiw and Merthyr Vale. Ironically the costs of doing so were relieved by a gift of £6,000 from Andrew Carnegie the steel magnate in America, after Lord Wimborne and W.T. Crawshay, heirs of iron and coal fortunes made in Merthyr, had both refused to help. Thomastown Park, Merthyr's first, had been opened in 1902 on what had once been a tip. This work was now carried forward as Merthyr Tydfil achieved county borough status in 1908. Talented and far-sighted individuals grasped the opportunity to deal with what had been sarcastically called 'the biggest room in Merthyr – the room for improvement'.[589]

Among the Liberals were Sydney Simons, Frank Treharne James and D.W. Jones – all three solicitors – and John Mathias Berry who had built a substantial business as an auctioneer. On the Labour side the outstanding figures were the colliers Enoch Morrell, Andrew Wilson, Rowland Evans and the railwayman David Davies (Dai Box). As a county borough Merthyr Tydfil acquired its own police force and a Court for Quarter Sessions with a Recorder. Above all, it had control of education. The majority of children left school at twelve; the boys went 'underground', the girls into domestic service or remained at home to look after younger children. The first task was to

[589] *ME*, 26 October 1901

provide new schools and these had been built at Troedyrhiw (1905), Heolgerrig and Georgetown (1907). However, Merthyr had three post-elementary schools with problems.

The County Intermediate School, opened in 1896 for 180 pupils had grown by 1908 to 296 boys and girls. It was a fee-paying school, primarily providing for children of the growing middle-class. At Zoar Chapel vestry in 'temporary' premises a Pupil Teacher Centre prepared students for entry to teacher training colleges. At Caedraw an Advanced Elementary School was overcrowded and with inadequate facilities. A Whitehall report had suggested a new building at considerable cost providing for working-class children an education that would 'make them efficient members of the class to which they belong'. The tone of the report and the expenditure envisaged aroused bitter controversy. The Trades Council began a campaign for a free secondary school, the councillors dithered and the ILP petitioned for an inquiry. Alongside these controversies D.W. Jones, the local solicitor for GKN and for Crawshay Brothers, began negotiations while Mayor in 1907-8 on behalf of the Council with W.T. Crawshay for the purchase of Cyfarthfa Castle and its grounds. By July 1908 terms were almost agreed and the County Borough Council took the decision to buy.[590] It was a stunning acquisition: but what to do with it?

On 18 September 1908 Enoch Morrell, as chairman of the education committee, met O.M. Edwards, Chief Inspector of Education for Wales to discuss the controversies. The idea of using Cyfarthfa Castle for a school had already been floated. Later that day Edwards toured the Castle and enthusiastically suggested that with very little alteration it could be adapted as a new Municipal Secondary School with provision for an Art

[590] Final terms were not settled until the following year when the Council paid £19,700.

Gallery and a Museum, both of which would add to the school's facilities. 'The decision is yours', he said.[591]

The decision was taken to site a Municipal Secondary School with departments for 200 boys and 300 girls at Cyfarthfa Castle with a Museum and Art Gallery. It would be the first secondary school in Wales conceived from its inception to be non-fee paying. Travel to the school for pupils would be free. In later years thousands of Merthyr people could say, 'I went to school in Crawshay's castle'. With full employment, a growing population and an ambitious Council the new County Borough seemed poised on the brink of a bright future.

[591] Joe England (ed.), *Cyfarthfa School: The First 100 Years 1913-2013* (Merthyr Tydfil, 2012); *ILP Conference Souvenir booklet* (Merthyr Tydfil, 1912), pp. 68-75.

Postscript

My first memory of Merthyr Tydfil dates back to 1938 when I was five. We lived in London, where my father worked, and my parents had brought me and my baby brother to see my grandparents who lived on Cilsanws mountain, Cefn Coed. Twelve months later we moved to Merthyr, where my father had been born, when he was appointed in charge of the Borough's parks and cemeteries. In later years it was my grandfather, Martin Luther England, who aroused my initial curiosity about Merthyr's history. He told about the Saturday night fights around the Iron Bridge; the Crawshays and 'God Forgive Me'; the Cyfarthfa Band and its brilliant arranger the Frenchman George D'Artney, frequently more drunk than sober. The Englands were the backbone of the Band, sixteen of them played in it. The connection began when Luther's grandfather, John England, a Bradford woolcomber in desperate poverty but an accomplished trombonist, was headhunted to join the Band in 1847.

When in 1938 I came out of Merthyr railway station I met an unforgettable sight. Lining the long length of its once prosperous High Street lounged the men who had made Merthyr one of the richest towns in the coalfield. In the vernacular of the day they were 'idle'. Many believed they would never work again. Unemployment, commented *The Times* in 1928, had 'descended like the ashes of Vesuvius and overwhelmed whole towns'. In Merthyr, unemployment rose to over 50 per cent of the insured population. In Dowlais it approached 80 per cent. In a reversal of the pre-1912 trend almost 27,000 people left the Borough between 1921 and 1939. These were years of widespread poverty and humiliation, the Means Test and Hunger Marches and declining public health. Children who should have entered universities went into dead-end jobs. The suffering to a greater or lesser degree was felt throughout South Wales but Merthyr, and Dowlais, to the poet Idris Davies that 'battered bucket on a broken hill', summed it all up. As Sir Wyndham Portal reported: 'I think it right to call special attention to the conditions of the County Borough of Merthyr Tydfil, as the circumstances relating to South Wales generally seem to be gathered together and epitomised in this single administrative area.' [592]

In November 1936 King Edward VIII shocked by the derelict appearance of the Dowlais Works, which his mother and father had triumphantly visited 24 years earlier, declared: 'These people were brought here by these works. Some kind of employment must be found for them'. In March 1939 the think-tank Political and Economic Planning (PEP) recommended that the town of Merthyr Tydfil should be abandoned. In its view

> ...the sole justification for a large town on this site has been the abundance of profitable coal and iron deposits, and no detached person would be likely to favour going to live at such a spot after the minerals have ceased to make it worthwhile. Nor does it seem reasonable to ask the taxpayers of the rest of the Britain indefinitely to pay hundreds of thousands of pounds a year in order to give large numbers of people the doubtful pleasure and benefit of continuing to live at subsistence level in one of the least habitable districts of England and Wales...[593]

---

[592] *An Investigation into the Industrial Condition of Certain Depressed Areas: South Wales and Pembrokeshire*. Cmnd. 427 (HMSO, London), 1934.

[593] *Location of Industry* (PEP, 1939), p. 247.

In September 1939 just six months after PEP had written it off, war was declared and Merthyr had two important economic advantages. Its geographic position, formerly a handicap to the attraction of industry was now an asset. It was an unlikely target for the Luftwaffe. Secondly, it had surplus colliers to work in the mines, and a large surplus of female labour available for assembly line work in munition factories. After the war the Labour Government, armed with the Distribution of Industry Act 1945 and the Town and Country Planning Act 1947, steered expanding firms away from overcrowded areas and into the newly created 'Development Areas', which naturally included Merthyr Tydfil. Unemployment fell dramatically. In 1938 there were 9,000 registered unemployed. In March 1965 there were 900.

Merthyr had been an iron town and then a mining town. Now it was a thriving factory town with ICI, Kayser Bondor, O.P. Chocolates, BSA Ltd., Remploy, Thorn Electrical Industries, Lines Brothers, Teddington Aircraft Controls, Croda Packaging, TBS (South Wales) and above all, Hoover Washing Machines, the largest washing machine factory in Europe employing over 5,000. By the 1960s more than 40 per cent of the Merthyr labour force was in manufacturing and only 15 per cent in mining. A revolution had taken place. For every eleven men working in 1938 one woman was in employment. In 1965 the ratio was one woman to just over two men employed. Two pay packets went into many homes.

From its eighteenth century industrialisation, its nineteenth century contrast of wealth and poverty, the juxtaposition of beer houses and chapels, riots and democratic yearnings, its twentieth century martyrdom and post-war revival, Merthyr had epitomised the changing face of Wales, and the reasons for it. It all happened again in the Thatcher years of globalisation and deindustrialisation in the 1980s as the factories disappeared, relocating to Eastern Europe and East Asia. Its collieries closed. Unemployment and deprivation returned. But, like the people, the local economic prospects, underpinned by the Council's Destination Management Plan, have proved to be resilient. Sited at the junction of the A470 and the A465 Merthyr is a major service centre with Prince Charles hospital, a large further education college, county borough offices, Rhydycar leisure centre, the Welsh Government regional office for South Wales, large comprehensive schools, BikePark Wales and Rock UK Summit Centre, Trago Mills and a modern retail park. Heritage Lottery money has restored a number of historic buildings including Vulcan House, St. John's Church Dowlais, and the Old Town Hall, now rebranded as Red House, an arts and cultural centre. Zoar Chapel has become Canolfan Soar, a centre for Welsh language learning. Penydarren Park football ground has been redeveloped. There are ambitious plans for the Cyfarthfa Heritage Area. The people of Merthyr, proud of the rich variety of their heritage, courageous survivors of so many severe trials, advance into an ever-changing future.

Acknowledgements

Writing this book was helped enormously by being an Honorary Fellow in the Department of History, Swansea University and by the efforts of the library staff at Swansea University, including those at the Miners' Library and the Richard Burton Archive. I am also indebted to the helpful staff at Merthyr, Dowlais, Aberdare and Cardiff public libraries; the Modern Records Centre, Warwick University; the Glamorgan Archive, Cardiff, and the National Library of Wales, Aberystwyth.

The cheerful Tuesday morning Merthyr WEA class provided food for thought. Sue Konieczny did valuable typing and Judy Evans and Miriam Ward helped in various ways, particularly with laughter. Mary and Wilf Owen, Carolyn Jacob and Steve Brewer provided valuable information. So did Dave Lyddon.

Enthusiastic encouragement came from those who read an initial draft of the text: my brother David England, Andy Croll, Chris Evans, Neil Evans, Dai Smith and Huw Williams. Neil Evans suggested various improvements and Dai Smith, as General Editor, gave the text meticulous attention and suggested its final shape and title.

Some of the material in this book has previously been published in *Merthyr Historian* and *Llafur*. Chapters 13, 14 and 16 contain material previously published in *Welsh History Review* and Chapter 20 makes use of an article published in *Historical Studies in Industrial Relations*, number 33 (2012). I am grateful to the editors and publishers concerned for permission to use this material. Chris Evans in *The Labyrinth of Flames* and Andy Croll in *Civilizing The Urban* have written in detail about the beginning and end of my period and I have freely used their work. Historians will be familiar with the research and work by various other authors that I have plundered. Any errors that remain are mine.

Index

Modern Wales by Parthian Books

In May 2017 Parthian Books, supported by the Rhys Davies Trust and edited by Dai Smith, launched a new series entitled Modern Wales. The series intends to look at places crucial to the development of modern Wales, such as Cardiff and Newport, as well as at the imagery and iconography which has shaped the culture and society of modern Wales. The series, in a new and distinctive livery, will include an impressive back catalogue of connected Parthian publications. The inaugural titles of the series are *To Hear the Skylark's Song* by Huw Lewis, and *Merthyr: The Crucible of Modern Wales* by Joe England. Future titles, already commissioned will include Angela John's Rocking the Boat, essays on Welsh women who pioneered the fight for equality, and Daryl Leeworthy's, *Labour Country*, a fresh and provocative look at the struggle through radical action for social democracy in Wales. In the pipeline already are new political and culturally-informed biographies of the pioneering socialist and feminist Minnie Palliser and of the great Welsh novelist, playwright and public commentator, Gwyn Thomas.

the RHYS DAVIES TRUST

PARTHIAN

WALES: ENGLAND'S COLONY?

Martin Johnes

From the very beginnings of Wales, its people have defined themselves against their large neighbour. This book tells the fascinating story of an uneasy and unequal relationship between two nations living side-by-side.

PB / £8.99
978-1-912681-41-9

RHYS DAVIES: A WRITER'S LIFE

Meic Stephens

Rhys Davies (1901-78) was among the most dedicated, prolific and accomplished of Welsh prose writers. This is his first full biography.

'This is a delightful book, which is itself a social history in its own right, and funny.'
– The Spectator

PB / £11.99
978-1-912109-96-8

MERTHYR, THE CRUCIBLE OF MODERN WALES

Joe England

Merthyr Tydfil was the town where the future of a country was forged: a thriving, struggling surge of people, industry, democracy and ideas. This book assesses an epic history of Merthyr from 1760 to 1912 through the focus of a fresh and thoroughly convincing perspective.

PB / £18.99
978-1-913640-05-7

TO HEAR THE SKYLARK'S SONG

Huw Lewis

To Hear the Skylark's Song is a memoir about how Aberfan survived and eventually thrived after the terrible disaster of the 21st of October 1966.

'A thoughtful and passionate memoir, moving and respectful.'
– Tessa Hadley

PB / £8.99
978-1-912109-72-2

ROCKING THE BOAT

Angela V. John

This insightful and revealing collection of essays focuses on seven Welsh women who, in a range of imaginative ways, resisted the status quo in Wales, England and beyond during the nineteenth and twentieth centuries.

PB / £11.99
978-1-912681-44-0

TURNING THE TIDE

Angela V. John

This rich biography tells the remarkable tale of Margaret Haig Thomas (1883-1958) who became the second Viscountess Rhondda. She was a Welsh suffragette, held important posts during the First World War and survived the sinking of the *Lusitania*.

PB / £17.99
978-1-909844-72-8

BRENDA CHAMBERLAIN, ARTIST & WRITER

Jill Piercy

The first full-length biography of Brenda Chamberlain chronicles the life of an artist and writer whose work was strongly affected by the places she lived, most famously Bardsey Island and the Greek island of Hydra.

PB / £11.99
978-1-912681-06-8

PARTHIAN **Parthian Voices**

A DIRTY BROTH: EARLY-TWENTIETH CENTURY WELSH PLAYS IN ENGLISH

VOLUME 1 OF TWENTIETH-CENTURY WELSH PLAYS IN ENGLISH

Edited by David Cottis

This anthology, the first in a series of three, brings together three plays from the beginnings of Welsh playwriting in English.

PB /£14.99
978-1-912681-71-6

A LADDER OF WORDS: MID-TWENTIETH CENTURY WELSH PLAYS IN ENGLISH

VOLUME 2 OF TWENTIETH-CENTURY WELSH PLAYS IN ENGLISH

Edited by David Cottis

A Ladder of Words explores the period either side of the Second World War, a time when Welsh playwrights enjoyed unprecedented commercial success.

PB / £14.99
978-1-913640-04-0

SAINTS AND LODGERS: THE POEMS OF W.H. DAVIES

Selected with an introduction by Jonathan Edwards

William Henry Davies (1871–1940) was a Welsh poet and writer. He was also a traveller and adventurer. In this collection he emerges as a poet of people, who never turns away from the suffering or the beauty of the saints and lodgers among whom he lives.

PB / £9.99
978-1-912681-34-1